FREEDOM OF ASSOCIATION

FREEDOM OF ASSOCIATION

Edited by

**Ellen Frankel Paul, Fred D. Miller, Jr.,
and Jeffrey Paul**

CAMBRIDGE
UNIVERSITY PRESS

PUBLISHED BY THE PRESS SYNDICATE OF THE UNIVERSITY OF CAMBRIDGE
The Pitt Building, Trumpington Street, Cambridge, United Kingdom

CAMBRIDGE UNIVERSITY PRESS
The Edinburgh Building, Cambridge CB2 8RU, UK
32 Avenue of the Americas, New York, NY 10013-2473, USA
477 Williamstown Road, Port Melbourne, VIC 3207, Australia
Ruiz de Alarcón 13, 28014 Madrid, Spain
Dock House, The Waterfront, Cape Town 8001, South Africa

http://www.cambridge.org

First published 2008

Printed in the United States of America

Typeface Palatino 10/12 pt.

A catalog record for this book is available from the British Library

Library of Congress Cataloging-in-Publication Data
Freedom of association / edited by
Ellen Frankel Paul, Fred D. Miller, Jr., and Jeffrey Paul.
p. cm.
Includes bibliographical references and index.
ISBN 978-0-521-73228-4 (pbk. : alk. paper)
1. Liberty. 2. Freedom of association. 3. Liberalism. 4. Academic freedom.
I. Paul, Ellen Frankel. II. Miller, Fred Dycus, 1944-
III. Paul, Jeffrey. IV. Title.

JC585.F742 2008
323.4'7-dc22

2008011274

The essays in this book have also been published,
without introduction and index, in the semiannual journal
Social Philosophy & Policy, Volume 25, Number 2,
which is available by subscription.

CONTENTS

ACKNOWLEDGMENTS

The editors wish to acknowledge several individuals at the Social Philosophy and Policy Center, Bowling Green State University, who provided invaluable assistance in the preparation of this volume. They include Program Manager John Milliken, Mary Dilsaver, and Terrie Weaver.

The editors also extend special thanks to Administrative Editor Tamara Sharp, for attending to innumerable day-to-day details of the book's preparation, and to Managing Editor Harry Dolan, for providing dedicated assistance throughout the editorial and production process.

INTRODUCTION

Freedom of association is a cherished liberal value, both for classical liberals who are generally antagonistic toward government interference in the choices made by individuals, and for contemporary liberals who are more sanguine about the role of government. However, there are fundamental differences between the two viewpoints in the status that they afford to associational freedom. While classical liberals ground their support for freedom of association on the core notion of individual liberty, contemporary liberals usually conceive of freedom of association as one among many values that are necessary for a liberal democracy to flourish. Which position provides a better grounding for freedom of association? Is liberal democracy the core value, or does a liberal democracy become defensible to the extent that it protects the core value of individual freedom?

On a classical liberal view, freedom of association flows logically from individual liberty: people have the right to choose their associates and to dissociate from people and groups whose beliefs and goals they do not share. As John Stuart Mill wrote in his famous essay *On Liberty* (1859): "[F]rom [the] liberty of each individual follows the liberty, within the same limits, of combination among individuals; freedom to unite, for any purpose not involving harm to others: the persons combining being supposed to be of full age, and not forced or deceived."[1]

On a contemporary liberal view, by contrast, freedom of association is not an absolute right; yet despite its conditional status, it weighs heavily in the balance against other important values when conflicts of rights arise. For contemporary liberals, the goal of curbing private discrimination counts as a compelling state interest that trumps freedom of association when a business-oriented club, such as Rotary International or the Jaycees,[2] seeks to exclude women from membership. For classical liberals — or their modern heirs, libertarians — freedom of association would be seen as sacrosanct, and an organization's right to exclude would be absolute.

The essays in this volume explore the history and development of the right of free association, and discuss the limits that may legitimately be placed on this right. Some essays address the constitutional status of freedom of association in the United States, exploring a range of legal decisions on association handed down by various courts, especially the

---

[1] John Stuart Mill, *On Liberty* (1859), in Mill, *On Liberty and Other Writings*, ed. Stefan Collini (Cambridge: Cambridge University Press, 1989), chap. 1.

[2] *Roberts v. United States Jaycees*, 468 U.S. 609 (1984); *Rotary International v. Rotary Club of Duarte*, 481 U.S. 537 (1987).

Supreme Court. Some look at freedom of association in the context of unionization, or university policies on military recruiting, or the treatment of subversive organizations. Other essays examine the tension between the right of individuals to associate and the interest of government in preventing discrimination against members of disadvantaged groups. Still others address the views of particular political theorists who have influenced the debate on associational freedom, theorists such as John Locke, James Madison, Alexis de Tocqueville, and John Rawls.

The collection opens with Larry Alexander's essay, "What Is Freedom of Association, and What Is Its Denial?" Alexander takes a classical liberal view of freedom of association, conceiving of it as the liberty of an individual to enter into voluntary relationships with others—relationships of any duration and for any noncoercive purpose. This freedom has both a positive and a negative aspect; it is the freedom to associate or to refuse to associate. Thus, freedom of association can be abridged by government in two ways: by prohibiting individuals from associating with others; or by compelling them to associate with others against their will. The central question of Alexander's essay concerns when government may legitimately force people to associate, or prohibit them from doing so, and for what reasons. He begins by considering what the denial of freedom of association entails in various domains, including intimate relationships, political and religious organizations, social clubs, and commercial transactions. He then goes on to consider the reasons government has for denying associational freedom through the implementation of antidiscrimination laws and regulations. Government can use such policies to pursue social-engineering goals, for example, by requiring employers to hire members of racial minorities or other protected groups. Government might also interfere with associational freedom for paternalistic reasons, in order to promote associations that are deemed to be beneficial to their members' welfare, and to forbid those that are putatively self-destructive. Alexander concludes by arguing that, on a classical liberal or libertarian view of rights, the goal of combating discrimination cannot justify coercive restrictions on private choices. What's more, he suggests that government lacks the wisdom to engage in social engineering or to make judgments about what contributes to the welfare of citizens, and that any government interference with freedom of association is bound to be messy and intrusive.

The next four essays look at the jurisprudential development of the freedom of association in the United States. Paul Moreno focuses on the development of American labor law in his essay, "Organized Labor and American Law: From Freedom of Association to Compulsory Unionism." Most legal scholars have held that the American labor movement has suffered from legal disabilities throughout its history, but Moreno argues that American constitutional law has never denied organized labor's freedom of association. He traces the history of the labor movement from the early decades of the nineteenth century to the post–World War II period, arguing that unions have generally enjoyed at least some favoritism in the law, and that this status has provided an essential element to their success and power. In the course of the essay, Moreno touches on a range of topics, including the recognition by early American courts of the right of union members to associate for lawful ends, the use of labor injunctions to curtail union violence, the application of antitrust laws to organized labor, and the impact of key legal decisions on the labor movement. He discusses the heyday of union power during the New Deal, when labor legislation such as the 1935 National Labor Relations Act sought to address the inequality of bargaining power between employers and employees by imposing requirements of collective bargaining. This sort of legislation, Moreno notes, instituted a radically new understanding of freedom of association, one under which state power was brought to bear in favor of unions and against employers and nonunion workers. He concludes by considering the causes of the decline of union power in the post–World War II period, contending that this decline has been due not to any legal disadvantage imposed on unions, but to increased immigration and a rise in market competition in the American and global economy.

In " 'Guilt by Association' and the Postwar Civil Libertarians," Ken I. Kersch explores developments in the status of the freedom of association during the mid-twentieth century. While contemporary discussions of associational freedom focus primarily on whether groups should be permitted to exclude women or minorities from their membership, mid-century theorists were concerned with a different set of questions: Do individuals have a right to keep their membership in associations private? Are there circumstances in which government should be able to require groups to reveal their membership lists? Can one legally be part of a subversive group (that is, a group committed to illegal objectives, such as the violent overthrow of the government), or does mere membership in such a group amount to participation in a criminal conspiracy? Kersch considers these questions, offering an overview of the way freedom of association was treated in the years immediately following World War II. He examines the writings of some of the era's most distinguished civil libertarian thinkers, including Leo Pfeffer, Milton Konvitz, Robert Cushman, Henry Steele Commager, Zechariah Chafee, Jr., and Sidney Hook. Kersch draws on these writings to illustrate how the doctrinal development of the right to freedom of association was driven by the right's central importance in two of the major political issues of the day: domestic security at the height of the Cold War, and civil rights. Turning his attention to the contemporary scene, he concludes that, in the aftermath of the September 11th attacks and in the context of the ongoing fight against terrorism, questions about freedom of association are likely to assume renewed prominence. Moreover, he suggests, contemporary theorists who deal with the most pressing freedom of association questions would profit by studying the highly relevant discussions of "guilt by association" offered by mid-twentieth-century civil libertarians.

The development of the idea of freedom of association in the middle of the twentieth century is also the subject of Keith E. Whittington's contribution to this collection, "Industrial Saboteurs, Reputed Thieves, Communists, and the Freedom of Association." Whittington describes how associational freedom, though not explicitly enumerated in the U.S. Constitution, was embraced by the Supreme Court as implicit in the First Amendment. In a series of cases in the mid-1930s and 1940s—cases involving crackdowns by local government officials against speakers and assemblies discussing strikes and labor unions—the Court endorsed the right of association as a fundamental freedom that was necessarily entwined with the freedom of speech. Government could legitimately intervene if a particular assembly was being used to advocate the commission of criminal acts, but the mere involvement of speakers or organizations who might elsewhere advocate such acts did not compromise the right of association. Whittington goes on to explain how the grounding of associational freedom in the First Amendment led to challenges for New Deal era justices. They sought to extend constitutional protections to the activities of union organizers, and in the process they had to carve out subtle distinctions between protected speech, on the one hand, and conduct subject to governmental regulation, on the other. The essay concludes with a discussion of the Supreme Court's more skeptical attitude toward free association claims from the mid-1940s through the early 1960s, when state and national government officials were pursuing a variety of anticommunist policies. During this period, the government sought to penalize those who associated with the Communist Party through measures such as forced disclosure of party membership and the questioning of suspected party members in public hearings. The Supreme Court generally deferred to the government in these matters. In the context of the Cold War, Whittington suggests, the Court was inclined to allow freedom of association to be outweighed by the government's responsibility to preserve the general welfare.

In "Expressive Association and the Ideal of the University in the Solomon Amendment Litigation," Tobias Barrington Wolff and Andrew Koppelman offer a critical analysis of a recent series of free association cases. These cases were initiated by law schools and their faculty in an effort to challenge the Solomon Amendment, a federal statute that requires law schools that receive federal funding to grant full and equal access to military recruiters during the student interview season. The law schools objected to this requirement on the grounds that the military discriminates against homosexuals under its "Don't Ask, Don't Tell" policy. As Wolff and Koppelman note, the law schools claimed a right to exclude military recruiters under the First Amendment doctrine of "expressive association," the idea that groups and institutions should be free to express their views and the views of their members through their policies. Given the military's practice of discriminating against homosexuals, the law schools argued, the presence of military recruiters on college campuses would interfere with their ability and the ability of their faculty members to express their own message of inclusion toward their gay students. The law schools' claims were ultimately rejected by the U.S. Supreme Court in *Rumsfeld v. FAIR* (2006),[3] and Wolff and Koppelman provide a detailed discussion of the context of the litigation and the reasoning the justices employed in rendering their decision. The authors contend that the law schools' litigation efforts, though well intentioned, were misguided, and were based on the untenable notion that faculty members must have the right to suppress and exclude divergent viewpoints from the campus environment in order to protect their own ability to express their views. This approach, the authors argue, is inconsistent with the ideals that should govern institutions of higher learning.

The collection continues with three essays on the tension between antidiscrimination principles and the right to free association. Richard A. Epstein defends a classical liberal view of freedom of association in his essay, "Should Antidiscrimination Laws Limit Freedom of Association? The Dangerous Allure of Human Rights Legislation." The classical liberal view gives strong protection to associational freedom, except in cases that involve the use of force or fraud or the exercise of monopoly power. As Epstein observes, the view stands in conflict with contemporary antidiscrimination or human rights laws, which seek to ensure equal opportunity in employment, housing, and other vital areas for members of disadvantaged groups (defined in terms of race, sex, age, and, increasingly, disability). Epstein argues that using the language of "human rights" to bolster the moral case for antidiscrimination laws gets matters exactly backwards, since any policy of forced association (e.g., requiring employers to hire certain employees, or landlords to rent to certain tenants) is inconsistent with a universal norm guaranteeing individuals the right to choose their associative relationships. In the course of his essay, Epstein discusses the tensions that arise under current constitutional law, which protects associational freedom arising out of expressive activities (e.g., allowing the NAACP to keep its membership lists private, or the Boy Scouts to exclude gay scoutmasters), but refuses to extend the same protection to other forms of association, such as those involving persons with disabilities. He contends that a strong social consensus against discrimination provides an insufficient reason to coerce those who disagree, given that holders of the consensus position can run their operations as they see fit even if others choose to operate differently. He concludes by offering a brief sketch of a model human rights statute, drafted in the classical liberal tradition: a statute that gives individuals the broadest freedom to

---

[3] *Rumsfeld v. FAIR*, 547 U.S. 47 (2006).

choose with whom they will interact and on what terms, and that avoids the awkward line-drawing and balancing that give rise to the bureaucracies needed to enforce contemporary antidiscrimination laws.

In "Freedom of Association in Historical Perspective," Stephen B. Presser conceives of the tension between antidiscrimination laws and associational freedom in terms of two conflicting strands of thought that have run through the U.S. Supreme Court's constitutional jurisprudence. The older, traditional conception of freedom of association sees a role for government in encouraging laudable associations (those that contribute to human flourishing), and it rejects the idea that members of associations should be forbidden from excluding others or forced into undesired interaction. The newer conception holds that individuals should be left free to work out their own lifestyles and should not be penalized for the choices that they make or for other irrelevant factors such as race, gender, sexual orientation, and so on. Thus, this contemporary conception embraces doctrines barring discrimination on the basis of these factors. The two conceptions still exist on the Court, Presser observes, and this has resulted in irreconcilable decisions such as those permitting the Boy Scouts to exclude gay scoutmasters, on the one hand, but forcing the Jaycees to accept women as members, on the other. He describes these two conceptions of freedom of association in detail, drawing on the work of three legal scholars: Herbert Wechsler (for the traditional model) and Cass Sunstein and Andrew Koppelman (for the newer model). Presser concludes by considering how best to account for the discontinuities in the Supreme Court's free association doctrine. The Court itself seems to ground its doctrine in the First Amendment's free speech clause, holding that discrimination in an organization's membership policies is permissible when it is essentially expressive, that is, when it sends a message about the organization's beliefs. Presser argues, however, that it makes more sense to regard free association cases as related to the First Amendment's free exercise of religion clause. On this view, internal decisions about an association's policies and membership reflect moral choices about how best to promote the good life. Thus, the Supreme Court's deference to an association's internal policies might be viewed as a recognition of the traditional role of associations, especially religious ones, in fostering human flourishing.

In "The Paradox of Association," Loren E. Lomasky explores the tension between what he terms negative freedom of association and positive freedom of association. Negative freedom provides the individual with a sphere of protected choice within which he is free to choose those relationships he favors and to avoid entanglement in other, disfavored relationships and social arrangements. Positive freedom involves an entitlement not to be excluded from valued associations and modes of activity. Lomasky begins by setting out several respects in which negative freedom of association is crucial to a liberal order. He seeks to show how the history of liberal societies is a history of expanding freedom in a number of important areas: with respect to religious belief and practice, speech and expression, travel and residence, choice of occupation, and ownership of property. Each of these crucially involves the right to dissociate, to reject undesired commitments and unwanted interactions. Lomasky then turns to positive freedom of association, asking whether there may be instances in which the right of some individuals to be included in valuable associations might outweigh the right of others to avoid such associations. A classic example would be government-mandated affirmative action, where the goal of including members of groups that have historically been excluded from certain jobs or educational opportunities is taken to justify imposing specific hiring or admissions policies. Lomasky addresses affirmative action along with several other cases in which the benefits of a particular institution or arrangement might be judged to trump the right of individuals to dissociate themselves from it (e.g., tax-supported public education, or national health care). Ultimately, he concludes, the importance of negative freedom of association to the maintenance of a liberal social order places it on a far stronger footing than positive freedom of association. Thus, any claim to a positive freedom of association must confront a strong presumption in favor of the right of individuals to dissociate, and, on Lomasky's view, only serious threats to the social and political order can overcome that presumption.

Each of the remaining four essays discusses the freedom of association from the perspective of a particular historical or contemporary figure. In "The Private Society and the Liberal Public Good in John Locke's Thought," Eric R. Claeys sets out to interpret Locke's teachings about "private societies," or free private associations. He proceeds by looking at Locke's mature writings on ethics, politics, and philosophy in the *Two Treatises of Government, An Essay Concerning Human Understanding,* and *A Letter Concerning Toleration.* Although Locke wrote about private societies primarily in the course of arguing for religious toleration, Claeys argues that throughout his mature corpus Locke develops an internally consistent general theory of associational freedom. At first glance, Locke seems to suggest that all citizens are entitled to associate for any end of their choosing, to control admission into and expulsion from their organizations, and to enforce their own internal rules of governance. However, Claeys shows how Locke qualifies this broad right in order to bar societies from organizing around ends that are inconsistent with the minimal moral and political conditions of liberalism. Ultimately, on Locke's view, citizens deserve a broad right of free association only to the extent that they are well enough formed by their social order and its private institutions to be capable of governing themselves in both private and public life. Claeys concludes his essay by comparing Locke's justification of the right of free association with contemporary understandings of this right, suggesting that Locke's justification is broader in some respects and narrower in others. On the one hand, for example, Locke's teachings may justify limiting the scope of antidiscrimination laws, since, on his view, an association's refusal to admit an individual as a member does not constitute a harm to that individual: his liberty and property are left intact, and he is free to join many other associations to pursue his ends. On the other hand, Locke's teachings may justify enlarging the scope of government efforts to dissolve seditious associations, on the grounds that they pose a threat to public morals or seek to advance foreign interests.

In "The Madisonian Paradox of Freedom of Association," Richard Boyd examines James Madison's thought on the right of free association. Boyd begins with the observation that the freedom of association holds an uneasy place in the pantheon of liberal freedoms. While freedom of association and the abundant plurality of groups that accompany it have been embraced by contemporary liberals, this was not always the case. Unlike more canonical freedoms of speech, press, property, assembly, and religious conscience, the freedom of association was seldom championed by liberal thinkers in the seventeenth and eighteenth centuries. Indeed, many of the political theorists of this period regarded the freedom of association with some trepidation because of the violent, irrational, and factional behavior of groups, and this attitude toward associational freedom was inherited by Madison and the other American Founders. Boyd sets out to illuminate this attitude by analyzing the anti-associational assumptions in Madison's writings. In *The Federalist,* Madison famously warned against political associations as sources of faction and civil dissension, and sought to demonstrate how the worst effects of faction could be mitigated through the sound design of political institutions. Nonetheless, as Boyd goes on to show, Madison was also a powerful defender of the freedom of association, as demonstrated by his opposition to the Alien and Sedition Acts of 1798 and his support for the "self-created societies" that arose in the 1790s (societies that espoused the principles of the French Revolution and were viewed by Federalists as posing a threat of domestic insurrection). With respect to these matters, Madison was a strong advocate of the rule of law, arguing that the same standards that applied to individuals should apply to associations, and that as long as a group undertook no illegal actions, it should not be subject to any penalty or censure. Thus, Boyd concludes, Madison's writings constitute an important step in overcoming the anti-associational bias present in earlier liberal thought.

Alexis de Tocqueville's observations on civil and political associations in America are the subject of Aurelian Craiutu's contribution to this volume, "From the Social Contract to the Art of Association: A Tocquevillian Perspective." Craiutu looks at Tocqueville's analysis of associations in the United States, paying special attention to the effects that associations have on promoting democratic citizenship, civility, and self-government. He notes that Tocqueville took a broad view of associations, using the term to encompass local institutions and municipal councils as well as news-

papers, political parties, and various voluntary organizations and societies. Moreover, Tocqueville drew a strong connection between local
institutions and liberty, holding that such institutions brought liberty
within the reach of the people and functioned as laboratories of democracy, teaching citizens the art of being free and giving them the opportunity to pursue their own interests in concert with others. Craiutu also
discusses the contrast that Tocqueville drew between America, where
decentralization allowed individuals to pool their efforts to achieve their
goals, and the countries of Europe, where centralized power tended to
undermine local initiatives. In Europe, associations were often viewed as
tools to be used in political battles, and thus collective action was often
linked to violence and unrest. In America, by contrast, widespread suffrage mitigated the violence of political organizations, and associations
turned their energies to a variety of causes, from building hospitals and
schools, to promoting ideas and distributing books, to sending mission-
aries to foreign lands. Craiutu concludes his essay by considering the
relevance of Tocqueville's thought to modern societies, which have wit-
nessed an increase in civic apathy and a decline in individuals' involvement in associational life. Yet despite this decrease in civic and political
participation, Craiutu suggests that associations still have a vital role to
play in promoting tolerance, cooperation, and civic virtue.

The collection's final essay, "The Rawlsian View of Private Ordering"
by Kevin A. Kordana and David H. Blankfein Tabachnick, explores John
Rawls's treatment of the right of free association. As Kordana and
Tabachnick note, Rawls's early work omits any mention of freedom of
association as among the basic liberties, but in his later work Rawls
explicitly includes freedom of association among these liberties. Moreover, the passages in his writings that deal with associational freedom are
ambiguous, and have led to sharp disagreements among interpreters of
Rawls regarding the breadth of what he calls the "basic structure" of
social institutions. At issue is whether Rawls's principles of justice govern
matters of "private ordering" (for example, the decisions of individuals to
associate for economic ends by entering into contracts, forming partnerships, or establishing corporations). In order to address this issue, Kordana
and Tabachnick focus on a specific passage from Rawls's *Political Liberalism* (1993), a passage that has led different commentators to divergent
conclusions about the proper conception of the basic structure. This passage discusses the freedom of individuals and associations to pursue their
ends, and Kordana and Tabachnick argue that disagreements in interpreting the passage stem from Rawls's failure to consistently distinguish
between two senses of "freedom." On the one hand, if freedom is understood in a pre-institutional sense, then freedom of association should be
considered as something like a preexisting natural right, and this would
provide grounds for arguing that matters of "private ordering" are not
subject to Rawls's principles of justice. On the other hand, if freedom is

understood in a post-institutional sense, then freedom of association must be viewed as a constructed right, as part of the basic structure governed by Rawls's principles. In particular, freedom of association would fall under the ambit of Rawls's difference principle, which requires that social arrangements (including, in this case, laws governing contracts, partnerships, and corporations) must be ordered so as to provide the greatest benefit to the least well-off. Kordana and Tabachnick conclude that the post-institutional sense of freedom is the relevant one for Rawls's argument, and that rules governing property and economic associations must conform to his principles of justice.

The right of individuals to associate with one another on mutually agreeable terms holds a central place in the ethos of modern liberal democratic societies. The essays in this volume offer valuable insights into the nature, development, and limits of this right.

CONTRIBUTORS

Larry Alexander is Warren Distinguished Professor at the University of San Diego School of Law. He is the author of four books, six anthologies, and more than 160 articles, essays, and chapters in legal and philosophical journals and collections, covering theories of constitutional law and criminal law, jurisprudence, and legal and moral philosophy. He is a founding coeditor of the Cambridge journal *Legal Theory* and serves on the editorial boards of *Ethics*, *Law and Philosophy*, *Criminal Law and Philosophy*, and the *Ohio State Journal of Criminal Law*.

Paul Moreno holds the Grewcock Chair in the American Constitution at Hillsdale College, and is a member of the James Madison Society at Princeton University. He is the author of *From Direct Action to Affirmative Action: Fair Employment Law and Policy in America, 1933–1972* (1997) and *Black Americans and Organized Labor: A New History* (2006). He is working on a book about the Michigan Supreme Court and another on the constitutional history of the New Deal. He has published articles in numerous journals, including the *Journal of Southern History*, the *Journal of Policy History*, *Labor History*, and *Academic Questions*.

Ken I. Kersch is Associate Professor of Political Science and Law at Boston College. He is the recipient of the American Political Science Association's Edward S. Corwin Award (2000), the J. David Greenstone Prize (2006) from APSA's politics and history section, and the Hughes-Gossett Award from the Supreme Court Historical Society (2006). He is the author of *The Supreme Court and American Political Development* (with Ronald Kahn, 2006), *Constructing Civil Liberties: Discontinuities in the Development of American Constitutional Law* (2004), and *Freedom of Speech: Rights and Liberties under the Law* (2003). He received his B.A. from Williams College, his J.D. from Northwestern University, and his Ph.D. (Government) from Cornell University.

Keith E. Whittington is William Nelson Cromwell Professor of Politics at Princeton University. He is the author of *Constitutional Construction: Divided Powers and Constitutional Meaning* (1999), *Constitutional Interpretation: Textual Meaning, Original Intent, and Judicial Review* (1999), and *Political Foundations of Judicial Supremacy: The Presidency, the Supreme Court, and Constitutional Leadership in U.S. History* (2007), and he is the coeditor of *Congress and the Constitution* (with Neal Devins, 2005) and the forthcoming *Oxford Handbook of Law and Politics* (with R. Daniel Kelemen and Gregory A. Caldeira). He has published widely on American constitutional theory and development, federalism, judicial politics, and the presidency. He has been a John M. Olin Foundation faculty fellow, an American Council of Learned Societies junior faculty fellow, and a visiting professor at the University of Texas School of Law. He is currently working on a political history of the judicial review of federal statutes and a casebook of materials in American constitutional law and politics.

Tobias Barrington Wolff is Professor of Law at the University of Pennsylvania Law School. Prior to joining the faculty at Penn, he was a professor at the University of California, Davis Law School and a visiting professor at Stanford Law School and Northwestern Law School. He works in two primary fields of scholarship: constitutional law and civil procedure. In constitutional law, he has written about free speech and the First Amendment, the rights of gay men and lesbians, and slavery and the Thirteenth Amendment, among other topics. In civil procedure, his work focuses on complex litigation, multijurisdictional disputes, and the conflict of laws. He is a member of the American Law Institute and sits on the executive board of the Equal Justice Society.

Andrew Koppelman is John Paul Stevens Professor of Law and Professor of Political Science at Northwestern University. He is the author of *Same Sex, Different States: When Same-Sex Marriages Cross State Lines* (2006), *The Gay Rights Question in Contemporary American Law* (2002), *Antidiscrimination Law and Social Equality* (1996), and more than fifty articles on topics including religious liberty, obscenity law, abortion, federalism, the theory of democracy, and the meaning of neutrality as a political ideal.

Richard A. Epstein is James Parker Hall Distinguished Service Professor of Law at the University of Chicago and Peter and Kirsten Bedford Senior Fellow at the Hoover Institution. He is a member of the American Academy of Arts and Sciences, a Senior Fellow of the Center for Clinical Medical Ethics at the University of Chicago Medical School, and a director of the John M. Olin Program in Law and Economics, University of Chicago. He has served as editor of the *Journal of Legal Studies* and the *Journal of Law and Economics*. He is the author of numerous books, including *Takings: Private Property and the Power of Eminent Domain* (1985), *Mortal Peril: Our Inalienable Right to Health Care?* (1997), *Skepticism and Freedom: A Modern Case for Classical Liberalism* (2003), *How Progressives Rewrote the Constitution* (2006), *Overdose: How Excessive Government Regulation Stifles Pharmaceutical Innovation* (2006), and *Antitrust Decrees in Theory and Practice: Why Less Is More* (2007).

Stephen B. Presser is Raoul Berger Professor of Legal History at Northwestern University School of Law and Professor of Business Law at Northwestern University's Kellogg School of Management. He is the legal affairs editor for *Chronicles: A Magazine of American Culture,* the author or coauthor of casebooks in constitutional law, legal history, and business organizations, and a frequently invited witness before congressional committees to testify on issues of constitutional law. He has written a treatise on shareholder liability for corporate debts, several monographs on modern and eighteenth-century constitutional law, and dozens of articles, book reviews, and essays on contemporary and historical legal topics. He is a graduate of Harvard College and Harvard Law School, and has taught at Rutgers University and the University of Virginia.

Loren E. Lomasky is Professor of Philosophy and Chair of the Philosophy, Politics, and Law Program at the University of Virginia. He has published numerous articles in moral and political philosophy, and is the author of *Persons, Rights, and the Moral Community* (1987) and *Democracy and Decision: The Pure Theory of Electoral Preference* (with Geoffrey Brennan, 1993). He has also held research appointments sponsored by the National Endowment for the Humanities, the Center for Study of Public Choice, the Australian National University, and the Social Philosophy and Policy Center, Bowling Green State University.

Eric R. Claeys is Associate Professor of Law at George Mason University. He has written extensively on property law and constitutional law, focusing especially on how those subjects are informed by classical liberal theories of rights and government. His articles include "Takings, Regulations, and Natural Property Rights" in the *Cornell Law Review* (2003), "Public-Use Limitations and Natural Property Rights" in the *Michigan State Law Review* (2004), and "The National Regulatory State in Progressive Political Theory and Twentieth-Century Constitutional Law" in *Modern America and the Legacy of the Founding* (2006).

Richard Boyd is Associate Professor of Government at Georgetown University. Previously, he taught at the University of Chicago, the University of Pennsylvania, the University of Wisconsin–Madison, and Deep Springs College. He is the author of *Uncivil Society: The Perils of Pluralism and the Making of Modern Liberalism* (2004), the editor and translator of two other books, and the author of journal articles and book chapters on a number of thinkers including Thomas Hobbes, John Locke, Adam Smith, David Hume, Jean-Jacques Rousseau, Edmund Burke, Frances Trollope, J. S. Mill, Alexis de Tocqueville, Michael Oakeshott, F. A. Hayek, and Frank H. Knight. He is currently completing a book-length manuscript entitled *Membership and Belonging: On the Boundaries of Liberal Political Theory.*

Aurelian Craiutu is Associate Professor of Political Science at Indiana University, Bloomington. He is the author of *Liberalism Under Siege* (2003) and *Le Centre introuvable* (2006), and serves as associate editor of the

European Journal of Political Theory. He is also editor and translator (with Jeremy Jennings) of *Alexis de Tocqueville, Letters and Other Writings: Tocqueville on America After 1840* (2008), and editor (with Jeffrey C. Isaac) of *America Through European Eyes* (2008).

Kevin A. Kordana is Professor of Law at the University of Virginia School of Law, where he has taught since 1996. He is a graduate of Yale Law School, where he served as a symposium editor of *The Yale Law Journal* and received the Olin Prize for the best paper in law and economics. Upon graduation, Kordana clerked for Chief Judge Richard A. Posner of the U.S. Court of Appeals for the Seventh Circuit. He has been a visiting professor at the University of Southern California Law School and the George Washington University Law School.

David H. Blankfein Tabachnick is a student at Yale Law School with interests in moral, political, and legal theory. He earned his Ph.D. in Philosophy from the University of Virginia. At UVA, he taught courses on philosophy of law, ethics and international relations, and political philosophy, and, at the UVA School of Law, he co-taught public health law and ethics, and lectured on philosophy of contract law. His recent publications include "On Belling the Cat: Rawls and Corrective Justice" in the *Virginia Law Review* (with Kevin A. Kordana, 2006), "Taxation, the Private Law, and Distributive Justice" in *Social Philosophy and Policy* (with Kevin A. Kordana, 2006), and "Rawls and Contract Law" in *George Washington Law Review* (with Kevin A. Kordana, 2005).

ACKNOWLEDGMENTS

The editors gratefully acknowledge Liberty Fund, Inc., for holding the conference at which the original versions of these papers were presented and discussed.

WHAT IS FREEDOM OF ASSOCIATION, AND WHAT IS ITS DENIAL?*

By Larry Alexander

I. Introduction

Freedom of association, as I understand it, refers to the liberty a person possesses to enter into relationships with others—for any and all purposes, for a momentary or long-term duration, by contract, consent, or acquiescence. It likewise refers to the liberty to refuse to enter into such relationships, or to terminate them when not otherwise compelled by one's voluntary assumption of an obligation to maintain the relationship. Thus, freedom of association is a quite capacious liberty.

Because there is both a positive and a negative aspect of freedom of association—the (positive) freedom to associate and the (negative) freedom to refuse to associate—governments can abridge freedom of association in two ways. They can do so by prohibiting individuals from associating with those with whom they would otherwise choose to associate, or by forcing individuals to associate with those with whom they would otherwise choose not to associate. If freedom of association in both its positive and negative aspects is the default position in a liberal society, the question becomes: What associations may government legitimately force or prohibit, and for what reasons may it do so?

I am going to approach the topic of freedom of association by attempting to illustrate what its denial would look like in each of several domains. I shall then ask why a government might seek to deny it, and on what grounds such a denial would violate the rights with respect to freedom of association of those affected.

II. The Landscape of Associations and Governmental Interferences with Association

A. Intimate associations

Let me begin with what are called "intimate associations." Suppose the government were to engage in picking people's spouses. "Preppy Jewish guys must marry pierced Wiccan girls." Or: "Unfashionable secular academics may not marry Evangelical Yalies." You get the picture. There is,

* I would like to thank Eric Claeys, Andy Koppelman, Ellen Paul, and Steve Smith for their helpful comments, and Caitlyn Obolsky for her excellent research assistance.

doi:10.1017/S0265052508080163

after all, some precedent here. Southern states forbade interracial marriages until the Supreme Court ended this in *Loving v. Virginia* (1967).[1]
And, of course, as of the time I write this, most states forbid same-sex
marriages, polygamous marriages, marriages of siblings, and so on.

Such laws by themselves, in denying the right to attain the status of
marriage, primarily deny the legal incidents of that status (for example,
with respect to intestate inheritance, income taxation, or guardianship in
case of incompetency). Beyond that, they do not forbid freedom of association. But they might be supplemented by other laws that encroach on
freedom of association more considerably.

Most obviously, such laws might forbid sexual contact outside of formal marriage. Adultery, cohabitation, and fornication statutes did this,
though in modern times they were rarely enforced, at least against het-
erosexuals.[2] But if the legal status of marriage is narrowly restricted in
terms of choice of spouse, and this restriction is buttressed by restrictions
on sexual contact outside of marriage, freedom of one kind of association—
sexual relations—will be effectively curtailed.

But the government might conceivably go further still than governments have traditionally gone in the past. It might restrict not only sexual
contact outside of marriage but also emotional attachments outside of
marriage—assuming government does not believe that social norms are
doing that job sufficiently. After all, many consider a spouse's emotional
attachment to another to be as grave a breach of the obligation of marital
fidelity as a spouse's sexual relations with another. And whatever governmental interest supports its enforcement of spouses' obligations of
sexual fidelity presumably also supports its enforcement of their obligations of fidelity more generally.

However, here things get very interesting. Sexual infidelity might be
relatively easy for government to define—Bill Clinton notwithstanding—
and to punish, but what acts would constitute the crime of emotional
infidelity? Presumably the emotions themselves are not a proper basis for
criminal punishment, so government would have to punish acts that (1)
were expressive of emotional infidelity, and (2) were under the voluntary
control of the actor (and thus fairly punishable). We might imagine, for
example, that government would have to forbid phone calls of more than
five minutes or more often than once a day to someone other than one's
spouse. But what if the recipient of the call were a professional colleague?
Of course, one can have an affair with a colleague. Or what about conversations with one's mother, or childhood best friend? These messy
details would have to be sorted out, and sorting them out might prove
practically impossible.

---

[1] *Loving v. Virginia*, 388 U.S. 1 (1967).
[2] *Lawrence v. Texas*, 539 U.S. 558 (2003) (striking down as violative of the Fourteenth
Amendment a Texas law criminalizing homosexual sodomy).

The government might then be tempted to enforce the spousal association by placing affirmative duties on the spouses rather than those difficult-
to-define negative ones. It might affirmatively require, with the backing
of sanctions, that the spouses "love, honor, and obey" one another, as they
have vowed to do. But the affirmative-duties approach to enforcing marital relations is even messier than the negative-duties approach. Love
cannot be commanded. And what affirmative acts would express true
honor? Obedience might be easier, though not without spouses ordering
each other about in code-like fashion, consistently with the principle of
legality.

Government could demand that spouses speak to each other a certain
amount each day (in terms of sentences? words? syllables? duration?
topics?), have sex with each other a specified number of times each week
(what kind? what quality?), or give each other gifts (of what amount?) or
flowers (which?).[3] And government could demand more than that spouses
share whatever incomes they earn during their marriage, as governments
currently do (although without micromanaging how the household bud-
get is actually allocated or how allocation decisions are actually made);
governments could go further and demand that spouses work at a specified occupation for a specified number of hours to ensure the other
spouse is not deprived because the first has independent means.

What all of the preceding demonstrates is that even with respect to an
"association" that the government has traditionally regulated, and regulated for reasons that I shall take to be proper bases for governmental
regulation, restricting freedom to associate and freedom not to associate
is an immensely complex and difficult task. Even where the choice of
one's legal spouse is restricted, and even with a government prepared to
enforce fidelity and other marital vows, government's task is daunting,
especially if social norms are not supporting its efforts. And that is true
not only with respect to affirmative duties, as one might expect, but also

---

[3] Jewish Law comes to mind here: "If a man [seeking to avoid his conjugal responsibil-
ities] forces his wife to take a vow to abstain from intercourse, the maximum length of the
vow may be two weeks—this according to the School of Shammai. But the School of Hillel
says for one week only. Those who are engaged in Torah study, and who are students of the
Sages, may leave their wives [i.e., avoid intercourse] for a period of 30 days. Laborers may
do so for one week. As for frequency of intercourse: for men of independent means [those
that are not working]: every day; for workmen: twice a week; for donkey drivers: once a
week; for camel drivers: once a month; for sailors: once every six months. This is the opinion
of Rabbi Eliezer." M. Ketubot 5:6.

Perhaps the most dramatic example of governmental attempts to dictate fine-grained
marital duties, both positive and negative, is the Taliban's attempt to enforce its interpretation of Islamic law with respect to marriage, under which women were restricted from
being seen by or speaking to men other than their husbands or male relatives. Qu'ran
24:30–24:31. See, e.g., Clark Benner Lombardi, "Islamic Law as a Source of Constitutional
Law in Egypt: The Constitutionalization of Sharia in a Modern Arab State," *Columbia Journal
of Transnational Law* 37 (1998): 81–123; and Karima Bennoune, "Secularism and Human
Rights: A Contextual Analysis of Headscarves, Religious Expression, and Women's Equality
under International Law," *Columbia Journal of Transnational Law* 45 (2007): 367, 389.

with respect to negative ones if one prohibits more than specific adulterous sexual acts. And imagine the difficulties if government ventured beyond marriage and tried to compel certain friendships or to disallow certain ones. What specific acts would it have to forbid or compel, and could it possibly achieve whatever purposes might motivate it?

Why does the government regulate marriage, the only intimate association it regulates at all? That is a question currently much mooted in the context of the debate over gay marriage.[4] Fostering the best environment possible for the rearing of children is one oft-cited reason.[5] And protecting reliance interests of spouses who become vulnerable to economic hardship by forgoing careers is another.[6] Conceivably, however, the government might decide that individuals are poor at choosing the mates most conducive to their flourishing, or that they need external pressures to forge the most beneficial intimate relationships. Or the government might decide that certain marriages—for example, interracial ones—would be socially beneficial (perhaps by destroying racial identities). Those are the reasons a benignly motivated government might attempt to curtail freedom of intimate association. What the previous paragraphs illustrate is just how difficult and intrusive such a task would be.

B. Associations regarding voting and political expression

Governments have attempted in various ways to curtail the associative freedoms of their citizens qua voters and political advocates. In some cases, as in modern Germany with respect to the Nazi Party, political parties with certain ideologies are prohibited from appearing on the ballot.[7] Those with Nazi sympathies can presumably meet somewhere and discuss their common political views, but they cannot deem their organization a "political party" such that its candidates can appear on the ballot as its candidates. Essentially, modern Germans with Nazi sympathies, though they may associate in other ways, may not "associate" their ballots.

In the United States, the Supreme Court in recent years has tended to support political parties' freedom to organize themselves as they choose.[8]

---

[4] See, e.g., William N. Eskridge, Jr., and Darren R. Spedale, *Gay Marriage: For Better or Worse? What We've Learned from the Evidence* (New York: Oxford University Press, 2006); and Mark Poirer, "Piecemeal and Wholesale Approaches Towards Marriage Equality in New Jersey: Is *Lewis v. Harris* a Dead End or Just a Detour?" *Rutgers Law Review* 59 (2007): 291.

[5] See generally Maxine Eichner, "Marriage and the Elephant: The Liberal Democratic State's Regulation of Intimate Relationships between Adults," *Harvard Journal of Law and Gender* 30 (2007): 25. But see also Brief for American Psychiatric Association as Amicus Curiae supporting Respondent, *Boy Scouts of America v. Dale,* 530 U.S. 640 (2000), at 13–24, No. 99-699 (March 29, 2000), 2000 WL 339884.

[6] Eichner, "Marriage and the Elephant," 42–57.

[7] German Basic Law of 1949, Article 21.

[8] *Cal. Democ. Party v. Jones,* 530 U.S. 567 (2000); *Tashjian v. Republican Party,* 479 U.S. 208 (1987); *Democ. Party of U.S. v. Wisconsin,* 450 U.S. 107 (1981).

In other words, the party members may choose, free from governmental interference, the terms on which they associate qua party members. For example, if they wish to hold a closed primary (an election of the party's candidates that is restricted to registered party members)—or an open one (one open to voters of any party)—that is their prerogative.[9]

By contrast, in the so-called White Primary cases, and especially in *Terry v. Adams*,[10] the last of those cases (decided in 1953), the Court itself restricted party members' freedom to associate on terms of their choosing. After the Fifteenth Amendment outlawed denials of the right to vote on racial grounds, many Southern states attempted to continue restricting blacks' votes through various other means, some subtle, some not. Overt discrimination moved from the general election, where it was constitutionally forbidden, to the primaries of the Democratic Party, which was the dominant political party in those states. In the White Primary cases, the Supreme Court held that the Democrats had to open their primaries to black voters.

In *Terry*, the Court prohibited a county in Texas from giving effect to what amounted to (successful) racial bloc voting. Democrats far outnumbered Republicans in the county, and thus the Democratic primary winners always prevailed in the general elections for county offices. Further, white Democrats appreciably outnumbered black Democrats within the county's Democratic Party. Although the Court in one of the earlier White Primary cases had forced the Democratic Party in Texas not to discriminate against black voters in its primaries[11]—which, after all, were run by the state itself out of tax revenues—and the Democratic primary in this county was indeed open to black voters, the white Democrats organized themselves into the Jaybird Club and held their own, privately supported "pre-primary primary." The winning Jaybird candidates then ran in the Democratic primary, in which they always won, and then in the general election, with the same results. In other words, the Jaybirds were successful racial bloc voters. The Court, in a most unedifying and poorly reasoned opinion even by its standards, held that something was constitutionally rotten about this and ordered it stopped.

A moment's reflection will reveal how strange the Court's decision was. Presumably, the Court wanted the Jaybirds either to admit blacks, to disband, or at least not to hold pre-primary elections. Admitting blacks to the Jaybirds would be pointless, at least as members entitled to vote, as that would make the Jaybirds merely a duplicate of the county's Democratic Party. That is so unless the white Jaybirds would then form the Bluebird Club and hold pre-pre-primary elections under *its* auspices—which would replicate the problem of the Jaybirds.

---

[9] See the cases cited in note 8.
[10] *Terry v. Adams*, 345 U.S. 461 (1953).
[11] *Smith v. Allwright*, 321 U.S. 649 (1944).

So suppose the Jaybird Club disbanded. And suppose, in its place, the white Democrats communicated with each other by phone or post (or today, e-mail) and came to an agreement among themselves to support a particular slate of white Democratic candidates. The ultimate results of this racial bloc voting scheme would be the same as those produced by the Jaybirds. The Supreme Court would not like this, but what could it do? Presumably, it could not prohibit white Democrats from talking politics with one another, as this would explicitly violate the First Amendment. Perhaps it could order them not to "agree" with one another—form a cohesive bloc—but it is not clear that it could do so. Nor is it clear that racial bloc voting is different in any principled way from interest-group bloc voting or from ideological bloc voting. (The Court has never argued that prohibitions on the government's taking race into account in governing entail prohibitions on the *citizens'* taking race into account in electing the government itself; and surely a candidate's race as well as ethnicity, gender, age, and religion have been central considerations for both party officials and citizens.)

C. Creedal organizations

One of the most common bases for association and non-association has been that of beliefs. Those who share certain beliefs associate with one another in order to discuss, strengthen, and promote such shared beliefs. The beliefs may be religious ones, and the associations may be churches, synagogues, mosques, campus ministries, and a multitude of orders, charities, study groups, and the like. Or the beliefs may be philosophical, political, or ethical.

Assuming the government is not attempting to stamp out the beliefs by forbidding speech that advocates or even merely transmits those beliefs, restrictions on this form of freedom of association make little sense. Yet governments have attempted to restrict such freedom. No government has, to my knowledge, ordered Catholics to admit women, homosexuals, or Jews to the priesthood[12]—or ordered the Ku Klux Klan to admit blacks into its ranks. But the state of New Jersey did forbid the Boy Scouts to revoke a scoutmaster's membership on the ground that he was a homosexual. In *Boy Scouts of America v. Dale* (2000),[13] the U.S. Supreme Court struck down this application of New Jersey's antidiscrimination law on the ground that forcing the Scouts to allow homosexuals to be members and scoutmasters would alter the Scouts' "messages" and thus violate their First Amendment right of freedom of expressive association. However, the New Jersey nondiscrimination law in question no more affected the Scouts' ability to send their preferred messages than any other law

[12] Nonetheless, it is not exactly transparent, after *Employment Div., Dept. of Human Res. of Oregon v. Smith*, 494 U.S. 872 (1990), how the Supreme Court would find such laws violative of the Constitution—which is not to say that the Court would not find a way to do so.
[13] *Boy Scouts of America v. Dale*, 530 U.S. 640 (2000).

affecting a group's ability to control its membership. If antidiscrimination laws dictate that the *New York Times* may not discriminate against blacks or women in hiring reporters or choosing columnists, the content of what appears in its pages will undoubtedly be affected. Laws regulating membership in *any* organization—including commercial ones—will affect the content of that organization's expression. In that respect, the *Dale* decision was correct. That "message effect," however, is only an incidental effect of a law that is not enacted for the purpose of affecting messages; and laws that are not aimed at messages and have only incidental message effects are not ordinarily violative of the First Amendment.[14] That is why Ollie's Barbeque could not rename itself Ollie's Racist Barbeque and then claim protection from public-accommodations laws on the ground that admitting blacks would denature its racist "message."[15]

The more basic interest at stake in *Dale* and in other collisions between antidiscrimination laws and membership criteria is the interest in associating with like-minded people around certain beliefs, including beliefs bearing on membership in the group itself. If that interest finds protection in a proper account of freedom of association, then the Black Panther Party should not have to admit whites on an equal basis even if those whites subscribe to all the tenets of the Black Panthers other than those regarding membership. Catholics should not have to admit women to the priesthood even if those women subscribe to all Catholic tenets other than that of a male priesthood. In short, a creedal organization should be able to organize around its creed, whatever the creed is, so long as it is not criminal, and even if that creed entails restrictions on membership. If it is part of the Boy Scouts' creed that homosexuals are not to be members, then it is logically impossible for a homosexual such as Dale to pledge adherence to the Scouts' creed and still wish to be a member. Government's forcing Dale's membership on the Scouts would be tantamount to government's denying the right to have a creedal association organized around a creed that endorsed discrimination of a prohibited type. The Supreme Court seems to agree up to a point: So long as it deems the organization to be an "expressive" organization rather than primarily commercial or civic, the Court will protect the organization's membership criteria from regulation under the First Amendment.[16] Nonetheless, as

[14] See Jed Rubenfeld, "The New Unwritten Constitution," *Duke Law Journal* 51 (2001): 289; and Jason Mazzone, "Freedom's Associations," *Washington Law Review* 77 (2002): 639. See also Richard A. Epstein, "The Constitutional Perils of Moderation: The Case of the Boy Scouts," *Southern California Law Review* 74 (2000): 119. See generally Larry Alexander, *Is There a Right of Freedom of Expression?* (Cambridge and New York: Cambridge University Press, 2005), 115–18.

[15] See *Katzenbach v. McClung*, 375 U.S. 294 (1964).

[16] Compare *Roberts v. U.S. Jaycees*, 468 U.S. 609 (1984); *Bd. of Dirs. of Rotary Int'l v. Rotary Club of Duarte*, 481 U.S. 537 (1987); *N.Y. State Club Ass'n v. City of New York*, 487 U.S. 1 (1988), with *Hurley v. Irish-American Gay, Lesbian, and Bisexual Group of Boston*, 515 U.S. 557 (1995); *Boy Scouts of America v. Dale*, 530 U.S. 640 (2000).

the next section illustrates, this places too great a burden on distinguishing creedal from noncreedal organizations and overlooks the "creedal"
aspects of all voluntary organizations.

D. Clubs and other voluntary organizations

Once we move beyond religious and political groups, which are obviously creedal, we enter the vast realm of voluntary nonmarketplace associations. There may be, for example, ascriptive identity groups of great
variety: the Downtown Women's Club; the Black Men's Fraternal Organization; the Greek-American Club; the Gay Men's Club; and so forth.
There may be groups devoted to certain hobbies and activities—the Harley-
Davidson Owner's Club; the Chess Club; the No-Carts Golf Association;
the World Affairs Discussion Group; the Debating Society; and so forth.
(The Boy Scouts and Girl Scouts and many other associations are both
ascriptive—restricted on the bases of gender as well as sexual orientation—
and also devoted to particular activities—as well as being creedal.) There
may be groups devoted to certain virtues or accomplishments—the Veterans of the Korean War; the Abstainers Club; the 20,000 Footers Moun-
taineers Club; and so forth.

It is again unclear why a government would want to regulate membership in such organizations. Would it make sense to require a Women's
Club or a college sorority to admit males? A Black Men's club to admit
Chinese? The Harley-Davidson Owners Club to admit Kawasaki owners?
The Greek-American Club to admit Italian-Americans? The Veterans of
the Korean War to admit nonveterans? The Debating Society to admit
nondebaters? And so on. Were government to do so, it would be tantamount to declaring that one may not have a women's club, a Greek-
American club, or a veterans club. But so long as the activities of these
associations are themselves noncriminal, why would government wish to
thwart voluntary associations formed around these activities or characteristics? (I suggest some answers to this question in Section IV below.)

Moreover, with a flashback to the earlier discussion of *Terry v. Adams*,[17]
what exactly would government be demanding by requiring these associations to admit unwanted members? Would the old members have to
talk to the new members? (If so, how much, and on which topics?) Be nice
to them? Take their opinions into account? If the new members must be
allowed to vote, must the old members refrain from bloc voting? Must
they refrain from organizing activities among themselves (i.e., forming a
club within a club)? Governmental regulation of membership in otherwise voluntary associations carries with it the impossible task of government's micromanaging the activities of those associations to make good
its promise of nondiscrimination.

---

[17] See text at notes 10–11 et seq.

E. Games and activities

The multitude of sports, games, and similar recreational activities affect both how associations are defined and whom they permit to participate. The 2001 *Casey Martin* case is famous for having put the U.S. Supreme Court in the position of questioning whether the PGA's "no cart" rule was essential to professional golf tournaments.[18] Justice Antonin Scalia, in his dissent, scoffed at the idea that there is some Platonic form of golf that does or does not require that competitors walk.[19] But the Court's majority felt compelled to decide the question. (It decided that the "no cart" rule was inessential and thus that Casey Martin, a golfer with a disability that made walking difficult, could use a golf cart in PGA competition.)

Justice Scalia's point remains and appears to expose the Court majority's position as completely arbitrary. As Scalia noted, the Court would be hard-pressed to justify a baseball league's refusal to allow a fourth strike to the myopic. He might also have pointed to Major League Baseball's rule barring midgets, a rule instituted after an owner, Bill Veeck, placed Eddie Gaedel, a midget, on the St. Louis Brown's roster and inserted him as a pinch hitter in order to draw a base on balls (which he did, on four pitches).[20]

The rules of sports and games are entirely artificial. But whatever they are, they will advantage some and disadvantage others. Were the basket in basketball four feet lower, the diminutive former NBA player Muggsy Bogues would be advantaged and giants like Shaquille O'Neal disadvantaged.

Moreover, sports and games frequently define not only how they are to be played but who can play. Most colleges and universities, for example, compete in "women's basketball" or "women's volleyball" or "women's soccer." Men are not eligible to play. In contrast, no university or conference of universities in the modern era would even think about offering "White basketball" or "Asian volleyball." Yet the typical rationalizations for gender-identified sports teams turn on *average* physical differences between men and women, and average physical differences are equally available to rationalize having racially-identified teams. When this point is pressed, the fallback explanation for the difference (between gender-identified sports teams and racially-identified ones) is that women's sports are just "different" from the men's versions, even if the rules are the same. But I imagine that one could make similar claims about racially-identified sports. Indeed, one frequently hears claims that black basketball players

---

[18] See *PGA Tour v. Casey Martin*, 532 U.S. 661 (2001).

[19] Id. at 691–705.

[20] See news stories in Louisville, KY, *The Courier-Journal*, August 18, 19, 20, 21, 1971; *New York Times*, January 21, 1972; *New York Times*, August 19, 2001. The American League president at the time, Al Harridge, immediately banned midgets from the league, a ban that apparently persists to this day.

play a "different game" from that played by whites, or perhaps the less controversial claim that Latin American or European soccer differs from North American soccer.

The *Casey Martin* case came to the courts as a case of discrimination against the disabled (Casey Martin) by a place of public accommodation (a PGA tournament). Even though that interpretation of federal civil rights statutes was strained,[21] it is nonetheless true that sports and games have a commercial aspect, and that how they define themselves and who is eligible to compete can look very much like ordinary marketplace criteria defining what products and services are available and who is best qualified to produce them.

F. Marketplace associations

Let me turn now to marketplace (a.k.a. commercial) associations. We are quite familiar with governmental interferences with individuals' freedom of association in the marketplace, principally through various antidiscrimination laws. Government does not tell employers specifically whom to hire. Rather, it tells them only on what grounds they may not refuse to hire (or on what grounds they may not fire), grounds such as race, ethnicity, gender, age, and religion.

This appears to be, and indeed has proven to be, a fairly manageable project. The employer may not refuse to hire, say, an otherwise qualified black or woman for a particular job. But suppose the employer replies, "Okay, I'll 'hire' so-and-so, but I won't put her to work or pay her." The government's response will undoubtedly be this: The employer can leave the worker in question idle if the employer so wishes, but the employer must pay her at the rate that the employer has set for the particular job in question. The employer will therefore either take a loss (by paying without receiving labor in return) or utilize the worker for the job in question.

But this point about whether the obligation not to discriminate on specified grounds in employment entails further obligations, such as to pay (yes), or to give work to (immaterial, given the obligation to pay), points out the ambiguities inherent in the obligation not to discriminate, ambiguities that have been bedeviling courts in the U.S. for several years. For example, does the obligation not to discriminate against Xs entail an obligation not to discriminate on grounds that have an adverse disproportionate impact on Xs?[22] Does it entail an obligation not to discriminate on the basis of traits highly correlated with Xs or with a subset of Xs?[23]

---

[21] See *supra* note 19.

[22] See *Griggs v. Duke Power Co.*, 401 U.S. 424 (1971).

[23] See generally Kimberly A. Yuracko, "Trait Discrimination as Sex Discrimination: An Argument Against Neutrality" *Texas Law Review* 83 (2004): 167. See also Thomas C. Grey, "Cover Blindness," in R. C. Post, ed., *Prejudicial Appearances* (Durham, NC: Duke University Press, 2001), 85–97.

And does it entail obligations regarding behavior toward Xs other than work and pay, such as refraining from making snide or condescending remarks to them, telling jokes about them, shunning them, engaging in speech that offends them or their religious beliefs, and so on?[24]

These reflections on freedom of association and antidiscrimination laws in the marketplace can lead in a multitude of directions. If government is really concerned with stamping out discrimination against Xs in the marketplace, the implications might be quite extreme. Consider discrimination on the bases of race, ethnicity, gender, age, and religion, the principal forbidden grounds in American antidiscrimination law. What should they entail for the following: Playboy clubs (which hire only *young women*)? Hooters restaurants (same)? The cover girls for *Vogue* magazine (same)? Beauty pageants (same)? The cover girls for *Ebony* magazine (same, plus they must be African-American)? The Miss Greek-American beauty pageant (open only to *young women of Greek ancestry*)? Business prayer meetings (which may make employees of certain faiths or of no faith feel like outsiders)? Hiring only Native-Americans to satisfy consumer demand for jewelry "handcrafted by Native Americans"? Hiring only Shakers to satisfy consumer demand for "furniture made by Shakers"? And so on, virtually ad infinitum. Race, ethnicity, gender, and religion often appear to be part of the product that is being sold in the marketplace. The courts usually do not allow employers to discriminate merely to satisfy the discriminatory preferences of their customers or their other employees, but both the courts and academic commentators have considerable difficulty with the kinds of examples I have just given.[25] Much of the value of goods in the market is bound up with aesthetics, notions of authenticity, aspects of the purchaser's identity, and so on. Authentic Shaker-made furniture or Native-American-handcrafted jewelry are different products from otherwise indistinguishable furniture and jewelry. Even more clearly, an old Chinese man on the cover of *Ebony* would change the magazine's message and appeal. And few go to Hooters for their hamburgers.

Indeed, even though, as I mentioned, the courts refuse to allow employers to discriminate against Xs merely because their other employees discriminate against Xs and will have their morale affected if Xs are hired, it is probably the case that the demographic make-up of the staff of a business has some effect on the staff's productivity. Indeed, one often hears the productive virtues of "diverse" staffs extolled. If demographic

---

[24] After all, employers have convictions—political, religious, and moral—that may conflict with the convictions of their employees. Or they may be providing services to a target group that has convictions at odds with those of the employees. As a consequence, employees may find the work environment quite ideologically uncomfortable. See, e.g., Kent Greenawalt, "Title VII and Religious Liberty," *Loyola University Chicago Law Journal* 33 (2001): 1. Similarly, one set of employees may express views in the workplace that offend another set of employees. See, e.g., Eugene Volokh, "Freedom of Speech, Religious Harassment Law, and Religious Accommodation Law," *Loyola University Chicago Law Journal* 33 (2001): 57.

[25] See *supra* note 23.

diversity might in some cases improve productivity, by the same token in other cases it might impede productivity.

If antidiscrimination laws threaten the loss of real value beyond that of a mere "taste for discrimination," one must ask what their ultimate goal is. They coexist uneasily with a marketplace that is otherwise governed only by consumer sovereignty on the demand side and the profit motive on the supply side. The foregoing examples illustrate this uneasy coexistence.

At this time, government principally intrudes on freedom of association and non-association in the marketplace in only two ways: by regulating employment practices through its antidiscrimination laws, and by barring discrimination on the same forbidden grounds by places of public accommodation in serving customers. Nonetheless, there are many choices within the marketplace where those antidiscrimination laws do not (now) apply, but could apply. For instance, why, if *employers* are prohibited from discriminating against *potential employees* on certain grounds, should *employees* not be similarly prohibited from discriminating against *potential employers*? Or, if restaurants and other places of "public accommodation" may not discriminate (on certain grounds) against potential customers, why should customers be allowed to discriminate against restaurants and other such businesses on those same forbidden grounds? (If I refuse to patronize restaurants owned by Moldovans, I am acting within my legal rights as they currently exist; I am not doing so if the restaurant I own refuses to serve Moldovans.) Likewise, a business that cannot discriminate in those ways in its employment practices may presumably do so when it comes to choosing its suppliers and other contractors. But given the quite slippery (if not illusory) distinctions between employing someone, on the one hand, and purchasing services from him, on the other hand, or between purchasing services and purchasing goods, the writ of freedom of marketplace association as a matter of principle would seem to cover either all such instances of discrimination or none at all.

(There are some other instances of governmental interference with freedom of marketplace association that are primarily designed to keep the marketplace competitive and free of fraud. Antitrust laws prohibit a narrow range of associations that have as their object price-fixing or monopolization.[26] The CEOs of corporations A and B may associate on any number of bases, but they may not agree not to compete with one another. And conflict-of-interest laws prohibit another narrow slice of associations as prophylaxes against fraud or deceptive practices.[27] All such laws do indeed restrict freedom of association in the marketplace in order to keep the marketplace functioning competitively and nondeceptively. And then

---

[26] Sherman Antitrust Act, 15 U.S.C.A. secs. 1–7 (West, Westlaw through 2007 Sess.).

[27] See, e.g., Public Company Accounting Reform and Corporate Responsibility, 15 U.S.C.A. sec. 7211 (West, Westlaw through 2007 P.L. 110-47).

there are, of course, laws that interfere with freedom of marketplace association precisely to counter marketplace competition, such as laws governing unions and their rights vis-à-vis employers and employees.)[28]

G. The nonexistent boundaries between these types of association

Having divided associations into various classifications, I now want to emphasize how arbitrary and misleading that division is. A great many, if not most, associations fall into more than one of the classifications I have mentioned. Social clubs, for example, are venues for close friendships, recreational activities, and commercial intercourse. The same is true of creedal groups, such as religions. Attempting to find the essential nature of any particular association in the terms that I have used to describe associations generally is a bootless quest, a misguided Platonism regarding human associations.

Because much of my attention in the remaining pages will be devoted to marketplace associations, my emphasis here will be on how permeable the boundary is between marketplace enterprises and creedal, social, recreational, and intimate forms of associations. The marketplace is not a sphere detached from these other human pursuits. The *New York Times* and Time Warner are businesses that compete in the marketplace, but they are also creedal. They sell a point of view in their editorials, their selections of stories to report, and in myriad less obvious ways. (I leave aside the question of who—which human beings—the "they" actually refers to in these cases.)

Universities, private academies, and other such institutions are both businesses and creedal (and recreational, social, and frequently somewhat intimate) associations. Recreational and social clubs compete in the marketplace for members; and their members form friendships, ideological commitments, and commercial relationships within their confines.

When parents choose a babysitter for their adolescent daughter and, in so doing, prefer a single, heterosexual female for the job over a heterosexual young male and a homosexual young female, are they to be regarded as associating commercially or as associating intimately? Likewise, if they are choosing someone to take their daughter camping? Likewise, if they choose an all-female private high school for her to attend? To ask these questions is to reveal how artificial the boundary is between commerce and the rest of human affairs. And if the parents are not acting commercially, then is an enterprise set up to provide such parents same-sex heterosexual babysitters or scoutmasters, or sex-specific schools, acting any more "commercially" than are the parents?

The same point can be made about many of the examples I gave earlier. If, to take one of those examples, *Ebony* magazine wants to

[28] See, e.g., Labor-Management Relations Act, 1947, 29 U.S.C.A. chap. 7.

target African-American women—and thus prefers to hire only such women to appear on its cover—there is surely a creedal and social aspect to its choice and the choice of its audience. The same may be true of the customers who want genuine Shaker-made furniture or Native-American handcrafted jewelry. And, as I pointed out earlier, neither employers nor their employees leave their creeds behind when they enter the office.

I cannot emphasize enough how impossible it is to divide any particular domain of associations from the other associative domains.[29] And from this point follows another: Any governmental interference with freedom of any form of association, including commercial association, will perforce result in interference with the other forms of association.

III. Freedom of Association and Liberalism

Freedom of association is a corollary of liberalism. On a standard, classical conception of liberalism, the role of government with respect to associations is to make sure that entrance and exit are consensual—nothing more, and nothing less. Citizens in a liberal state are entitled to deal or not to deal with whomever they choose—intimately, socially, recreationally, and commercially. They may do so for good reasons or for bad ones. Their affirmative obligations are to provide public goods (defense, police, infrastructure)—and, on some versions, a level of material support for their fellow citizens (welfare, free education, subsidized health care)—to abide by the rules prohibiting force, fraud, theft, promissory breach, and dangerous conduct, and to stand ready to defend the liberal framework from enemies foreign and domestic. With respect to the market, the liberal government's writ runs to enforcing contracts, and preventing force and fraud; and on most conceptions, it runs as well to overcoming market imperfections, such as natural monopolies, collective action problems, and the like.

In a modern, Western nation, classical liberalism of this type will spawn a great deal of diversity, the result of diverse beliefs and preferences. Equality at the level of rights of citizens will result in unequal, discriminatory treatment at the level of the exercise of those rights. For when we exercise our rights, we choose, and when we choose, we discriminate—whether it's in choosing our mates, our friends, our pastimes, our creeds, or what we produce and buy. The liberalism of nondiscrimination rests upon the "illiberalism" of individual discriminatory choices.[30] Equality cannot coherently be prized as a value "all the way down."[31] Nor can

---

[29] This makes it puzzling why even some of the most ardent supporters of freedom of association make an exception when it comes to commerce. See, e.g., Mark Hager, "Freedom of Solidarity: Why the Boy Scout Case Was Rightly (But Wrongly) Decided," *Connecticut Law Review* 35 (2002): 129.

[30] See Alexander, *Is There a Right of Freedom of Expression?* 165–66.

[31] See Larry Alexander, "Illiberalism All the Way Down: Illiberal Groups and Two Conceptions of Liberalism," *Journal of Contemporary Legal Issues* 12 (2002): 625.

diversity. For as the Boy Scouts put it in their brief to the Supreme Court in *Dale*, "A society in which each and every organization must be equally diverse is a society that has destroyed diversity."[32] Liberalism as a cosmopolitan perfectionism is self-undermining. Without nonliberal choices and associations, there is no diversity upon which the liberal cosmopolitan can rest his cosmopolitanism; cosmopolitanism as an ideal inevitably homogenizes and shallows out the diversity upon which it depends.[33]

It is against this general background that governmental interferences with freedom of association must be assessed.

IV. Governmental Reasons to Regulate Associations

Why does government interfere with freedom of association to the extent it does, and why might it be tempted to interfere even more? Let me put to the side certain regulations of marriage premised on protection of the welfare of children or protection of economically vulnerable spouses. Let me also put aside the following: those interferences with freedom of association in the name of collective bargaining, which are *sui generis*; regulations of political parties, which have, since the White Primary cases, been largely held unconstitutional by the courts; antitrust and conflict-of-interest legislation; and prophylactic criminal restraints, such as "no contact" orders, anti-stalking orders, and conditions of parole and probation. That leaves, as the principal form of interference, antidiscrimination laws and their outgrowths. Such laws—real and hypothesized—are usually justified by their proponents as legitimate forms of social engineering, as perfectionist-paternalism, or as legal moralism.

A. Social engineering

On their face, antidiscrimination laws appear inconsistent with classical liberalism. However, there is a plausible case that they are not—or, at least, that they are not when applied to: (1) a relatively large, public corporation; (2) that is solely engaged in commerce; (3) that is producing a good or service with no ascriptive or ideological content (say, rivets); and (4) the law prohibits intentional discrimination on a few ascriptive grounds and does not extend to disparate impact discrimination (discrimination based on criteria that correlate more highly with some ascriptive groups than others), trait-based discrimination (discrimination based on criteria typically identified with a particular ascriptive group), (some) hostile-environment discrimination, and perhaps statistical ("rational") discrimination. So limited, antidiscrimination laws might be justifiable attempts to overcome collective action problems that existed in various

---

[32] Brief for Petitioners, *Boy Scouts of America v. Dale*, 530 U.S. 640 (2000).
[33] See Alexander, *Is There a Right of Freedom of Expression?* 169.

parts of the country during the last century and that prevented employers, employees, and consumers from hiring and dealing with African-Americans, women, and sometimes homosexuals. In many areas of the South, for example, even after the demise of the Jim Crow laws, there was tremendous social pressure not to cross the "color line" in commerce, pressure often backed by fear of violent retaliation and undependable law enforcement protection. To a lesser extent, this may also have been true of hiring homosexuals. And there was surely social pressure, if not the threat of violence, deterring the hiring of women. Antidiscrimination laws may have been welcomed as the means for overcoming this collective action problem.

There are other similar "social engineering" rationales that can be offered in support of limited antidiscrimination laws and their interference with freedom of association. One rationale takes us back to the discussion of cosmopolitan liberalism and the perhaps paradoxical fact that liberalism in its classical form is a big tent housing "illiberal" choices and the illiberal associations that are their outgrowths. It may be argued that a liberal polity cannot exist if certain liberal attitudes are not cultivated and sustained, and that racism, sexism, and similar prejudices must be extirpated for the liberal project to succeed. Freedom of association must be limited to secure a regime in which freedom of association can flourish.

There is, of course, some plausibility to this argument, particularly where African-Americans in the United States in the mid-twentieth century were concerned. There may also be some plausibility to it with respect to women, homosexuals, and members of certain religious groups. But notice that there is an ever-present danger with such arguments, a danger that in the name of saving liberalism, we shall have to destroy it.

Antidiscrimination laws might also be supported on welfare-maximizing grounds, apart from the collective-action market imperfection mentioned previously. Normally, in a free market economy, if we put aside market imperfections, including information deficits, wealth is maximized by consumer/producer sovereignty. Redistribution of wealth, to the extent it is justified, is better accomplished by direct transfers through taxation/spending than by interfering with market choices. Moreover, the standard concern of liberal redistributionists is the income of individuals, not the income of ascriptive groups.[34]

---

[34] Groups as such are not the objects of concern for liberal redistributionists, and especially not ascriptive groups. If the worst off *individual* is better off under policy A than under policy B, then the liberal redistributionist would instruct us to choose policy A, even if, say, African-Americans or women as a group fared less well under A than under B. And although it is true that John Rawls, an archetypical liberal redistributionist, referred to a representative of the least well off *group* as the bellwether for just policies, he was referring to income groups (e.g., the poor), not to ascriptive groups. See generally John Rawls, *A Theory of Justice* (Cambridge, MA: Harvard University Press, 1971). And Rawls's theory is otherwise quite individualistic in its concerns, emphasizing the separateness of persons. Ibid., 22–46.

However, antidiscrimination laws might be viewed as aimed at affecting social attitudes regarding race, religion, and the like, with the ultimate goal of improving the welfare of certain groups and, perhaps as a consequence, increasing the welfare of most individuals. In the marketplace, assuming a free, competitive economy, if there were no change of racial attitudes among employers, employees, and customers, antidiscrimination laws would merely transfer wealth from some individuals to others and would cause a net decline in welfare. The hope—and the hope has been realized almost completely—was that the existing racist, sexist, and similar attitudes would be extinguished and that the total welfare would ultimately be increased—because the allocation of resources would be improved by antidiscrimination laws once those old attitudes disappeared.

Notice that in terms of overall social welfare, as opposed to a reallocation of welfare among groups, antidiscrimination laws would have been a gamble. They would have been a bet that racial and like attitudes could be altered by forced associations of certain kinds, and that, so altered, the individuals whose attitudes they were would attain more satisfaction and fulfillment in the newer forms of association than they would have if the old forms had persisted. With the racial premium removed, for example, not only could blacks find employment commensurate with their skills, and opportunities to consume commensurate with their wealth, but employers would receive more productivity from employees and provide more satisfaction to consumers. And the same is true regarding gender, religion, and the other "forbidden grounds."

As I said, the bet was won. But some are dissatisfied with the results, as dramatic as they have been. They are dismayed that blacks—at least those not from immigrant families—have made less economic progress as a group than they would have hoped. Or they are dissatisfied that women, though now nearly equal in numbers to men in medicine and law, are still disproportionately underrepresented in the sciences, engineering, and top corporate management, and overrepresented in unpaid household and childcare labor.

Those dissatisfied with the results of current antidiscrimination laws sometimes argue for compelled proportionate representation, usually maintaining that the tastes and attitudes that result in the current underrepresentation of certain groups in certain occupations can give way with no net loss of aggregate welfare. (Sometimes the mantra that these attitudes are "socially constructed" is a shorthand way of making this claim.)

Moreover, races and ethnic groups are quite artificial constructs. Biologically, human beings are one interbreeding species, with no bright-line biological divisions. Sociologically, races and ethnic groups can be (and are) defined in different ways for different purposes and by different people. See Larry Alexander and Maimon Schwarzschild, "Grutter or Otherwise: Racial Preferences and Higher Education," *Constitutional Commentary* 21 (2004): 3; and Larry Alexander, "Equal Protection and the Irrelevance of 'Groups,'" *Issues in Legal Scholarship* (2002), http://www.bepress.com/ils/iss2/art1.

If government were to bet on such claims, I strongly doubt that the bet would pay off. The kinds of blatantly racist and sexist attitudes that the current antidiscrimination laws eroded were pretty thin and superficial, at least for most who held them. And the amount of welfare that was sacrificed to honor those attitudes was quite high. The attitudes and tastes that result in "underrepresentation" are quite different in all relevant respects. The preference for, say, good math skills is thin and superficial only for those who do not care whether the walls of their house will meet at right angles, whether their monthly bank balance is correct, or whether the plane they are flying in is safe. Moreover, the social groups whose identity and salience as groups were themselves the products of racist and sexist attitudes have lost their identity and salience with the eradication of those attitudes and the practices that embodied them, the identity-politics hustlers to the contrary notwithstanding.

The fact that the preferences that result in "underrepresentation" are now quite different from those that animated "no blacks or women need apply" forms of discrimination explains the difficulties the courts have had with "trait-based" preferences (those based on a trait usually identified with a particular ascriptive group), "sex-plus" preferences (those directed at a subgroup of one sex), and other forms of preferences that have a local, though not necessarily a global, adverse disproportionate impact on certain groups. Requiring women to wear dresses, men to shave and to wear non-baggy pants fastened at the waist rather than the groin, and similar requirements are sometimes assimilated by advocates and more than a few courts to the "no Xs need apply" forms of discrimination. But although the genesis of these preferences might pass through certain race- or sex-linked ideas of propriety, they will, I suspect, prove hardier and more difficult to dislodge than the blatantly sexist and racist ones. The amount of re-engineering of our preferences necessary to rid them of all connections to ideas with a racial, ethnic, national, religious, or sexual component would be staggering if not impossible even to conceive. Our preferences for authentic Native-American-made pottery or Shaker furniture are just the tips of the iceberg of preferences that undergird our intimate, ideological, recreational, and other associations in addition to our marketplace ones.

I say that the current antidiscrimination laws have proven successful as social engineering. Nonetheless, it should be pointed out that although these laws are often thought of as harm-preventing intrusions on freedom of association—because they are thought of as shielding racial and religious minorities and women from harm—they are surely violative of libertarian principles and also, in their wager on overall welfare improvement, more than a little paternalistic. Although the employer, employees, and customers with racially or sexually bigoted views were, in discriminating, acting within their libertarian rights (assuming *their* wealth was justly acquired), the antidiscrimination laws interfered with their associating with whom they chose on the ground of overall social good, not a ground that a libertarian would accept as a justification. Moreover, the overall social good in no small part depended for its achievement on the paternalistic assumption that a forced change in attitudes would enhance the welfare of those forced to change.

B. Paternalism: Compelling associations that are beneficial to flourishing and forbidding those that are self-destructive

A second principal reason government might have for interfering with freedom of association is its concern that its citizens choose the good and eschew the bad. Most of the laws that currently interfere with freedom of association are not paternalistically justified; but there are hints of paternalism in some of the rationales for extending (or "interpreting") antidiscrimination laws in various directions. For example, Kimberly Yuracko argues that gender discrimination laws can best be rationalized and justified by reading into them a "perfectionist" rationale, that is, a concern for women's flourishing.[35] Certain jobs are degrading to women, and employers should not be allowed to offer them to women (and, necessarily, women should not be allowed to accept them on the terms offered).

Yuracko's basic perfectionist approach can easily be extended to racial and other forms of discrimination. Moreover, it is not confined to employment. If some jobs are bad for us—they represent shallow or base values and thus take us off the path to our true flourishing—then so are some noncommercial activities, organizations, creeds, and intimates.

Now I am not a skeptic about whether there are better and worse paths to flourishing, or whether some jobs, activities, organizations, creeds, and friendships are shallow, base, or degrading. What I *am* skeptical about is the competency of government to make judgments about the paths to flourishing. It has not been my experience that government is a repository for that kind of wisdom. Nor do I find the processes of governmental decision-making in the modern mass democracy well-designed to produce that wisdom. But even if government were generally reliable with respect to identifying the paths to flourishing, there would remain the question of government's entitlement to act paternalistically.

C. Legal moralism

There is another rationale for antidiscrimination laws and their infringements of freedom of association apart from how they affect consumer satisfaction in the economy, the welfare of certain groups, or the flourishing of those who discriminate. That rationale is simply that certain

[35] See Kimberly A. Yuracko, "Private Nurses and Playboy Bunnies: Explaining Permissible Sex Discrimination," *California Law Review* 92 (2004): 147, 201–12.

forms of discrimination are just morally wrong, and government is entitled to forbid them for that reason alone.

Now the question of when and why private discrimination is morally wrong is a difficult one, as the literature on the subject reveals.[36] But putting that question aside, there is the more basic issue of whether governments may legitimately prohibit conduct that is merely immoral. Joel Feinberg presented the most sustained case against legal moralism.[37] Other liberals have taken the opposite point of view.[38] Even they, however, have suggested that there is a strong presumption in favor of liberty and against prohibitions based on mere immorality.[39]

V. THE RIGHT OF (BAD) ASSOCIATION

Suppose that government knew better than most of us what kinds of association were conducive to our flourishing and what kinds were detrimental thereto. Suppose as well that government could effectively control our associations without unduly consuming resources and without becoming a dangerous Leviathan. One still might object to its paternalistic interferences with freedom of association on the ground that we have the right to choose the bad—the shallow, the base, the degrading—and eschew the good, so long, that is, as others' rights are not infringed by our choices.

Surely the libertarian liberal would agree with this. All interferences with associative freedom look suspect to her, including the antidiscrimination laws currently governing employers and public accommodations. Freedom of association to the greatest extent possible follows naturally from libertarian premises, even so-called left-libertarian ones. If the avoidance of social strife requires an end to, say, racial discrimination, that may be a matter of prudential exercise of one's rights, but not a ground for coercive interference with private choices that are otherwise legitimate.

The same result follows from versions of neutralist welfare liberalism that give the right priority over the good. The welfare liberal may support redistribution of wealth, which will in turn have major effects on which associations look attractive. Nevertheless, the neutralist welfare liberal would not, if consistent, redistribute wealth by interfering with freedom of association itself.

[36] Symposium, "The Rights and Wrongs of Discrimination," *San Diego Law Review* 43 (2006): 733; Larry Alexander, "What Makes Wrongful Discrimination Wrong?" *University of Pennsylvania Law Review* 141 (1992): 149.

[37] Joel Feinberg, *The Moral Limits of the Criminal Law*, vol. 4: *Harmless Wrongdoing* (New York: Oxford University Press, 1988).

[38] See generally Joseph Raz, *The Morality of Freedom* (Oxford: Clarendon Press, 1986); and Michael S. Moore, *Placing Blame* (Oxford: Clarendon Press, 1997), 70, 662–63, 756.

[39] See Moore, *Placing Blame*, 763–77.

The perfectionist liberal is a different matter. Joseph Raz, for example, argues that so long as a range of valuable alternatives are available, government may legitimately curtail choice for paternalistic reasons.[40] Raz, however, would only allow government to subsidize good choices.[41] He would not allow it to prohibit bad choices that do not impose harmful externalities.

I find the moral rationale for Raz's distinction between subsidies and penalties elusive.[42] Indeed, I find the distinction itself to be so. I suspect that Raz believes that subsidies do not curtail the freedom of the non-subsidized, whereas penalties obviously do. A stronger version of liberal perfectionism would self-confidently allow government to ban bad associations and allow autonomous choice to operate only among choiceworthy options. In any event, as I said earlier, I for one lack the confidence in governmental wisdom to endorse that form of paternalism, even if I had no libertarian or neutralist liberal objection to perfectionist liberalism as a theory of governmental authority and individual rights.

VI. Conclusion

Governmental interference with freedom of association is a messy, intrusive business; and even when it is warranted, it is difficult to pull off entirely successfully in a non-Orwellian regime. Moreover, even rather minimal restrictions raise serious questions of legitimacy. Governmental attempts to engineer our preferences or to foreclose our associating for shallow, base, or degrading reasons contravenes libertarian and neutralist liberal principles. Such attempts place government in the role of writing the rules of golf.

Law, University of San Diego

---

[40] See Raz, *The Morality of Freedom*, 380–81, 410–12.
[41] Ibid., 418–22.
[42] See Larry Alexander, "The Legal Enforcement of Morality," in R. G. Frey and Christopher Heath Wellman, eds., *A Companion to Applied Ethics* (Oxford: Blackwell Publishing, 2003), 128–141.

ORGANIZED LABOR AND AMERICAN LAW: FROM FREEDOM OF ASSOCIATION TO COMPULSORY UNIONISM

By Paul Moreno

I. Introduction

Labor unions have long presented a conundrum for the principle of freedom of association in American history. In pursuit of their associative goals, unions must compromise the freedom of association of others—employers, nonunion workers, and consumers.[1] Yet most American historians maintain that the legal system has deprived workers of their freedom to form effective labor associations. A composite account goes something like this: Unions were outlawed as criminal conspiracies before 1842. Even after courts recognized their legal existence, their methods (strikes, picketing, boycotting) were useless because laissez-faire, "free-labor" formalism hid the overwhelming economic power of employers behind a façade of equality. Courts then subverted the Fourteenth Amendment from its purpose of protecting black civil rights and turned it into a shield for the property rights of big business. In the Gilded Age, courts fashioned the labor injunction to recriminalize unions. Worse still, when Congress enacted antitrust laws to curb big business, judges used them to crush organized labor. Judges also vitiated congressional and state acts to exempt unions from injunctions and antitrust laws. When Congress finally acted in the 1930s, either it did so primarily to dampen truly radical working-class activism, or the federal courts and administrators "deradicalized" congressional intent. In either case, national labor relations legislation ended up as a net loss for organized labor. Union power eroded after World War II and collapsed after 1980, largely due to political and legal disadvantages.[2]

[1] Sheldon Leader, *Freedom of Association: A Study in Labor Law and Political Theory* (New Haven, CT: Yale University Press, 1992), 6.

[2] This caricature is not far from Leon Fink, "Labor, Liberty, and the Law: Trade Unionism and the Problem of the American Constitutional Order," *Journal of American History* 74 (1987): 904–25. Fink sketches "an era of repressive conspiracy indictments followed by an era of equally demobilizing dependency on government by labor." It is notable that, in this issue of the *Journal of American History* memorializing the bicentennial of the Constitution, the "American constitutional order" rather than "trade unionism" is the "problem." For a recent overview of the literature, see Josiah B. Lambert, *"If the Workers Took a Notion": The Right to Strike and American Political Development* (Ithaca, NY: ILR Press, 2005), 16; and Melvyn Dubofsky, "The Federal Judiciary, Free Labor, and Equal Rights," in *The Pullman Strike and the Crisis of the 1890s: Essays on Labor, Politics, and the State*, ed. Richard Schneirov et al. (Urbana: University of Illinois Press, 1998), 159–61.

doi:10.1017/S0265052508080175

At least since the early twentieth century, American historiography has displayed an anticapitalist bias, especially in matters of labor relations.[3] A half-century ago, a historian of employer associations noted that students of labor relations "almost universally have had a bias in favor of the laborer or the trade union."[4] So deep is this orientation that a recent and overtly "conservative" history observes that nineteenth-century "laborers were not free to bargain with business owners over wages and work conditions because government stacked the deck against them. Federal and state politicians outlawed union membership, issued court injunctions to halt strikes and cripple labor activism, and sent in federal and state troops to protect the interests of powerful businessmen."[5]

Legal history echoes these conclusions. Reflecting the influence of "critical legal studies," legal academics assume that the ruling class wields law as an instrument of capitalist hegemony. In 2002, for example, the University of Pennsylvania Law School built a conference around the theme of the "essential role of law in reinforcing and rationalizing class distinctions in the twentieth century." "Historically," the conference description stated, "law and legal theory have shaped, maintained, and justified class hierarchies, as well as hidden them from political view."[6] One prominent historian of labor law claims that unions have been "down by law," with nineteenth-century courts keeping them in "semi-outlawry, suppressing peaceful boycotts and strikes."[7] Indeed, even the standard textbook in American constitutional history observes: "Since the landmark case of *Commonwealth v. Hunt* in 1842 labor unions were held not to be illegal, but by the 1890s they might as well have been for all the restraints that courts had placed upon them."[8]

---

[3] Louis M. Hacker, "The Anticapitalist Bias of American Historians," in *Capitalism and the Historians*, ed. F. A. Hayek (Chicago: University of Chicago Press, 1954), 72. Hacker notes that the general anticapitalist bias among American historians is not due to Marxist or communist influence, but more from native Jeffersonian-populist traditions. But this is less so in the case of "labor history," a self-consciously "movement" history that flowered in the 1960s. It is important to note that, in the Marxist view, historical writing, as much as law, is a weapon in the class struggle. That is to say, bourgeois historians will write history in the interests of their class, and so will proletarians—or intellectuals who understand the true interests of the proletariat. This should remind a reader to treat Marxist-inspired labor history with more than the usual critical distance.

[4] Clarence E. Bonnett, *History of Employers' Associations in the United States* (New York: Vantage Press, 1956), 14; W. H. Hutt, *The Theory of Collective Bargaining, 1930–1975* (Washington, DC: Cato Institute, 1980), 76.

[5] Larry Schweikart and Michael Allen, *A Patriot's History of the United States* (Norwalk, CT: Sentinel, 2004), 418.

[6] "Call for Papers," *Law and History Review* 19 (2001).

[7] William E. Forbath, "Down by Law? History and Prophecy about Organizing in Hard Times and a Hostile Legal Order," in *Audacious Democracy: Labor, Intellectuals, and the Social Reconstruction of America*, ed. Steven Fraser and Joshua B. Freeman (Boston, MA: Mariner Books, 1997), 132.

[8] Alfred H. Kelly, Winfred A. Harbison, and Herman Belz, *The American Constitution: Its Origins and Development*, 7th ed. (New York: W. W. Norton, 1991), 398.

Though some scholars have dissented from this orthodox view, they have not made much of an impression on mainstream historiography.[9] This is unfortunate, and it is the argument of this essay that American law has never denied organized labor's freedom of association. Quite the contrary, unions have always enjoyed at least some favoritism in the law, which has provided the essential element to their success and power. Nonetheless, even during the heyday of union power (1930–1947), organized labor never succeeded in gaining all of the privileges that it sought, and, indeed, it has not made sufficient gains to stem its current (private-sector) decline back to historically normal levels. This essay will examine the legal standing of labor unions in three periods (discussed in Sections II through IV below). In the first period, American law liberated itself from old English common law principles of master-and-servant, and especially from the remnants of conspiracy doctrine, culminating in *Commonwealth v. Hunt* (1842). This liberated status was supplemented by the mid-nineteenth-century antislavery, free-labor doctrine, and during this period the nation's predominant labor organization (the American Federation of Labor) emerged. In the second period (from the 1870s to the 1930s), unions sought legal relief from developments in the law of labor relations (most markedly, the development of the labor injunction in equity), and also from federal antitrust statutes. Most especially, this period saw the major Progressive departure from the founding constitutional ideas of law and rights. The Progressive ideology culminated in the third, New Deal period, especially in the Norris-LaGuardia and National Labor Relations Acts. In this period, classical "freedom of association" finally gave way to a fundamentally different principle, the entitlement to collective bargaining. With law and the administrative state clearly on their side, unions made impressive gains, which provoked a reaction in the Taft-Hartley Act and other acts after 1947. However, though organized labor remained privileged, the state began to take back some of what it had

---

[9] In a generally outstanding recent revisionist work, Daniel R. Ernst dismisses the work of "several scholars [Barry Poulson, Sylvester Petro, Richard Epstein, and Howard Dickman] writing from a libertarian perspective," noting that they "were not trained as professional historians, and they displayed so little interest in understanding the past on its own terms that their work had little impact. It remains a historiographic dead end." Daniel R. Ernst, *Lawyers Against Labor: From Individual Rights to Corporate Liberalism* (Urbana: University of Illinois Press, 1995), 237. It is more than a little doubtful that these authors' lack of academic background or their disinterestedness accounts for the neglect of their works in comparison to the near-universal resort to the work of Felix Frankfurter and Nathan Greene, neither of whom (unlike Dickman) possessed a doctorate in history, and whose famous work, *The Labor Injunction* (New York: Macmillan, 1930), has been aptly and often called "a brief for the Norris-LaGuardia Act." See P. F. Brissenden, "The Campaign Against the Labor Injunction," *American Economic Review* 23 (1933): 43; John Minor Wisdom, "Rethinking Injunctions," *Yale Law Journal* 89 (1980): 826; Dianne Avery, "Images of Violence in Labor Jurisprudence: The Regulation of Picketing and Boycotts, 1894–1921," *Buffalo Law Review* 37 (1988–89): 5; and Catherine Fisk, "Still 'Learning Something of Legislation': The Judiciary in the History of Labor Law," *Law and Social Inquiry* 19 (1994): 166. For works by Poulson, Petro, Epstein, and Dickman, see notes 12, 17, 44, 46, 106, 129, and 134 below.

given in the New Deal era, and market forces returned unions to roughly the place they had occupied at the beginning of the twentieth century.

II. Labor Combinations Before 1842

The Anglo-American common law imposed a variety of restrictions on laborers, recognizing a broad spectrum of rights and obligations between chattel slavery at one end and autonomy at the other. English law criminalized any kind of labor combination to raise wages, a restriction that went back at least as far as the Statute of Laborers, enacted in 1349 to prevent workers from taking advantage of the labor scarcity caused by the Black Death. As late as 1800, Parliament enacted an Anti-Combinations Act for similar ends.[10] English labor law—the law of "master and servant," sometimes referred to as the "Tudor Industrial Code"—treated not just slaves but also apprentices and indentured servants as part of the family, household, or property of their employers, in order for employers to be able to control the labor supply and keep the poor working.[11] Guild members, in contrast, had a property right in certain trades, within legal limits.[12]

American courts recognized the common law principle that conspiracies—concerted actions to achieve illegal ends, or using unlawful means to achieve lawful ends—could be criminally prosecuted. But colonial American restrictions were less effective, and the general movement in antebellum American law was to free the individual worker from medieval personal restraints.[13] In short, employment law followed the general transition "from status to contract" elaborated by Sir Henry Maine.[14] By one estimation, unions faced twenty-one labor-conspiracy prosecutions before 1842, losing fifteen.[15] No court condemned an American trade union as a criminal conspiracy per se, apart from questions of

[10] Leonard W. Levy, *The Law of the Commonwealth and Chief Justice Shaw: The Evolution of American Law, 1830–1860* (Cambridge, MA: Harvard University Press, 1957), 183.

[11] William E. Nelson, *Americanization of the Common Law: The Impact of Legal Change on Massachusetts Society, 1760–1830* (Cambridge, MA: Harvard University Press, 1975), 51.

[12] Howard Dickman, *Industrial Democracy in America: Ideological Origins of National Labor Relations Policy* (La Salle, IL: Open Court, 1987), 26–29.

[13] For two recent works that emphasize that modern, free-labor status was not necessarily an improvement for workers, and that feudal labor restrictions persisted into the twentieth century, see Robert J. Steinfeld, *The Invention of Free Labor: The Employment Relation in English and American Law and Culture, 1350–1870* (Chapel Hill: The University of North Carolina Press, 1991); and Karen Orren, *Belated Feudalism: Labor, the Law, and Liberal Development in the United States* (New York: Cambridge University Press, 1991).

[14] Henry Maine, *Ancient Law* (1861; New York: Macmillan, 1931); Jay M. Feinman, "The Development of the Employment at Will Rule," *American Journal of Legal History* 20 (1976): 124; Lawrence M. Friedman, *A History of American Law* (New York: Simon and Schuster, 1973), 275.

[15] Anthony Woodiwiss, *Rights Versus Conspiracy: A Sociological Essay on the History of Labour Law in the United States* (New York: St. Martin's Press, 1990); John T. Nockleby, "Two Theories of Competition in the Early Nineteenth Century Labor Cases," *American Journal of Legal History* 38 (1994): 471.

means employed to achieve their ends. Labor union attorneys often won acquittals when they could show that union members had not used coercive means, and those convicted received negligible punishments—small fines, and never any jail time.[16] "There is not a single case in which the courts in America held that a peaceful strike by a union for higher wages, standing alone, constituted a criminal conspiracy," another study concludes.[17] However, factual and doctrinal questions are often difficult to discern in the records of these early cases.[18] In the earliest recorded labor-conspiracy case, the 1806 Philadelphia Cordwainers (shoemakers) case, the trial record revealed "some minor injuries and verbal threats" by the striking workers, but this was not part of the prosecutor's indictment or the jury verdict.[19] Another account notes that these early cases involved violence, but adds: "Nevertheless, striking laborers were inclined to think that it was their right."[20]

The great Massachusetts chief justice Lemuel Shaw put to rest any question about the legality of trade unions in the famous case of *Commonwealth v. Hunt,* decided in 1842. The Boston Journeymen Bootmakers' Society maintained a "closed shop" agreement with Isaac B. Wait, a master cordwainer, in which Wait agreed to employ no journeymen who were not members of the society. The society's members forced Wait to dismiss Jeremiah Horne, who then sought a criminal prosecution against the society. The trial court convicted the society of an illegal conspiracy. Shaw, on the Supreme Judicial Court, overturned the conviction. He held that, while Massachusetts had adopted the English common law of criminal conspiracy, "we cannot perceive that it is criminal for men to agree together to exercise their own acknowledged rights, in such manner as best to subserve their own interests." While the prosecutors did not allege a "conspiracy or even an intention to raise their wages," Shaw noted, "Such an agreement . . . would be perfectly justifiable," unless it were accompanied by illegal means like "coercion, or duress, by force or fraud." The chief justice noted "the established principle, that every free man . . . may work or not work, or work or refuse to work with any company or individual, at his own option, except so far as he is bound by contract." A monopolistic combination's legality depended upon the means that it used to maintain its power. Unless it used illegal means, involving force or fraud, it was legal. Shaw concluded with an analogy to show how competition curtailed the ill effects of producer conspiracies. "Suppose a baker in a

[16] Lambert, *"If the Workers Took a Notion,"* 22.

[17] B. W. Poulson, "Criminal Conspiracy, Injunctions, and Damage Suits in Labor Law," *Journal of Legal History* 7 (1986): 215.

[18] Feinman, "The Development of the Employment at Will Rule," 122–23.

[19] Woodiwiss, *Rights Versus Conspiracy,* 53; Nockleby, "Two Theories of Competition," 464.

[20] Herbert Hovenkamp, *Enterprise and American Law, 1836–1937* (Cambridge, MA: Harvard University Press, 1991), 228.

small village had the exclusive custom of his neighborhood, and was making large profits by the sale of his bread. Supposing a number of those neighbors, believing the price of his bread too high, should propose to him to reduce his prices, or if he did not, that they would introduce another baker; and on his refusal, such other baker should, under their encouragement, set up a rival establishment, and sell his bread at lower prices; the effect would be to diminish the profit of the former baker, and to the same extent to impoverish him. And it might be said and proved, that the purpose of the associates was to diminish his profits, and thus impoverish him, though the ultimate and laudable object of the combination was to reduce the cost of bread to themselves and their neighbors. The same thing may be said of all competition in every branch of trade and industry; and yet it is through that competition, that the best interests of trade and industry are promoted."[21]

For those expecting consistently antiunion bias in the law, the *Hunt* decision has posed something of a problem, especially since it came from Chief Justice Shaw, a "conservative," natural-rights-respecting Whig. Reducing the decision to political motives and economic policy, Yale law professor Walter Nelles argued that Shaw and the Whigs were attempting to placate organized labor in order to win its support for protective tariffs.[22] Others have pointed out that Shaw offered *Hunt* as a small concession to organized labor to take some of the edge off of his more significant antiunion decision in the 1842 *Farwell* case, which established the "fellow servant rule" (holding that employers are not liable for injuries to workers if due to the negligence of other employees). Shaw's mere sop, though, could not disguise the fact that *Hunt* was "a perpetuation of that same [antilabor] bias skillfully reconstituted the more ably to serve the needs of an evolving capitalism." Since it did not protect the *means* of labor combination (strikes, picketing, boycotts), *Hunt* left the door open to criminal conspiracy prosecution, which would "prove devastating in the late nineteenth century."[23]

These views of *Hunt* conform to the general view of the antebellum legal system as being manipulated by capitalists to secure economic benefits for themselves. In his pathbreaking 1977 book *The Transformation of American Law,* Harvard law professor Morton Horwitz purported to show how the common law of property, liability, and contract was altered by judges in order to shift the economic burden of industrialization onto small farmers and workers, "to force those injured by economic activities

---

[21] *Commonwealth v. Hunt,* 45 Mass. 111, 130–34 (1842).

[22] Walter Nelles, "*Commonwealth v. Hunt,*" *Columbia Law Review* 32 (1932): 1128–70. See also discussion in Levy, *The Law of the Commonwealth,* 192–96; and Christopher L. Tomlins, *Law, Labor, and Ideology in the Early American Republic* (Cambridge: Cambridge University Press, 1993), 209–10.

[23] Tomlins, *Law, Labor, and Ideology,* 210, 216. *Farwell v. Boston and Worcester Railroad Corp.,* 45 Mass. 49 (1842).

to bear the cost of the improvements." Horwitz argues that nineteenth-century courts applied a "ruthless" conceptualism when it came to labor contracts, but not to other contracts, displaying their class bias.[24] As the standard constitutional history textbook puts it, "State courts in effect subsidized the development of the economy by fashioning legal doctrines and rules that shifted the cost of economic and technological change from the entrepreneur to the community."[25]

This thesis has undergone a thorough revision in the last generation. One study concludes that, far from subsidizing the rich, American judges consistently used the law to aid the weak and the poor. These judges were neither tools of rapacious capitalists nor engaged in a law-and-economics calculus of social utility. Rather, nineteenth-century jurists were "arguing earnestly over basic principles of law and justice," in which religion figured more prominently than economics.[26] "Jurists seem ultimately to have been more concerned with inspiring what they thought of as morally and socially responsible behavior than economic efficiency, and these two ends were often *not* the same."[27]

In short, we have no reason to regard *Hunt* as anything more or less than a recognition of the status that labor unions had long enjoyed under the American common law. They were free to associate for lawful ends, including the raising of wages or reduction of hours or even, in Massachusetts, to establish a closed shop. Though these were combinations to reduce competition, to control the labor supply, or otherwise to extract resources from employers and consumers, workers were as free as any other economic associations to attempt to do so by lawful means—without force or fraud.

Leaders of the antebellum labor movement, however, regarded this formal legal equality and freedom to combine as a sham. They denigrated the individualistic "free-labor" philosophy of northern liberalism as a mask for "wage slavery." Labor activists claimed that capitalism had produced what later generations would call the "inequality of bargaining power," which actually left workers with no choice but to accept the terms that their employers offered. Indeed, the fear of potential competition from Southern slaves led many antebellum labor unionists to take an "anti-anti-slavery" stance, and sometimes an outright pro-slavery one. As one scholar notes, "even radical historians have not been able to show

[24] Morton Horwitz, *The Transformation of American Law, 1780–1860* (Cambridge, MA: Harvard University Press, 1977), 187–88.

[25] Kelly, Harbison, and Belz, *The American Constitution*, 239.

[26] Peter Karsten, *Heart Versus Head: Judge-Made Law in Nineteenth-Century America* (Chapel Hill: The University of North Carolina Press, 1997), 224. On the religious content in the education of nineteenth-century federal judges, see Mark Warren Bailey, *Guardians of the Moral Order: The Legal Philosophy of the Supreme Court, 1860–1910* (DeKalb: Northern Illinois University Press, 2004); and Herbert Hovenkamp, "The Political Economy of Substantive Due Process," *Stanford Law Review* 40 (1988): 420.

[27] Karsten, *Heart Versus Head*, 299; italics in original.

convincingly that the antebellum labor movement in the United States had much sympathy with the antislavery campaign."[28] Abolitionists, for their part, tended to object to labor unions as contrary to individual liberty. "The liberating ideology of 'free labor' was as hostile toward unionism as it was toward enslavement," one historian notes.[29] They continued this opposition into the postwar years. Abolitionist Frederick Douglass, for example, wrote an editorial titled "The Folly, Tyranny, and Wickedness of Labor Unions."[30] Similarly, the liberal *Independent* spoke out against union violence in the great 1877 railroad strike. "Shall we, who have fought and conquered that we might forbid capital to rob and enforce labor, now allow labor to rob and enforce capital?"[31]

Though historians have emphasized the "ambiguities" of the free-labor doctrine and express "surprise" at abolitionist suspicion of organized labor, in the late nineteenth century the individualist, voluntarist, contractual view articulated in the *Hunt* decision guided the operation of the American labor market.[32] But it took several decades for American unions to decide what they wanted to do with their freedom of association. The Civil War saw the rise of the first national labor unions, organized into the National Labor Union, which lasted until the depression of 1873. The Noble and Holy Order of the Knights of Labor established itself as the next major union federation, with over half a million members. It suffered a major blow when the Haymarket bombing of 1886 (in which a bomb set off at an anarchist protest killed several Chicago police officers) discredited the whole labor movement. These organizations were "reform" union federations, more interested in abolishing the wage-labor system than in securing a greater economic share for workers, and tended to move into partisan political activity. By the late nineteenth century, these organizations gave way to the trade unionism of the American Federation of Labor (AFL).[33]

One of the chief disputes between reform and trade unionists was over the use of the strike. The reformers disdained it as a usually ineffective tactic that at best treated the symptoms rather than the disease itself. As one

[28] Marcus Cunliffe, *Chattel Slavery and Wage Slavery: The Anglo-American Context, 1830–1860* (Athens: University of Georgia Press, 1979), 23. For a recent effort, see Philip S. Foner and Herbert Shapiro, eds., *Northern Labor and Antislavery: A Documentary History* (Westport, CT: Greenwood Press, 1994).

[29] Hovenkamp, *Enterprise and American Law*, 222.

[30] *New National Era*, May 7, 1874.

[31] *Independent*, July 26, 1877.

[32] William E. Forbath, "The Ambiguities of Free Labor: Labor and the Law in the Gilded Age," *Wisconsin Law Review* (1985): 767. Eric Foner adopted "The Ambiguities of Free Labor" as the title of the fourth chapter of his book *Reconstruction: America's Unfinished Revolution, 1863–1877* (New York: HarperCollins, 1988). Henry F. May, *Protestant Churches and Industrial America*, 2d ed. (1949; New York: Octagon Books, 1977), 29, expresses "surprise" at abolitionist antiunionism.

[33] Gerald N. Grob, *Workers and Utopia: A Study of Ideological Conflict in the American Labor Movement, 1865–1900* (Evanston, IL: Quadrangle Books, 1961).

historian observes, the reformers "did not understand what the trade unions of the 1880s were beginning to realize, namely that often only the potential or actual use of coercion would compel employers to negotiate with their employees."[34] Here was the rub: the use of coercion against employers and nonstriking workers was more than an exercise of freedom of association; it abridged the freedom of association of employers and nonstrikers. The public was unwilling to extend this freedom to coerce to unions. The use of violence and intimidation is what brought an end to almost all strikes. "With few exceptions," one study notes, "labor violence in the United States arose in specific situations, usually during a labor dispute. The precipitating causes have been attempts by pickets and sympathizers to prevent a plant on strike from being reopened by strikebreakers, or attempts of company guards, police, or even National Guardsmen to prevent such interference."[35] Such strike violence became increasingly widespread in the late nineteenth century, beginning with the great railroad strike of 1877.

Scholars have tended to ignore the issue of union violence, or to attribute it to employer provocation or to the coercion inherent in apparently nonviolent capitalism; or they have regarded the whole issue as a subjective matter of class perspective. One scholar claims, for example, that judicial notice of union violence "can only *partly* be explained by the reality of labor violence which *at times* existed outside the courtroom," much of which was "a response to direct acts of violence against workers by employers, their agents, police, militia, and federal troops, as well as to the more diffuse *structural violence* of the workplace." According to this scholar, one's evaluation of violence "depends on the facts and *one's own social vision*."[36] But the fact remained that "[w]hile employer obduracy might lead to rejection of [union] recognition, such conduct was legally permissible. Had workers passively accepted such decisions, the level of violence in American labor disputes would have been reduced."[37] But strikers continued to behave as if they were free to use force, as if their "right to organize and to strike was meaningless if the strikers' jobs were taken by strikebreakers."[38] As Henry George told Pope Leo XIII in 1891, "Labor associations can do nothing to raise wages but by force. . . . Those who tell you of trades unions bent on raising wages by moral suasion alone are like those who would tell you of tigers who live on oranges."[39]

---

[34] Ibid., 72.

[35] Hugh Davis Graham and Ted Robert Gurr, *The History of Violence in America: A Report to the National Commission on the Causes and Prevention of Violence*, rev. ed. (New York: Bantam Political Science, 1970), 281.

[36] Avery, "Images of Violence," 8; italics added. For a similar analysis, see Robert L. Hale, "Coercion and Distribution in a Supposedly Non-Coercive State," *Political Science Quarterly* 38 (1923): 470.

[37] Graham and Gurr, *History of Violence in America*, 294.

[38] Avery, "Images of Violence," 13.

[39] Henry George, *The Condition of Labor: An Open Letter to Pope Leo XIII* (New York: John W. Lovell, 1891), 86.

In response to increased labor organization in the late nineteenth century, employers formed their own associations to resist such coercion.[40] They benefited from several legal developments: the labor injunction, the Interstate Commerce Act (1887), and the Sherman Antitrust Act (1890). These devices, labor historians claim, reduced unions to "semi-outlawry" and were part of the general Gilded Age judicial antipathy to socioeconomic reform often called "laissez-faire jurisprudence" in the "*Lochner* era."[41] However, this general view of pre–New Deal jurisprudence has undergone a major revision in the last generation. The old Progressive view that there was "a veritable slaughter of legislation in the name of liberty of contract on the state court level" has been overturned, and we are coming to realize that "the hidden truth about the judges of 'substantive due process' is that they used that weapon very rarely."[42] A similar revision is in order with regard to labor law in particular. In short, "Gilded Age" law was no more a weapon of class warfare than antebellum law had been.

III. The Search for Privilege

Unionists remained liable for criminal conspiracy after the *Hunt* decision if their ends or means were unlawful—indeed, there were more conspiracy prosecutions in the second half of the nineteenth century than in the first.[43] But such prosecutions could not end most strikes, and few

[40] Hutt, *The Theory of Collective Bargaining*, 19–22; William E. Forbath, *Law and the Shaping of the American Labor Movement* (Cambridge, MA: Harvard University Press, 1991), 64, following Bonnett, *History of Employers' Associations*.

[41] Forbath, *Law and the Shaping of the American Labor Movement*, chap. 4; William E. Forbath, "Labor," in *The Oxford Companion to the Supreme Court of the United States*, 2d ed., ed. Kermit L. Hall (New York: Oxford University Press, 2005), 565. In *Lochner v. New York*, 198 U.S. 45 (1905), the U.S. Supreme Court struck down a state act that prohibited workers from working more than ten hours in a day or sixty hours in a week.

[42] Richard C. Cortner, *The Wagner Act Cases* (Knoxville: University of Tennessee Press, 1964), 3; Hadley Arkes, "*Lochner v. New York* and the Cast of Our Laws," in *Great Cases in Constitutional Law*, ed. Robert P. George (Princeton, NJ: Princeton University Press, 2000), 112. The revisionist works are legion. A few major ones are Charles Warren, "A Bulwark to the State Police Power—The United States Supreme Court," and "The Progressivism of the United States Supreme Court," *Columbia Law Review* 13 (1913): 294, 667; Melvyn Urofsky, "Myth and Reality: The Supreme Court and Protective Legislation in the Progressive Era," *Supreme Court Historical Society Yearbook* 19 (1983): 53; Michael Phillips, *The Lochner Court, Myth and Reality: Substantive Due Process from the 1890s to the 1930s* (New York: Praeger Publishers, 2001); and Michael Les Benedict, "Laissez-Faire and Liberty: A Re-Evaluation of the Meaning and Origins of Laissez-Faire Constitutionalism," *Law and History Review* 3 (1985): 293.

In substantive due process analysis, the Supreme Court claimed that the Fourteenth Amendment's provision that "no state shall . . . deprive any person of life, liberty, or property, without due process of law" protected certain fundamental rights against legislative interference. Among these rights was "liberty of contract," which permitted competent, adult males in ordinary occupations to make employment contracts on whatever terms they thought advantageous.

[43] Benjamin J. Taylor and Fred Witney, *U.S. Labor Relations Law: Historical Development* (Englewood Cliffs, NJ: Prentice-Hall, 1992), 11.

were instituted after 1880. Instead, employers began to seek injunctions against strikes in the 1870s. Courts of equity issued injunctions in situations where ordinary common law courts were inadequate. If someone faced immediate and irreparable harm, and could not prevent it by normal criminal or civil procedure, he could ask a judge (originally a "chancellor") for a writ of injunction to prevent the harm. If faced with a strike, an employer could not sue a union, since unions were almost never incorporated; nor could he wait to sue each individual union member. The local criminal justice forces were often unwilling or unable to protect the employer against strikers. Chancellors could issue temporary restraining orders quickly (which could be made permanent after a hearing), without hearing defendant testimony, and without jury consideration.

Scholars repeatedly point out that courts enjoined even "peaceful picketing," but rarely point out that judges almost never enjoined picketing that *began* peacefully.[44] Sylvester Petro has shown that violence, intimidation, and coercion were involved in every case in which a federal or state court issued an injunction. Even after picketing received Supreme Court protection as "free speech," the Court allowed injunctions of picketing conducted in an atmosphere of violence.[45] Admittedly, intimidation could be defined loosely, and employers might provoke violence in order to gain an injunction or state intervention. But there was more than enough evidence and history of overt union lawlessness to support most claims of coercion. Moreover, injunctions were only as good as the agents who enforced them. They were often ignored and failed to stop determined strikes.[46] "If anything, the courts bent over backwards to protect the rights of unionists and in some states such as New York the courts granted the unions special privileges and immunities that were not available to other organizations," one study concludes. "Far from abusing their equity power, the courts used those powers with care so as to protect the rights of union members as well as employers and non-union employees."[47]

Other public policies in the late nineteenth century compounded organized labor's inability to control much of the labor market. It may be said that late-nineteenth-century public policy—rather than the era's

[44] Sylvester Petro, "Injunctions and Labor Disputes: 1880–1932," *Wake Forest Law Review* 14 (1978): 462. The one exception was the Michigan case of *Clarage v. Luphringer*, 202 Mich. 612 (1918). On this case, see Coreen Derifield, "Defining Peaceful Picketing: The Michigan Supreme Court and the Labor Injunction, 1900–1940" (M.A. thesis, Western Michigan University, 2005), 80–96.

[45] *Thornhill v. Alabama*, 310 U.S. 88 (1940); *Milk Wagon Drivers v. Meadowmoor Dairies*, 312 U.S. 287 (1941).

[46] Petro, "Injunctions and Labor Disputes," 471–72; Sylvester Petro, "Unions and the Southern Courts: Part II—Violence and Injunctions in Southern Labor Disputes," *North Carolina Law Review* 59 (1981): 896, 906; Duane McCracken, *Strike Injunctions in the New South* (Chapel Hill: The University of North Carolina Press, 1931), 143; Taylor and Witney, *U.S. Labor Relations Law*, 94; Derifield, "Defining Peaceful Picketing," 8, 50, 65–73, 91.

[47] Poulson, "Criminal Conspiracy, Injunctions, and Damage Suits in Labor Law," 226; Petro, "Unions and the Southern Courts: Part II," 901, 905.

jurisprudence—was biased against labor. For while the government attempted to maintain a free and competitive labor market (at least for adult white males), it used government power for a range of purposes that did more for capital than for labor. The railroad industry, the sector first beset by violent labor uprisings, was largely the product of federal assistance. A host of American manufacturers were protected from foreign competition by the imposition of tariffs, while there were virtually no restrictions on European immigration, thus increasing the labor supply and depressing wages. At the same time, organized labor supported the protective tariff, in the belief that higher prices permitted employers to pay higher wages. Most important, the United States remained short on labor; few employers had "monopsony" (single-purchaser) power to dictate wages.[48] And while organized labor did lead the charge to curtail Asian immigration, it was ambivalent about restricting European sources. Federal banking policy also aided capital accumulation. However, the federal and state judiciary, using such doctrines as "liberty of contract" and "substantive due process," attempted to maintain a neutral, competitive attitude toward business and labor alike.[49]

The Sherman Antitrust Act of 1890 also brought more government power to bear against unions. The act prohibited "every contract, combination ... or conspiracy" in restraint of interstate commerce. The Sherman Act reintroduced the idea that conspiracy per se was punishable, apart from the means and ends pursued. Although there was some dispute about whether Congress intended to apply the law to labor as well as to producer combinations, it seems most likely that it did.[50] Historians usually regard it as ironic, if not insidious, that an act aimed at the steel and oil trusts ended up being applied to labor unions. However, Herbert Hovenkamp notes that the courts, "far from being aligned with big business ... applied the same stricter standards to business and labor alike, although the consequences for labor were far more devastating." The Sherman Act, he says, turned out to be "a savage weapon against labor combinations."[51] The law ended up promoting what Hovenkamp calls "one of the most embarrassing failures of classical economics: its notion that combinations of capital and combinations of labor should be treated in exactly the same way."[52] However, it is more likely that the situation that prevailed from *Hunt* until

---

[48] Richard Posner, "Some Economics of Labor Law," *University of Chicago Law Review* 51 (1984): 992; Hovenkamp, *Enterprise and American Law,* 213; Morgan O. Reynolds, "The Myth of Labor's Inequality of Bargaining Power," *Journal of Labor Research* 12 (1991): 167.

[49] Hovenkamp, *Enterprise and American Law,* 188, 208. Cf. Haggai Hurvitz, "American Labor Law and the Doctrine of Entrepreneurial Property Rights: Boycotts, Courts, and the Juridical Reorientation of 1886–1895," *Industrial Relations Law Journal* 8 (1986): 349.

[50] Hovenkamp, *Enterprise and American Law,* 229.

[51] Ibid., 208.

[52] Ibid., 22.

the Sherman Act—which allowed conspiracies but made their agreements unenforceable—was probably the wisest and most just.[53] Indeed, as Hovenkamp points out, once the U.S. Supreme Court introduced the "rule of reason," holding that some combinations in restraint of trade might be "reasonable" and beneficial to the public, it did no good for unions, whose combinations never benefited the public.[54] Antitrust law might have benefited unions if they could have found a way to use it against more efficient worker-competitors. (This is essentially what a picket line tries to do.) They would have had to make a case that employers and efficient workers (whom they tended to call "cheap" workers) were engaged in a combination in restraint of trade. Antitrust law has most often been used by small, less efficient firms against larger, more efficient rivals, and there is at least some evidence that the framers of the Sherman Act sought to protect small, inefficient competitors.[55] But to make such a case in the labor market would have been entirely too far-fetched.

The combination of national power to regulate interstate commerce, the antitrust laws, and the injunction put an end to the Pullman strike in 1894. When employees of the Pullman Palace Car Company began a strike, Eugene V. Debs's American Railway Union supported them by refusing to handle any Pullman cars. This action is known as a "secondary boycott," in which employers who had no dispute with their own employees faced strike activity because of those employees' support for another union. The federal courts issued injunctions prohibiting interference in the conduct of the railroads' business. When Debs and other union officers violated the injunction, they were jailed for contempt of court. The Supreme Court upheld President Grover Cleveland's resolute efforts, as the Court put it in the 1895 *Debs* decision, "to brush away all obstructions to the freedom of interstate commerce or the transportation of the mails."[56] While the Democratic Party took up organized labor's condemnation of "government by injunction" in the 1896 presidential election, the Republicans won an overwhelming victory.[57] And while criticism of the judiciary as unfairly hostile to unions persisted, the public reaction to such complaints was markedly tepid. The populist-progressive-union campaign against the judiciary reflected, as a recent history puts it, "a muted fury."[58]

---

[53] Dickman, *Industrial Democracy in America*, 4.

[54] *Standard Oil Co. v. United States*, 221 U.S. 1, 179 (1911).

[55] Dominick T. Armentano, *Antitrust: The Case for Repeal* (Auburn, AL: Ludwig von Mises Institute, 1999); Thomas W. Hazlett, "The Legislative History of the Sherman Act Re-Examined," *Economic Inquiry* 30 (1992): 263.

[56] *In re Debs*, 158 U.S. 564, 582 (1895).

[57] "Gov. Altgeld's Message," *New York Times*, January 11, 1895, p. 10; Democratic Party Platform, July 9, 1896.

[58] William G. Ross, *A Muted Fury: Populists, Progressives, and Labor Unions Confront the Courts, 1890–1937* (Princeton, NJ: Princeton University Press, 1994).

After the Pullman strike, unions continued to pursue legislative assistance. It is a hearty myth in American labor history that, in contrast to the nineteenth-century reform-utopian unionists, the AFL was strictly "voluntarist"—apolitical, distrustful of the state, and limited to pure-and-simple, bread-and-butter, wages-and-hours "business unionism." In fact, the AFL sought numerous legislative enactments at the local, state, and federal levels. These included restrictions on all Asian and European "pauper" immigration, health and safety legislation that would limit competition from nonunion members, and occupational licensing that unions could control. Above all, the AFL sought special exemptions from injunctions and the antitrust laws.[59]

Legislative ambivalence characterized the first major piece of federal labor law, the Erdman Act of 1898. Intended to prevent nationally disruptive railway strikes like that of 1894, section 10 of the act made it a crime for employers (at least those engaged in interstate commerce) to make contracts with employees in which the employee agreed "not to become or remain a member of any labor corporation, association, or organization." Such agreements were known as "yellow-dog contracts." The Erdman Act further forbade employers to "unjustly discriminate against any employee" on account of union activity.[60] The Supreme Court struck down this section of the act ten years later. The Fifth Amendment's guarantee that Congress could not deprive any person of "liberty, or property, without due process of law" prohibited such a statute. Justice John Marshall Harlan wrote, "An employer has the same right to prescribe terms on which he will employ one to labor as an employee has to prescribe those on which he will sell his labor, and any legislation which disturbs this equality is an arbitrary and unjustifiable interference with liberty of contract."[61] This decision is usually depicted as the first of many pieces of laissez-faire judicial activism that foiled the democratic achievement of the labor movement. In fact, unionists were divided and never satisfied with the Erdman Act. The railroad brotherhoods supported it, but the AFL opposed it. The act's provision for government arbitration seemed to limit the right to strike and offended the federation's "voluntarist" principles. Union leader Samuel Gompers denounced it as "destructive of the best interests of labor, ruinous to the liberties of our people," threatening to create "an autocracy or an empire on the one side and a class of slaves or serfs on the other." The AFL dropped its opposition to the Erdman Act after

---

[59] Ruth O'Brien, *Workers' Paradox: The Republican Origins of New Deal Labor Policy, 1886–1935* (Chapel Hill: University of North Carolina Press, 1998), 23; Dickman, *Industrial Democracy in America*, 224, 253.

[60] Erdman Act, 30 Stat. L. 428 (1898).

[61] *Adair v. United States*, 208 U.S. 161, 162 (1908). The Court struck down a virtually identical state law, as violating the Fourteenth Amendment's equivalent due process clause, in *Coppage v. Kansas*, 236 U.S. 1 (1915).

street railway workers and seamen were exempted from it. The act typified the ambivalent attitude in Congress about organized labor, and signified a willingness to leave contentious policy questions to the courts to decide.[62]

The Supreme Court also explicitly applied the Sherman Antitrust Act to labor unions in 1908 (something it had done only implicitly in the earlier *Debs* case). The 1908 decision, *Loewe v. Lawlor*, arose out of a case in which the United Hatters Union, in collusion with hat manufacturers, called a strike against the Loewe Company in Danbury, Connecticut. Although Dietrich Loewe's own workers had no complaints against him, some of those he employed were not union members. Thus, "even though Loewe, with tears in his eyes, begged [United Hatters members] to stay, they left rather than be blacklisted by the union and barred from the industry."[63] The union also began a nationwide boycott of Loewe's hats. Like the Pullman strike, this was a secondary boycott. An ordinary or primary strike was difficult enough when it involved more than employees quitting and interfered with the employer's ability to carry on his business and with replacement workers' right to work. In a secondary boycott, striker *A* in dispute with employer *B* tries to cut off anyone else from doing business with *B*. Thus, employer *C* (for example), who had no quarrel with *A*, suffers for his relations with *B*. The ultimate extension of the secondary boycott was the syndicalist "general strike," in which any dispute between workers and employers would prompt all workers to quit work and bring about a fundamental reordering of the economy. Several general strike attempts occurred in England (1926), Canada (1919), and Spain (1919); the United States experienced general strikes in several cities in 1919 and 1934. State law on the secondary boycott was unclear. The Supreme Court held that this kind of strike was actionable under the Sherman Act—open to criminal prosecution as a misdemeanor, to an injunction sought by a U.S. attorney, or, as in the *Loewe* case, to a civil suit with treble-damage liability.[64]

Although Loewe won money damages from union members, the effect of the *Loewe* decision on union power was rather limited. It only "deprived organized labor of a particular type of organizing strategy, the distributor-targeted secondary boycott, effective only in industries in which manufacturers sold their goods through independent distributors to a largely working-class clientele."[65] However, the decision coincided with the high-profile prosecution of Samuel Gompers and other AFL leaders for contempt of court when they violated an injunction in the 1906 Buck's Stove boycott. Buck's Stove and Range Company had secured an injunction

---

[62] George I. Lovell, *Legislative Deferrals: Statutory Ambiguity, Judicial Power, and American Democracy* (Cambridge: Cambridge University Press, 2002), 72, 88–90.

[63] Ernst, *Lawyers Against Labor*, 16.

[64] *Loewe v. Lawlor*, 208 U.S. 274 (1908); Ernst, *Lawyers Against Labor*, 16, 56, 109.

[65] Ernst, *Lawyers Against Labor*, 122.

against an AFL boycott, and then won a criminal contempt case against Gompers when the AFL newspaper, *The American Federationist*, continued to publicize the boycott. The Supreme Court overturned the criminal conviction in 1911, and then overturned a subsequent conviction for civil contempt in 1914 because the statute of limitations had expired.[66]

Unions would also not suffer from the *Loewe* decision because they were seldom legal entities, and thus could seldom be sued in court. Loewe had to sue and recover damages from dozens of individual members of the union, which was both tedious for him (he was bankrupt by the time he collected a judgment, almost a decade after the Supreme Court decision) and unfair for the individual union members (who were often unaware of what their union had conspired to do). The Supreme Court straightened out this anomaly, and again extended the labor reach of the commerce clause, in the 1920s. When the Coronado Coal Company attempted to operate its mines with nonunion labor, the United Mine Workers (UMW) responded with threats and violence against replacement workers and the owners, ultimately committing several murders and flooding and dynamiting the mines. In 1922, the Supreme Court held that the UMW, though unincorporated, could be sued under federal antitrust laws; however, the Court denied that the union's activity had enough of an effect on interstate commerce to be covered by the antitrust laws.[67] In a second suit, the company was able to convince the Court that the strike did affect interstate commerce and won a judgment against the union.[68]

Loewe and *Buck's Stove* pushed the AFL into closer cooperation with the Democratic Party in the union's effort to win exemption from injunctions and antitrust law. The AFL claimed victory when Congress passed the Clayton Antitrust Act in 1914. The sections relevant to organized labor held that "the labor of a human being is not a commodity or article of commerce," and that the law did not "forbid or restrain individual members of such organizations [i.e., unions] from lawfully carrying out the legitimate objects thereof" (section 6). The act also prohibited federal courts from issuing injunctions "in any case between an employer and employees ... unless necessary to prevent irreparable injury to property, or to a property right"; nor could the courts prohibit "peaceful" strikes or boycotts (section 20).[69] This language was broad and evasive enough to allow both employers and labor organizations to claim victory. Gompers called it "the greatest measure of humanitar-

---

[66] Ken I. Kersch, "The *Gompers v. Buck's Stove* Saga: A Constitutional Case Study in Dialogue, Resistance, and the Freedom of Speech," *Journal of Supreme Court History* 31 (2006): 28–57. The cases were *Gompers v. Buck's Stove and Range Co.*, 221 U.S. 418 (1911) and 233 U.S. 604 (1914).

[67] *United Mine Workers of America v. Coronado Coal Co.*, 259 U.S. 344 (1922).

[68] *Coronado Coal Co. v. United Mine Workers of America*, 268 U.S. 295 (1925).

[69] Clayton Antitrust Act, 38 Stat. L. 323 (1914).

ian legislation in the world's history" and "the industrial Magna Carta upon which the working people will rear their construction of industrial freedom."[70] In fact, "Congress delegated the decision about organized labor's status under the antitrust laws to the courts."[71] Employers, and eventually the courts, believed that the new act did nothing more than give statutory expression to the law as it stood, and unions continued to be liable under antitrust law and to injunctions. Moreover, the Clayton Act now allowed private parties, rather than just U.S. attorneys, to seek injunctions, so unions were in fact in worse shape than before the act. As one historian notes, "Never did an act backfire so badly."[72] Congress had again deferred to the courts, which really had no choice but to make an independent policy judgment.[73]

Organized labor gained much more from the national mobilization of World War I than it had from earlier legislative efforts. The AFL's traditional reluctance to seek state power to promote union goals—its oft-mischaracterized "voluntarism"—was swept away by the prounion government policy of the Great War.[74] The war saw a major step forward in the union ideal of "industrial democracy." Unions claimed that, since the nation was fighting against the autocracy of the German Empire, it ought to curtail the despotic power of American employers by compelling them to bargain with organized labor.[75] Shortly after the Clayton Act, Congress enacted the La Follette Seamen Act (1915) to promote organization among sailors. More dramatically, the railroad brotherhoods threatened a strike that would cripple defense mobilization and "virtually extorted Congress" into enacting an eight-hour-day law for railroad labor.[76] Squeezed by government policies that raised their labor costs, capped their shipping rates, and made it difficult to raise or borrow capital, the industry was overwhelmed by the demands that national mobilization placed on it, and the federal government took control of the railroads under the terms of the 1916 Army Appropriations Act.[77] Though restored to private ownership in 1920, the railroads were highly regulated in a government-enforced cartel system. Railway labor legislation served as a model or rehearsal for New Deal

[70] Joseph A. McCartin, *Labor's Great War: The Struggle for Industrial Democracy and the Origins of Modern American Labor Relations, 1912–1921* (Chapel Hill: The University of North Carolina Press, 1997), 17.

[71] Ernst, *Lawyers Against Labor*, 166.

[72] Herbert Hovenkamp, "Labor Conspiracies in American Law, 1880–1930," *Texas Law Review* 66, no. 5 (1988): 964.

[73] Kelly, Harbison, and Belz, *The American Constitution*, 450.

[74] Lovell, *Legislative Deferrals*, 210; Ross, *Muted Fury*, 172–80; McCartin, *Labor's Great War*, 224.

[75] McCartin, *Labor's Great War*, 7.

[76] Robert Higgs, *Crisis and Leviathan: Critical Episodes in the Growth of American Government* (New York: Oxford University Press, 1987), 118; Dickman, *Industrial Democracy in America*, 241.

[77] Higgs, *Crisis and Leviathan*, 143–47.

labor legislation.[78] Indeed, the whole World War I experience of national economic regulation was a training period for many New Dealers. The War Industries Board coordinated national industrial production in a way that New Dealers tried to repeat in the National Industrial Recovery Act; Army camps served as a model for the Civilian Conservation Corps; government munitions production projects presaged the Tennessee Valley Authority; the U.S. Housing Corporation adumbrated the Federal Housing Administration. In short, the command economy of "war socialism" showed Progressives that the American people would give government extraordinary powers in extraordinary circumstances. The National War Labor Board served as the model for New Deal labor policy. Though it had no official power to compel unionization, the board had significant influence on labor-management relations; its mediation and conciliation efforts helped to increase union membership to over five million by the time of the armistice.[79]

When Washington ended its wartime support, unions lost most of their wartime gains. Employers and government retained the antiunion legal devices that they possessed before the war. Hundreds of injunctions were issued to break the 1922 railway shopmen's strike, for example, a conflict that produced 1,500 cases of assault, fifty-one cases of dynamiting, and sixty-five kidnappings.[80] The Supreme Court continued to uphold traditional protections for employers and nonunion workers against unions. In 1917, it upheld the yellow-dog contract, in which workers agreed not to join a union as a condition in the employment contract. Employers were thus able to seek injunctions to prevent union attempts to organize their workers, since such efforts were unlawful inducements to breach a contract.[81] Shortly after the war, the Court held that a state law prohibiting the issuing of injunctions in labor disputes violated the Fourteenth Amendment's protection of property, as well as the amendment's guarantee of the equal protection of the law.[82] The same year, it construed the Clayton Act's labor provisions very strictly: secondary boycotts were not lawful, and therefore not protected by section 6 of the act; section 20, proscribing the issuing of injunctions, did not apply to secondary activity, either.[83] The Court also held unions to a strict standard when evaluating whether strike activity was "peaceful," and permitted injunctions against intimidating activity.[84] It also stretched its standard of what affected interstate

[78] Dickman, *Industrial Democracy in America*, 243; O'Brien, *Workers' Paradox.*

[79] William E. Leuchtenburg, "The New Deal and the Analogue of War," in *The F.D.R. Years: On Roosevelt and His Legacy* (New York: Columbia University Press, 1995); McCartin, *Labor's Great War*, 90–105.

[80] Morgan O. Reynolds, "An Economic Analysis of the Norris–LaGuardia Act, the Wagner Act, and the Labor Representation Industry," *Journal of Libertarian Studies* 6 (1982): 237.

[81] *Hitchman Coal & Coke Co. v. Mitchell*, 245 U.S. 229 (1917).

[82] *Truax v. Corrigan*, 257 U.S. 312 (1921).

[83] *Duplex Printing Co. v. Deering*, 254 U.S. 443 (1921).

[84] *American Steel Foundries v. Tri-City Central Trades Council*, 257 U.S. 184 (1921).

commerce in a way that made it easier to apply federal antitrust laws to strikes.[85]

While these cases reinforced the impression of a judicial double standard against organized labor, an unrestrained interpretation of Congress's commerce power ultimately provided the basis for an array of union privileges in the 1930s and 1940s. At the same time, the judiciary was becoming more sympathetic to union goals, as it moved from nineteenth-century liberalism to Progressive-era "corporate liberalism."[86] American business and political leaders began to think that labor unions, if they behaved in a peaceful, lawful, orderly fashion, could be legitimate parties in the political economy, and these leaders tried to encourage "responsible unionism."[87] Even Chief Justice William Howard Taft, often depicted as typifying the antiunion reaction of the 1920s, referred to the strike as "a lawful instrument in a lawful economic struggle or competition between employer and employees as to the share or division between them of the joint product of labor and capital," and remarked that "the day of the industrial autocrats is passing and should pass."[88] Congress enacted a new Railway Labor Act in 1926, one which guaranteed the right to join a union.[89] Many employers (other than interstate railroad operators), though still able to use yellow-dog contracts and other legal devices to thwart unions, moved away from strident opposition and toward more sophisticated "industrial relations" systems. The most prominent of these was the employee representation plan or "company union."[90] The courts, employers, and voters retained their Progressive-era ambivalence about labor unions through the 1920s, during which organized labor reverted to roughly its prewar share of the American labor force.[91]

IV. "FULL" FREEDOM OF ASSOCIATION

The Great Depression finally swept away the principal obstacles to organized labor and produced a wave of prounion legislation. The surge began after the Democrats won control of Congress in 1930 and at last

---

[85] *Bedford Cut Stone Co. v. Journeymen Stone Cutters Association of North America*, 274 U.S. 37 (1927).

[86] Ernst, *Lawyers Against Labor*; Petro, "Injunctions in Labor Disputes," 355.

[87] O'Brien, *Workers' Paradox*, 14.

[88] *American Steel Foundries*, 257 U.S. at 209; McCartin, *Labor's Great War*, 186.

[89] But the act did not impose exclusive majority unionism nor prohibit company unions. The Supreme Court upheld the act, though it did not explicitly overrule *Adair*, in *Texas & New Orleans Railroad Co. v. Brotherhood of Railway and Steamship Clerks*, 281 U.S. 548 (1930).

[90] While some authorities see an increase of yellow-dog contracts in the 1920s (Irving Bernstein, *The Lean Years: A History of the American Worker, 1920–1933* [Boston, MA: Houghton Mifflin, 1960], 200; Taylor and Witney, *U.S. Labor Relations Law*, 30), others see a decline (Lovell, *Legislative Deferrals*, 177; Daniel R. Ernst, "The Yellow-Dog Contract and Liberal Reform, 1917–1932," *Labor History* 30 [1989]: 261). But in a later work Ernst refers to the "spread of yellow-dog contracts" in the 1920s (*Lawyers Against Labor*, 231).

[91] Taylor and Witney, *U.S. Labor Relations Law*, 148.

passed an effective anti-injunction act. The Norris-LaGuardia Act of 1932 recognized organized labor's argument that employer and employee were not on equal bargaining terms, and that "the individual unorganized worker is commonly helpless to exercise *actual* liberty of contract"; therefore "it is necessary that he have *full* freedom of association."[92] Since government policy had aided capital through the corporate form of organization, it now ought to balance the scales by promoting union organization. The act made yellow-dog contracts unenforceable, and prohibited federal courts from issuing injunctions in labor disputes absent actual fraud or violence. It protected "giving publicity to the existence of, or the facts involved in, any labor dispute, whether by advertising, speaking, patrolling, or by any other method not involving fraud or violence."[93] It also tightened the procedural requirements for gaining an injunction to stop fraud and violence. Although the act did not mention antitrust laws, it did declare that no federal court could hold that "any persons participating in a labor dispute constitute or are engaged in an unlawful combination or conspiracy."[94] Many states enacted their own versions of the act, and labor injunctions dropped off substantially.[95]

These provisions might have satisfied the AFL of 1900, but organized labor now sought greater government promotion of unionization.[96] President Franklin D. Roosevelt displayed a Progressive-era ambivalence about organized labor, but made the promotion of collective bargaining part of his comprehensive plan for industrial recovery and reform, the National Industrial Recovery Act (NIRA) of 1933. This was a fantastically ambitious scheme in which Congress allowed American industries to devise their own "codes of fair competition," essentially an invitation to establish enforceable cartels.[97] Section 7(a) of the act endeavored to promote labor cartels. It stated:

> Every code of fair competition shall contain the following conditions: (1) That employees shall have the right to organize and bargain collectively through representatives of their own choosing, and shall be free from the interference, restraint, or coercion of employers of labor, or their agents, in the designation of such representatives or in self-organization or in other concerted activities for the purpose of collective bargaining or other mutual aid or protection; (2) that no employee and no one seeking employment shall be required as a

[92] Norris-LaGuardia Act, 47 Stat. L. 70 (1932), sec. 2; emphasis added.
[93] Ibid., sec. 4(c).
[94] Ibid., sec. 5.
[95] Woodiwiss, *Rights Versus Conspiracy*, 178.
[96] Lovell, *Legislative Deferrals*, 210.
[97] Ellis Hawley, *The New Deal and the Problem of Monopoly: A Study in Economic Ambivalence* (Princeton, NJ: Princeton University Press, 1966), 25; Kelly, Harbison, and Belz, *The American Constitution*, 471–74.

condition of employment to join any company union or to refrain from joining, organizing, or assisting a labor organization of his own choosing.[98]

Though it failed on the whole, the NIRA encouraged and inspired union organizers. The federal government had gone beyond merely exempting unions from laws and judicial processes that restrained other persons and organizations; it was now lending its power to the promotion of unions. It was the common phrase of the day that "President Roosevelt wants you to join a union." The Depression itself had not increased militancy among American workers—it followed the historical pattern that depressions usually weaken unions.[99] The NIRA, though, induced a significant "strike wave" in 1934, as organizers battled with company unions or other employer attempts to maintain the open shop. The Supreme Court finally held the act unconstitutional in 1935, but Congress adopted a more far-reaching version of section 7(a) later that year.

The National Labor Relations Act—known as the Wagner Act after its sponsor, New York Senator Robert F. Wagner—revolutionized American labor law. The act purported to be an exercise of Congress's power "to regulate commerce . . . among the states," and thus began with the claim that employers' refusal to recognize unions "leads to strikes and other forms of industrial strife or unrest, which have the intent or the necessary effect of burdening or obstructing commerce."[100] Yet the industrial unrest that preceded the Wagner Act had resulted from the NIRA's attempt to promote unionization. And the Wagner Act would produce an even greater outbreak of industrial unrest in 1936–37. New Deal labor law is a prime example of what has been called "the phenomenon of self-generating interventions," in which "every problem brought forward as a reason for further government intervention is the result of a *prior* intervention."[101]

The Wagner Act, like Norris-LaGuardia, tried to redress "the inequality of bargaining power between employees who do not possess full freedom of association or actual liberty of contract and employers who are organized in the corporate or other forms of ownership association." It compelled employers to bargain exclusively with the organization chosen by a majority of their workers to represent them. It banned "company unions" and any employer interference with employee organization.[102] The Wagner

[98] National Industrial Recovery Act, 48 Stat. L. 194 (1933), sec. 7(a).

[99] Foster Rhea Dulles, *Labor in America: A History*, 3d ed. (New York: Thomas Y. Crowell, 1960), 261; Mark Barenberg, "The Political Economy of the Wagner Act: Power, Symbol, and Workplace Cooperation," *Harvard Law Review* 106 (1993): 1401–2, 1436–37.

[100] National Labor Relations Act, 49 Stat. L. 449 (1935).

[101] M. Stanton Evans, "The Liberal Twilight," *Imprimis* 5 (August 1976); Morgan O. Reynolds, *Power and Privilege: Labor Unions in America* (New York: Universe, 1984), 163.

[102] National Labor Relations Act, 49 Stat. L. 449 (1935). Some argued that the NIRA, and even Norris-LaGuardia, had already imposed a similar duty to bargain. See Dickman, *Industrial Democracy in America*, 241, 260.

Act established a National Labor Relations Board to oversee representation elections and to enforce rulings. President Roosevelt initially opposed the act, until the Supreme Court struck down the NIRA in May 1935. He then threw his support behind the Wagner Act, perhaps assuming (and hoping) that the Court would strike it down as well. Many congressmen similarly voted for the act on the assumption that they could placate organized labor with an act that was doomed in light of recent Court decisions.[103]

Despite the Wagner Act's claim to be an effort to foster "industrial peace," it provoked a major wave of strike activity in 1936–37, especially after FDR's landslide reelection.[104] As employers continued to resist collective bargaining, awaiting an adverse Supreme Court decision, union organizers became more aggressive, culminating in the famous "sit-down" strikes in early 1937. In a sit-down strike, striking workers occupied the factory and refused to vacate it until their demands were met. This was a more effective way of preventing nonunion workers from breaking the strike. This tactic, even more than most ordinarily menacing picketing, was unlawful, but many officials—most notably Michigan governor Frank Murphy—refused to enforce court orders against it. Some prominent employers, like General Motors and U.S. Steel, came to terms with the new industrial unions, and most other employers stopped resisting after the Supreme Court upheld the Wagner Act in April 1937. Although no satisfactory explanation has yet been given for the Court's capitulation in the Wagner Act cases, the Court's preference for the act over the anarchy of the sit-down strikes is not an unlikely one.[105]

The Wagner Act provided much more than a guarantee of labor's freedom of association. It furnishes a good illustration of the New Deal's transformation of American liberalism from a rights-based to an entitlement-based system.[106] From the founding until the twentieth century, the American regime assumed that government's purpose was to

[103] Attorney General Homer Cummings advised Roosevelt to veto the bill on constitutional grounds. Marian C. McKenna, *Franklin D. Roosevelt and the Great Constitutional War: The Court-Packing Crisis of 1937* (New York: Fordham University Press, 2002), 195, 327, 425; Peter Irons, *The New Deal Lawyers* (Princeton, NJ: Princeton University Press, 1982), 110; Irving Bernstein, *The Turbulent Years: A History of the American Worker, 1933–1941* (Boston, MA: Houghton Mifflin, 1970), 341. At the same time, Roosevelt hoped that the Supreme Court would continue to strike down New Deal legislation, and thus alienate public opinion enough so that the public would support his effort to bring the court to heel. See William E. Leuchtenburg, *The Supreme Court Reborn: The Constitutional Revolution in the Age of Roosevelt* (New York: Oxford University Press, 1995), 100.

[104] Woodiwiss, *Rights Versus Conspiracy*, 179.

[105] Drew D. Hansen, "The Sit-Down Strikes and the Switch in Time," *Wayne Law Review* 46 (2000): 50; James Pope, "Worker Lawmaking, Sit-Down Strikes, and the Shaping of American Industrial Relations, 1935–1938," *Law and History Review* 24 (2006): 45. The Court upheld the Wagner Act in a set of cases beginning with *National Labor Relations Board v. Jones & Laughlin Steel Corp.*, 301 U.S. 1 (1937).

[106] Leuchtenburg, *The F.D.R. Years*, 19; Reynolds, *Power and Privilege*, 251; Sylvester Petro, "Civil Liberty, Syndicalism, and the N.L.R.A.," *Toledo Law Review* 5 (1974): 496–97. The definition of "entitlement" that I employ follows Harvey Mansfield, *America's Constitutional Soul* (Baltimore, MD: The Johns Hopkins University Press, 1991), 56. A more technical,

secure preexisting natural rights—such as life, liberty, property, or association. Everyone can exercise such rights simultaneously; nobody's exercise of his own rights limits anyone else's similar exercise. Your right to life or to work or to vote does not take anything away from anyone else. We can all pursue happiness at once. Entitlements, in contrast, require someone else to provide me with the substantive good that the exercise of rights pursues. The right to work, for example, is fundamentally different from the right (entitlement) to a job; the right to marry does not entitle me to a spouse; the right to free speech does not entitle me to an audience. The Wagner Act provided not freedom of association, but an entitlement to association—compulsory collective bargaining. "*Full* freedom of association" was something fundamentally different from the traditional understanding of freedom of association.[107] The New Deal gave unions a power to compel association by nonunion members and employers, while the classical standard of a right to associate would have prevented such compulsory association.

The Wagner Act removed both employers' and workers' ability to decline to associate with unions. Congress contributed to this effort by exposing the most egregious instances of employer resistance that seemed to violate old-fashioned freedom of association. The La Follette Committee, which met from 1936 until 1941, brought to light the industrial spies, private detectives, blacklists, professional strikebreaking firms, and corporate arsenals of machine guns and tear gas. "During [the 1930s] many American workers undoubtedly did not want to join unions," the chief historian of the committee wrote. "But the framers of the Wagner Act and the members of the La Follette Committee were concerned with those who did. 'Labor,' in the context of the La Follette investigations, meant those workers who wished to become union members."[108] The power of the state was required, not to protect unionists' freedom of association, but to compel employers and nonunion workers to accept unionization. Thus, an entirely new definition of "civil liberties" arose in the 1930s. The American Civil Liberties Union, like the AFL, gave up traditional liberal voluntarism and came to embrace state power.

---

philosophical definition can be found in Robert Nozick, *Anarchy, State, and Utopia* (New York: Basic Books, 1974).

[107] Barenberg, "Political Economy of the Wagner Act," 1437, 1441.

[108] There is little doubt that the La Follette Committee was engaged in a prounion publicity effort, largely to counteract the negative public reaction to the sit-down strikes. Many historians take the committee's work at face value; one pair of historians calls it "the most complete study" of employer antiunion abuses and of "unquestionable accuracy" (Taylor and Witney, *U.S. Labor Relations Law*). But the most careful study of the committee notes, more modestly: "The La Follette Committee certainly did not fabricate its findings; through its choice of incidents and witnesses, however, it painted a picture that indicated occasional blindness to shadings of gray. Nuance and complexities were obscured by the committee's zeal to accelerate and justify the C.I.O. [Congress of Industrial Organizations] organizing drives." Jerold S. Auerbach, *Labor and Liberty: The La Follette Committee and the New Deal* (Indianapolis, IN: Irvington Publishers, 1966), 8–9, 28, 108.

Unions often claimed that a legal double standard worked against them (especially in antitrust cases); now it clearly worked in their favor. In the 1930s, the Supreme Court largely abandoned its protection of property rights under the Fifth and Tenth Amendments (with regard to federal law) and the Fourteenth Amendment (with regard to state law). In the *Carolene Products* case of 1938, Justice Harlan F. Stone wrote that the Court would henceforth give greater protection to nonproperty rights. The Court would now assume that laws affecting "ordinary commercial transactions" were constitutional. But it would apply a more stringent standard for laws that affected provisions in the Bill of Rights, or "particular religious, or national, or racial minorities." [109] Advocates of New Deal labor legislation had adumbrated this "preferred freedoms" idea in Congress.[110]

Roosevelt's proposal that Congress increase the size of the Supreme Court, to allow him to appoint up to six new justices—the infamous "court-packing plan" of 1937—prompted a widespread political reaction against the New Deal. The sit-down strikes and the sharp economic downturn (the "Roosevelt recession") of that year also brought the New Deal effectively to an end. But Roosevelt was able to appoint two liberals to replace conservatives George Sutherland and Willis Van Devanter in 1937–38, and by the end of his presidency he had appointed every member of the Court but one. This New Deal Supreme Court continued to extend the privileges of organized labor. In the 1940 case of *Thornhill v. Alabama*, for example, the Court declared that peaceful picketing constituted "free speech" under the First Amendment, and thus states could not prohibit it. Justice Frank Murphy, whom Roosevelt had appointed to the Court in the prior year, wrote the opinion. Although there was some dispute about the peaceful nature of the picketing at issue, Murphy stressed its democratic-communication character, citing the *Carolene Products* precedent.[111]

The *Thornhill* case also represented an important extension of federal judicial power in its application (known as "incorporation") of provisions of the Bill of Rights to the states. Well into the twentieth century, the Supreme Court had held that the Bill of Rights applied only to the federal government. In the 1920s and 1930s, it began to apply some provisions to the states; by the end of the century, nearly all of the Bill of Rights had been incorporated.[112] This process helped to facilitate the agenda represented by the *Carolene Products* decision. Since the Bill of Rights concerns

---

[109] *U.S. v. Carolene Products*, 304 U.S. 144, fn. 4 (1938).

[110] William E. Forbath, "The New Deal Constitution in Exile," *Duke Law Journal* 51 (2001): 179.

[111] *Thornhill v. Alabama*, 310 U.S. 88, 95 (1940).

[112] Richard C. Cortner, *The Supreme Court and the Second Bill of Rights: The Fourteenth Amendment and the Nationalization of Civil Liberties* (Madison: University of Wisconsin Press, 1981). *Gitlow v. New York*, 268 U.S. 652 (1925), is usually cited as the beginning of the incorporation of the Bill of Rights, but the Court acted in a similar fashion in *Chicago, Burlington, and Quincy Ry. Co. v. Chicago*, 166 U.S. 226 (1897).

many noneconomic rights, the Court was able to strike down state acts through incorporation, as it had struck down state economic regulations via the "substantive due process" doctrine before 1937. With regard to picketing, however, the Court almost immediately stepped back; in 1941, it declared that peaceful picketing could be prohibited after a strike had manifested an atmosphere of intimidation and violence.[113] The Court "moved consistently toward the position that picketing was so bound up with elements of economic coercion, restraint of trade, labor relations, and other social and economic problems that a large measure of discretion in regulating it must be restored to the states."[114]

In 1940, a month after the *Thornhill* picketing-as-free-speech decision, the Court decided (in *Apex Hosiery v. Leader*) that a business could not recover damages under the antitrust acts after a sit-down strike had prevented the interstate shipment of its goods (in this case, stockings). While the Court did not hold that unions were completely exempt from antitrust action, it severely narrowed the bounds of union liability. In doing so, the Court evinced a definition of interstate commerce and federalism quite at odds with the tendency of its recent decisions regarding congressional economic regulation. Though the Court would soon hold that a farmer could be fined under the Agricultural Adjustment Act for cultivating eleven acres more wheat than he was allotted—even though none of the wheat left his farm[115]—in *Apex* it held that, since the strike did not affect the market price of stockings, interstate commerce was not substantially affected. Justice Stone admitted that the strike evinced "a lawless invasion of petitioner's plant and destruction of property by force and violence of the most brutal and wanton character, under [union] leadership and direction," but this did not justify the application of the federal antitrust laws. Such mayhem was the responsibility of state and local powers, though he noted here that the strike was carried on "without interference by the local authorities."[116] Chief Justice Charles Evans Hughes's dissent called attention to an anomaly: the Wagner Act applied to employers because of the putative effect that antiunionism had on interstate commerce, but here employers were unprotected from "the

---

[113] *Milk Wagon Drivers v. Meadowmoor Dairies*, 312 U.S. 287 (1941).

[114] Kelly, Harbison, and Belz, *The American Constitution*, 524. Needless to say, strikes often interfered with First Amendment as well as other freedoms. In 1950, a newspaper publisher in Norfolk, Virginia, was resisting unionization by using his "daughters, sons-in-law, nieces and nephews" to carry on publishing during a strike. C.I.O. Committee on Civil Rights member Boyd Wilson suggested that "[a] daughter's head will bleed just like a head that isn't a daughter's. You simply have to apply that kind of tactics." When the chairman of the committee objected, Wilson replied, "We put a picket line out there and that daughter, mama or nobody else is going in." Proceedings of Civil Rights Staff Conference, National C.I.O. Committee to Abolish Discrimination, May 24, 1950, pp. 205–6, 234, R.G. 9-001, Box 7, George Meany Memorial Archives, Silver Spring, Maryland.

[115] *Wickard v. Filburn*, 317 U.S. 111 (1942).

[116] *Apex Hosiery v. Leader*, 310 U.S. 469 (1940). See Bernard D. Meltzer, "Labor Unions, Collective Bargaining, and the Antitrust Laws," *Journal of Law and Economics* 6 (1963): 158–60.

direct and intentional obstruction or prevention of such [interstate] shipments by the employees." [117]

The next year, in *U.S. v. Hutcheson*, the Court decided that a secondary boycott, part of a jurisdictional conflict between two unions, could not be enjoined under the antitrust acts. The majority decision noted, "So long as a union acts in its self-interest and does not combine with non-labor groups, the licit and the illicit ... are not to be distinguished by any judgment regarding the wisdom or unwisdom, the rightness or wrongness, the selfishness or unselfishness of the end of which the particular union activities are the means." [118] In what Justice Owen Roberts called "a process of construction never, as I think, heretofore indulged by this court," the Court found that the Norris-LaGuardia Act had repealed criminal penalties for unions under the Sherman Act. "I venture to say that no court has ever undertaken so radically to legislate where Congress has refused to do so." [119] Nor were the holdovers from the pre-Roosevelt court the only dissenters in this line of double-standard cases. In 1945, the Court held that a union, from motives of revenge, could compel an employer to cease doing business with another firm so as to drive that firm out of business—reiterating the *Hutcheson* principle that the Court would not scrutinize the rightness or wrongness of union motives. Justice Robert H. Jackson, who had been FDR's attorney general and a supporter of the court-packing plan, noted:

> With this decision, the labor movement has come full circle. The working man has struggled long, the fight has been filled with hatred, and conflict has been dangerous, but now workers may not be deprived of their livelihood merely because their employers opposed and they favor unions. Labor has won other rights as well. . . . This Court now sustains the claim of a union to the right to deny participation in the economic world to an employer simply because the union dislikes him. This Court permits to employees the same arbitrary dominance over the economic sphere which they control that labor so long, so bitterly and so rightly asserted should belong to no man.[120]

Thus, national policy at once tried to preserve competition in product markets while tolerating or promoting labor monopolies.[121]

[117] *Apex Hosiery v. Leader*, 310 U.S. at 528 (Hughes, C.J., dissenting).
[118] *U.S. v. Hutcheson*, 312 U.S. 219, 232 (1941).
[119] Id. at 245 (Roberts, J., dissenting). See Meltzer, "Labor Unions, Collective Bargaining, and the Antitrust Laws," 160–61.
[120] *Hunt v. Crumboch*, 325 U.S. 821, 830 (1945) (Jackson, J., dissenting).
[121] Meltzer, "Labor Unions, Collective Bargaining, and the Antitrust Laws," 167, 170; Ralph K. Winter, "Collective Bargaining and Competition: The Application of Antitrust Standards to Union Activities," *Yale Law Journal* 73 (1963): 16.

In 1940, Chief Justice Hughes had mused, "Suppose . . . there should be a conspiracy among the teamsters . . . in New York City to prevent the hauling of goods and their transportation in interstate commerce, can it be doubted that the Sherman Act would apply?" [122] But two years later, in the case of *U.S. v. Local 807*, not only was the Sherman Act of no avail in an obvious case of a conspiracy to obstruct interstate commerce, but the Court held that the federal antiracketeering laws did not apply to union violence. In the events that led to this case, New York City teamsters forced their way into trucks coming into the city from other states, and demanded either to take over the delivery or to receive payment of a day's union wage to leave the out-of-state truckers alone. The Federal Anti-Racketeering Act of 1934 declared it a felony for any person to use force in interstate commerce to extort the payment of money, "not including, however, the payment of wages by a *bona fide* employer to a *bona fide* employee." Despite the lack of *bona fides* or any employer-employee relation in this case, the Supreme Court found that this teamster activity was not extortion but a "traditional labor union activity," one acceptable even when it involved resort to "violence and threats." [123] Although Congress tried to overturn this decision with the Hobbs Act of 1946, the Court ultimately continued to hold union violence exempt from the antiracketeering laws.[124]

V. CONCLUSION: POLICY AND MARKET REACTION

The power and privileges of organized labor peaked during World War II, and a reaction began to set in during and after the war. The outbreak of strikes in the middle of the war led Congress to enact (over President Roosevelt's veto) the War Labor Disputes (Smith-Connally) Act of 1943, which gave the United States the power to take over industries that were affected by strikes, provided criminal penalties for strike leaders, and prohibited expenditure of union funds on political campaigns. Though the act had little effect on most workers, "[l]abor discovered to its chagrin that government protection exacted a price in the form of greater supervision of union affairs." [125] By the end of the war, the President's Committee on Fair Employment Practice and the federal courts had begun to impose a duty of "fair representation" on unions, to make sure that they did not use their majority and compulsory unionism to discriminate against members who were racial minorities.[126] The courts here recognized that

[122] *Apex Hosiery v. Leader*, 310 U.S. at 526.

[123] *U.S. v. Local 807*, 315 U.S. 521, 530, 526 (1942).

[124] R. Alton Lee, *Truman and Taft-Hartley: A Question of Mandate* (Lexington: University of Kentucky Press, 1966), 44; *U.S. v. Enmons*, 410 U.S. 396 (1973).

[125] Richard Polenberg, *War and Society: The United States, 1941–1945* (Philadelphia, PA: Lippincott, 1972), 158.

[126] See *Steele v. Louisville & Nashville R.R.*, 323 U.S. 192 (1944); *Tunstall v. Brotherhood of Locomotive Firemen & Enginemen*, 323 U.S. 210 (1944).

federal labor relations law had delegated extraordinary power to unions—
"power not unlike that of a legislature," as the U.S. Supreme Court put
it—and, therefore, unions had to abide by constitutional standards of
equal protection. The Wagner Act had, as one historian puts it, "created
a hybrid social organization, private in origin but exercising public power
over individual rights; the majority union became something akin to a
private government, a legally created 'state within the state.' " [127]

The War Labor Disputes Act provided a model for the Taft-Hartley Act
of 1947, which preserved the basic principles of the Wagner Act but tried
to balance the respective rights of management and unions. While the
Wagner Act outlawed only "unfair labor practices" by employers, Taft-
Hartley enumerated certain unfair labor practices that unions could not
engage in. It outlawed the closed shop and secondary boycotts, required
that union officers forswear Communist Party membership, and gave the
president powers to forbid strikes that might imperil national security.
Perhaps most important, it permitted states to prohibit the "union shop"
or any kind of requirement that an employee join or pay dues to a union.
This provision led many southern and western states to enact such "right-
to-work" laws. Ironically, organized labor made an unsuccessful effort to
get the Supreme Court to hold such laws unconstitutional on the "liberty
of contract" basis that underlay the old understanding of freedom of
association.[128]

While virtually no one accepts the contemporary union claim that Taft-
Hartley was a "slave labor act," it did restrict union freedom in unprec-
edented ways. Even if the closed shop were a mutually acceptable
arrangement for employer and union, they were forbidden voluntarily to
adopt it. Taft-Hartley also established the first real prohibition on the
right of employees to strike, by giving the president power to suspend
strikes and to impose federal mediation. Nevertheless, the act did not
seriously clip the wings of organized labor, especially as it was interpreted by the National Labor Relations Board.[129] Union membership continued to grow, peaking at about one-third of the nonfarm private sector
labor force in the mid-1950s.

During the 1950s, union violence, corruption, and connections to organized crime led to further calls for restrictions on union power. Perhaps
the most revealing observation came from Harvard law professor Roscoe Pound. Pound had been the principal theorist of "sociological jurisprudence," which attacked the natural law tradition that underlay
the nineteenth-century individualist, voluntarist common law of labor

---

[127] Dickman, *Industrial Democracy in America*, 283.

[128] *Lincoln Federal Labor Union v. Northwestern Iron & Metal Co.*, 335 U.S. 525 (1949). See
Charles W. Baird, "Right to Work Before and After 14(b)," *Journal of Labor Research* 19 (1998):
471–93.

[129] Sylvester Petro, *How the N.L.R.B. Repealed Taft-Hartley* (Washington, DC: Labor Policy
Association, 1958).

relations. But by the mid-twentieth century, he concluded that legislation intended to compensate workers for their unequal bargaining power and to secure "real" liberty of contract had done more harm than good. Unions, he said, were free to commit torts against persons and property, interfere with the use of transportation, break contracts, deprive people of the means of livelihood, and misuse trust funds—"things no one else can do with impunity. The labor leader and labor union now stand where the king and government . . . stood at common law." Rather than a countervailing force to limit corporate power, unions had themselves gained "a despotic centralized control." American labor law had "substitute[d] tyranny of centralized employee oligarchies for tyranny of the employers."[130] "There can be no question," the economist F. A. Hayek wrote around the same time, "that the basic principles of the rule of law have nowhere in recent times been so generally violated and with such serious consequences as in the case of labor unions. . . . Most people, however, have so little realization of what has happened that they still support the aspirations of the unions in the belief that they are struggling for 'freedom of association,' when this term has in fact lost its meaning and the real issue has become the freedom of the individual to join or not to join a union."[131] This perception was reinforced by the exposés of the McClellan Committee hearings in Congress, which revealed to a mass television audience the deep influence of organized crime in national unions. The award-winning Hollywood film *On the Waterfront* (1954), directed by Elia Kazan and starring Marlon Brando, also popularized the image of gangster-dominated unions. The 1959 Landrum-Griffin Act established a "bill of rights" for union members, and imposed greater reporting requirements on unions, particularly involving their finances.[132]

Not surprisingly, the academic world that blamed the law for the failure of organized labor before the New Deal now blames the law for the decline of union power since the 1960s.[133] Though Taft-Hartley,

[130] Roscoe Pound, "Legal Immunities of Labor Unions," in *Labor Unions and Public Policy*, ed. Edward H. Chamberlin et al. (Washington, DC: American Enterprise Association, 1958), 145–63. Pound's early progressivism can be seen in his essay "Liberty of Contract," *Yale Law Journal* 18 (1909): 454–87. By the post–World War II period, his sociological jurisprudence had been surpassed by the more radical "legal realist" school, which Robert Wagner credited as the basis of the NLRA. See Barenberg, "Political Economy of the Wagner Act," 1409; and Cortner, *The Wagner Act Cases*, 193.

[131] Friedrich A. Hayek, *The Constitution of Liberty* (Chicago: University of Chicago Press, 1960), 266, 268.

[132] Landrum-Griffin Act, 73 Stat. L. 519 (1959). See James A. Gross, *Broken Promise: The Subversion of U.S. Labor Relations Policy, 1947–1994* (Philadelphia, PA: Temple University Press, 1995), 138, 191.

[133] Gross, *Broken Promise*; Karl E. Klare, "The Judicial Deradicalization of the Wagner Act and the Origins of Modern Legal Consciousness, 1937–1941," *Minnesota Law Review* 62 (1978): 265; Matthew W. Finkin, "Revisionism in Labor Law," *Maryland Law Review* 43 (1984): 23; Karl E. Klare, "Traditional Labor Law Scholarship and the Crisis of Collective Bargaining: A Reply to Professor Finkin," *Maryland Law Review* 44 (1985): 731; David M. Rabban, "Has the N.L.R.A. Hurt Labor?" *University of Chicago Law Review* 54 (1987): 407.

Landrum-Griffin, and other laws and court decisions (such as those against racial discrimination) weakened union power in the second half of the twentieth century, much more important to the erosion of union power was the return of competitive market forces in the American and global economy.[134] Taft-Hartley permitted industries to relocate in right-to-work states or abroad, and shifted employment from unionized to nonunionized industries. At the same time, the United States became more open to immigration, and women entered the labor force in greater numbers. The unionized percentage of the American workforce began to decline after 1953, and the absolute number of union members began to fall in 1970. The only growth of union numbers has been in government employment, where workers began to be permitted to unionize in the late 1950s and 1960s.[135] Despite the growth of their legal privileges over the course of the twentieth century, unions entered the twenty-first century at about the same place they had occupied before those legal privileges were granted. "Economic forces, competition and economic change have eroded the power of the N.L.R.A.," one economist notes, "just as economic forces have always undermined regulation of markets throughout history."[136] The mixed, often contradictory set of policies that marked the twentieth century (most notably in the antitrust realm) has remained. There has been no fundamental alteration in American union policy since the 1935 Wagner Act. But the new, entitlement understanding of "real" freedom of association only went so far, because the old, rights-based tradition remained resilient.[137]

Historians have fundamentally misunderstood the relationship between American unions and state power. Rather than suffering from legal disabilities, unions have depended on government privileges for their success. The great boon of federal legislation in the mid-twentieth century is what accounted for the temporary expansion of organized labor's numbers. In 2005, seventy years after the Wagner Act and fifty years after the merger of the American Federation of Labor and the Congress

---

[134] On the impact of federal antidiscrimination laws, see Judith Stein, *Running Steel, Running America: Race, Economic Policy, and the Decline of Liberalism* (Chapel Hill: The University of North Carolina Press, 1998); and Reuel E. Schiller, "From Group Rights to Individual Liberties: Postwar Labor Law, Liberalism, and the Waning of Union Strength," *Berkeley Journal of Employment and Labor Law* 20 (1999): 1; and Richard A. Epstein, *How Progressives Rewrote the Constitution* (Washington, DC: Cato Institute, 2006), 98.

[135] Leo Troy, "The Right to Organize Meets the Market," in *Liberty, Property, and the Future of Constitutional Development*, ed. Ellen Frankel Paul and Howard Dickman (Albany, NY: SUNY Press, 1990), 314–16; Harry S. Farber and Bruce Western, "Accounting for the Decline of Unions in the Private Sector," in *The Future of Private Sector Unionism in the U.S.*, ed. James T. Bennett and Bruce E. Kaufman (Armonk, NY: M. E. Sharpe, 2002), 53.

[136] Troy, "The Right to Organize Meets the Market," 319.

[137] Seymour Martin Lipset and Ivan Katchanovski, "The Future of Private Sector Unionism in the U.S.," in Bennett and Kaufman, eds., *The Future of Private Sector Unionism*, 23; Barry T. Hirsch and Edward J. Schumacher, "Private Sector Union Density and the Wage Premium," ibid., 103; Dubofsky, "The Federal Judiciary, Free Labor, and Equal Rights," 173–74; Epstein, *How Progressives Rewrote the Constitution*, 126.

of Industrial Organizations (CIO), reacting to the moribund condition of the AFL-CIO, a group of dissident unions broke away and formed a rival federation, called "Change to Win." Its leaders complained that the AFL-CIO spent too much time and money on political activities rather than trying to organize workers at the grass roots. But the history of American labor law suggests that, absent any major change in labor legislation, this effort will bear little fruit.

History, Hillsdale College

"GUILT BY ASSOCIATION" AND THE POSTWAR CIVIL LIBERTARIANS

By Ken I. Kersch

In the course of our discussion we have found one phrase crop-
ping up again and again which constitutes a stone of stumbling
on the path to an intelligent position. This phrase is "guilt by
association."[1]

—Sidney Hook

In the whole discussion of the tangled questions of national security,
professional integrity, and personal freedom, now raging throughout
the country, "guilt by association" is the most overworked phrase in
circulation.[2]

—Sidney Hook

The phrase "guilt by association" is in constant use.[3]

—Robert Cushman

Now, for the first time in our history, the principle of voluntary
association is seriously jeopardized by the doctrine of guilt by association. It is a new doctrine. It appeared in our law only in 1940; since
then it has grown and spread until this cloud, no larger than a man's
hand, covers the whole horizon.[4]

—Henry Steele Commager

[T]he constitutional status of the Communist Party [is] perhaps the
most complex subject in constitutional law, one that has divided both
the Court and the scholars.[5]

—Milton Konvitz

---

[1] Sidney Hook, *Heresy, Yes; Conspiracy, No* (New York: John Day & Co., 1953), 83.

[2] Ibid., 85.

[3] Robert E. Cushman, *Civil Liberties in the United States: A Guide to Current Problems and
Experiences* (Ithaca, NY: Cornell University Press, 1956), 185.

[4] Henry Steele Commager, "The Pragmatic Necessity for Freedom," in Henry Steele Commager and Clair Wilcox, eds., *Civil Liberties Under Attack* (Philadelphia: University of Pennsylvania Press, 1951), 17.

[5] Milton R. Konvitz, *Expanding Liberties: The Emergence of New Civil Liberties and Civil
Rights in Postwar America* (New York: Viking Press, 1967), 109.

doi:10.1017/S0265052508080187

53

I. Introduction

The freedom of association has assumed a relatively low profile in contemporary accounts of civil liberties. Today, major textbooks on the subject treat the free association right as an afterthought. These books accord pride of place to the right's presumably more foundational First Amendment neighbors: the freedoms of speech, press, and religion, and the proscription on religious establishments.

One possible explanation for the lower level of attention paid to free association could be its absence from the constitutional text. The right to free association technically has no First Amendment neighbors since, strictly speaking, it doesn't exist. The freedom of association is not specifically enumerated in the First Amendment's text. Rather, it has been derived by implication from the amendment's tag-end provisions providing for "the right of the people peaceably to assemble, and to petition the Government for a redress of grievances," read in conjunction with the ostensible purpose attributed to the First Amendment as a whole by modern civil libertarians: to create a "system of freedom of expression."[6] But does the fact that the constitutional free association right is nontextual explain its status as a relatively neglected right in the contemporary civil liberties firmament? The fact that a right is nontextual and generated, by implication, out of other textual provisions, in conjunction with some general spirit of the Constitution, hardly disqualifies it from marquee status—the "right to privacy" (like the earlier "liberty of contract") being a classic case in point.[7] Moreover, in the immediate post–World War II years, the free association right's status as an unenumerated right did not preclude its being widely discussed as one of our most important constitutional rights. What is determinative is political, social, and ideational context. The American constitutional order may be understood, in significant part, as a web of complex (and often countervailing, and contradictory) rights claims. Different rights do—and are imagined to do—different things at different times, and they buttress, or run up against, other rights claims as they do so. Mapping these interactions between rights in distinctive historical contexts is crucial in understanding the prominence of a particular right at a particular developmental moment.

[6] Thomas I. Emerson, *The System of Freedom of Expression* (New York: Random House, 1970).

[7] See *Griswold v. Connecticut*, 381 U.S. 479 (1965); *Roe v. Wade*, 410 U.S. 113 (1973); *Allgeyer v. Louisiana*, 165 U.S. 578 (1897); and *Lochner v. New York*, 198 U.S. 45 (1905). The freedom of association was the most prominent unenumerated right of its time. It is notable that, although the Supreme Court's rulings based on it were criticized, so far as I can tell, associational freedom was not attacked with any special vehemence on the specific ground that it was unenumerated. See generally Ken I. Kersch, "The Right to Privacy," in David Bodenhamer and James W. Ely, Jr., eds., *The Bill of Rights in Modern America*, 2d ed. (Bloomington: Indiana University Press, 2008). In its lead-up to declaring the new right to freedom of association, however, the Supreme Court considered the issue under the rubric of the (enumerated) right to assembly. See *Adler v. Board of Education*, 342 U.S. 485 (1952); and *Wieman v. Updegraff*, 344 U.S. 183 (1952), discussed in note 16 below.

As taught and considered today, the relatively underdiscussed free association right is, in two senses, a second-order right. First, it is commonly considered as an instrument for vindicating high-status (First Amendment) rights claims, like freedom of religion and freedom of speech, which, as first-order rights, are defended not as instruments indispensable to the exercise of other rights but rather on their own substantive terms.[8] Second, in the most high-profile contemporary free association cases, the right is asserted defensively, as a countervailing claim, in cases involving the highest status group-rights claims made in modern American law—those involving civil rights. That, today, the free association right is considered a second-order rather than a first-order right is not determined by some property inherent in the right itself; it is, rather, historically and developmentally determined. That is to say, it is a matter of context.[9]

What does the freedom of association mean today? The contemporary freedom of association is primarily apprehended as a potentially countervailing claim in civil rights cases. It is invoked most prominently in cases involving rights for women and gays and lesbians. In *Roberts v. United States Jaycees* (1984), for example, the Supreme Court spurned the claim of a private young men's civic association that Minnesota's requirement that it admit women as regular members trenched upon the group's free association rights.[10] In *Boy Scouts of America v. Dale* (2000), by contrast, the Court narrowly held that New Jersey's requirement that the Boy Scouts of America admit gay scoutmasters violated the group's right to free (expressive) association.[11]

Although decided on different grounds doctrinally, these cases represent, in many respects, the extension of earlier Supreme Court "right to exclude" decisions involving blacks. Those cases also pitted claims of private individual rights against civil rights. In *Heart of Atlanta Motel v. United States* (1964), for example, the Supreme Court issued a landmark opinion upholding Congress's power under the commerce clause to forbid hotels from barring black guests, and rejected the hotel owners' claim that they should be free to admit only guests of their own choosing pursuant to their Fifth Amendment property and liberty rights, and their Thirteenth Amendment right against involuntary servitude.[12]

---

[8] See Tobias Barrington Wolff and Andrew Koppelman, "Expressive Association and the Ideal of the University in the Solomon Amendment Litigation," elsewhere in this volume.

[9] See generally Ken I. Kersch, *Constructing Civil Liberties: Discontinuities in the Development of American Constitutional Law* (New York: Cambridge University Press, 2004).

[10] *Roberts v. United States Jaycees*, 468 U.S. 609 (1984). In the *Jaycees* case, the Court specifically rejected the club's claims to freedom of intimate association and freedom of expressive association. See also *Frank v. Ivy Club*, 120 N.J. 73, 576 A.2d 241 (1990) (holding that, free association claims notwithstanding, the state of New Jersey could require private all-male eating clubs at Princeton University to admit women).

[11] *Boy Scouts of America v. Dale*, 530 U.S. 640 (2000). In *Dale*, the Court recognized the Boy Scouts' claims to freedom of expressive association.

[12] *Heart of Atlanta Motel v. United States*, 379 U.S. 241 (1964).

The companion case of *Katzenbach v. McClung* (1964) issued a similar landmark ruling applying to restaurants.[13]

Contemporary freedom of association cases (like the mid-twentieth-century Fifth Amendment liberty and property rights cases—not incidentally known today as civil rights cases) raise questions of the rights of ownership, the significance of personal identity, and the right to exclude. It is for this reason that they have been taken up for consideration by contemporary Rawlsian liberal academics, and others.[14] The question for these scholars, in essence, is how far we should go in according recognition to a second-order right in the teeth of the claims of a first-order one. Since the question is framed in this way in advance by these scholars, the answer, of course, is "not very."

To read the overviews of civil libertarian scholars writing in the mid-twentieth century, however, is to enter another country, where the freedom of association is not a second-order but rather a first-order right. This is evident from the fact that, at that time, the freedom of association arrayed itself not at the margins but rather at the core of civil liberties discussions. For example, in Milton Konvitz's *Expanding Liberties: The Emergence of New Civil Liberties in Postwar America* (1967), three of the book's five chapters on First Amendment liberties were devoted to matters of associational rights.[15] The era's other major civil liberties texts and scholars devoted considerable space to the subject not as a potentially countervailing second-order consideration but, rather, in its own right. Indeed, it was at this time that the term "freedom of association" was invented and accorded constitutional status by the Supreme Court.

Foremost in the minds of those who first announced this new first-order right were not matters of personal identity, and the group's right to exclude, but rather the question of "guilt by association": that is, to what degree is it legitimate to hold an individual accountable, in public or private relations, for his association with others as a member of a group? Questions of freedom of association were raised, and developed, in two types of cases in this period. The first involved civil rights, but in an entirely different posture from the identity/right-to-exclude cases (which, at this time, did not expressly take up free association issues). These civil rights cases involved the question of the state's ability to require groups (either civil rights groups or "subversive" political parties like the Communists) to reveal their membership lists, and the right of individual members of groups to keep their membership in a group private. The cases involved, that is, not claims of intimate and expressive association

---

[13] *Katzenbach v. McClung*, 379 U.S. 294 (1964).

[14] See, e.g., Amy Gutmann, ed., *Freedom of Association* (Princeton, NJ: Princeton University Press, 1998).

[15] Those chapters were titled "Freedom of Association," "Academic Freedom," and "The Communist Party and the Freedom of Association." The other two First Amendment chapters were titled "Religious Liberty" and "Censorship of Literature."

(as in the modern free association cases) but rather claims of associational privacy.[16] The second group of cases involved the attribution of "guilt" to individuals on the basis of their membership in the allegedly subversive Communist Party. These cases involved questions of membership rights: Could one legally be a part of this group? Problems with group membership arose either because the group itself was ostensibly collectively committed to illegal objectives or because (other) individual members of the group had presumably engaged in illegal conduct. Under these circumstances, the question was whether membership in the group alone amounted to participation in a criminal conspiracy. Thus, in this earlier era, free association cases were cases involving the right to privacy and criminal procedure.

II. "Guilt by Association" Through the Eyes of the Mid-Century Civil Libertarians: Pfeffer, Cushman, Konvitz, Commager, and Chafee

The problem of "guilt by association" was a major theme of civil libertarian scholars writing in the middle years of the twentieth century. Indeed, as they saw it, it was a problem that had occasioned the invention of a new constitutional right. Far from denying the right's newness—a requirement in our later, more conservative age—mid-century civil libertarians openly trumpeted, and celebrated, free association's novelty. "The First Amendment does not mention the right of association," Leo Pfeffer explained in his chapter on petition, assembly, and association rights in his book *The Liberties of an American* (1956):

> [I]t speaks only of "the right of the people peaceably to assemble, and to petition the Government for a redress of grievances." Moreover, the right of assembly was historically conceived merely as an incident or aid to the right of petition, as if the Amendment had read "the right of the people peaceably to assemble *in order to* petition the Government for a redress of grievances." Today, however, it is universally recognized and accepted that the right of peaceable assembly for a lawful

[16] *Adler v. Board of Education*, 342 U.S. 485 (1952) (upholding, against a freedom-of-assembly claim, the constitutionality of New York State's 1949 Feinberg Law requiring the state's board of regents to compile a list of subversive organizations, membership in which constituted a prima facie case for dismissal from employment in the state's public schools); *Wieman v. Updegraff*, 344 U.S. 183 (1952) (striking down an Oklahoma statute requiring all state employees to take an oath that they were not members of any group listed by the U.S. attorney general as a subversive or Communist front group on the grounds that the law did not distinguish between innocent and culpable membership); *Barenblatt v. United States*, 360 U. S. 109 (1959) (upholding the criminal conviction of a Vassar College professor for contempt of Congress for refusal to answer questions about his membership in the Communist Party); *NAACP v. Alabama*, 357 U.S. 449 (1958) (upholding, on freedom of association grounds, the right of the NAACP to refuse to provide its membership list to the state of Alabama pursuant to a state statute requiring corporations doing business in the state to provide such a list).

purpose is an independent right, as fundamental as free speech and a free press to a democratic society. . . . Association is nothing more than continuing assembly, and, therefore, though not expressly mentioned in the Bill of Rights, is equally a constitutionally protected, basic liberty of Americans.[17]

Although contemporary conservative and communitarian critics of the mid-twentieth-century "rights revolution" commonly denounce the hyper-individualism of the mid-century civil libertarians, Pfeffer, for one, cited the new association right not as an indication of a trend toward hyper-individualism, but as a sign of a movement toward the group-orientation of modern society.[18] He explained:

> The Constitution and Bill of Rights were written in a generation and a milieu that emphasized individualism and the rights of individuals. The experiences the fathers of our republic had with associations undoubtedly conditioned them toward a suspicious approach to associations, to the extent that they thought of associations at all. The associations they were familiar with were the religious associations constituting the established churches and the political associations constituting the British government and colonial agents. The political associations known as political parties were looked on with suspicion and mistrust by many of the founding fathers, and Washington in his Farewell Address warned against "factions" in the political life of the new nation.[19]

Along these lines, "When . . . the Supreme Court in *Hague v. CIO* [1939] dismissed the companion action of the American Civil Liberties Union (which too had been denied a permit to hold a public meeting) on the ground that it was a corporation and that the constitutional liberty of freedom of assembly was secured only to individuals, it was reflecting truly the philosophy of the founding fathers."[20]

The predominance of individualism was an understandable by-product of the politics and culture of an earlier era. "The individualistic spirit of the [founding] fathers," Pfeffer explained, "was a natural consequence of the expanding frontier and, at least in its pristine purity, was

---

[17] Leo Pfeffer, *The Liberties of an American: The Supreme Court Speaks* (Boston, MA: Beacon Press, 1956), 97–98. See also ibid., 110: "The Bill of Rights nowhere makes specific reference to freedom of association. . . ."

[18] For a reading of contemporary civil liberties consistent with this, focusing on the relationship of civil liberties with modern pluralist political thought, see Ronald Kahn, *The Supreme Court and Constitutional Theory, 1953–1993* (Lawrence: University Press of Kansas, 1994).

[19] Pfeffer, *The Liberties of an American*, 110.

[20] Ibid., 110. See *Hague v. CIO*, 307 U.S. 496 (1939).

doomed to disappearance with the frontier."[21] Modern, less individualistic times, however, demanded new understandings of constitutional
rights:

> Today we are beginning to recognize that associations, even those
> competing in some degree with the state for [the] loyalty and sov-
> ereignty of individuals, need not be inimical to democracy. Quite
> the contrary, with the ever-expanding scope of governmental activ-
> ities and jurisdiction, and the magnitude and increasing complex-
> ity of modern social life, voluntary associations, political, religious,
> economic, cultural, fraternal, [and] social, have become an indis-
> pensable ally in the struggle to preserve democracy against totali-
> tarianism. To take one simple illustration: the industrial associations
> known as labor unions have probably been the most important
> single force in the struggle for industrial democracy.[22]

Like all students of legal history, Pfeffer was well aware that the
problem of unlawful association was not a new one: throughout American history, various types of associations had been outlawed. "Just as
assembly for an unlawful purpose is not constitutionally protected, so
too association for an unlawful purpose is not made immune from
governmental interference by the First Amendment. Today, unlawful
associations in the context of civil liberties are generally taken to refer
to political associations whose purpose is to overthrow the government; but surprisingly the constitutional law concerning unlawful associations goes back more than half a century and grew out of religious,
not political association."[23] Pfeffer finds the progenitor cases here to be
the Mormon polygamy cases, where the defendant "was not himself
charged either with practicing or with teaching polygamy; he was
charged only with being a member of the Mormon Church which, he
knew, advocated polygamy." "Congress, said the [Supreme] Court, has

---

[21] Pfeffer, *The Liberties of an American*, 110.

[22] Ibid., 110–11. On the profound conceptual significance of this understanding of the
political function of labor unions in twentieth-century constitutional thought concerning
rights, see Kersch, *Constructing Civil Liberties;* and Ken I. Kersch, "The New Deal Triumph
as the End of History? The Judicial Negotiation of Labor Rights and Civil Rights," in Ronald
Kahn and Ken I. Kersch, eds., *The Supreme Court and American Political Development* (Lawrence: University Press of Kansas, 2006). In these works, I emphasize the developmental
significance of conceptualizing New Deal era labor rights as a form of group rights. In his
essay in the present volume, Richard Boyd notes that Thomas Hobbes had warned against
associations on the grounds alluded to here by Pfeffer, calling them "lesser commonwealths
in the bowels of a greater, like worms in the entrails of a natural man." Boyd, "The Madisonian
Paradox of Freedom of Association," citing Thomas Hobbes, *Leviathan,* ed. Edwin Curley
(Indianapolis, IN: Hackett, 1994), chap. 29, 218.

[23] Pfeffer, *The Liberties of an American*, 112.

the power to dissolve this unlawful association and to prevent its funds from being used for the unlawful purpose of promoting polygamy."[24]

In his overview of civil liberties at mid-century, *Civil Liberties in the United States: A Guide to Current Problems and Experience* (1956), Cornell University political scientist Robert Cushman observed that "[t]he phrase 'guilt by association' is in constant use," but that it was tossed about all too casually. "It is often loosely employed by those who condemn the drawing of any unfavorable inferences from a man's association with other persons under any circumstances," Cushman wrote. "This of course is nonsense," he noted, "for there are many instances in which we are bound to consider a man's associations in making various kinds of judgments about him."[25]

Cushman insisted that "[t]he whole problem posed by 'guilt by association' should be considered against the background of well-established principles in the law which relate to presumptions of guilt.[26] These rules have been developed over the years to protect persons from the injustices resulting from improper presumptions of guilt."[27] He went on to distill three such rules: first, that guilt must be personal; second, that the accused must be afforded the due-process opportunity to rebut the presumption; and, third, that there must be a rational connection between the fact offered as evidence and the inference of guilt drawn from it.[28] He then undertook a critical assessment of the array of contemporary efforts to fight domestic communism in light of these three rules.[29] Cushman discussed guilt by association as exerting a chilling effect on a specifically enumerated constitutional right—the right to petition the government for a redress of grievances: "Discouragement of the exercise of the right of petition, informal but nonetheless effective, is one of the end results of the doctrine of guilt by association. Stigma attaches to one who signs a petition (many did petition the President in 1933 to recognize Russia) which has also been signed by Communists and fellow travelers. Names on petitions will be carefully checked by officers administering loyalty and security programs."[30]

---

[24] Ibid., 113. See *Davis v. Beason*, 133 U.S. 333 (1890) (unanimously upholding an Idaho territorial statute disenfranchising those who advocated or practiced plural marriage or belonged to an organization that did); and *Church of Jesus Christ of Latter Day Saints v. United States*, 136 U.S. 1 (1890) (upholding the revocation of the Mormon Church charter and the confiscation of Church property).

[25] Cushman, *Civil Liberties in the United States*, 185.

[26] Here Cushman is emphasizing rule of law aspects of the freedom of association similar to those emphasized by James Madison. See Boyd, "The Madisonian Paradox of Freedom of Association."

[27] Cushman, *Civil Liberties in the United States*, 185–86.

[28] Ibid., 186.

[29] Ibid., 186–205.

[30] Ibid., 65. See also Pfeffer, *The Liberties of an American*, 99: "In our own day persons who signed the Stockholm peace petition, or a petition for clemency for the Rosenbergs, or a Communist Party or even a Progressive Party nominating petition are very likely to have that fact count against them in applying for or seeking to retain government employment or employment in private industry working on defense contracts, or in resisting deportation,

Milton Konvitz opened his discussion of the freedom of association in *Expanding Liberties* by citing Alexis de Tocqueville and James Bryce (and Max Weber) for the proposition that the United States was, from its inception, "a nation of joiners."[31] "The picture in the middle of the twentieth century," Konvitz noted, in contrast to Pfeffer's reading of American history, "was not, in essentials, different. If individualism, in some significant sense, characterizes American life, it is of a special kind that has been described as 'group individualism.' . . . [A]ssociation remains a distinguishable and significant characteristic of American society."[32]

Like Pfeffer, and despite this heritage, Konvitz too recognized the novelty of the constitutional right to free association—to the point of subtitling one of the sections of his free association chapter "A New First Amendment Freedom."[33] "Despite this proclivity of Americans to form or join associations," he wrote, "it was not until 1958 in *National Association for the Advancement of Colored People v. Alabama* that the United States Supreme Court, for the first time, directly recognized freedom of association as a liberty guaranteed by the First Amendment. . . . Nowhere in the Bill of Rights of the Constitution is association mentioned. . . ."[34] Moreover, asserted Konvitz, "the omission was not due to bungling or an oversight. No draft of the Bill of Rights submitted by James Madison, nor any amendment proposed by any other member of Congress, which debated the Bill of Rights in 1789, mentioned association. Indeed, Madison's best-known contribution to *The Federalist* is an attack on voluntary associations, political or economic, which he called 'factions.' "[35] Madison, accordingly, "was not one to urge a constitutional guarantee of freedom of association."[36] In a similar vein, Konvitz went on to quote George Washington's warning in his Farewell Address against "the spirit of party."[37] Konvitz concluded that "the Founding Fathers felt hostile towards

---

or in a variety of other situations where their loyalty is called into question. The fact that the American public does not uniformly believe that 'there is no harm in asking' and that exercise of the right of petition does not entail punitive consequences is indicated by the difficulties encountered not long ago by a reporter of a Midwestern newspaper who vainly sought to obtain signatures from street passers-by to a petition incorporating part of the Declaration of Independence." The Stockholm Peace Petition, which called for a ban on atomic weapons, occasioned considerable controversy in 1950, as the petition was championed by the communist movement around the world. Julius and Ethel Rosenberg were New York City communists who were tried and executed for passing U.S. nuclear secrets to the Soviet Union. Although they were championed by the left at the time as the prototypical dissenters victimized by the excesses of McCarthyism, it was later confirmed by documents from the Soviet archives that Julius Rosenberg was indeed a Soviet spy. Note that both Cushman and Pfeffer consider guilt by association inappropriate in both criminal and noncriminal contexts.

[31] Konvitz, *Expanding Liberties*, 48.

[32] Ibid., 49–50.

[33] Ibid., 59.

[34] Ibid., 50.

[35] Ibid. Konvitz is referring to *Federalist* No. 10, written by Madison.

[36] Konvitz, *Expanding Liberties*, 51.

[37] Ibid.

the idea of voluntary association."[38] When the Supreme Court issued its ruling in the *NAACP* case in 1958, it thus "broke away from the views of Madison and the other Founding Fathers, which had stood in the way of this constitutional development."[39] Nonetheless, Konvitz judged that "[t]hese decisions are a clear, significant gain. It is obvious that they are a gain for freedom of association, and they mark a considerable advance on the democratic philosophy of John Locke, James Madison, and the other thinkers who contributed to the hopes and fears that went into the framing of the First Amendment."[40]

The Supreme Court's invention of this new right, Konvitz explained, was prompted by southern efforts to destroy the NAACP and to cripple its attempts to mount a sustained legal campaign against racial segregation in the South.[41] It was civil rights cases such as *NAACP v. Alabama* "which fixed the constitutional principles."[42] These cases, in turn, intersected with others involving allegations of subversive activity and raising questions of "guilt by association."[43] Given their diverging fact scenarios, these cases might not have been related, except conceptually. But Konvitz noted that state legislators looking to undermine the efforts of civil rights organizations decided: "Why not look for subversives in the N.A.A.C.P., just as New Hampshire had looked for them in World Fellowship?"[44]

In inventing the freedom of association, the Supreme Court also marked a clear advance for civil rights—and for the right to litigate, which is

---

[38] Ibid.

[39] Ibid., 57.

[40] Ibid., 84. On the Founders' ambivalence toward the freedom of association, see Boyd, "The Madisonian Paradox of Freedom of Association." The degree to which the Founders' negative views toward faction and the spirit of party were coextensive with their views on other, potentially quite different and more benign forms of association remains an open question. Of course, even if they were positively disposed toward the more benign forms of associations—the equivalents of, say, 4-H clubs—they would likely have understood that these sorts of benign groups would be much less likely to need to invoke a constitutional freedom specifically enumerated in the constitutional text: it would likely be the self-seeking troublemakers who would appeal to such a freedom.

[41] Konvitz, *Expanding Liberties*, 62. That it led the Court to the invention of a new constitutional right, which subsequently developed a life of its own, is yet another way in which *Brown v. Board of Education*, 347 U.S. 483 (1954), had a major effect on the shape of the law, revealing one of the many limits of Gerald N. Rosenberg's popular account of *Brown*'s limits. See Gerald N. Rosenberg, *The Hollow Hope: Can the Courts Bring about Social Change?* (Chicago: University of Chicago Press, 1991).

[42] Konvitz, *Expanding Liberties*, 84.

[43] Ibid., 75. See, e.g., *Wieman v. Updegraff*, 344 U.S. 183 (1952), and *Gibson v. Florida Legislative Committee*, 372 U.S. 539 (1963).

[44] Konvitz, *Expanding Liberties*, 80. World Fellowship, Inc., under the leadership of Willard Uphaus (a labor, peace, and civil rights activist, and a Methodist minister), ran a summer camp in Conway, New Hampshire, for progressive activists. Suspecting the camp was involved in subversive activities—chiefly by inviting communists and members of subversive groups as speakers at the camp—the New Hampshire legislature subpoenaed the Fellowship's records, including the registry of all those who had attended the camp's programs. Uphaus refused, citing in part the group's rights to associational privacy, and was sent to jail for nearly a year. He lost the appeal of his conviction in a 5-to-4 decision by the U.S. Supreme Court. *Uphaus v. Wyman*, 360 U.S. 72 (1959).

important to the vindication of all the other rights: "for if Alabama or Arkansas or Florida or Louisiana had won in the Court, a way would have opened for the South to paralyze the N.A.A.C.P. and any other civil rights or civil liberties organization; and since the Bill of Rights is not self-executing, but is dependent upon vindication through litigation, the struggle for freedom and equality would have been effectively arrested."[45] One of the most precious rights of associations is the right

> to litigate, and thereby to vindicate the constitutional and legal rights of Americans. Without this right of association for civil rights and civil liberties litigation, our Bill of Rights might remain as abstract and insignificant as is the part of the Constitution of the U.S.S.R. that purports to guarantee personal freedoms and rights. There are no civil rights or civil liberties organizations in the U.S.S.R. or in any other totalitarian or one-party state. It took the attacks on the N.A.A.C.P. to demonstrate that, "under the conditions of modern government"—and ... given the conditions of the complexity and high cost of legal actions—"litigation may well be the sole practicable avenue open to a minority to petition for the redress of grievances."[46]

Konvitz devoted a separate chapter of *Expanding Liberties* to "Academic Freedom," whose opening section was subtitled "Emergence of a New Constitutional Liberty."[47] He noted: "In the more important cases the problem of academic freedom arose in the context of freedom of association. Here we shall consider academic freedom only insofar as it may involve, or be involved with, freedom of association."[48] Konvitz then discussed the progression of Supreme Court decisions leading up to the Court's landmark defense of academic freedom. In *Adler v. Board of Education* (1952), spurning a freedom of assembly claim, the Court upheld the constitutionality of New York State's 1949 Feinberg Law requiring the state's board of regents to compile a list of subversive organizations, membership in which constituted prima facie grounds for dismissal from employment in the state's public schools. But in *Wieman v. Updegraff* (1952), the Court struck down an Oklahoma statute requiring all state employees to take an oath that they were not members of any group listed by the U.S. Attorney General as a subversive or Communist-front group on the grounds that the Oklahoma law did not distinguish between innocent and culpable membership. Finally, in *Sweezy v. New Hampshire* (1957),

---

[45] Konvitz, *Expanding Liberties*, 84.

[46] Ibid., 85, quoting *N.A.A.C.P. v. Button*, 371 U.S. 415 (1963) (invalidating, on free expression and free association grounds, Virginia's prosecution of NAACP litigators for improper solicitation of legal business).

[47] Konvitz, *Expanding Liberties*, 86.

[48] Ibid., 86.

the Court (particularly in a concurrence written by Justice Felix Frankfurter) delivered a ringing defense of the value of academic freedom in
voiding New Hampshire's prosecution of a University of New Hampshire professor for his failure to answer questions on the contents of a
lecture he delivered on the Progressive Party (as well as on his knowledge
of the party). "With the decision in the *Sweezy* case," Konvitz wrote, "we
can say that the Court gave academic freedom full and equal First Amendment status, so that it is on a par, for dignity and sanction, with the
freedoms expressly enumerated in the Bill of Rights, and with freedom of
association."[49]

In his contribution to a book titled *Civil Liberties Under Attack* (1951),
"The Pragmatic Necessity for Freedom," Henry Steele Commager wrote:

> Now, for the first time in our history, the principle of voluntary asso-
> ciation is seriously jeopardized by the doctrine of guilt by association.
> It is a new doctrine. It appeared in our law only in 1940; since then it
> has grown and spread until this cloud, no larger than a man's hand,
> covers the whole horizon. Yet already its consequences are apparent.
> They are, in brief, that men and women are afraid to join anything. As
> it is dangerous to join an organization unless you know that all other
> members—past and future as well as present—are above suspicion,
> and as it is impossible ever to know this, the easiest thing is simply to
> stand aloof. But once this process gets under way, democracy itself is
> threatened—threatened at the grass roots. For the same principle that
> prevents people from joining, let us say, an organization to help ref-
> ugees, prevents them from joining a political party or even a church.[50]

After quoting at length from the chapter in Tocqueville's *Democracy in
America* titled "The Uses Americans Make of Public Organizations," Commager warned: "Every day it becomes more difficult to organize new
associations, or to maintain old ones. Every day it becomes more difficult
to undertake any program of reform or even change. But the instinct for
voluntary association is the instinct for democracy, and the instinct for
change is the instinct for life."[51]

In "Investigations of Radicalism and Laws Against Subversion," another
contribution to *Civil Liberties Under Attack*, Zechariah Chafee, Jr. linked associational rights to the importance of deliberation to life in a democracy. There
are, he wrote, "great dangers ... [to] ... interfering by law with freedom
of discussion through organizations. [Contemporary anti-subversion leg-
islation] proposes to twist out of all recognizable shape one of the leading

---

[49] Ibid., 94. See *Adler v. Board of Education*, 342 U.S. 485 (1952); *Wieman v. Updegraff*, 344
U.S. 183 (1952); and *Sweezy v. New Hampshire*, 354 U.S. 234 (1957).
[50] Commager, "The Pragmatic Necessity for Freedom," 17.
[51] Ibid., 18.

traditions of American life: the possibility of freely forming associations for all sorts of purposes—religious, political, social, and economic."[52] Chafee then went on to note the historical importance of associations as a spur to social change, citing William Lloyd Garrison's Anti-Slavery Society, and the Granger and Populist movements.[53]

III. SIDNEY HOOK

Sidney Hook's *Heresy, Yes; Conspiracy, No* (1953) was one of the most prominent mid-century works reflecting seriously on questions relating to the freedom of association. In this book, Hook sought to chart a middle path on the question of the legality of Communist Party membership between the "cultural vigilantes" of the right (the staunch supporters of Joseph McCarthy) and the "ritualistic," "professional" liberals of the liberal left, "who are more hostile to anti-Communists than to communists."[54] Hook characterized both groups as "calamity howlers and hysteria mongers."[55] "Both groups flourish on each other's misapprehension," he worried, "and their outcries have drowned out the voice of intelligence."[56]

Hook, a professor of philosophy at New York University, was perhaps the most accomplished student of Columbia University professor and pragmatist philosopher John Dewey. Hook began as a Marxist and made the reconciliation of Marx's thought with Dewey's his primary intellectual project. An early supporter of the Soviet Union, Hook spurned the international communist movement and the USSR in the wake of the Hitler-Stalin Pact, though he remained a committed Marxian socialist for the rest of his life. Beginning in the 1930s, Hook became an indefatigable critic of communism and totalitarianism—indeed, one of the country's most prominent. This commitment endeared him to many on the right, and they came to consider Hook, if not a conservative himself, a hero to conservatives. He ended his career as a scholar at Stanford University's conservative Hoover Institution.

Although celebrated by many conservatives as a fierce anticommunist, Hook always considered himself not a traditionalist but a modern. In seeking to position himself within the currents of American history, he counted himself clearly on the side of the nascent civil libertarians of the early twentieth century who had fought for modern understandings of the freedom of speech:

Having when young experienced the years of the Palmer Raids, massed physical assaults on peaceful meetings, systemic violations

---

[52] Zechariah Chafee, Jr., "Investigations of Radicalism and Laws Against Subversion," in Commager and Wilcox, eds., *Civil Liberties Under Attack*, 76.

[53] Ibid., 76–77.

[54] Hook, *Heresy, Yes; Conspiracy, No*, 11.

[55] Ibid.

[56] Ibid.

of due process of law by courts and police in relation to the rights of citizens, I regard the period since then, on the whole, as a progressive improvement with some serious but transitory setbacks like the forcible relocation of the Japanese during World War II.[57]

But heresy—which Hook approved of, and invited—was readily distinguishable from conspiracy. Hook observed that all rights have their legal limits, and guarantees for the freedom of ideas are not guarantees for absolute freedom of conduct. "Freedom to worship God according to one's conscience is one of the historical cornerstones of the structure of American liberties," Hook noted, "but it cannot be invoked to protect rituals which require human sacrifice or practices like plural marriages or refusal to submit to vaccination against plagues." [58]

For Hook, conspiracy may have had an involvement with ideas, but its essence was in working together toward the performance of an illegal act. It also differed in other significant ways from heresy. Hook considered the elements of subterfuge, dishonesty, and deceit to be among the crucial distinctions between heresy and conspiracy. Heresy, Hook argued, was loud, open, and invited publicity. Conspiracy was furtive, secretive, and shunned the light.[59]

Like Konvitz and Commager, Hook praised the Tocquevillian vision of an America brimming with associative life: "No program to safeguard American democracy can be anything but self-defeating which discourages the existence and multiplication of such voluntary associations." [60] But he did not understand Communists as simply another addition to a nation of lively associations. As such, the appeal made to Tocqueville in defending them was misplaced. Communists were not pro-association; they were anti-association. Communists did not truly join associations: they infiltrated them. Many may have considered the Communist Party to be a free-standing association (putting aside, for the time being, its subservience to the Soviet Union). But, if so, it was on a mission to infiltrate and destroy the independence of other free-standing associations. It was viral. It was predatory. Its cells infiltrated healthy associations through deceit, took them over, and killed them. This was conduct, not belief. The Party's object was, through its conduct, to repress dissent

[57] Ibid., 12. The Palmer Raids (1919–1921) were crackdowns on radical political groups, pursuant to the Espionage Act of 1917 and the Sedition Act of 1918, initiated by President Woodrow Wilson's attorney general, A. Mitchell Palmer, in the aftermath of a series of bomb attacks launched across the country by anarchists—including one on the home of Palmer himself.

[58] Ibid., 20.

[59] The Communist conspiracy, Hook insisted, would not warrant the approval of even Karl Marx himself; after all, Marx in the *Communist Manifesto* thundered: "The Communists disdain to conceal their views and aims. They openly declare that their ends can be attained only by the forcible overthrow of all existing social conditions" (quoted in ibid., 26).

[60] Ibid., 92.

and reduce the varieties of belief and purpose that help constitute a vital civil society. As was said repeatedly at the time, the Communist Party USA (CPUSA) was not simply another political party: it was a fifth column moving to attack the innards of the Tocquevillian civil society, with the aim of ultimately felling the liberal-democratic body politic itself.[61]

This view of the CPUSA sheds an informative light on labor legislation such as the Taft-Hartley Act (1947), which required every labor union officer to file an annual affidavit with the National Labor Relations Board swearing that he was not a member of the Communist Party, and neither belonged to nor believed in any organization that "believes in or teaches the overthrow of the United States Government by force or by any illegal or unconstitutional methods," as a condition for maintaining the rights of the union under the 1935 National Labor Relations Act. Given the view of the CPUSA as a fifth column, Taft-Hartley amounted not to a set of restrictions on the freedom of association, but rather to a government-administered effort to protect the autonomy of the union, and the democratic control of its membership. That is, these provisions of Taft-Hartley were designed to protect the union from being secretly invaded, and its legitimate, democratically-elected government from being overthrown.[62]

Many considered Communists to be simply another voice in the American tradition of dissent, speaking truth to power, expressing unwelcome and unorthodox ideas.[63] On this view, Communists were yet another addition to the marketplace of ideas.[64] Hook insisted, however, that it was the chief purpose of Communists to suppress heterodoxy and the free expression of ideas, to move forward inside the Trojan Horse of dissent and nonconformism (which seemed to him to have obviously fooled many civil-libertarian liberals, who would welcome them inside the gates of the city), and ultimately to lay siege to and destroy the marketplace:

[61] "The members of the Communist Party are literally the fifth column of the Red Army, and the success and strategic position of that Army are certainly relevant in considering the danger, not merely of Communist advocacy, but of Communist organization in this country" (ibid., 111). The phrase "fifth column" is attributed to the Spanish Civil War's General Emilio Mola, who said that he had four columns encircling Madrid, and a fifth column working for him in the city. See The Wordsworth Dictionary of Phrase and Fable, ed. Ebenezer Cobham Brewer, revised by Ivor H. Evans (London: Wordsworth Editions, 1993), 409.

[62] Cushman, Civil Liberties in the United States, 50–52; Harry A. Millis and Emily Clark Brown, From the Wagner Act to Taft-Hartley: A Study of National Labor Policy (Chicago: University of Chicago Press, 1950): 552–54. See American Communications Association v. Douds, 339 U.S. 382 (1950) (upholding as constitutional these provisions of Taft-Hartley). See also Kersch, Constructing Civil Liberties, 159–67, on the democratic design behind the collective bargaining provisions of the National Labor Relations Act that, Hook argued, these provisions of Taft-Hartley were designed to preserve. Hook's teacher, John Dewey, was one of the major theorists of "industrial democracy."

[63] See Stephen Feldman, Free Expression and Democracy in America: A History (Chicago: University of Chicago Press, 2008).

[64] See Abrams v. United States, 250 U.S. 616 (1919) (Holmes, J., dissenting). See generally Howard Gillman, "Preferred Freedoms: The Progressive Expansion of State Power and the Rise of Modern Civil Liberties Jurisprudence," Political Research Quarterly 47 (1994): 623–53.

A conspiracy, as distinct from a heresy, is a secret or underground movement which seeks to attain its ends not by normal political or educational processes but by playing outside the rules of the game. Because it undermines the conditions which are required in order that doctrines may freely compete for acceptance, because where successful it ruthlessly destroys all heretics and dissenters, a conspiracy cannot be tolerated without self-stultification in a liberal society. A heresy does not shrink from publicity. It welcomes it. Not so a conspiracy. The signs of conspiracy are secrecy, anonymity, the use of false names and labels, and the calculated lie. It does not offer its wares openly but by systematic infiltration into all organizations of cultural life, it seeks to capture strategic posts to carry out a policy alien to the purposes of the organization. There is political conspiracy, which is the concern of the state; but there may also be a conspiracy against a labor union, a cultural or professional association, or an educational institution which is not primarily the concern of the state but of its own members. In general, whoever subverts the rules of a democratic organization and seeks to win by chicanery what cannot be fairly won in the process of free discussion is a conspirator. Communist *ideas* are heresies, and liberals need have no fear of them where they are freely and openly expressed. They should be studied and evaluated in the light of all the relevant evidence. No one should be punished because he holds them. The Communist *movement*, however, is something quite different from mere heresy. . . .[65]

"Under present conditions of political and military warfare," Hook warned, "it is not hard to see what immense dangers to the security of liberal institutions [are] implicit in this strategy of infiltration and deceit."[66] Communists, he wrote, "operate through 'fronts,' . . . because they fear that, given a free choice of honestly labeled alternatives, they will be rejected; once they slip into power, they consolidate their position by terror."[67]

Free governments are, and have always been, empowered to act against illegal conspiracies through criminal prosecution. The law of the United States was no exception: "Under existing law punishment is provided for criminal conspiracy, whether this be conspiracy in restraint of trade or conspiracy to overthrow the government by insurrection or to advocate such overthrow in time of clear and present danger."[68] That said, Hook believed that "there are noncriminal conspiracies in sectors of life which are not affected by legislative power. These sectors of life are social and

---

[65] Hook, *Heresy, Yes; Conspiracy, No*, 22 (emphasis in the original).
[66] Ibid., 23.
[67] Ibid., 24.
[68] Ibid.

cultural and are regulated by tradition, common standards of propriety or decency in personal relations, and sometimes by explicit rules."[69] Twentieth-century totalitarianism, however, presented society with unique problems, since it operated against the government through its predatory and viral infiltration and control of private associations in a society built upon vibrant associations:

> The transfer of some of the techniques by which conspirators in the past have seized the state to capturing control of benevolent associations, social, chess, and athletic clubs, literary societies, research groups, professional and trade unions, even philanthropic agencies is unique to modern totalitarian movements. In the past, it was here, if anywhere, that honest opposition openly declared itself. The elaborate devices adopted by Communists to disguise the nature of their opposition and to prevent others from functioning in opposition to them when they seize control may have been anticipated in earlier times by other groups but they never were previously employed with such fanaticism, rationalized by such body of doctrine, and executed with such lack of scruple.[70]

The problem was particularly acute when it came to labor unions. After all, the political order created by the institution of the modern liberal state at the time of the New Deal was built upon the decision to accord broad governing powers to private labor unions.[71] The CPUSA set its sights on labor unions, the very type of association that earlier in the century had helped to advance commitments to free speech, freedom of assembly, and democracy—the type of association that, to achieve its successes, had been obliged to overcome the obstacles set in its way by the law of conspiracy.[72] "Every large labor organization in the United States," Hook explained, "had been compelled to take administrative action against Communist party elements not because of their beliefs—their heresies— but because their pattern of conduct made the Communist party, and ultimately the Kremlin, the decisive power in the life of the union, and not the needs and wishes of the membership."[73]

In addition to its secrecy and its commitment to deceit, the second aspect of the CPUSA that made it distinctive as an association was that it was dictatorial, hierarchical, and suppressed even the slightest hint of

---

[69] Ibid., 25.

[70] Ibid.

[71] See Kersch, *Constructing Civil Liberties;* and Steven Fraser, "The 'Labor Question,'" in Gary Gerstle and Steven Fraser, eds., *The Rise and Fall of the New Deal Order, 1930–1980* (Princeton, NJ: Princeton University Press, 1989). The crucial legislation was the National Labor Relations Act (1935), commonly known as the Wagner Act.

[72] See Kersch, "The New Deal Triumph as the End of History?"

[73] Hook, *Heresy, Yes; Conspiracy, No,* 24.

dissent. The Communist Party, Hook recounted, was "rigorously controlled by an iron-clad discipline which excludes those who are inactive or in disagreement with the line of the party on *any* question."[74] "Very few individuals who have discussed the issues posed by the existence of the Communist movement," he lamented, "have paid proper attention to the existence of the mechanisms of control by which the Communist parties in all countries purge their ranks of the inactive, the doubtful, the half-hearted, or the critical—in short, of all whose conformity is less than total."[75]

What, then, was to be done? Given the nature of the Communist conspiracy, there were, in Hook's estimation, very good reasons to exclude Communists from government posts. Communists could be expected to work at cross purposes to the government. In many cases, their ultimate goal was to thwart it, if not to overthrow it. Civil libertarian platitudes notwithstanding, there was good reason to consider the ideas an individual held when considering him for employment in a government (or other) position, particularly if his ideas were held fanatically.[76] If we were to reflect upon this dispassionately for a moment, we would know this, of course. After all, as Hook noted, "No one questioned Senator [William] Borah's right to know whether Mr. Thurman Arnold believed that the anti-trust laws should be enforced before approving his appointment to a post whose responsibility included prosecution of violators of those laws."[77] And no one would argue that the fact that a man is a Ku Klux Klan member or sympathizer should be irrelevant to considering his fitness to serve as a schoolteacher or a federal judge. To make such determinations regarding governmental employment, Hook insisted, is a different decision from criminalizing Communist Party membership.

Hook, nevertheless, recognized the special problems posed by situations in which an individual was judged not for his membership in the Communist Party itself, but for his membership in a Communist front organization. These were the situations where questions of "guilt by association" became a problem: they raised questions involving the "lumping together [of] the sheep and the goats."[78] These situations, the pragmatist Hook averred, posed real concerns. Unfortunately, he concluded, "No single formula can be a guide to intelligent decision in such situations,

---

[74] Ibid., 28 (emphasis in the original).

[75] Ibid., 30.

[76] Ibid., 74.

[77] Ibid., 75. In 1938, President Franklin Roosevelt appointed the controversial Thurman Arnold, the author of the bestselling 1937 book *The Folklore of Capitalism* (which was highly critical of both antitrust enforcement and the capitalist economic system itself), to head the U.S. Justice Department's antitrust division. In his Senate confirmation hearings, Arnold faced a lengthy and heated encounter with the trust-busting Senator Borah, a populist Republican from Idaho, whose views on antitrust law had been singled out for criticism in Arnold's book.

[78] Hook, *Heresy, Yes; Conspiracy, No*, 90.

but only tested knowledge acquired in long and close study of front organizations."[79]

Hook was characteristically critical of both the detractors and the defenders of the Smith Act (1940), which criminalized the teaching or advocacy of the violent overthrow of the government or associating with any person or group conspiring to teach, advocate, or organize for doing so.[80] Hook suggested that the nation keep the act, but with amendments: "The proscription should have been placed," he wrote, "not on speech to achieve revolutionary overthrow, but on organization to achieve it, and not merely any organization but an organization set up and controlled by a foreign power."[81]

IV. The Freedom of Association Today in Developmental Perspective

As Keith Whittington has noted, political controversies over the scope of a freedom of association predated the mid-twentieth century. Under the (emergent) modern constitutional order, free association issues were taken up most prominently in disputes over the scope of the right of individuals to join and participate in the collective activities of labor unions.[82] Many labor union activities today considered ordinary— picketing, threatening to strike, organizing a boycott—were once considered illegal infringements of a company owner's property rights. Accordingly, workers associating together in a labor organization with the purpose of engaging in these activities were understood as conspiring for illegal ends. After a long political struggle over the course of the late nineteenth and early twentieth centuries, however, employers were held not to have any sort of property right against these activities, and the tactics of the labor movement were considered legitimate means of achieving ends—better working conditions and wages—that were newly understood as advancing not simply private interests but the broader public good. The tactics, moreover, once considered tortious *conduct*, were newly reconceptualized as amounting to the exercise of (desirable) First Amendment freedom of *speech*.[83] All of these free association "problems," however, were ultimately settled by New Deal labor legislation, which, under the regulatory auspices of the National Labor Relations Board, recognized labor unions as an integral part of a pluralist system of group-based

[79] Ibid.

[80] Smith Act, 18 U.S.C. sec. 2385. See *Dennis v. United States*, 341 U.S. 494 (1951).

[81] Hook, *Heresy, Yes; Conspiracy, No*, 106.

[82] Keith E. Whittington, "Industrial Saboteurs, Reputed Thieves, Communists, and the Freedom of Association," elsewhere in this volume.

[83] See Kersch, *Constructing Civil Liberties*; and Ken I. Kersch, "How Conduct Became Speech and Speech Became Conduct: A Political Development Case Study in Labor Law and the Freedom of Speech," *University of Pennsylvania Journal of Constitutional Law* 2 (March 2006): 255–97.

workplace governance.[84] Accordingly, under the state-sanctioned collective bargaining arrangements, the group was deemed presumptively to speak for and represent the views of its individual members. Along the way, a controversy over the freedom of association was transmogrified into a matter of administration.

Free association controversies, of course, did not suddenly disappear. As it happened, the middle years of the twentieth century were crucial in spurring the Supreme Court to fashion the outlines of our modern constitutional doctrine concerning the freedom of association as a first-order right. In this era, of course, free association rights were part and parcel of the Supreme Court's accelerating focus on the Bill of Rights in the 1950s and 1960s.[85] In the wake of the free association right's involvement in the labor question, the right became associated chiefly with political controversies over subversion and civil rights.

Free association questions involving an individual's association with the Communist Party raised questions of possible subversive activity, in an era of heightened threats to, and fears about, national security. Real political events contributed to the framing of communist (and, often, progressive) groups as conspiratorial. The collapse of the popular front, the fall of China to the Communists, and the outbreak of the Korean War and the Cold War—all tied to an avowedly subversive international communist movement—raised suspicions among many about the motives of domestic Communists and fellow travelers.[86]

The closer one's membership in a group is tied to an illegal conspiracy, of course, the less weight is accorded to claims of the freedom of association. The practical problem, however, is the question of whether mere membership in a group amounts to collusion in a criminal conspiracy. Does membership alone constitute participation, if not by acts, then by signaling support of the broader project? As Sidney Hook noted, these questions can only be answered after a close consideration of the facts of the case at hand.

In the new context, following the pioneering settlements arrived at in response to the labor question, and the Red Scare free speech cases, matters relating to group membership were also considered as raising important questions of the freedom of speech.[87] As such, free association

---

[84] See generally Victoria C. Hattam, *Labor Visions and State Power: The Origins of Business Unionism in the United States* (Princeton, NJ: Princeton University Press, 1993).

[85] See, e.g., *Roth v. United States*, 354 U.S. 476 (1957); *Mapp v. Ohio*, 367 U.S. 643 (1961); *Engle v. Vitale*, 370 U.S. 421 (1962); *Gideon v. Wainwright*, 372 U.S. 335 (1963); *New York Times v. Sullivan*, 376 U.S. 254 (1964); *Miranda v. Arizona*, 384 U.S. 436 (1966); and *Tinker v. Des Moines*, 393 U.S. 503 (1969).

[86] Michael J. Klarman, "Rethinking the Civil Rights and Civil Liberties Revolutions," *Virginia Law Review* 82 (1996): 1.

[87] On the labor settlements, see Kersch, *Constructing Civil Liberties*, 134–234; and Hattam, *Labor Visions and State Power*. The seminal Red Scare free speech cases are *Schenck v. United States*, 249 U.S. 47 (1919), and *Abrams v. United States*, 250 U.S. 616 (1919).

questions would henceforth raise factual questions about the distinction between conduct and speech. Is a certain group proscribable as a group committed either to overthrowing the government or to committing a violent attack on the country? If so, is one obligated to disclose one's membership in the organization? Can the government keep a list of pro-scribed organizations? Can it engage in surveillance of the activities of the group? Does membership in the organization alone imply complicity in the group's purposes? What of so-called "innocent" members, who may be committed to some, but not all, of the group's purposes? What of members who do not actually know the group's full slate of purposes, or the purposes (and actions) of some subset of its members? What debilities can be visited upon members of such a group? For example, can they be denied public employment on the basis of their group membership? Can they be dismissed from private employment on the same basis?

Interestingly enough, the current "war on terror" has raised similar questions about guilt by association. The McCarran-Walter Act (1952), passed at the height of the Cold War, permitted the exclusion or depor-tation of aliens on ideological grounds—that is, on the grounds that they had engaged in, or had the purpose of engaging in, activities that were subversive or contrary to the national interest.[88] Under McCarran-Walter, the government has repeatedly relied upon an individual's articulated beliefs (such as statements critical of U.S. foreign policy) and associations (such as links to radical, communist, or communist front groups) as grounds for his deportation and exclusion from the United States. McCarran-Walter was repealed in 1990. In the aftermath of the Oklahoma City bombing, however, its relevant provisions were revived in the Antiter-rorism and Effective Death Penalty Act (AEDPA) of 1996, which replaced McCarran-Walter's provisions on subversion with new language appli-cable to terrorism and supporters of terrorism.[89] At the same time, the AEDPA gave the secretary of state essentially unreviewable discretion to designate foreign groups as "terrorist" organizations.[90]

The AEDPA also criminalized the provision of any financial or material support for such organizations. Under the 1996 law, an individual can be charged with aiding a terrorist group even if he had no knowledge that the group was on the terrorist watch list, had no intention of supporting ter-rorism, and had no ties to particular acts of terror. Working in conjunction

[88] McCarran-Walter was officially known as the Immigration and Nationality Act, 66 Stat. 163 (1952), as amended, 8 U.S.C. Sec. 1101 et seq. (1982 & Supp. II 1984). President Harry Truman had vetoed the law, claiming, "The basic error of this bill is that it moves in the direction of suppressing opinion and belief . . . [in a manner] that would make a mockery of the Bill of Rights and our claims to stand for freedom in the world." His veto was overridden.

[89] Antiterrorism and Effective Death Penalty Act of 1996, 110 Stat. 1214, P.L. 104-132 (April 24, 1996).

[90] The Intelligence Reform and Terrorism Prevention Act (2004) makes the secretary of state's designation of a group as a terrorist group permanent.

with the AEDPA, the USA Patriot Act (2001), passed shortly after the September 11 terrorist attacks, makes aliens deportable for having any association whatsoever with a "terrorist organization." The Patriot Act defines terrorism to include any use of, or threat of the use of, violence, and defines a "terrorist organization" as any group of two or more that has used or threatened to use violence, a definition that sweeps broadly to cover, potentially, a wide array of groups (such as, for example, radical environmentalist and anti-abortion groups). Under the Patriot Act, domestic, and not just foreign, groups may be designated as terrorist organizations.[91]

The Patriot Act puts the full force of the federal government's investigatory powers behind efforts to find out whether or not individuals are either members of, or have contributed to, such groups. Since September 11, 2001, the federal government has availed itself of the AEDPA and the USA Patriot Act, along with the president's Article II executive and commander-in-chief powers to protect national security, to engage in heightened scrutiny (often on the basis of secret evidence) of the associational ties of Muslim aliens or immigrants, and of (sometimes charitable) groups with ties to the Middle East.[92]

When it comes to questions of guilt by association in the national security area, it is very difficult to say that these matters were "settled" in the mid-twentieth-century free association decisions of the Supreme Court in the same way that New Deal statutory and administrative orders settled the free association questions raised by labor unions. These matters will always turn on factual determinations concerning the severity of the threat, the nature of the group in question, and the individual's relationship to the group and its purposes.

This means that the ongoing "war on terror" raises many of the same questions that the mid-century civil libertarians grappled with during the height of the Cold War. Today, the issues concern membership in organizations designated as terrorist organizations by the federal government. Like the Communist Party USA at mid-century, organizations listed by the government as terrorist groups are likely to be transnational organizations. Just as the CPUSA was involved in labor and civil rights organizing, in addition to promoting worldwide revolution, groups like Hamas or the Popular Front for the Liberation of Palestine will be involved in an array of charitable and humanitarian initiatives in addition to their more violent endeavors. One may join or contribute to the group in order to advance one of what one considers to be the group's legitimate projects, but may end up being tarred with collusion in one of its other (violent or illegal) activities, of which one may or may not have been aware. Or one may be interested in supporting the full range of the group's activities, and may

---

[91] USA Patriot Act, P.L. 107-56 (October 26, 2001). See David Cole and James X. Dempsey, *Terrorism and the Constitution: Sacrificing Civil Liberties in the Name of National Security* (New York: New Press, 2002), 153.

[92] Cole and Dempsey, *Terrorism and the Constitution*, 118.

hide behind its charitable initiatives when called upon to justify one's membership. The civil libertarian case law arising out of the line of mid-century Communism cases holds that one cannot be charged with guilt by association unless one had the intent to support the specific ends of the group. So far, this principle has not been followed with respect to today's terrorism designation under the 1996 Antiterrorism Act and the USA Patriot Act.

In these circumstances, it is not surprising that, for the first time in many years, contemporary scholars are devoting significant attention to guilt by association.[93] The question remains: Will the mid-century associational precedent be applied to these laws, or will constitutional doctrine change? Already, individuals have challenged in court the designation of groups they belong to as terrorist groups.[94] The law in this area remains very much in flux.

V. CONCLUSION

For those whose eyes have been trained for many years now on the freedom of association as a second-order identity politics and civil rights question involving the right to exclude—and a cursory glance at most contemporary civil liberties textbooks makes clear that the eyes of many students and scholars alike have been so trained—an airing of the full spectrum of questions concerning guilt by association will mark a notable departure in focus. If these questions remain on the front burner in American politics in the years to come, new civil liberties textbooks, and updated editions of established ones, may once again come to reflect the interests and concerns of the now largely forgotten mid-twentieth-century civil libertarians rather than the interests of the currently more familiar identity/exclusion-focused liberals who succeeded them.

There is a strong tendency on the part of legal academics to consider the nature of rights only in light of the pressing problems that the rights seem to implicate at the time they are writing. More comprehensive descriptions, however, allow us to give fuller accounts not simply of the history of constitutional rights, but of their nature. We may be entering a historical moment with more similarities to the era in which the free association right was first named than to the era in which, subsequently, it was eclipsed. If so, the rich complexities of the constitutional right to free association will be increasingly discussed in the years to come.

Political Science and Law, Boston College

---

[93] See ibid., 108.

[94] See *United States v. Rahmani*, sub nom. *United States v. Afshari*, 426 F.3d 1150 (9th Cir. 2005).

INDUSTRIAL SABOTEURS, REPUTED THIEVES, COMMUNISTS, AND THE FREEDOM OF ASSOCIATION

By Keith E. Whittington

I. Introduction

In the early and mid-twentieth century, the United States confronted a shadowy enemy. There were fears that the nation had been, or might be, infiltrated by covert agents of a foreign power, that the U.S. was faced with "tightly organized, highly disciplined, international revolutionary . . . organization[s]" capable of working against American interests from within the United States itself.[1] Moreover, the members of these organizations and those associated with them might well work against American interests through actions that were themselves legal, or they might spend long periods covertly preparing for a catastrophic revolutionary act. The U.S. government responded creatively and aggressively to this perceived threat, which, in turn, fostered new thinking about the constitutional limits on government powers.

This essay is concerned with one aspect of that new thinking, the jurisprudential development of the idea of "freedom of association." The difficulty of addressing the perceived threat created the temptation to look for and make use of "guilt by association" and to undertake measures to prevent harmful acts from occurring in the first place by breaking up, harassing, or monitoring dangerous or potentially dangerous associations. Of course, we are familiar with that temptation today from the war on terror, and freedom of association and related concerns have been raised in the context of antiterrorism efforts as well.[2] The idea that freedom of association is constitutionally protected is now well entrenched,

[1] Ellen Schrecker, *Many Are the Crimes: McCarthyism in America* (Boston: Little, Brown, 1998), 6 (characterizing the American Communist Party).

[2] See *United States v. Al-Arian*, 308 F. Supp. 2d 1322 (M.D. Fla. 2004) (applying the Antiterrorism and Effective Death Penalty Act of 1996 [AEDPA] to individuals accused of supporting fundraising activities of a terrorist organization); *Linde v. Arab Bank, PLC*, 384 F. Supp. 2d 571 (E.D. N.Y. 2005) (applying the Anti-Terrorism Act of 1990 to a bank accused of providing financial assistance to a terrorist organization); *United States v. Goba*, 220 F. Supp. 2d 182 (W.D. N.Y. 2002) (upholding AEDPA against challenge that it was unconstitutionally vague); *United States v. Marzook*, 383 F. Supp. 2d 1056 (N.D. Ill. 2005) (upholding AEDPA against challenge that it violated First Amendment freedom of association); *United States v. Assi*, 414 F. Supp. 2d 707 (E.D. Mich. 2006) (same); *Humanitarian Law Project v. Reno*, 205 F. 3d 1130 (9th Cir. 2000) (upholding AEDPA against challenge that it unconstitutionally infringed on freedom of association, but restricting its application on grounds that it was unconstitutionally vague).

doi:10.1017/S0265052508080199

however, and the legal and political response to the war on terror has necessarily been shaped by that Cold War constitutional inheritance.

The idea of a constitutionally protected freedom of association posed a problem for those who initially advanced it in the early decades of the twentieth century: namely, the U.S. Constitution does not mention a freedom of association. Like a right to contract or a right to privacy, the freedom of association was to be a judicially recognized and protected unenumerated right. Worse, it was an unenumerated right being advocated against government in a post–New Deal context in which many of the justices of the Supreme Court were committed to deferring to the actions of elected officials. Even so, the New Deal justices had inherited some jurisprudential resources that could make sense of the idea of freedom of association but could also limit its scope.

Although the freedom of association is not enumerated in so many words in the Constitution, the Court has nonetheless looked for a textual home for such a right. In the context of the U.S. Constitution, a freedom of association is often located in the First Amendment. A particular freedom of association may be regarded as implicit in the free exercise clause of the First Amendment. As Justice Hugo Black noted, English laws to suppress those "terming themselves Catholicks . . . [who] do secretly wander and shift from Place to Place within this Realm, to corrupt and seduce her Majesty's Subjects" bore a striking resemblance to twentieth-century American laws aimed at other "seditious" (though explicitly antireligious) sects.[3] No doubt due in part to the explicit constitutional securities provided to the free exercise of religion, the specific freedom of religious association has had little jurisprudential significance. Nonetheless, the presence of the free exercise clause and the historical background that led to its inclusion in the Constitution helps provide the conceptual underpinnings for recognizing a broader right to a freedom of association.[4] Prohibiting the organizational activities of dissenters, whether religious or otherwise, makes dissent more difficult, and the First Amendment, broadly conceived, prevents the government from brushing aside inconvenient dissenters.

Of greater significance for the judicial recognition and elaboration of a constitutional freedom of association has been the free speech clause of the First Amendment. The First Amendment, of course, includes within it a distinct clause securing "the right of the people peaceably to assemble," but this provision has rarely stood by itself. In effect, the right peaceably

---

[3] *Communist Party of the United States v. Subversive Activities Control Board,* 367 U.S. 1, 149 (1961) (quoting English acts of 1593).

[4] See also Ernst Freund, *The Police Power: Public Policy and Constitutional Rights* (Chicago: Callaghan and Company, 1904), 496–97: "Whether freedom of religion requires freedom of association . . . is a question upon which the courts have not passed. The right of association is enjoyed and exercised to the fullest extent without any attempt at legislative restraint or interference. It may be safely asserted that legislative restraint on the right of association for religious purposes . . . would be unconstitutional."

to assemble has been taken to be a natural extension of the right to free speech, and it is the right to free speech that has been taken to define the purpose, extensions, and proper limitations on a right to assemble and a freedom of association. How the justices have conceptualized the free speech clause itself has been critical to how they have understood and applied the freedom of association over time.

This essay will consider the development of freedom of association in four contexts. Section II considers the U.S. Supreme Court's linkage of the freedom of association with the First Amendment and the freedom of speech in the New Deal era. Section III examines an earlier history of freedom of association in the state courts that relied on general notions of personal liberty rather than the specific context of speech and assembly. Section IV returns to the New Deal and the challenges that the First Amendment framework created for the Court as it extended freedom of association protections to its allies in the labor movement. Section V examines the ultimate unwillingness of the post–New Deal Court to allow the freedom of association to be used to block anticommunist measures at the height of the Cold War.

II. *De Jonge*, Industrial Saboteurs, and the Right to Assembly

The U.S. Supreme Court first seriously addressed the question of the meaning of the right to assembly in the case of *De Jonge v. Oregon*. The case was argued just after Franklin D. Roosevelt's 1936 reelection as president and was decided during the same term as the Court's famous 1937 "switch in time." In attempting to understand what elements of a right to assembly might be applied to the states via the Fourteenth Amendment, Chief Justice Charles Evans Hughes linked the right to speak with the right to assemble as part of a unified whole.

At issue in *De Jonge* was Oregon's criminal syndicalism law, which banned presiding over, conducting, or assisting in conducting "any assemblage of persons, or any organization, or any society, or any group which teaches or advocates the doctrine of criminal syndicalism or sabotage." The law had been used to break up a public meeting sponsored by the Communist Party to protest police tactics during a longshoremen's strike in Portland, and the Oregon Supreme Court had upheld this application of the law against constitutional challenges.[5] In ruling on the appeal of the case, Hughes observed that the

> right of peaceable assembly is a right cognate to those of free speech and free press and is equally fundamental. . . . These rights may be abused by using speech or press or assembly in order to

---

[5] *De Jonge v. Oregon*, 299 U.S. 353, 357 (1937).

incite violence and crime. The people through their Legislatures may protect themselves against that abuse. But the legislative intervention can find constitutional justification only by dealing with the abuse. The rights themselves must not be curtailed. The greater the importance of safeguarding the community from incitements to the overthrow of our institutions by force and violence, the more imperative is the need to preserve inviolate the constitutional rights of free speech, free press and free assembly in order to maintain the opportunity for free political discussion, to the end that government may be responsive to the will of the people and that changes, if desired, may be obtained by peaceful means.[6]

The government could intervene if a particular assembly was being used to advocate or conspire to commit criminal acts, but the mere involvement of those who might elsewhere advocate such acts did not itself vitiate the right to assemble or legally endanger those who might so associate with syndicalists. In the midst of the Great Depression and the New Deal, the Supreme Court emphasized that the government should not attempt to squelch the voices of radicalism but instead should channel the pressures for change into democratic processes of reform.

By contrast, the Oregon Supreme Court had earlier concluded that the legislature had ample discretion to determine how best to address this threat to public safety. It was the "exclusive province of the legislature to determine what acts are inimical to the public welfare, and to declare that such acts when done shall constitute crimes," and there was little question that curtailing the activities of organizations that advocated criminal acts was a "reasonable condition" that the legislature might impose on the general "possession and enjoyment" of constitutionally protected rights. The members of the state constitutional convention that included a provision for peaceful assembly in Oregon's constitution would never have "supposed that a statute prohibiting assemblages from counseling the commission of a crime would be an unconstitutional interference with the right of assemblage."[7] The Oregon Supreme Court focused on the general question of whether criminal syndicalism statutes that banned organizing certain assemblies could be consistent with the state constitutional right to assembly, and answered that they could by observing, as courts have often done, that liberty is not license and that the constitutional right was not intended to protect criminal conspiracies.

The U.S. Supreme Court, by contrast, reached a different outcome in part because it placed the case firmly in the context of the First Amendment's free speech clause and not simply the right of assembly. Although the Communist Party advocated industrial sabotage (and thus its assemblies

---

[6] Id. at 364–65.
[7] *State v. Laundy*, 103 Or. 443, 458, 462 (1922).

were banned under the criminal syndicalism statute), the particular public meeting that the defendant Dirk De Jonge helped conduct was in content a lawful discussion of and protest against police strikebreaking activity. Suggesting that the Court's own prior cases from the 1920s upholding the convictions of those charged with directly advocating revolutionary action ought to be read narrowly in light of the "fundamental" importance of the freedom of speech, Hughes emphasized that federal constitutional protections applied to such cases and that a freedom to associate to engage in lawful advocacy and protest had to be secured even for those who might, in other circumstances, associate for unlawful purposes.[8]

III. Reputed Thieves and Guilt by Association

In upholding De Jonge's conviction, the Oregon Supreme Court took note of an additional feature of such emerging freedom of association cases. When defense attorneys raised a claim that individuals had a freedom to associate with whom they pleased, the judges pointed to such traditional crimes as incitement as providing limits on the personal liberty of individuals. No one was at liberty to cause harm to others by inciting criminal acts or organizing to engage in criminal acts. "[J]oining with" those who would commit a crime or advocate crime had to be distinguished from "the act of merely associating with persons having the reputation" of being criminals.[9] For the *De Jonge* case, however, this might imply that those who merely attended a public meeting sponsored by the Communist Party did not incur the legal risk that the actual members of the Party did, a possibility that seemed to weigh on Chief Justice Hughes in evaluating the application of the act to the Portland meeting.[10] But the distinction is one that other courts had likewise made. In upholding a similar criminal syndicalism statute in 1921, the supreme court of Washington state had argued, "An ordinance or act which makes it unlawful to associate with persons having the reputation of being thieves, and so forth, is different from an act which makes it unlawful for any one to organize or help to organize a group of persons to advocate and teach crime, and so forth, for the purpose which is specified in the syndicalism

[8] *Gitlow v. New York*, 268 U.S. 652 (1925) (upholding conviction for distribution of socialist manifesto advocating unlawful acts); *Whitney v. California*, 274 U.S. 357 (1927) (upholding conviction for organizing the Communist Labor Party); *Fiske v. Kansas*, 274 U.S. 380 (1927) (striking down conviction on grounds that no evidence was presented that unlawful acts were advocated).

[9] *State v. Laundy*, 103 Or. 443, 459 (1922).

[10] "While defendant was a member of the Communist Party, that membership was not necessary to conviction on such a charge. A like fate might have attended any speaker, although not a member, who 'assisted in the conduct' of the meeting. However innocuous the object of the meeting, however lawful the subjects and tenor of the addresses, however reasonable and timely the discussion, all those assisting in the conduct of the meeting would be subject to imprisonment as felons if the meeting were held by the Communist Party." *De Jonge v. Oregon*, 299 U.S. at 362.

act. If it were in the legislative province as we have found to make it a penal offense to do the prohibited things in the act including the organization of a group of persons, it would seem to follow that it were likewise within the power of the Legislature to make it a penal offense for any one to become a member of such a group of persons or organization." [11] It was one thing to know a member of the Communist Party, or perhaps even to attend a public meeting on matters of general interest sponsored by the Communist Party, as in *De Jonge*, but it was quite another to be a member of the Communist Party yourself.

The distinction was of some significance in the criminal syndicalism cases of the early twentieth century precisely because the Missouri Supreme Court had three decades earlier (in 1896) invalidated a St. Louis vagrancy ordinance that sought to forbid residents from "knowingly . . . associat-[ing] with persons having the reputation of being thieves, burglars, pickpockets, pigeon droppers, bawds, prostitutes or lewd women or gamblers, or any other person, for the purpose or with the intent to agree, conspire, combine or confederate, first, to commit any offense, or, second, to cheat or defraud any person of any money or property." It was here, in a context far removed from public meetings and speeches, that lawyers and judges first considered a right to freedom of association. Unsurprisingly, their reference point had to do with common-law notions of personal liberty rather than the text of the First Amendment. Simply put, did one have a right to associate with reputed thieves?

In evaluating the St. Louis vagrancy ordinance, the Missouri Supreme Court readily agreed with the habeas petitioner that it would be an invasion of "the right of personal liberty . . . to forbid that any person should knowingly associate with those who have the reputation of being thieves, etc." Indeed, if the legislature could "forbid one to associate with certain classes of persons of unsavory or malodorous reputations, by the same token it may dictate who the associates of any one may be," and the court denied "the power of any legislative body in this country to choose for our citizens whom their associates shall be." [12] One might well think that the first portion of the relevant clause in the ordinance had to be read along with the last portion, prohibiting not mere association but association with intent to conspire. The judges chose to read the two portions separately, but they had difficulty with the latter portion as well, "for with

[11] *State v. Hennessy*, 114 Wash. 351, 365 (1921).

[12] *Ex parte Smith*, 135 Mo. 223, 224 (1896). See also *City of Watertown v. Christnacht*, 39 S.D. 290 (1917) (invalidating ordinance declaring that any male "found associating with" prostitutes "shall be deemed a pimp"); *Ex parte Cannon*, 94 Tex. Crim. 257 (1923) (invalidating ordinance "prohibiting male and female persons from associating together for immoral purposes" defined as, among other things, being "found together in a house of prostitution"). But cf. *Brannon v. State*, 16 Ala. App. 259 (1917) ("There is no truer saying than that 'birds of a feather flock together,' and, in this class of cases [vagrancy statutes], the law recognizes it."); and *Williams v. State*, 98 Ala. 52 (1893) (evidence of defendant's associates admissible to support prostitution charge).

mere guilty intention, unconnected with overt act or outward manifestation, the law has no concern."[13] The "guilty intention" at issue here was
simply the one to conspire or confederate, so the court was not requiring
an overt act of committing "any offense" or fraud but simply an actual
agreement or combination to commit such an offense. Merely being in the
presence of thieves and lewd women was not action enough to trigger the
police powers of the state, even for the low bar of conspiracy.

Besides the fact that the petitioner in the 1896 case, Walter Smith, was
apparently convicted of vagrancy on just that basis, the Missouri court
may have been particularly watchful since, according to the ordinance as
originally passed in 1871, "mere association" "with persons having the
reputation of thieves and prostitutes" *was* criminal. In the 1873 case *City
of St. Louis v. Fitz*, when reviewing the original 1871 vagrancy ordinance,
the Missouri Supreme Court had pointed out that this went "beyond the
common law crime of conspiracy," and thus probably beyond the constitutional power of the city. The judges were not impressed by how the
ordinance was applied in practice either. In the *Fitz* case, the factual basis
for the prosecution—that the associates of the defendant had reputations
as thieves—was provided entirely by the testimony of the police, while
"all the witnesses outside the police force, including some fifteen or twenty
of the neighbors and associates of the defendant, contradict[ed] the statements of the police officers concerning the reputation of the persons
alleged to be thieves and in whose society the defendant was found."
(The police themselves apparently reached their conclusion largely on the
basis of the fact that alleged thieves "lived in the neighborhood of the
defendant . . . and this neighborhood was infested with thieves and
prostitutes.")

This early Reconstruction era case grounded the freedom of association in a broader understanding of the proper role of the state. Whereas
Chief Justice Hughes in *De Jonge* was concerned with identifying the
specific value of the "fundamental right" of free speech and the utility
of the freedom of association to advancing that right, the judges of the
Missouri Supreme Court in the 1870s drew a line between the regulation of acts that caused harm to others and those that did not. The
police powers of the legislature entitled it to regulate the sale of liquor
or houses of prostitution but not "to regulate the morals or habits of
individual citizens." The law could interfere "[w]hen a positive breach
of law is reached, or when the act of the citizen is such as to justify an
implication of an intended breach of law," but "a citizen has the right
of selecting his associates," no matter how unsavory they may be. It
was "not the business of the Legislature to guard over individual morality" or to "correct the evil consequences which such an association may

---

[13] *Ex parte Smith*, 135 Mo. 223, 224 (1896). See also *Lanzetta v. New Jersey*, 306 U.S. 451
(1939) (invalidating as excessively vague a statute imposing penalties for being a "gangster").

bring on the individual." It was the state's role "to protect society from actual or anticipated breaches of the law," which meant that a person's association with others could not be criminal unless "such person so associates with a design or intent to aid, abet, promote, or in any way to assist" in the commission of a crime. The Missouri court noted that, although "once a thief always a thief would be the maxim upon which police officers would act," the state could hardly "mark" someone "as a leper in society, to be avoided by his former associates." (The alleged thieves in the *Fitz* case, as it happened, did not even have criminal records.) Henceforth, the lower courts in Missouri were to instruct juries that individuals could only be convicted under the 1871 ordinance when there was evidence of "an identification or community of interest" and "an intent to assist or encourage" a criminal act. Only by this means could the Missouri Supreme Court save the St. Louis ordinance from being invalid, make "clear . . . the intent of the ordinance," and prevent it from criminalizing "mere casual association, or an association for honest purposes." [14]

The city council of St. Louis took the hint and amended the ordinance, but twenty years later police were still conducting themselves in much the same way as they had in the *Fitz* case. In *City of St. Louis v. Roche* (1895), the Missouri Supreme Court took a tough stance: "Our constitution and laws guaranty to every citizen the right to go where and when he pleases, and to associate with whom he pleases, exacting from him only that he conduct himself in a decent and orderly manner, that he disturb no one, and that he interfere with the rights of no other citizen." The ordinance still authorized too much. [15]

Unsurprisingly, the *Fitz* and *Roche* cases did not ground a freedom of association in a right to free speech. The freedom for which they contended was to be found in a general "personal liberty"—in the inherent limits on the police powers of a republican government. The right to associate with others was an extension of the most basic, Blackstonian "right of locomotion, to go where one pleases, and when, and to do that which may lead to one's business or pleasure, only so far restrained as the rights of others may make it necessary for the welfare of all other citizens." This right was of a piece with a then-recent Michigan case holding that the city of Kalamazoo could not empower its police officers to arrest a woman merely because she was present on the street at "unseasonable hours" and the subject of gossip in the police department. A justifiable arrest for "street walking" required an overt "act indicating that the party is there for that purpose" and not "mere suspicion" that a woman was on the street to ply her illicit trade. [16]

[14] *City of St. Louis v. Fitz*, 53 Mo. 582 (1873).
[15] *City of St. Louis v. Roche*, 128 Mo. 541, 543 (1895).
[16] *Pinkerton v. Verberg*, 78 Mich. 573, 584, 586 (1889), cited in *City of St. Louis v. Roche*, 128 Mo. 541, 542 (1895).

The 1937 *De Jonge* case decisively threw aside this personal-liberty approach in order to fasten the freedom of association to the freedom of speech. The same notion of personal liberty could easily have underwritten the liberty of contract that had obstructed the expansion of economic regulation and redistribution legislation, and at the end of the battles over the New Deal, Chief Justice Hughes was looking forward, not back; free speech as a fundamental right would survive the constitutional revolution of 1937. Free speech was also a seemingly narrow platform on which to erect a right like freedom of association. Nonetheless, the personal-liberty background was not irrelevant to the U.S. Supreme Court's thinking about the freedom of association. From its narrow opening, the range of applications for the freedom of association expanded over time, and, as that range of applications expanded, many of the same considerations that had arisen in the earlier context carried over as well.

IV. Labor, the New Deal, and the Freedom of Association

In 1945, not long after *De Jonge* but with the New Deal no longer a matter of controversy on the Court or in politics, the U.S. Supreme Court again emphasized the connection between the various components of the First Amendment and the freedom of association. As part of a larger regulatory scheme, the government of Texas required that union organizers register with the state. As part of a tour to encourage workers to join the United Auto Workers (UAW), R. J. Thomas, the president of the union, passed through Texas and was scheduled to speak at a meeting in Bay Town on the Gulf Coast. A few hours before the meeting, Thomas was served with a restraining order barring him from participating in organizing activities until he had registered with the Secretary of State's office in Austin. Thomas went ahead with his planned speech and was arrested. He later challenged the registration requirement as a prior restraint on speech, but the state courts upheld the law as routine commercial regulation (comparable to similar requirements for other commercial agents such as real estate brokers and securities salesmen) with only incidental effects on speech. Of course, the central feature of the constitutional revolution of 1937 was that commercial regulations and the balancing of economic interests were to be left in the hands of the elected branches and administrative agencies, and such regulations were routinely upheld by the courts. The union organizer and the securities salesman were presumably in the same boat and could find their proper remedy in the legislature. Moreover, Thomas, unlike De Jonge, was not speaking at a public meeting about government officials and their actions. Thomas was simply organizing an economic association. But Thomas was giving a speech, and labor was not simply an economic organization but a central component of the New Deal coalition, and that left him well positioned to transform both freedom of association and traditional understandings of freedom of speech.

In an opinion written by Justice Wiley Rutledge, a recent appointee of Franklin Roosevelt's, the Supreme Court placed union organizing well within the zone of liberty protected by the First Amendment, and built on the *De Jonge* case to connect the freedom of speech with the right to assembly. In *Thomas v. Collins* (1945), the Court held that Thomas's activities fell within the "preferred place" of the "democratic freedoms secured by the First Amendment." As such, "[t]he rational connection between the remedy provided and the evil to be curbed, which in other contexts might support legislation against attack on due process grounds, will not suffice. These rights rest on firmer foundation." Only the narrowest restrictions on speech could be tolerated, "particularly when this right is exercised in conjunction with peaceable assembly. It was not by accident or coincidence that the rights to freedom of speech and press were coupled in a single guaranty with the rights of the people peaceably to assemble and to petition for redress of grievances. All these, though not identical, are inseparable. They are cognate rights." [17]

Significantly, the *Thomas* Court understood the protections of the First Amendment to extend beyond the realm of politics and religion. Shifting the jurisprudential ground of the freedom of association from personal liberty to the First Amendment potentially limited the purposes for which the freedom could be claimed. If the freedom of association was a mere adjunct of the First Amendment's free exercise clause, then it was of concern only to religious worshipers. If it was an adjunct of the free speech clause—as *De Jonge* held—then perhaps it was only of concern to those associating in order to advance a political message, the constitutional value Hughes emphasized in *De Jonge*. But the New Deal Court was unconcerned that Thomas was assembling with others and giving speeches in order to mobilize workers to join a labor union and pressure their employers for higher wages, rather than speaking about public policy. The First Amendment, Justice Rutledge explained, was concerned with the redress of grievances generally, "not confined to any field of human interest." "The right thus to discuss, and inform people concerning, the advantages and disadvantages of unions and joining them is protected not only as part of free speech, but as part of free assembly." The First Amendment did not merely protect "intellectual pursuits"; it protected "action," and the organizing activity of unions fell within its ambit.[18] It was not until an organizer undertook "the collection of funds or securing subscriptions" that the state's regulatory interest could make itself felt, and it was not until that point that the regulated action became "free speech *plus* conduct." [19]

---

[17] *Thomas v. Collins*, 323 U.S. 516, 530 (1945).

[18] Id. at 532.

[19] Even then, however, the regulated conduct must not be too "intertwined" with protected speech. Ibid., 540, 541. Four dissenters, led by Justice Owen Roberts, thought that the Texas statute was merely a reasonable occupational regulation that did not in fact regulate

As the legal scholar Ken Kersch has noted, the Supreme Court's extension of First Amendment protections to such union activities required redrawing the line between protected "speech" and governable "conduct."[20] The confluence of Thomas's roles as a speaker and as an organizer allowed the Court to easily assimilate the latter into the former, while at the same time building on its earlier efforts to extend the realm of constitutionally protected speech and assembly beyond the "free political discussion" that Hughes had highlighted in *De Jonge* to simple labor disputes. It is not entirely surprising that "peaceful assemblies" seeking "redress" for grievances would now be read to include labor organizing. In the decades leading up to the New Deal, the notion of freedom of association had been developing within the economic context. As early as 1893, in the law journal of the New York Law School, S. C. T. Dodd, general counsel for Standard Oil, observed the rise of "peculiar criminal laws" that "undertake to limit freedom of association for business purposes," namely, antitrust legislation punishing conspiracies in restraint of trade.[21] More common, however, was the connection made between freedom of association and labor unions. In recounting the status of trade unions in English law, W. M. Geldart pointed out: "Freedom of association has never been looked upon as a privilege requiring constitutional guarantees." There were no legal restraints on the formation of such "voluntary societies" as trade unions, though they were bound by the same limits as to what "one man may lawfully do."[22] The "principle of freedom of association" was advocated as an international human right that should be integrated into treaties and domestic legislation.[23] And the "full freedom of association"

---

or implicate public speeches but only regulated "transaction[s]" between professional labor organizers and potential union members (and thus, in order to insure his arrest, Thomas took pains not only to deliver his planned speech but also to personally register workers into the union at the meeting). Ibid., 551.

[20] Ken I. Kersch, "How Conduct Became Speech and Speech Became Conduct: A Political Development Case Study in Labor Law and the Freedom of Speech," *University of Pennsylvania Journal of Constitutional Law* 8 (2006): 255.

[21] S. C. T. Dodd, "Peculiar Legislation," *Counsellor* 2 (1893): 195. See also John W. Burgess, "The Ideal of the American Commonwealth," *Political Science Quarterly* 10 (1895): 404, 413–14. In this guise, freedom of association made a brief comeback in the early New Deal as necessary to the management of production. Malcolm P. Sharpe, "Monopolies and Monopolistic Practices," *University of Chicago Law Review* 2 (1934): 301, 310. More critically, see John P. Davis, *Modern Corporations* (New York: G. P. Putnam's Sons, 1905), 267: "Distrust of the state as organized caused the accumulation of political powers in the hands of minor states, corporations, which excited no apprehensions because they were democratically organized. . . . [W]ere they not based substantially on individual contract and was not 'freedom of association' one element of liberty? . . . But there is much evidence that the true nature of corporations is gradually becoming plainer, though least in the system of law."

[22] W. M. Geldart, "Status of Trade Unions in England," *Harvard Law Review* 25 (1912): 579, 580.

[23] "Report of the Commission on International Labor Legislation," *American Labor Legislation Review* 9 (1919): 364, 374; "Report of the Special Committee of the American Bar Association on a League of Nations," *American Bar Association Journal* 6 (1920): 136, 177; "Treaty of Peace between the Allied and Associated Powers and Hungary," *American Journal of International Law* 15 (1921): 1, 134.

had been integrated into the rhetoric of the anti–labor injunction movement and incorporated into the Norris-LaGuardia Act.[24] The International Labor Organization titled its multivolume comparative review
of labor legislation *Freedom of Association*.[25] Before the Court appended
it to the First Amendment, the idea of freedom of association had already
gained considerable resonance in the context of labor organizing. The
Colorado Supreme Court recognized this in 1944, after *De Jonge* and
similar cases: "[W]e think the decisions indicate that the constitutional
guarantee of the people is not restricted to the literal right of meeting
together 'to petition the Government for a redress of grievances.'" The
"right of workmen to organize and operate as a voluntary labor association" was effectively "within the area of the guarantees of assembly
and free speech."[26] The New Jersey Supreme Court had concluded
even before *De Jonge* that the text of the constitutional right of assembly "must be given the most liberal and comprehensive construction"
so as to encompass the "right of the people to meet in public places to
discuss in an open and public manner all questions affecting their substantial welfare, and to vent their grievances, to protest against oppression, economic or otherwise, and to petition for the amelioration of
their condition, and to discuss the ways and means of attaining that
end." So long as such an assembly did not display by "overt acts" a
"common understanding" among the participants of the assembly that
was "of such a nature as to inspire well-grounded fear in persons of
reasonable firmness and courage," it was constitutionally protected.[27]
The innovative New Jersey Supreme Court was charting the course
that the U.S. Supreme Court would later follow, somewhat more ten-
tatively. The freedom of association may have been tied textually to the
freedom of speech, and initially justified by the U.S. Supreme Court as
a fundamental freedom because of the importance of protecting political dissent in a democracy, but, with the New Deal coalition politically
and intellectually ascendant, freedom of association was also understood to be the right to organize against economic "oppression."

V. COMMUNISTS AND THE POST–NEW DEAL COURT

Such developments set the background for the Court's encounter with
anticommunism measures in the early Cold War period. The postwar
Communist threat gave new salience and meaning to the possibility of
"guilt by association." Former secretary of state Henry Stimson declared

---

[24] Felix Frankfurter and Nathan Greene, "Labor Injunctions and Labor Legislation," *Harvard Law Review* 42 (1929): 766, 795; Norris-LaGuardia Act, 47 Stat. 70 (1932).

[25] International Labour Office, *Freedom of Association*, 5 vols. (Geneva: International Labour
Office, 1927–1930).

[26] *American Federation of Labor v. Reilly*, 113 Colo. 90, 98 (1944).

[27] *State v. Butterworth*, 104 N.J.L. 579, 580, 585 (1928).

soon after World War II that "those who now choose to travel in company with American Communists are very clearly either knaves or fools."[28] In 1920, Charles Evans Hughes had written a memorial for the New York City bar association calling on the state legislature to accept the election of five Socialists to its chambers and to respect the fact that "it is of the essence of the institutions of liberty that it be recognized that guilt is personal and cannot be attributed to the holding of opinion or to mere intent in the absence of overt acts."[29] The petition did little good then, in the midst of the first "Red Scare," and the Socialists were expelled from the legislature. In the Red Scare of the late 1940s through the early 1960s, legislators were similarly unconvinced by calls to assume the innocence of Communist Party members and associates in the absence of individual overt acts of criminality.

Besides the most direct attacks on Communist speakers and activists (with sedition charges leveled against those who either advocated or engaged in criminal activity), the state and federal governments adopted a variety of tactics for penalizing those who associated with such Communists.[30] Notably, over the course of nearly two decades the U.S. Supreme Court heard cases in which the government sought to deport Communist resident aliens,[31] denaturalize and deport Communist immigrant citizens,[32] force disclosure of Communist Party membership or affiliation,[33] question in public hearings those suspected of association with the Party,[34] require registration of the Communist Party and affiliated groups as subversive organizations,[35] and criminalize active membership in the Communist Party.[36]

Although the Court provided some resistance to these anticommunist measures, on the whole it adopted a posture of judicial restraint and deferred to the government. In the range of cases addressing these issues, the Court recognized that a freedom of association that linked with considerations of free speech was at stake. The jurisprudential

[28] Henry Lewis Stimson, "The Challenge of Americans," *Foreign Affairs* 26 (1947): 8.

[29] Quoted in John Lord O'Brian, "Loyalty Tests and Guilt by Association," *Harvard Law Review* 61 (1948): 592, 594.

[30] The federal government also refused to issue passports to known Communists, but this did not raise particular issues of freedom of association. See *Kent v. Dulles*, 357 U.S. 116 (1958); *Aptheker v. Secretary of State*, 378 U.S. 500 (1964). The government also pursued espionage charges against suspected spies, of course.

[31] *Bridges v. Wixon*, 326 U.S. 135 (1945); *Harisiades v. Shaughnessy*, 342 U.S. 580 (1952).

[32] *Schneiderman v. United States*, 320 U.S. 118 (1943); *Knauer v. United States*, 328 U.S. 654 (1946). *Knauer* involved a Nazi rather than a Communist, but the principles are consistent with the other cases considered here.

[33] *American Communications Association, et al. v. Douds*, 339 U.S. 382 (1950).

[34] *Sweezy v. New Hampshire*, 354 U.S. 234 (1957); *Watkins v. United States*, 354 U.S. 178 (1957); *Barenblatt v. United States*, 360 U.S. 109 (1959); *Braden v. United States*, 365 U.S. 431 (1961).

[35] *Communist Party of the United States v. Subversive Activities Control Board*, 367 U.S. 1 (1961).

[36] *Scales v. United States*, 367 U.S. 203 (1961).

groundwork for such freedom of association claims had been laid, and the justices were prepared to recognize that there was such a freedom and that it was implicated in such cases. But the Court rarely held that the liberty interests protected by freedom of association were sufficient to override the government's interest in protecting national security and its assessment of how best to realize that goal. In general, the Court was sharply divided in these cases. All the cases were decided with dissents, and in nearly all the majorities were further fragmented by concurring opinions.

Politically speaking, it is little surprise that the Supreme Court proved fairly deferential in these years. A total of eighteen justices sat in one or more of these cases (from the late 1940s through the early 1960s). Nearly all of them adopted a fairly consistent posture in deciding the cases. Seven of the justices overwhelmingly voted to reject the government's efforts in the cases; nine voted with similar consistency to uphold the government's actions against the objections of the individuals or organizations involved. Only two justices (Robert Jackson and Stanley Reed) split their votes to a significant degree; one of those (Jackson) voted in only two cases, and the other (Reed) leaned toward the government. With this tendency toward the appointment of deferential justices, it is not surprising that the Court tended to see things the government's way in these cases. The dissent on the Court might have been even less if not for the fact that two of the most forceful advocates for the freedom of association in these cases (William O. Douglas and Hugo Black) also happened to be particularly long-serving justices. Those two justices, countered only by the similarly long-serving Felix Frankfurter, voted in cases throughout the period, which meant that presidents had more opportunities to replace justices who were deferential to the government than to replace justices who took a more aggressive stance.

Beyond the question of opportunity, presidents clearly had different outlooks in selecting their justices, which translated into different patterns of behavior on the bench. Perhaps surprisingly, a majority of Franklin Roosevelt's appointees fell into the activist camp. From the perspective of Felix Frankfurter, the self-appointed voice of the Progressive legacy of judicial deference, this pattern might be unexpected, given Roosevelt's own problems with an activist Court and the Progressives' history of opposition to the active exercise of judicial review. Roosevelt clearly was committed to selecting justices who would support the New Deal and the expansion of government authority over the economic arena, and the justices he appointed were reliable on that front. It is not at all clear that Roosevelt was more broadly committed to judicial restraint or sought it in his justices. Supporters of Roosevelt and his Court-packing plan, for example, were explicit that what was needed was not judicial restraint but a "liberal-minded judiciary." The administration wanted to shape the direction of constitutional law, not put an end to it.[37] As the direction the state and federal courts were moving in in the late 1930s suggested, the new judges were finely attuned to the fact that the activities of Democratic constituencies (i.e., unions) were to be protected and not swept within a general disposition to unleash government power to make reasonable regulations. Harry Truman's appointees, by contrast, uniformly lined up on the side of government on this issue. The Truman administration was on board with the general anticommunist agenda, if not with all its particulars, and Truman's justices were closely aligned with his administration. They did not exhibit the diversity or the civil libertarian streak in regard to Communists that the New Deal justices did. Likewise, Dwight D. Eisenhower's justices were generally deferential to the government on this issue. The two exceptions were, of course, big ones, in the form of Earl Warren and William Brennan. The nominations of those two justices were also the most politically driven of the Eisenhower presidency. Warren, Eisenhower's first nomination to the Court, was political payback for the former California governor's critical assistance in securing the Republican presidential nomination for Eisenhower. Brennan's nomination was made on the eve of the 1956 elections, and it was hoped that nominating the New Jersey state judge would help shore up support among northeastern Catholic Democrats for the president's reelection. There are good reasons to believe that John Marshall Harlan more closely fit Eisenhower's preferences for a justice than did Earl Warren or William Brennan. Eisenhower famously groused that the appointments of the latter two justices were mistakes, and it is likely that their votes in the anticommunism cases were precisely what he had in mind in making those complaints.[38]

VI. Conclusion

Freedom of association grew out of various roots, but finally found a home under the rubric of the First Amendment. The Supreme Court proved most sympathetic to such claims when they were made within the core context of free speech situations—in the case of speakers at public rallies—and in the context closest to the New Deal's concern with economic justice—the activity of labor unions. As the assertion of freedom of

---

[37] See Keith E. Whittington, *Political Foundations of Judicial Supremacy* (Princeton, NJ: Princeton University Press, 2007); and Kevin McMahon, *Reconsidering Roosevelt on Race* (Chicago: University of Chicago Press, 2003). Roosevelt's Court-packing plan would have allowed the president to appoint a new justice to the U.S. Supreme Court for every justice over the age of seventy. It would have had the effect of giving Roosevelt an immediate and solid majority on the Court, but the plan was defeated amid concern that it would dangerously empower the president and as the Court retreated from its opposition to the New Deal.

[38] David Yalof, *Pursuit of Justices* (Chicago: University of Chicago Press, 1999), 65, 229 nn. 108–9.

association moved to a different context, one in which the justices had substantially less sympathy for the defendants, the claim proved harder to sustain before the Court. The choice to affiliate with the Communist Party seemed rather unlike the possibility of innocent citizens stumbling into public rallies sponsored by dubious organizations, and much more like the action of one who is forming an intent to promote illegal activities. As a result, in this context the Court tended to take a different view of how far the freedom of association could legitimately extend before it was outweighed by the government's responsibility to preserve the general welfare. From the very earliest cases, when state courts worked with notions of personal liberty rather than fundamental rights of free speech, courts had emphasized that individuals should be able to freely associate to engage in lawful activities. But courts had also emphasized that joining an organization such as the Communist Party was quite different from hanging out on the street corner with reputed thieves or attending a public meeting to air general grievances. Over the course of prior decades, the state and federal courts had laid the jurisprudential foundations for recognizing a constitutional freedom of association that had implications for the government's domestic anticommunism efforts during the mid-twentieth century, but the courts hoped to reserve that freedom for those they regarded as exercising traditional and fundamental freedoms and as being in danger of becoming swept up by an overly aggressive state. Although some of Franklin Roosevelt's appointees to the Supreme Court looked with such sympathy upon those individuals being targeted by anticommunism measures, most of the post–New Deal justices instead emphasized the necessary limits of the freedom of association. Guilt by "mere association" was unacceptable, but sometimes "guilt by association" made sense.

Politics, Princeton University

EXPRESSIVE ASSOCIATION AND THE IDEAL OF THE UNIVERSITY IN THE SOLOMON AMENDMENT LITIGATION

By Tobias Barrington Wolff and Andrew Koppelman

I. Introduction

More than any other area of constitutional law, the doctrines that govern the free speech clause of the First Amendment suffer from the risk that form may come to override function. The potential ambit of free speech doctrine is huge, since most types of collective human activity necessarily involve speech, and the rise of robust constitutional protection for freedom of speech in the modern era has been accompanied by an inevitable proliferation of complex doctrines. These free speech doctrines must distinguish between expression that should enjoy protection from state interference and conduct that should not, even when the conduct in question is accomplished in part through the medium of speech. When at its best, First Amendment doctrine uses sensitive, contextual analysis to identify and protect those forms of expression that play some role in democratic self-governance, human flourishing, and the expansion of collective knowledge. When not at its best, however, the First Amendment can become a self-propelled and self-justifying juggernaut, demanding outcomes that claim to be the inevitable, algorithmic result of established free-speech precedents but are in fact profoundly disconnected from the underlying reality and the animating values to which they purport to give voice.

The series of lawsuits that sought to challenge the constitutionality of the federal Solomon Amendment under the First Amendment doctrine of "expressive association" fell decisively into the latter category. The Solomon Amendment requires that universities afford equal and unfettered access to military recruiters during the on-campus interview process, despite the military's discriminatory behavior toward gay recruits—behavior that would otherwise call for the recruiters to be excluded from portions of the recruitment process under the nondiscrimination policies of many institutions. Born of a well-intentioned effort to express tangible support for the gay, lesbian, and bisexual students who are excluded by the military's Don't Ask, Don't Tell policy, these lawsuits threatened to bring about a crisis in the doctrine of expressive association. That potential crisis became acute when the law-professor plaintiffs secured a pair of victorious opinions from federal courts in the U.S. Court of Appeals for

doi:10.1017/S0265052508080205

the Third Circuit[1] and the District of Connecticut[2] that had appalling implications for the enforceability of other important laws and progressive reforms. Ultimately, the Supreme Court defused the situation by reversing the Third Circuit and upholding the constitutionality of the Solomon Amendment in a unanimous opinion that was more an exercise in damage control than in analytical cogency.

The doctrinal crisis provoked by the Solomon litigation offers a picture in microcosm of the current state of expressive association and the crossroads at which that doctrine stands. This essay will undertake to illustrate that picture. It begins, in Section II, with a brief overview of the Solomon Amendment and the history of enforcement that led the law professors to mount their challenge. Section III then identifies the unstable analytical fault lines of equality and speech that currently characterize expressive association doctrine. Those fault lines underwent a major shift when the Supreme Court issued its misguided decision in *Boy Scouts of America v. Dale* (2000),[3] a shift that the law professors sought to exploit and accelerate in their lawsuits in ways that threatened to push the American constitutional landscape in a regressive direction. Finally, Section IV turns the lens of analysis inward, stripping away the distracting veneer of First Amendment rhetoric and examining the set of values that the law professors embraced with their invocation of the free speech clause. Section IV argues that the account that many law faculties gave of their institutional self-definition in this litigation effort was deeply inconsistent with the principles that lie at the heart of the modern university. Well intentioned or not, these constitutional challenges were misbegotten, and it was both correct and fortunate that they failed in their doctrinal goals.

II. MILITARY RECRUITMENT AND THE SOLOMON AMENDMENT

One of the earliest victories of the gay rights movement came when some institutions in mainstream America embraced the view that discrimination against gay people is, in at least some respects, analogous to racism. Quite early on, some elite institutions became persuaded that the two kinds of discrimination were equally pernicious. For example, as early as 1978, Yale Law School extended its nondiscrimination policy (which had first been promulgated in 1972) to bar sexual-orientation discrimination.[4]

Gradually, these nondiscrimination policies spread across many law school campuses, were adopted by the Association of American Law

---

[1] *Forum for Academic and Institutional Rights [FAIR] v. Rumsfeld*, 390 F.3d 219 (3d Cir. 2004); rev'd, 547 U.S. 47 (2006).

[2] *Burt v. Rumsfeld*, 354 F. Supp. 2d 156 (D. Conn. 2005).

[3] *Boy Scouts of America v. Dale*, 530 U.S. 640 (2000).

[4] The facts that follow are drawn largely from the summary provided in *Burt v. Rumsfeld*, 354 F. Supp. 2d 156 (D. Conn. 2005).

Schools (AALS), and became the norm at accredited institutions around the country. The policies also expanded to include the activities of employers who sought to recruit law students from these institutions. In 1990, the AALS added sexual orientation to its nondiscrimination policy, requiring both public and private employers to sign a pledge that they would not discriminate against a law school's gay, lesbian, and bisexual students before the employers would be given full access to the recruitment apparatus and permitted to come on campus to conduct interviews.[5]

Such nondiscrimination policies were an unwelcome development for the military, which recruits, among many other places, on law school campuses, seeking to fill the ranks of its Judge Advocate General's Corps, or JAG. As an arm of the military, JAG overtly discriminates against gay, lesbian, and bisexual employees as a matter of official policy.[6] When law schools began to enforce their antidiscrimination policies and exclude military recruiters from the campus interview process, the Pentagon and the military grew upset with this highly visible expression of institutional disapproval, and also with what they claimed to be a threat to their ability to staff JAG ranks.[7] Congress responded by enacting a law, the Solomon

---

[5] See *FAIR*, 390 F.3d at 224–25 (recounting AALS's expansion of its nondiscrimination policy).

[6] The current policy, colloquially known as "Don't Ask, Don't Tell," was enacted by statute in 1993 and took effect in early 1994. See 10 U.S.C. sec. 654, "Policy Concerning Homosexuality in the Military." The policy imposes unique and extraordinarily burdensome restrictions on speech and conduct upon gay, lesbian, and bisexual servicemembers, effectively forcing them to remain closeted and celibate, and to affect a straight identity, as the condition of military service. See generally Tobias Barrington Wolff, "Political Representation and Accountability under Don't Ask, Don't Tell," *Iowa Law Review* 89 (2004): 1633 (describing operation of policy). Prior to Don't Ask, Don't Tell, the military maintained a blanket ban on service by gay, lesbian, and bisexual soldiers, a policy that it imposed through executive and administrative command rather than statutory mandate. In practice, Don't Ask, Don't Tell has operated in a manner very similar to the blanket ban that preceded it; indeed, the rate at which gay servicemembers are discharged has gone up under Don't Ask, Don't Tell, despite President Clinton's promise at the time of its enactment that the new policy would create a space within which gay men and lesbians could serve. See generally Servicemembers Legal Defense Network, "Ten Year Timeline of 'Don't Ask, Don't Tell'," available at http://www.sldn.org/templates/dadt/record.html?section=183&record=1449 (last visited August 9, 2007).

[7] This essay is not the place to take up the unresolved question of what actual impact the law school policies might have had upon the ability of the military to satisfy its recruitment goals in the various Judge Advocate General's Corps, but that threat is easily overstated. The common shorthand description that one often hears of the manner in which law schools sought to enforce their nondiscrimination policies—"The law schools were trying to exclude military recruiters"—can easily give the false impression that JAG was being prevented from interviewing law students altogether. The reality is far different.

No law school ever forbade its students to interview with JAG, and most permitted JAG to participate in some fashion in the normal interview season. Generally, schools merely requested that JAG conduct their interviews off campus and contact interested students without the assistance of the law school placement office. See Brief for the Respondents, *Rumsfeld v. FAIR*, No. 04-1152 (September 21, 2005) (hereinafter FAIR Main Brief), at 7–8 (setting forth undisputed account of accommodations requested by objecting law schools). Such policies imposed inconvenience on JAG recruiters, to be sure, and may have had some marginal impact on JAG's overall recruitment efforts. But the number of law students who interview with JAG

Amendment, that put financial pressure on law schools to excuse the military from complying with their antidiscrimination rules, by denying certain types of federal funding to institutions that barred military recruitment on campus. That pressure has steadily increased and is now overwhelming for law schools that exist as part of larger research universities.

The Solomon Amendment was first enacted in 1995, and has since been amended several times.[8] The amendment originally was interpreted to remove federal funding only from the part of the university that placed limitations on military recruiters. Thus, for example, if a university's law school barred military recruiters from portions of the hiring process, only the law school, not the entire university, would lose funding.[9] In 1999, however, the statute was amended to bar funding for an entire university if any part of it treated military recruiters less favorably than other recruiters.[10] Almost all American universities receive large amounts of federal funds, and the prospect of losing those funds would have been a financial disaster. So law schools gave in to this financial pressure and allowed military recruiters on campus.[11]

---

recruiters is very small at most institutions; and law schools often do not offer a very affirming or friendly atmosphere for those interested in the military, for reasons having as much to do with class bias as with political views. This is particularly the case at rich and selective private institutions. As a consequence, those students who do wish to interview with JAG are usually a highly motivated and self-directed group. While they may find it less pleasant and less convenient to interview under the conditions that the law schools sought to impose, law students who are interested in careers as military lawyers are likely to find their way to JAG even if they must overcome administrative inconvenience to do so.

[8] The Solomon Amendment currently provides as follows (10 U.S.C. sec 983[b]):

(b) Denial of funds for preventing military recruiting on campus.—No funds described in subsection (d)(1) may be provided by contract or by grant to an institution of higher education (including any subelement of such institution) if the Secretary of Defense determines that that institution (or any subelement of that institution) has a policy or practice (regardless of when implemented) that either prohibits, or in effect prevents—

(1) the Secretary of a military department or Secretary of Homeland Security from gaining access to campuses, or access to students (who are 17 years of age or older) on campuses, for purposes of military recruiting in a manner that is at least equal in quality and scope to the access to campuses and to students that is provided to any other employer; or

(2) access by military recruiters for purposes of military recruiting to the following information pertaining to students (who are 17 years of age or older) enrolled at that institution (or any subelement of that institution):

(A) Names, addresses, and telephone listings.

(B) Date and place of birth, levels of education, academic majors, degrees received, and the most recent educational institution enrolled in by the student.

[9] See 61 Fed.Reg. 7739, 7740 (February 29, 1996). Law schools do not typically receive a large amount of federal funding.

[10] 10 U.S.C. sec. 983(c)(2), as modified by Pub.L. No. 106-65, sec. 549(a)(1) (1999); Defense Federal Acquisition Regulation Supplement: Institutions of Higher Education, 65 Fed.Reg. 2056 (January 13, 2000). The effect of this redefinition was that a violation in any part of the university would put federal funding for the entire university in jeopardy. 48 C.F.R. sec. 252.209-7005.

[11] Judge Richard Posner's criticism of the depth of the law schools' commitment is unfair in this respect. In describing the choice that law schools made to bow to the Solomon

Some law schools and individual law professors then sued to challenge the constitutionality of the Solomon Amendment. Two of these cases produced constitutional rulings: *FAIR v. Rumsfeld* (2004), a suit instituted by a large array of institutions and groups of faculty members, and *Burt v. Rumsfeld* (2005), a suit brought solely by members of the faculty of Yale Law School.[12] After producing a remarkably broad victory on behalf of the plaintiffs in the U.S. Court of Appeals for the Third Circuit (a victory that was subsequently echoed in the Yale Law School suit), the former suit came before the Supreme Court, styled as *Rumsfeld v. FAIR* (2006).

The constitutional argument that the plaintiffs in these cases offered was based on the First Amendment. They made two claims. First, they argued that, by enacting their antidiscrimination policies, law schools were communicating a message: "Discrimination against gay men and lesbians is wrong and will not be tolerated." By forcing them to allow recruiters on campus who discriminate against gay students, the professors and law schools argued, the Solomon Amendment impeded their ability to communicate or exemplify this inclusive message. Second, they argued that the military had its own message that it conveys when it recruits: "Discrimination against gay men and lesbians is acceptable and necessary for the military mission." The law schools argued that, by forcing them to facilitate the dissemination of that message, the Solomon Amendment was compelling them to say things with which they disagreed.

Both First Amendment arguments depended heavily upon expansive interpretations of one recent Supreme Court decision, *Boy Scouts of America v. Dale* (2000),[13] which held that the Boy Scouts had the right to discriminate against gay people in setting its membership requirements.

Amendment, Posner writes, "The law school merely wants to have its cake and eat it—and who doesn't? It is not an edifying desire—it is embarrassing for a law school to have to tell its irate homosexual students that it loves them but loves federal money even more—but the reality is that universities nowadays are giant corporations and behave accordingly, whatever their pretensions." Richard A. Posner, "A Note on *Rumsfeld v. FAIR* and the Legal Academy," *Supreme Court Review* 2006 (2007): 47, 52. When law schools had the option of refusing their own federal funds as the price of enforcing their antidiscrimination policies, one could legitimately use their willingness to take that step as a measure of their commitment. But when Congress amended Solomon to threaten the wholesale destruction of other programs throughout their universities as the price of law schools' noncompliance, any semblance of a true "choice" was eliminated.

[12] See notes 1 and 2 above. The University of Pennsylvania Law School also brought a Solomon suit, which placed much greater emphasis on a claim that the institution was actually in compliance with the statutory mandate and asserted constitutional claims only in a subsidiary posture. That suit was partially dismissed at the district court level (for lack of standing and failure to state a cause of action on respective counts), and was then superseded by the decision of the Supreme Court before it produced any substantial constitutional ruling. See *Burbank v. Rumsfeld*, 2004 WL 1925532 (E.D. Pa., August 26, 2004).

Professor Wolff joined the faculty of the University of Pennsylvania Law School after the termination of this suit (and after the Supreme Court's decision in *FAIR*) and played no role in that litigation.

[13] *Boy Scouts of America v. Dale*, 530 U.S. 640 (2000).

Before *Dale,* the treatment of freedom of association claims in similar cases had followed what Professor Dale Carpenter calls a "message-based approach":[14] Only if an association was organized for the purpose of expressing a viewpoint would a statute requiring it to accept unwanted members raise constitutional difficulties, and then only if that requirement would impair the association's ability to convey its message. *Dale* moved expressive association doctrine well beyond those limitations. The opinion in *Dale* did not state a clear rule to guide lower courts, but it suggested two bases for its decision: first, that the Boy Scouts had a right to exclude gay people on the mere basis of their claim that a nondiscrimination law would prevent the Scouts from sending a message about the morality of homosexual conduct, even in the absence of a robust factual showing that they satisfied the other requirements previously associated with the doctrine; and second, that the Scouts could legitimately claim that obedience to the law would compel them to convey a message of approval of homosexual conduct, allowing them to take advantage of the Court's vigorous prohibition against compelled speech. The plaintiffs in *Rumsfeld v. FAIR* argued that their position was exactly the same as that of the Boy Scouts and that the expansive doctrines of the *Dale* case should apply with equal force to the claims of any association that asserts that it has an expressive mission.

III. Equality and Speech in the Law of Expressive Association

To appreciate the doctrinal crisis that the Solomon litigation provoked, it is necessary to understand in detail the nature of the shift that the *Dale* decision effectuated in the law of expressive association and the manner in which the Solomon plaintiffs proposed to amplify that shift. That understanding must operate on both a doctrinal and a conceptual level. On the level of doctrine, the Solomon plaintiffs embraced a ruling that vastly expanded expressive association rights in one particular context—an organization, the Boy Scouts, that was engaged in quintessentially noncommercial activity, operated predominantly in small and local groups, and faced a challenge to control over its membership and leadership positions— and sought to explode that context, asking for these expanded rights to apply to enormous and powerful quasi-corporate institutions that had elaborate involvement in commerce and were under no threat to their control over membership. On a conceptual level, the Solomon plaintiffs sought to entrench and expand the signature move of the *Dale* opinion: the framing of expressive association claims exclusively in terms of speech values, rather than as a composite of speech and equality principles (the

[14] Dale Carpenter, "Expressive Association and Anti-Discrimination Law after *Dale:* A Tripartite Approach," *Minnesota Law Review* 85 (2001): 1515, 1517.

frame employed by *Dale's* predecessors). In both respects, the litigation sought to push the law of expressive association in unsustainable directions.

A. *Expressive association before and after* Dale

An expressive association claim focuses on the particular features of "associations"—collections of individuals that operate as a cohesive group, institution, or entity—that state laws may interfere with when such entities engage in communicative or expressive activities. The doctrine recognizes the possibility that regulation can sometimes intrude upon an organization's ability to undertake its chosen form of expression, and it provides the organization with an opportunity to demonstrate that speech values entitle it to an exemption from the law's operation.

One of the Supreme Court's earliest articulations of this proposition came in the 1958 case of *NAACP v. Alabama ex rel. Patterson*.[15] As part of their concerted resistance to desegregation and the enfranchisement of Black voters, Alabama and other states invoked state corporation laws in an effort to compel the National Association for the Advancement of Colored People and its local affiliates to disclose the names of their members. In the atmosphere of intimidation and violence that prevailed in many quarters at the time, the NAACP asserted that compelled disclosure of its membership lists would effectively destroy the organization's ability to function by intimidating members from contributing their money or their efforts to the organization's advocacy. The Court agreed. Laying the foundation for the expressive association doctrine, the Court unanimously held that "[e]ffective advocacy of both public and private points of view, particularly controversial ones, is undeniably enhanced by group association" and that "[i]t is beyond debate that freedom to engage in association for the advancement of beliefs and ideas is an inseparable aspect of the . . . freedom of speech."[16] Alabama failed to show an interest in its generic disclosure laws that was sufficient to justify a threat to that freedom, and the NAACP was allowed to continue protecting its members' anonymity.[17]

Though it had its roots in a decision that was supportive of the civil rights movement's impulse toward promoting equality values, expressive association doctrine quickly came to be embraced by organizations seeking to resist the application of antidiscrimination laws and other forms of progressive regulation. This second generation of expressive association petitioners has come to define the dominant paradigm for the doctrine, and, in resisting antidiscrimination laws, these petitioners have claimed a different and subtler form of interference with their ability to engage in

---

[15] *NAACP v. Alabama ex rel. Patterson*, 357 U.S. 449 (1958) (Harlan, J.).
[16] Id. at 460.
[17] Id. at 463–66.

advocacy and expression. In *Alabama ex rel. Patterson*, the NAACP argued (with good reason) that the Alabama regulation threatened to destroy their association altogether. The second generation of associational claimants, in contrast, have argued that antidiscrimination laws, in depriving them of control over whom they accept as members, threaten to alter, undermine, or obscure the message that a given association wishes to convey. The claim is either that the newly admitted members will not themselves be interested in conveying the association's message, or that the newly admitted members will compromise the ability of the association to communicate its message to an external audience. A frequently invoked example—as absurd as it is effective, given its counterfactual conceit—calls upon one to imagine a law that compels the Ku Klux Klan to admit Black or Jewish members. Such individuals would presumably both resist the KKK's message of White gentile supremacy within the organization and, at the same time, deprive the KKK of credibility in its ability to communicate that message to an external audience, since a visibly mixed membership would belie the message of segregation.[18]

In *Alabama ex rel. Patterson*, the Court did not require the NAACP to make an extensive factual showing at the trial level in support of its claim that the forced disclosure of membership lists would effectively destroy the organization. As the Court explained, the NAACP had "made an uncontroverted showing that on past occasions revelation of the identity of its rank-and-file members [had] exposed these members to economic reprisal, loss of employment, threat of physical coercion, and other manifestations of public hostility."[19] These facts, considered against the backdrop of hostility toward civil rights workers and organizations in the Deep South that was a matter of common understanding during this era, were sufficient for the Court to conclude on appeal that the NAACP was entitled to the First Amendment shield that it sought.

With the second generation of expressive association cases, however, the Supreme Court adopted a more stringent view toward claims of interference with expression. Since the threat to an association's expressive

---

[18] At least one court has issued such a holding in a related situation. In *Invisible Empire of the Knights of the Ku Klux Klan v. Mayor et al. of Thurmont*, 700 F. Supp. 281, 289–91 (D. Md. 1988), a district court found that the KKK could not be denied a permit to march on a town's public streets because of the group's objection to a demand by the mayor that they comply with a nondiscrimination condition in their choice of whom to include as marchers. (No issue of membership in the KKK chapter itself was presented.) From the discussion in the opinion, it appears that Black and Jewish protesters would have marched with the KKK, if allowed, in order to spoil their message. Id. at 289. Prefiguring the result in *Hurley*, the district court essentially treated the KKK's choice of whom to include in a parade as a question of pure expression and invalidated the attempt to mandate the inclusion of unwanted members. Id. at 290–91. See *Hurley v. Irish-American Gay, Lesbian, and Bisexual Group of Boston*, 515 U.S. 557 (1995) (holding that a private parade organizer has a First Amendment right to exercise control over the groups that will march under their own banners in the parade, as that feature of the parade's composition itself constitutes protected expression).

[19] *Alabama ex rel. Patterson*, 357 U.S. at 462.

activities is more attenuated in this class of cases—relying upon assertions about symbolic impact or prevailing attitudes rather than threats of
violence and economic reprisal—the Court came to demand a concomi-
tantly more demanding standard of First Amendment claimants. Associations seeking an exception to an antidiscrimination law or other generally
applicable provision had to make a factual showing at trial, and a robust
one, establishing the nature of their expressive activities and demonstrat-
ing how the law threatened to undermine those activities. Where the very
existence of an association was not clearly being placed in jeopardy, as
had been the case in *Alabama ex rel. Patterson*, the Court was not willing
to take the factual underpinnings of the claim on faith.

The leading case before *Dale* that addressed the right to exclude, and that
most powerfully embodied this shift, was *Roberts v. United States Jaycees*
(1984).[20] In *Jaycees*, the Court held that a state could constitutionally require
an all-male association of young businessmen to admit women as full
voting members, where previously they had been admitted only as non-
voting participants. The Court's opinion reaffirmed the proposition that the
freedom of speech that the First Amendment guarantees is often exercised
collectively, and so entails a certain degree of freedom of association. That
liberty, in turn, sometimes entails a right to exclude unwanted members:

> There can be no clearer example of an intrusion into the internal
> structure or affairs of an association than a regulation that forces the
> group to accept members it does not desire. Such a regulation may
> impair the ability of the original members to express only those
> views that brought them together. Freedom of association therefore
> plainly presupposes a freedom not to associate.[21]

At the same time that it embraced this more expansive view of the type
of interference that might give rise to a First Amendment claim, the Court
also imposed doctrinal limits upon the right it had thus created. First and
foremost, it demanded the factual showing that had been implicitly deemed
unnecessary in *Alabama ex rel. Patterson*. While interference with membership "*may* impair" the association's expressive activities,[22] it falls to
the association to establish the nature of its expressive practice and to
demonstrate just how changes in its membership will undermine that
practice. The Jaycees failed in their claim, in part, because of their inability to make a sufficient showing on that score.[23] In addition, the Court

---

[20] *Roberts v. United States Jaycees*, 468 U.S. 609 (1984).
[21] Id. at 623.
[22] Id. (emphasis added).
[23] In one of the key passages of the *Jaycees* decision (id. at 627–28), the Court explained:

> While acknowledging that "the specific content of most of the resolutions adopted
> over the years by the Jaycees has nothing to do with sex," the Court of Appeals

held that even interference with membership that demonstrably interferes with expressive practice could be justified by "compelling state interests, unrelated to the suppression of ideas, that cannot be achieved through means significantly less restrictive of associational freedoms." [24] The result was a balancing test: antidiscrimination norms could legitimately be imposed on associations in the absence of a convincing showing of expressive burden, and perhaps even where such a burden existed, if the state interest were great enough. In practice, free association claims unrelated to viewpoint discrimination lost in the Supreme Court under this standard.[25]

Then came *Dale*. The decision in *Dale* represented an enormous departure from its predecessors. Despite a litigation context that appeared to be a natural progression from *Jaycees* and its progeny—a case firmly within the second generation of expressive association claims—the *Dale* majority shifted to an extraordinarily permissive standard in the factual showing that it demanded of associational claimants. Going further even than *Alabama ex rel. Patterson* (where, recall, the very existence of the NAACP had been placed in jeopardy by terroristic threats), the Court adopted a posture of almost complete deference to an association's claim that an antidiscrimination law's interference with decisions about a small number of members would undermine the group's expressive practice.

The *Dale* case involved a New Jersey public accommodations statute that prohibited discrimination on the basis of sexual orientation. The Boy Scouts revoked the membership of James Dale, an Eagle Scout and assistant scoutmaster, after a newspaper story (which did not mention his affiliation with the Scouts) identified him as an officer of his college's lesbian and gay student organization. Dale successfully sued under the statute. The Boy Scouts of America claimed that the application of the law to their New Jersey chapters would violate their freedom of expression, but the New Jersey Supreme Court, applying the *Jaycees* test, was "not persuaded . . . that a shared goal of Boy Scout members is to associate in order to preserve the view that homosexuality is immoral." [26] The court noted that the Scouts had not, in their public materials, taken any position whatsoever concerning the morality of homosexuality prior to litigation.

---

nonetheless entertained the hypothesis that women members might have a different view or agenda with respect to these matters so that, if they are allowed to vote, "some change in the Jaycees' philosophical cast can reasonably be expected." It is similarly arguable that, insofar as the Jaycees is organized to promote the views of young men whatever those views happen to be, admission of women as voting members will change the message communicated by the group's speech because of the gender-based assumptions of the audience. Neither supposition, however, is supported by the record.

[24] Id.

[25] See, e.g., *Board of Dirs. of Rotary Int'l v. Rotary Club of Duarte*, 481 U.S. 537 (1987); and *New York State Club Ass'n v. City of New York*, 487 U.S. 1 (1988).

[26] *Boy Scouts of America v. Dale*, 160 N.J. 562, 613, 734 A.2d 1196, 1223–1224 (1999) (internal quotation marks omitted), quoted in *Dale*, 530 U.S. at 647.

It therefore held "that Dale's membership does not violate the Boy Scouts' right of expressive association because his inclusion would not 'affect in any significant way [the Boy Scouts'] existing members' ability to carry out their various purposes.' "[27] The Boy Scouts, in other words, had failed to make the robust factual showing that *Jaycees* demanded.

The U.S. Supreme Court reversed the New Jersey court's decision. The Supreme Court's opinion is muddled and its reasoning imprecisely rendered, but the steps of its analysis essentially proceed as follows: (1) The Scouts are an association that "engages in expressive activity"[28] protected by the First Amendment. (2) Forced inclusion of a member therefore violates the First Amendment if it "would significantly affect the Boy Scouts' ability to advocate public or private viewpoints."[29] (3) The Boy Scouts assert that homosexual conduct is inconsistent with the values embodied in the Scout Oath and Law, particularly those values represented by the requirement that Scouts be "morally straight" and "clean." (4) The Court must give deference to an organization's assertions regarding the nature of its expression. (5) "[W]e must also give deference to an association's view of what would impair its expression."[30] (6) "Dale's presence in the Boy Scouts would, at the very least, force the organization to send a message, both to the youth members and the world, that the Boy Scouts accepts homosexual conduct as a legitimate form of behavior."[31] (7) Therefore, the First Amendment prohibits application of the antidiscrimination law to the Scouts.

In essence, the Court held that the Scouts were entitled to an exception to New Jersey's antidiscrimination law because they said in their litigation papers that they needed it. The Scouts had taken positions in the litigation about the nature of their expressive practice and the manner in which state law would interfere with that practice, the Court found, and that was all the Court needed to know. The Boy Scouts were an association that "engages in expressive activity," and that was sufficient.

The opinion in *Dale* does not state a clear rule to guide lower courts, but it seems to imply two shocking propositions: that all antidiscrimination laws are unconstitutional whenever they are applied to associations that object; and that citizens are allowed to disobey laws whenever obedience would be perceived by others as endorsing some unwanted message. As to the first proposition, almost any noncommercial organization can make the *de minimis* showing that is necessary to classify it as an "expressive association," and *Dale* appears to impose only that threshold requirement for full access to the broad rights it articulates. Steps (1) through (5) of the

---

[27] *Dale*, 160 N.J. at 615, 734 A.2d at 1225, quoting *Board of Directors of Rotary Int'l v. Rotary Club of Duarte*, 481 U.S. 537, 548 (1987); quoted in *Dale*, 530 U.S. at 647.

[28] *Dale*, 530 U.S. at 650.

[29] Id.

[30] Id. at 653.

[31] Id.

Court's reasoning, taken together, appear to permit any such litigant to resist an antidiscrimination law merely by asserting in litigation that the law interferes with some inchoate expressive practice. (In the *Dale* case, the expressive practice that entitled the Boy Scouts to a victory consisted largely of the Scouts' traditional camping and wilderness activities.)[32] If courts must then give "*Dale* deference" to that assertion, as the opinion itself implies, then the case is over and the litigant must receive its First Amendment exemption.

As to the second proposition, the Supreme Court appears to embrace the view in step (6) of its reasoning that the state impermissibly imposes a message upon an unwilling speaker whenever it forces compliance with a law that would be perceived as having symbolic implications with which the subject disagrees. The Scouts could refuse to admit gay members, the Court apparently held, because they said that the presence of gay Scouts might have symbolic meaning to the outside world and the Scouts would be the unwilling billboards of that message. Once again, the Court appears to "defer" to the litigant's assertions as to when an impermissible imputation of a message is present. The implications of this second, "compelled speech" holding are even broader than the first proposition outlined above. The compelled speech doctrine is available to *any* claimant, even the largest for-profit corporation.[33] If the Court really meant what it said in *Dale*, it appeared to be licensing any litigant to resist any form of state regulation, merely by arguing that compliance with the regulation would impose an unwelcome symbolic message upon the subject.[34]

Cases after *Dale* revealed the unsustainably broad implications of the Court's opinion, along with lower courts' reluctance to follow out those implications. Courts have rejected *Dale*-based challenges to a city ordinance prohibiting commercial sex clubs;[35] a gun control statute limiting the use of certain weapons to licensed gun clubs (effectively pressuring nonmembers to join such clubs);[36] the use of undercover officers to enforce

---

[32] This analysis of the Court's opinion is developed in detail in Andrew Koppelman, "Signs of the Times: *Dale v. Boy Scouts of America* and the Changing Meaning of Nondiscrimination," *Cardozo Law Review* 23 (2002): 1819. For a more detailed analysis of the doctrinal confusion introduced by *Dale*, see David McGowan, "Making Sense of *Dale*," *Constitutional Commentary* 18 (2001): 121.

[33] See, e.g., *Pacific Gas & Elec. v. Public Utils. Comm'n*, 475 U.S. 1 (1986) (empowering PG&E to resist a California law requiring it to bundle environmental literature with bills mailed to customers during some months on the grounds that the regulation forced the corporation to facilitate speech that was not of its choosing). For an exposition of some of the contours of the compelled speech doctrine, see Tobias Barrington Wolff, "Compelled Affirmations, Free Speech, and the U.S. Military's Don't Ask, Don't Tell Policy," *Brooklyn Law Review* 63 (1997): 1141, 1193–1201.

[34] The implications of *Dale* for compelled speech doctrine are of great importance, but they also raise a distinct and complex set of issues and must remain the subject of another essay. See Koppelman, "Signs of the Times." Having identified the issue, we will focus only on expressive association doctrine from this point forward.

[35] *Recreational Developments of Phoenix v. City of Phoenix*, 220 F. Supp. 1054 (D. Ariz. 2002).

[36] *Gun Owners' Action League, Inc. v. Swift*, 284 F.3d 198 (1st Cir. 2002).

a prohibition against "lap dancing";[37] a statute banning children's access to a public clothing-optional park;[38] a state university's decision to strip a fraternity of its status as a recognized student organization where it was found that members had abused illegal drugs;[39] and, not least, a city ordinance prohibiting discrimination on the basis of sexual orientation.[40] The logic of the *Dale* opinion made the claimants' arguments colorable in all these cases, but the lower courts were unwilling to follow that opinion's logic to its conclusions.

Prior to the Solomon litigation, only three reported cases relied upon *Dale* in upholding a claim of freedom of association. The Boy Scouts themselves were a party in two of these, one of which carves out a category of "nonexpressive" jobs in the Scouting organization, to which *Dale* does not apply.[41] The other involved a males-only meeting conducted by the Nation of Islam, and thus raised questions of the autonomy of religious groups that are different from those presented by ordinary association claims.[42] Until the Third Circuit's decision in *FAIR v. Rumsfeld* (2004),[43] no lower court had upheld a *Dale* claim involving a nonreligious association other than the Boy Scouts. The lower federal courts seemed to be on their way to confining *Dale* to its facts.[44]

---

[37] *City of Shoreline v. Club for Free Speech Rights*, 36 P.3d 1058 (2001).

[38] *Central Texas Nudists v. County of Travis*, 2000 WL 1784344 (Tex. App. Austin 2000).

[39] *Pi Lambda Phi Fraternity v. University of Pittsburgh*, 229 F.3d 435 (2000).

[40] *Hyman v. City of Louisville*, 132 F. Supp. 2d 528 (W.D. Ky. 2001).

[41] *Chicago Council of Boy Scouts of America v. City of Chicago*, 748 N.E.2d 759 (Ill. 1st Dist. 2001), appeal denied, 763 N.E. 2d 316 (Ill. 2001); *Boy Scouts of America v. D.C. Commission on Human Rights*, 809 A.2d 1192 (D.C. 2002). But even the Scouts have gotten only limited mileage from *Dale*. The City of Berkeley was not prevented from revoking the Scouts' privilege of docking their boats rent-free in the city's marina. See *Evans v. City of Berkeley*, 129 P.2d 394 (Cal.), cert. denied, 127 S. Ct. 434 (2006). Nor was the state of Connecticut barred from excluding the Scouts from its state employee's charitable campaign. See *Boy Scouts of America v. Wyman*, 335 F.3d 80 (2d Cir. 2003), cert. denied, 541 U.S. 903 (2004).

[42] *Donaldson v. Farrakhan*, 762 N.E. 2d 835 (Mass. 2002). The internal autonomy of religious groups is a well-established doctrine which has been held to survive the holding of *Employment Division v. Smith*, 494 U.S. 872 (1990), that (as a general matter) the free exercise clause does not authorize the courts to carve out exemptions to generally applicable laws when such laws burden religious activities. See *Combs v. Central Texas Annual Conference of the United Methodist Church*, 173 F.3d 343 (5th Cir. 1999); and *E.E.O.C. v. Catholic University of America*, 83 F.3d 455 (D.C. Cir. 1996).

[43] *Forum for Academic and Institutional Rights [FAIR] v. Rumsfeld*, 390 F.3d 219 (3d Cir. 2004); rev'd, 547 U.S. 47 (2006).

[44] In recent years, federal courts have been considering several challenges brought by Christian student organizations seeking exemptions from their institutions' antidiscrimination policies. In one such challenge, decided following the Supreme Court's decision in *FAIR*, the Seventh Circuit provided the organization with the exemption that it sought. See *Christian Legal Soc'y v. Walker*, 453 F.3d 853 (7th Cir. 2006). The court in that case appears to have employed a much more robust form of factual analysis than would be called for under the "*Dale* deference" doctrine. In addition, the court concluded that the defendant sought to apply its policy to the student group because of its disapproval of the group's viewpoint—an assertion that, if true, would bring the holding of the case squarely within the ambit of *Jaycees*, with no need even to advert to the more expansive features of *Dale*. See *Jaycees*, 468 U.S. at 623–24.

And, indeed, for all its broad language, the *Dale* decision involved a factual situation that could be understood as placing many limitations on the new doctrine that it had announced. Unlike many technically not-for-profit entities, the Boy Scouts really do engage almost entirely in activities that are far removed from commerce. It is an organization of teenagers, largely supervised by volunteer adults, who go camping and participate in other recreational and community activities. Earlier Supreme Court decisions had made clear that the noncommercial character of an organization's pursuits would weigh in favor of an expressive association claim. Moreover, the State of New Jersey had sought to compel the Boy Scouts to accept, not just a member (i.e., another scout), but a person in a leadership position, placing the Scouts on much firmer ground in arguing that the *Jaycees* decision, with its references to membership and interference with expression, supported their claim. And the Boy Scouts, though a national organization, operated on a small scale in locally organized troops, painting a sympathetic picture of an informal entity that should remain free from state regulation. The *Dale* decision was still wrong, and dangerously so, in exempting the Scouts from making the factual showings (about the nature of their expressive activities and the alleged interference with those activities) that *Jaycees* had long since required. But it was still possible to approach the *Dale* case as articulating a rule that would apply, if at all, only in a limited context in future cases.

The law professor plaintiffs in the Solomon litigation sought to explode that context. The expansion of *Dale* that the Solomon plaintiffs called for would have disassembled all the implicit limitations that kept that beast at bay. American law schools, unlike the Boy Scouts, are deeply and directly enmeshed with powerful commercial forces. The credentialing and regulatory rules that govern the practice of law make law schools almost the sole gatekeepers to that powerful and highly compensated profession. The activity at issue in the Solomon litigation—the manner in which law schools would manage the recruitment of their students at this high-stakes commercial job fair—was unquestionably a "commercial" activity, even if undertaken by institutions that formally operated on a not-for-profit basis. (As a point of comparison, the Jaycees also operate as a not-for-profit corporation,[45] but the Supreme Court found that they engaged in "various commercial programs" that served as important gateways to professional advancement[46] and that this "commercial nature" militated in favor of their amenability to state regulation.)[47] And law schools are powerful economic entities with clear quasi-public features: they employ large numbers of workers, collect steep tuition from students, and are presumptively open to any applicant who can qualify for admission.

[45] See U.S. Junior Chamber Jaycees, http://www.usjaycees.org/learn_more.htm (last visited July 4, 2007).
[46] *Jaycees*, 468 U.S. at 625–26.
[47] Id. at 629–30.

What is more, the type of interference that the law schools were claiming with their expressive activities—their ability to be effective and credible in communicating a message of inclusiveness toward their gay, lesbian, and bisexual students—was a far cry from the interference that the Court had recognized in the cases stretching from *Jaycees* to *Dale*. There was no question of "membership" in the Solomon litigation.[48] The Solomon Amendment does not require law schools to admit anyone as a faculty member, staff employee, or student. All the law requires is that law schools permit JAG recruiters to participate on an episodic basis—typically, once or twice per year—in the job fairs that law schools host for potential employers who wish to interview their students. Presenting quite the opposite of a "membership" question, these job fairs explicitly involve the invitation of outsiders into the law school as temporary guests. The form of interference with expression that the Court recognized as a matter of principle in *Jaycees*, and found as a matter of fact in *Dale*, is entirely absent on law school campuses under Solomon.

Finally, the actual core of the argument for interference with expression in the Solomon litigation was simply not credible. In plain language, the law professors claimed that their ability to express a message of inclusiveness toward their LGBT students was fatally undermined by the presence twice each year of JAG recruiters at the schools' commercial job fairs.[49] As FAIR put it in their main brief before the Supreme Court: "To the distress of law deans and faculty, members of their communities have concluded that the schools are not committed to antidiscrimination, and that the law schools have lost credibility to preach values of equality, justice, and human dignity."[50] One is invited to imagine that law students, upon seeing the presence of the military recruiters on campus, will either assume that the law school has invited them there as a sign of its approval of Don't Ask, Don't Tell, despite their knowledge of the law school's vigorous protests; or else that the mere presence of the recruiters at the commercial job fair "poisons the atmosphere" at a law school for the entire rest of the year, so that even students who understand that the

[48] The law professors emphasized this distinction and explicitly invited the Court to extend *Dale* beyond the context of membership interference. See, e.g., FAIR Main Brief, *supra* note 7, at 17: "The freedom of association is not limited to circumstances in which the government interferes with an organization's internal composition, but extends to the full range of causes an expressive organization may choose to embrace or reject." See also id. at 31–32 (elaborating on this argument).

[49] We will sometimes use the shorthand "LGBT" to refer to students who identify as lesbian, gay, bisexual, or transgendered. Don't Ask, Don't Tell itself does not deal directly with gender identity or the treatment of transgendered individuals, though the military treats transgendered people with swift and reliable hostility through other policies.

[50] FAIR Main Brief, *supra* note 7, at 14. See also id.: "Faculty attest to student expressions of cynicism and cries of hypocrisy when the lessons turn to topics such as equality, human dignity, and other underpinnings of a just society. They feel inhibited to preach about integrity, adhering to principle, and fighting for a worthy cause" (citations omitted). As a side note, one might question whether "preach" is a felicitous term to use in describing the pedagogical responsibility of a law professor offering a lesson.

school does not share the military's views will never again be able to hear that message from the administration or faculty with open ears.[51]

These suggestions blink reality. To be sure, faculty, staff, and students who care about these issues might be very unhappy about the presence of military recruiters and what they believe those recruiters to represent. They might even feel differently about messages of inclusiveness and equality when they must occasionally confront the discordant reality that one of our most important public institutions rejects that message. But this is not interference with the expression of law schools or law faculty. It is merely the fabric of reality against which that expression must attempt to take hold. It is no more the case that the participation of military recruiters in law school job fairs impairs faculty expression about gay equality than it is that the requirement of paying taxes impairs expression about the philosophical belief in anarchism.[52]

If the expansive rule of *Dale* applied, in full force, to institutions and regulations such as these, then there would truly be nothing left of the limits that *Jaycees* and its progeny imposed. Any "expressive association"—which, in essence, could include almost any organization that does not pursue commercial profit as its primary activity—would have the authority to resist

[51] Under *Dale*, it was arguably the case that the law professors were required only to show that the inclusion of the military recruiters "significantly affect[ed]" their ability to propound their message, even if it did not undermine the message altogether. This is the standard that the Third Circuit purported to apply—see *FAIR v. Rumsfeld*, 390 F.3d 219, 231–34 (3d Cir. 2003)—and FAIR adopted the Third Circuit's analysis wholesale in its briefs. See FAIR Main Brief, supra note 7, at 30. However, any such distinctions are rendered irrelevant by the Third Circuit's further conclusion that it was required to apply "*Dale* deference" to any claim that FAIR made of interference with its expression, whatever the magnitude of that claimed interference. See *FAIR*, 390 F.3d at 233–34. As Justice David Souter once wrote in a different context, "The sequence of the Court's positions prompts a suspicion of error, and skepticism is confirmed by scrutiny of the Court's efforts to justify its holding." *Alden v. Maine*, 527 U.S. 706, 761 (1999) (Souter, J., dissenting).

Of course, had the Supreme Court accepted the invitation to place substantial weight on the lesser "significantly affects" standard, the results would have been dire. Although the more permissive standard might have made the plaintiffs' claims somewhat more plausible on the facts (though not much), it would also have resulted in a change in the law—the application of even more expansive "*Dale* deference" to every entity that engages in any form of expression—that would have been all the more breathtaking and catastrophic in scope.

[52] Focusing primarily on the compelled speech argument, Judge Posner expresses his skepticism on this point in the following terms:

> [N]o one reading the notices sent to students or employers by law school placement offices would think that the law school was expressing its agreement with the policies of prospective employers. Law firms that represent cigarette companies or pornographers, the law departments of giant corporations that pollute the atmosphere or sell munitions to Third World dictators, the offices of the general counsel of the CIA and the Defense Department, right-wing and left-wing public interest firms—all are welcome to "meet the employer" nights. No one, least of all the law schools themselves, thinks that by extending this welcome the law schools or their faculties endorse the policies of their employer guests. All that the law school is "expressing" by its hospitality gestures to prospective employers of its students is its desire to help the students, for the law school's sake as well as the students' own, get good jobs.

Posner, "A Note on *Rumsfeld v. FAIR* and the Legal Academy," 50–51.

any form of regulation that it claimed would interfere with its ability to express its purported message.

The resulting rule would have placed in serious jeopardy the very antidiscrimination principles that the law professors sought to promote in their challenge. Under *Jaycees*, it was already well established that laws affecting the ability of organizations to control their membership might sometimes infringe upon expressive rights in violation of the First Amendment. Until *Dale*, that proposition was carefully limited by the requirement of a robust factual showing and a constitutional balancing test. In the *Dale* case, the Court relieved the Boy Scouts of those important limitations, but it still left a good deal of room for arguing that the expansive rights it had recognized were limited to the idiosyncratic context of that particular case. Imagine, however, if the Court had granted the Solomon plaintiffs their wish and accorded all "expressive associations" the licentious deference that it gave to the Boy Scouts. What impact would such a ruling have had upon equality values?

To recap, the Solomon plaintiffs argued that an expressive association has the right to resist any form of state or federal regulation that is inconsistent with its values, undermines its credibility in communicating a message about its values to the outside world, or forces it to take actions that are inconsistent with its desire to teach by doing and thereby exemplify its values. The plaintiffs further argued that such claimants need offer no factual proof of the centrality of the "values" in question to their broader expressive mission, nor of the interference that they claim with their credibility in the public sphere, nor of the extent to which the regulation interferes with their ability to exemplify their values by acting upon them; rather, claimants could demand that courts defer to their assertions on all these matters. Consider how these arguments might be used in other contexts:

- Title IX of the federal Education Amendments of 1972 has been the primary vehicle by which women have gained broader access to sports opportunities in the United States. Broadly speaking, the law requires universities that accept federal funds to make roughly equal facilities and resources available to their female and male students in their sports programs. Under the position urged by the Solomon plaintiffs, a university could invoke the First Amendment to resist this requirement, simply by asserting that it values more traditional forms of activity by women and wishes to encourage its students to pursue activities that reflect more traditional gender roles. Title IX would obviously undermine the ability of the university to communicate with credibility about the traditional roles of women as much as, if not more than, the Solomon plaintiffs claimed that the presence of military recruiters interfered with their message about inclusiveness. Title IX would obviously interfere with the ability of such an institution to exemplify its values concerning traditional gender roles by structuring extracurricular programs to reflect those roles, just as the Solomon Amendment interferes with the law schools' ability to exemplify antidiscrimination values. If the Solomon plaintiffs had prevailed, it appears that Title IX could have been resisted by any university willing to claim a different worldview.[53]

- An increasing number of states provide some form of protection to gay men and lesbians against discrimination in employment. Under the proposed rule in the Solomon litigation, however, any expressive association—including huge, multi-billion-dollar organizations like elite private universities—could resist the enforcement of those laws simply by asserting a contrary worldview. If a university were willing to say that it "values" traditional ideas of sexual morality under which homosexuality is unacceptable, then, under the rule proposed by the Solomon plaintiffs, the university could claim a First Amendment right to fire gay or lesbian faculty members, or any other employee. For that matter, such an institution could exclude and expel gay and lesbian students, state law notwithstanding. After all, if the institution's values held homosexuality to be categorically unacceptable, it would surely interfere with their credibility in communicating that message, to the same degree claimed by the Solomon plaintiffs, if they were forced to

---

[53] Title IX, like the Solomon Amendment, operates as a condition upon the receipt of federal funds, and any institution seeking to pursue such a claim might have to grapple with the particular set of requirements associated with spending clause doctrine (U.S. Constitution, Article I, section 8). But the very fact that Title IX would be subject to the threat of a robust First Amendment defense in such cases would constitute a dramatic change. In *Grove City College v. Bell*, 465 U.S. 555 (1984), in contrast, the Court avoided any First Amendment analysis by concluding that individual recipients of federal funds were free to decline them, presenting no threat to First Amendment values. The entirety of the Court's analysis is contained in the following passage:

> Grove City's final challenge to the Court of Appeals' decision—that conditioning federal assistance on compliance with Title IX infringes First Amendment rights of the College and its students—warrants only brief consideration. Congress is free to attach reasonable and unambiguous conditions to federal financial assistance that educational institutions are not obligated to accept. Grove City may terminate its participation in the BEOG program and thus avoid the requirements of § 901(a). Students affected by the Department's action may either take their BEOGs elsewhere or attend Grove City without federal financial assistance. Requiring Grove City to comply with Title IX's prohibition of discrimination as a condition for its continued eligibility to participate in the BEOG program infringes no First Amendment rights of the College or its students.

Id. at 575–76. This dismissive holding clearly could not survive a robust application of *Dale*, and it has questionable continuing vitality in any event due to the passage by Congress of the Civil Rights Restoration Act of 1987, 20 U.S.C. sec. 1987, which overruled *Grove City's* interpretation of Title IX and threatened the withdrawal of federal funds from entire educational institutions when any component or program of the institution engages in discrimination, resulting in significantly greater coercive pressure.

allow gay people to teach, work, and study as members of their community. Similarly, if the university cannot maintain a putatively gay-free environment, how can it "walk the walk" and exemplify its antigay values?

This same set of arguments could be deployed as easily under the Americans with Disabilities Act, or even under laws outlawing racial discrimination. The type of discrimination involved might affect a court's assessment of the state's interest in enforcing its laws. But all antidiscrimination laws would be subject to this form of First Amendment scrutiny, and—as we suggested in deliberately alarmist terms above—perhaps all such laws would be subject to a mandatory constitutional exemption for any organization willing to embrace discriminatory values as a litigation position.[54] The *Dale* decision seemingly opened the door for this catastrophic reconfiguration of the constitutional landscape.[55] That result is one that should be resisted, not embraced.

Indeed, the Supreme Court avoided these dangers in reversing the Third Circuit in *Rumsfeld v. FAIR* (2006), rejecting the law professors' claims and resolving the case very narrowly. "The Solomon Amendment," Chief Justice John Roberts wrote for a unanimous Court, "neither limits what law schools may say nor requires them to say anything,"[56] bringing the case outside the ambit of both expressive association and compelled speech doctrines. For the most part, the Chief Justice distinguished *Dale* by ignoring it. He did not even cite the decision until he took up the forced association claim, which he rejected because "the Solomon Amendment does not force a law school 'to accept members it does not

---

[54] The Supreme Court dismissed an argument along these lines out of hand in *Runyon v. McCrary*, 427 U.S. 160 (1976), where it upheld the constitutionality of the Civil Rights Act as applied to a private school that wished to remain all White and teach principles of segregation and White supremacy. While "it may be assumed that parents have a First Amendment right to send their children to educational institutions that promote the belief that racial segregation is desirable," the Court held, "it does not follow that the practice of excluding racial minorities from such institutions is also protected by the same principle." Id. at 175–76. *Runyon* was decided at a time when the Court's expressive association doctrine was still at an early stage of development, and the brevity of its treatment of the issue in an opinion that was primarily focused on other matters has meant that *Runyon*'s impact in this arena has been limited. Nonetheless, it is difficult to imagine the Court overruling the result in that case.

Members of the Harvard Law School faculty raised a similar set of concerns about the impact of FAIR's arguments on antidiscrimination laws in an *amicus curiae* brief, urging the Supreme Court to confine its ruling to statutory rather than constitutional grounds. See *Rumsfeld v. FAIR*, Brief of Professors William Alford et al., 2006 WL 2367595.

[55] FAIR's response to this threat was to argue that, as a matter of constitutional policy, antidiscrimination laws should continue to prevail even in the face of robust *Dale*-style First Amendment arguments, because discrimination suffers from particular disfavor under the Constitution. See FAIR Main Brief, supra note 7, at 34–35. Of course, this argument did not prevail in the *Dale* case itself.

[56] *Rumsfeld v. Forum for Academic and Institutional Rights [FAIR]*, 547 U.S. 47, 126 S. Ct. 1297, 1307 (2006).

desire' " [57]—perhaps limiting *Dale* (and the *Jaycees* case as well?) to actual interference with membership. Roberts did not even deign to discuss the idea that compliance with an unwelcome law imposed symbolic behavior that would compromise a speaker's credibility or constitute compelled speech—one of the central themes of *Dale*. When he addressed the compelled speech cases, he simply distinguished them with the assertion that, in those cases, the speaker's own message was directly affected because it was forced to accommodate speech.[58] Expressive conduct, the Chief Justice held, is not compelled speech if it is not inherently expressive, as marching in a parade or burning a flag would be.[59]

Thus, at the close of the Solomon litigation, the law of expressive association remains in flux. The Court did not expand the *Dale* decision in the dramatic manner that the law professors had sought, but neither did it impose clear and explicit limitations on *Dale*. Indeed, the one explicit gesture of limitation contained in *Rumsfeld v. FAIR*—the Court's suggestion that interference with membership lies at the heart of the *Dale* doctrine—appears to keep the door open for the litany of consequences regarding the enforcement of equality values explored in the scenarios above. While antidiscrimination laws are apparently not in imminent danger of a fundamental restructuring, their fate under the *Dale* doctrine remains unclear.

B. Equality and speech paradigms in expressive association analysis

The radical nature of the *Dale* decision, and of the effort of the law professors in the Solomon litigation to expand that ruling, was not confined to the decision's impact upon the mechanics of expressive association doctrine. The *Dale* opinion also effectuated a shift in how we conceptualize the involvement of the state in the administration of constitutional claims. That shift moved the boundary between equality and speech paradigms in expressive association analysis. As with the purely doctrinal ramifications of *Dale*, this conceptual revision was both discontinuous with what came before and unsustainable going forward.

An important structural feature of the Court's constitutional equality jurisprudence is its substantive rejection of certain factual or legislative conclusions about different groups. In other words, the Court has found that the equal protection clause of the Fourteenth Amendment and its Fifth Amendment correlate simply "take off the table" certain factual or

---

[57] Id. at 1312, quoting *Dale*, 530 U.S. at 648 (which in turn was quoting *Jaycees*, 468 U.S. at 623).

[58] *Rumsfeld v. FAIR*, 126 S. Ct. at 1307–10.

[59] This unsatisfying explanation leaves in place *Dale*'s nasty suggestion that the inclusion of a gay member is inherently expressive (and hence raises First Amendment problems that are particular to gay people), but at least the Court's opinion did not give any further credence to that idea.

legislative conclusions. In the case of laws that classify on the basis of race, for example, the Court has categorically rejected the conclusion that non-White people are inherently inferior in their intellectual capacities to Caucasians. With respect to gender discrimination, the Court has categorically rejected the conclusion that women have an inherent predisposition for certain roles in society or the workplace, or that women have "delicate sensibilities" that must be protected from full participation in public life. It does not matter if the legislature reaches these prohibited conclusions "in good faith," nor even if there is empirical evidence to support them in particular contexts. Even so, these conclusions are "off the table," categorically unavailable as a basis for regulation.

This feature of equal protection jurisprudence is independent of, and in addition to, the classic definition of "heightened" or "strict" scrutiny, which focuses upon state interests, narrow tailoring, and least restrictive means of regulation. Thus, even if a legislature has a compelling reason for adopting a race or gender classification and tailors its law narrowly to effectuate that purpose, its regulation is still invalid if the classification rests upon one of these substantively impermissible factual conclusions about a protected group, regardless of the empirical support for the conclusion.

An important structural feature of the Court's free speech jurisprudence, in contrast, is its near-absolute deference to, and protection of, the opinions of private speakers, even when the state believes that it has good reason for disagreeing with those opinions. In other words, the Court has categorically prohibited the state from restricting speech that is otherwise protected simply because the state disagrees with the opinions, conclusions, or premises of that speech. This is even true—indeed, especially so—in the case of speech that rests on factual premises that the state itself rejects. Thus, it is a particular point of pride for the Court that it gives undiminished protection to "unpopular" speech like that of the Ku Klux Klan, even though that speech is often founded upon the very conclusions—about inherent White gentile supremacy, in the case of the KKK—that the Court has rendered unavailable when the state seeks to craft its own regulations.

The expressive association cases have always operated at the interface of these two opposing jurisprudential forces. In part, such claims are about speech and the creation of meaning. In the paradigm expressive association case, a group of speakers, operating as an association, claims that the content and credibility of their speech is being compromised by intrusive state regulations, usually in the form of laws that forbid discrimination in membership or hiring. The group offers an account of its distinctive message and its preferred mode of expression in communicating that message, an account that places the identity of its speakers and representatives at center stage. In this respect, an expressive association argument makes powerful claims upon the presumption of inviolability that has surrounded the speaker's prerogative to select the mode and vernacular of his chosen message since early in the modern free speech era.[60]

But expressive association claims are also partly about equality values — about groups and the popular perception of their status in society. The particular form of intrusion at issue in an expressive association case is not a direct interference with the association's choice of words and arguments. Rather, such cases involve indirect interference. An expressive association claim generally asserts that the conditions created by the forced inclusion of a group of individuals whom the claimant would prefer to exclude (or any other challenged law) make it difficult or impossible for the association to convey its message with the same meaning, efficacy, and credibility as it could in the absence of state regulation.

The plaintiff in such a case calls upon the court to accept the speaker's own assessment of the social meaning that will attach to the inclusion of the disputed group. He argues for a particular account of the social status of a group in the public mind. In this respect, an expressive association claim appears to inscribe itself within the continuing constitutional discussion about the assumptions that it is and is not permissible for institutions of the state to make about the social roles that different groups occupy. An expressive association claim, in others words, seeks to measure the impact of membership and admission ("equality" issues) upon the content and meaning of a message ("speech" issues) in light of the belief system that the association believes to be held by the audience of private individuals that it is trying to reach.

The Supreme Court offered an account of that impact in its ruling in the *Jaycees* case. In this respect, the significance of *Jaycees* extends well beyond its restatement of the purely doctrinal elements of the law of expressive association for second-generation claims. The case also offers the clearest articulation of the relationship between speech values and equality values, and of the boundary between courts as detached protectors of private preferences, on one side, and as engaged participants in the elevation of private prejudices to legal proscriptions, on the other.

Recall that *Jaycees* involved the desire of the U.S. Jaycees to exclude women as full voting members from their organization and to keep them as only partial participants. The Jaycees claimed that they wished to communicate a distinctively "male" message and that the admission of women as fully enfranchised members would change the nature of their message. They based that claim upon their own set of views about two

---

[60] See, e.g., *Cohen v. California*, 403 U.S. 15 (1971) (holding that political protestors retain the right to choose their mode of expression, even when they use offensive or tasteless terms to do so); and *Hustler Magazine v. Falwell*, 485 U.S. 46 (1988) (rejecting "outrageousness" exception to protected status of political and social commentary). For an extended analysis of the potential relationship between the identity of a speaker and the meaning of the message that the speaker conveys, see Wolff, "Political Representation and Accountability under Don't Ask, Don't Tell."

distinct but related matters: their beliefs about the attitudes that women generally exhibit, and their assumptions about the manner in which female speakers generally are perceived by an audience. In analyzing this speech claim, the Court was forced to determine how to assess the premises and conclusions underlying the Jaycees' perception of their own message—premises and conclusions that would be forbidden to the state if it sought to use them as the basis of its own regulations. Were such beliefs purely a part of the Jaycees' definition of their message, and hence not subject to reexamination by a court? Or were they a component of the Jaycees' legal claim for relief that would require the complicity of a court, rendering them subject to the limitations arising out of the Supreme Court's equality jurisprudence?

The *Jaycees* Court embraced the latter answer. It found that, while the Jaycees' speech and message were their own, the assumptions that the Jaycees wished the Court to adopt concerning the relationship between identity and communicative impact were subject to independent review and must be scrutinized in light of the substantive limitations bound up in the Court's equality jurisprudence. In reaching this conclusion, the Court drew upon a seemingly out-of-place precedent, but one that, upon reflection, should not be at all surprising: *Palmore v. Sidoti* (1984).[61] *Palmore* is the leading case in the Court's equality jurisprudence for the proposition that courts cannot enforce or confer approval upon private prejudices when entertaining claims for relief or judicial assistance. The relevant passage from *Jaycees* is worth quoting at length in order to capture the interplay of equality and speech values at this key analytical juncture:

> While acknowledging that "the specific content of most of the resolutions adopted over the years by the Jaycees has nothing to do with sex," 709 F.2d, at 1571, the Court of Appeals nonetheless entertained the hypothesis that women members might have a different view or agenda with respect to these matters so that, if they are allowed to vote, "some change in the Jaycees' philosophical cast can reasonably be expected," ibid. It is similarly arguable that, insofar as the Jaycees is organized to promote the views of young men whatever those views happen to be, admission of women as voting members will change the message communicated by the group's speech because of the gender-based assumptions of the audience. Neither supposition, however, is supported by the record. In claiming that women might have a different attitude about such issues as the federal budget, school prayer, voting rights, and foreign relations, see id. at 1570, or that the organization's public positions would have a different effect if the group were not "a purely young men's association," the Jaycees

---

[61] *Palmore v. Sidoti*, 466 U.S. 429 (1984).

relies solely on unsupported generalizations about the relative interests and perspectives of men and women. See Brief for Appellee 20–22, and n. 3. *Although such generalizations may or may not have a statistical basis in fact with respect to particular positions adopted by the Jaycees, we have repeatedly condemned legal decisionmaking that relies uncritically on such assumptions. See, e.g., Palmore v. Sidoti, 466 U.S. 429, 433–434, 104 S.Ct. 1879, 80 L.Ed.2d 421 (1984).* In the absence of a showing far more substantial than that attempted by the Jaycees, we decline to indulge in the sexual stereotyping that underlies appellee's contention that, by allowing women to vote, application of the Minnesota Act will change the content or impact of the organization's speech.[62]

The *Jaycees* Court makes a clear choice here in defining the juridical category within which expressive association claims will operate. The stage of analysis that examines the relationship between membership and communicative impact in such a claim is a component of "legal decisionmaking" and hence is the province of the court, not the private speaker. It is therefore subject to the substantive limitations that equality principles impose upon governmental action. Under *Jaycees*, an identifiable, tangible interference with a group's ability to communicate its message is necessary in order to make out an expressive association claim. Reliance on stereotyped assumptions about the attitudes possessed by a group, or the way in which that group will be perceived, is impermissible not merely because such stereotypes may be flawed as a factual matter but also because they involve the court in an impermissible mode of decision-making.

This feature of the *Jaycees* doctrine bears a deep structural relationship to the varied formulations of the state action doctrine. The administration of legal rules within a constitutional framework always raises questions about the degree of intimacy with which the state can become involved in enforcing private actions that would be forbidden to the state itself—a dilemma that is most notably exemplified in the American constitutional tradition by *Shelley v. Kraemer* (1948),[63] where the Court found racially restrictive covenants in contracts for the sale of real estate to be constitutionally unenforceable. As Professor Louis Henkin wrote in his classic treatment of that case:

The question . . . is not whether a state has "acted," but whether its role in the circumstances has denied equal protection—whether because of the character of state involvement, or the relation of the

---

[62] *Jaycees*, 468 U.S. at 627–28 (emphasis added).
[63] *Shelley v. Kraemer*, 334 U.S. 1 (1948).

state to the private acts in issue, there has been a denial for which the state should be held responsible.[64]

Professor Henkin is speaking here of the enforcement of private acts of discrimination by facially neutral rules, which can sometimes involve the state too intimately in the perpetuation of inequality. But the same dilemma is posed by the enforcement of private discriminatory attitudes within the administration of facially neutral constitutional doctrines. In both circumstances, the state is asked to become a participant in the endorsement, validation, or vigorous enforcement of actions or views that derogate from its larger constitutional commitments.[65] When the Supreme Court ruled in *Palmore v. Sidoti* that it would not give weight to private racial prejudices in the administration of a family law system, it was carrying forward a constitutional policy that it had already articulated in its more traditional state action cases. Similarly, when the *Jaycees* Court incorporated the *Palmore* ruling into the element of expressive association analysis that requires plaintiffs to make a factual showing of the interference that they claim with their speech activities, and forbade them from relying upon broad stereotypes or prejudicial private attitudes for that purpose, it was making a consistent statement of constitutional policy. In both contexts, the Court has forbidden the state from directly endorsing, validating, or giving vigorous enforcement to private attitudes that derogate from important constitutional values.

The *Dale* Court significantly disrupted this consistent statement of constitutional policy. In embracing its posture of almost complete deference in the analysis of expressive association claims, the majority in *Dale* shifted

---

[64] Louis Henkin, "*Shelley v. Kraemer*: Notes for a Revised Opinion," *University of Pennsylvania Law Review* 110 (1962): 473, 481.

Professor Charles Black offered another much-noted account of state action, this one more trenchant and polemical, that takes similar aim at any effort to define state action with bright, formal analytical lines:

> The "state action" concept [in the field of equal protection] has just one practical function; if and where it works, it immunizes racist practices from constitutional control. . . . If it were impelled by anything in authority, or in the nature of the issues arising in life, that were perhaps another matter, but the very contradictory is true on both scores. Such a formula, whatever its foresightedness in statement, would decide in advance hundreds of classes of cases, without focal consideration of the issues they will raise. As long as the "state action" concept is looked to, even pro forma, for significant limitations, it will either remain vague and ambiguous or become arbitrary, losing correspondence to the varieties of life. At this stage of the game, as racism runs about searching for a sheltered place, solution is to be sought not in the clarification of "lines" now vague, but in a radical shift in approach, attitude, and expectation—a shift which one may hope will move the entire profession.

Charles L. Black, Jr., "Foreword: 'State Action,' Equal Protection, and California's Proposition 14," *Harvard Law Review* 81 (1967): 69, 90–91.

[65] See also *Reitman v. Mulkey*, 387 U.S. 369 (1967) (striking down a facially neutral California law that authorized acts of private discrimination in housing sales because the law involved the state too intimately in the validation and encouragement of that discrimination).

the examination of the relationship between state regulation and communicative impact to the province of the individual speaker. It made that analysis a "private" speech matter rather than a question of legal decision-making constrained by equality values. In so doing, the majority authorized courts to endorse, validate, and give vigorous enforcement to private discriminatory attitudes in a manner that it had previously found to be forbidden to the institutions of the state.

In this respect, *Dale* cannot be rehabilitated by observing that the particular context in which the claim arose—an entity that operates primarily on a local scale, engages in quintessentially noncommercial activities, and so forth—might serve as a doctrinal basis for distinguishing the holding in future cases. *Dale* effectuated a conceptual shift, and an important one, in the manner in which such claims will be administered in every context. Following *Dale*, private prejudice and offensive stereotypes appear to be a component of the "deference" that courts must give "to an association's view of what would impair its expression."[66] That license on the part of courts to validate private prejudice constitutes an alteration in constitutional policy that is potentially bound up with the doctrine of state action in every context.

The plaintiffs in the Solomon litigation sought to extend this pernicious component of *Dale* as well, entrenching it as part of the broader restatement of expressive association doctrine that they read that case to effectuate. Without qualification or caveat, FAIR embraced the breathtaking account of "*Dale* deference" contained in the opinion of the Third Circuit and urged that it be applied to every case in which an institution claims that its value system is being burdened by state regulation. Such an amplification of *Dale* would have resulted in immense practical and normative damage to equality values.

In rejecting that effort, *Rumsfeld v. FAIR* might be understood to have limited the doctrinal consequences of *Dale*'s paradigm shift to cases where the claimed interference with an association's expression results from an interference with its control over membership. (Recall that Chief Justice Roberts explained his rejection of the plaintiffs' "*Dale* deference" argument by pointing out that the Solomon Amendment did not compel any law school "to accept members it does not desire.")[67] This is small comfort, however, since judicial deference to private prejudice or stereotype is likely to be most damaging in the context of membership disputes, where it is precisely the social status of disfavored groups that is at issue. The pernicious influence of *Dale* survives any gesture of limitation that one might read into *Rumsfeld v. FAIR*, inviting courts into a much more active and intimate partnership with the private prejudices of expressive association claimants than *Jaycees* had permitted.

---

[66] *Dale*, 530 U.S. at 653.
[67] *Rumsfeld v. FAIR*, 126 S. Ct. at 1312 (quotation marks omitted).

IV. The Solomon Litigation and the Ideal of the University

Beyond all the discussion of constitutional doctrine and conceptual framing—important as those matters are—there is a more basic critique of the Solomon litigation that it is important to articulate. That critique operates on the level of ethics, responsibility, and institutional self-definition. In seeking to promote the welfare of their gay, lesbian, and bisexual students, the faculty and institutions who initiated these suits set forth a vision of their own role, and of the expressive environment of a law school, that is fundamentally at odds with the values and ideals that should guide the mission of a university.

To understand the significance of the Solomon litigation for the ideal of the university, it is necessary to begin with a basic question: On whose behalf were these lawsuits brought? Any nonlawyer (indeed, any non-specialist) would be forgiven for assuming that the gay, lesbian, and bisexual law students who served as the rhetorical justification for these suits were also the individuals whose rights were formally being invoked. That assumption, however, would be incorrect. The Solomon lawsuits were brought on behalf of law professors. It was the rights of faculty members that lay at the foundation of these suits, and around which their arguments were structured.[68] What right were the law faculty members asserting? The right to express their own views about inclusion and affirmation of LGBT students, a right that they claimed was jeopardized by the periodic presence of military recruiters. The Solomon litigation, in other words, was an occasion for law faculty to take a formal position on the manner in which they engage in their own expression, along with the conditions that they require to do so successfully.

Recall that the specific nature of the threat to their expression that the law professors claimed was twofold. First, they argued that the presence of the JAG recruiters in the job fair process, refusing to conform with the school's nondiscrimination policy, would undermine their credibility in expressing support for their LGBT students and compromise their ability to communicate a message of inclusion. Second, the law professors emphasized the fact that recruiters brought along their own message when they participated in the job fair—a message that expressly lauded the virtues of a military career and, by implication, reaffirmed the legitimacy and wisdom of the policy that excluded gay students from that profession. The *FAIR* plaintiffs, in particular, emphasized the gravity of this second threat. The presence of JAG recruiters, bringing with them a message that

---

[68] The University of Pennsylvania suit (supra note 12) was the only one that included students as parties and attempted to assert student rights. Tellingly, the district court found that "the students and the student organization are not the proper parties to bring the associational claim because the Law School faculty here sets the rules of association by resolution," and, "[s]imilarly, the claim of injury to the ability to convey the Law School policy of anti-discrimination belongs to the faculty, not to the students or student group." *Burbank*, 2004 WL 1925532, at *3.

diverged so fundamentally from the beliefs of the law faculty, formed the vital core of their argument about threats to the law professors' ability to express themselves effectively.[69]

It is worth taking a moment to restate these arguments in the plainest language possible, in order to emphasize the nature of the claims that the law professors were making in their constitutional challenges to the Solomon Amendment. They asserted:

(1) We cannot express ourselves effectively as faculty members when there are people in our community who refuse to act in conformity with our system of beliefs. We need to be able to exclude such nonconforming behavior in order to be effective speakers.

(2) We cannot express ourselves effectively as faculty members when there are people in our community who propound ideas that conflict with our system of beliefs. We need to be able to exclude such divergent viewpoints in order to be effective speakers.

We dare say that, when viewed without the elaborate doctrinal and rhetorical apparatus of the Solomon litigation to surround them, these statements would be shocking to most academics, and properly so.

A university does not merely prepare young adults to become professionals, though that is unquestionably an important part of its mission. A university is an institution devoted to teaching young adults how to think.[70] This is no less true of a law school, despite its focused institutional affiliation with one particular profession. Faculty members undertake their work within an ethical framework that calls for a strong commitment to critical rigor. That rigor must include a willingness to test one's ideas against strong expressions of disagreement.

In the modern university, faculty members are given elaborate forms of institutional protection in order to facilitate this ethical and intellectual vocation. The most frequently identified of these protections is tenure, which gives those academics who receive it nearly absolute job protection when they choose to pursue a scholarly or expressive agenda that is

---

[69] See FAIR Main Brief, supra note 7, at 1–5 (emphasizing introduction of government message into job fair); and id. at 33–35 (same). The lawyer for FAIR began his presentation to the Court by framing the issue in the following terms: "This case is not about whether military recruiters will be barred at the campus gates. Congress had a law on the books that guaranteed entry to campus, but that was not what Congress really wanted. So, it passed a new law. What Congress really wants is to squelch even the most symbolic elements of the law schools' resistance to disseminating the military's message, which is why it gave us the current version of the statute. The current version isolates for regulation the most communicative aspects of the law schools' resistance" (2005 WL 3387694, at 28–29).

[70] This characterization of the function of a university, and the discussion that follows, are influenced to some extent by the noted discussion of the philosopher Robert Paul Wolff in his 1969 volume on the subject. See Robert Paul Wolff, *The Ideal of the University* (Boston, MA: Beacon Press, 1969).

controversial or unpopular.[71] But tenure is not the only such protection, and it may not even be the most important. The credentialing effect of the title "Professor" is of inestimable discursive value. There must surely be few academics who have not been amazed to discover how much more credibility and weight their opinions are afforded when they are identified as "Professor So-and-So"—and, better still, when they are described as an "expert" in a particular field. While that deference is no doubt deserved in many cases, it is frequently a product of the office and the credentialing effect that it carries, not the audience's ability to make an independent and confident assessment of the qualifications that underlie the speaker's opinions. Of similar importance is the effect of the podium. Social and institutional rules define academics as the ultimate authority in shaping discussion within the classroom and proclaiming upon the value of ideas there. That authority inevitably translates outside the classroom to the larger university environment. In some sense, faculty members carry a virtual podium with them whenever they navigate around the campus community. In these and many other respects, academics are extremely powerful speakers.

This position of extraordinary privilege can only be justified if faculty members use it to further the intellectual mission of the university: the expansion of knowledge and understanding through the creation of an environment in which individuals can grapple with diverse ideas and subject them to critical analysis. Stated in such terms, this account of the university and the position that faculty occupy within it is one with which few academics would be likely to disagree. But this ideal of the university is realized, not just in a shared account of its abstract definition, but also in the manner in which it is implemented. It is in this regard that the Solomon litigation—well intentioned though it may have been—went seriously astray.

There is every reason for law schools to enforce regulations that prohibit employers who discriminate against their LGBT students from participating in on-campus job fairs. The discrimination is reprehensible, and it is highly desirable for faculty to take active steps to combat that behavior, whether through policies that seek to pressure employers into reforming or through other means.[72] But it is another matter entirely for faculty

---

[71] The tenure system was an innovation of the mid-twentieth century and came largely in response to vicious forms of recrimination that some academics faced for politically unpopular ideas during the Red Scare and McCarthy eras. See generally Christopher Jencks and David Riesman, *The Academic Revolution* (Garden City, NY: Doubleday, 1968) (discussing the evolution of the university in twentieth-century America).

[72] Judge Posner does not contribute to the debate when he refers to the efforts of law schools to enforce antidiscrimination policies as themselves constituting "discrimination." See Posner, "A Note on *Rumsfeld v. FAIR* and the Legal Academy," 49: "All [the] largesse [of extra assistance from the placement office] is denied to military recruiters and other employers who do not promise not to discriminate against homosexuals. The law schools are discriminating against such recruiters." To reduce the word "discriminate" to a thin,

members to suggest that their own ability to communicate their views and their values will be compromised by the presence of discriminatory recruiters twice a year at commercial job fairs. That suggestion is an unworthy denial of the position of privilege and responsibility that faculty occupy in their expressive lives.

More unworthy still is the suggestion that faculty must have the right to exclude divergent viewpoints from their environment in order to protect their own ability to express themselves. It represents an act of embarrassing self-deprecation for faculty to assert that their ideas are not robust enough to find effective expression when confronted with disagreement, and it represents a betrayal of the institutional function of a university to attempt to elevate that self-deprecation to a statement of official university policy. Even if these assertions constituted a potential avenue for victory following the *Dale* decision—indeed, even if one were to take the view that *Dale* is a correct statement of the law and should be available as a doctrinal weapon to any association willing to articulate the views necessary to invoke its protections—this is not an avenue that the academy should have chosen.[73]

It is probably the case that many faculty members did not fully understand the nature of the arguments that were being made in their names in the Solomon litigation. Even among law professors, only those who specialize in the Constitution and free speech are likely to appreciate the precise nature of the doctrinal claims that *Jaycees* and *Dale*

---

generic term for any form of differential treatment and then make the implicit suggestion that there is some parity between the military's abusive treatment of gay and lesbian servicemembers and the law schools' response to that abusive treatment seems almost willfully perverse.

[73] We therefore disagree with the license that Judge Posner implicitly extends to members of the legal academy to behave like "any other litigant" when they are parties to a lawsuit urging constitutional claims. In criticizing the statutory arguments made by the Harvard faculty in their *amicus* brief in the *FAIR* case, Judge Posner draws a contrast with the standards of behavior that might have applied to the Harvard faculty had they been acting as litigants rather than expert *amici*. He writes:

> A lawyer whom you hire to represent you can in perfect good faith make any argument on your behalf that is not downright frivolous. But the [Harvard] professors were not parties to *Rumsfeld v. FAIR* and so a reader of their amicus curiae brief might expect the views expressed in it to represent their best professional judgment on the meaning of the Solomon Amendment. The brief identifies them as full-time faculty members of the Harvard Law School rather than as concerned citizens, and one expects law professors when speaking *ex cathedra* as it were to be expressing their true belief rather than making any old argument that they think might have a 5 percent chance of persuading a court.

Posner, "A Note on *Rumsfeld v. FAIR* and the Legal Academy," 52. There is a considerable distance between that which is legally or ethically permissible and that which is desirable or admirable. To suggest that law professors should not be held to a higher standard than "any other litigant" in the choice of arguments that they press as litigants, without regard for intellectual integrity or potential impact upon larger systemic values, is to embrace an unfortunate measure of cynicism about the norms of the profession. It is not only when members of the academy are "speaking *ex cathedra*" that those norms are important.

require a plaintiff to assert in order to invoke the associational protections of the First Amendment. Be that as it may, however, the Solomon litigation purported to represent the collective voice of the legal academy in articulating, not just a commitment to support and affirm LGBT students, but a statement of self-definition and institutional values.[74] It will require time, introspection, and a degree of humility for the academy to recover from the portions of that statement that were so poorly chosen.

V. Conclusion

Form eclipsed proper function in the Solomon lawsuits. A set of First Amendment doctrines, articulated with overbroad language in a poorly written and wrongly decided Supreme Court opinion, appeared to provide a prefabricated toolkit that could deliver victory in a litigation effort. It is fortunate—for the coherence and sustainability of our First Amendment jurisprudence and for the academy itself—that the effort failed. Though undertaken in good faith, the constitutional challenges to the Solomon Amendment led many in the legal academy to endorse an account of their own institutional commitments that few faculty members would be happy with if considered in a broader context.

When the First Amendment leads to such distortions, it is a sign that something is amiss in that complex web of doctrines. Perhaps the saga of Solomon will provide the impetus for a reexamination of the pernicious and unsustainable decision that led the academy down this path. Let us hope so. If the Solomon litigation ultimately contributes to the overthrow of *Dale,* it will be able to claim a measure of redemption.

Law, University of Pennsylvania
Law and Political Science, Northwestern University

---

[74] When the Supreme Court decided to review the Third Circuit's decision in *FAIR,* Professor Wolff published an op-ed essay in which he levied criticisms similar to the ones developed in this essay. See Tobias Barrington Wolff, "'Don't Ask, Don't Tell' Harms the Constitution, but So Does This Cure," *Los Angeles Times* (May 15, 2005). To the authors' knowledge, this was the only prominent public statement by a member of the academy generally identified as liberal or progressive expressing opposition to the arguments that were pressed in the Solomon cases, prior to the Supreme Court litigation itself.

SHOULD ANTIDISCRIMINATION LAWS LIMIT FREEDOM OF ASSOCIATION? THE DANGEROUS ALLURE OF HUMAN RIGHTS LEGISLATION*

By Richard A. Epstein

I. Introduction

In this essay I plan to explore, from my classical liberal perspective, the role that freedom of association plays in organizing political and social institutions. The essay is organized as follows. Section II deals with the intellectual preliminaries by defining the principle of freedom of association. It also explains how that principle works within both the libertarian and the classical liberal positions. Finally, it shows how, in the latter, but not the former, an antidiscrimination norm has a vital but limited role to play as a strategy to counteract private monopoly power.

Section III offers two concrete illustrations of how the freedom of association norm clashes with the antidiscrimination norm in circumstances devoid of any monopoly power. One illustration examines the extent to which private "expressive" organizations are able, under modern American constitutional law, to obtain protection against the antidiscrimination norm. This illustration contrasts two associational claims based on the First Amendment. One involves the First Amendment associational right of the NAACP to keep its membership lists out of the hands of the Attorney General of Alabama during the civil rights movement, as articulated in the well-known decision of *NAACP v. Alabama*. The other claim involves the ultimately successful efforts of the Boy Scouts to invoke their First Amendment freedom of association to exclude gay scoutmasters. The second illustration in Section III examines the inability of organizations to protect against the antidiscrimination norm in situations where First Amendment expressive rights are not in play. Here I focus on the failure of free association claims against the 1990 Americans with Disabilities Act. In dealing with this range of expressive and nonexpressive claims, I argue that the classical liberal theory of freedom of association leads to better and more consistent social outcomes insofar as it protects all types of associations from the application of the antidiscrimination norm, whether these associations are "expressive" or "nonexpressive."

Once the particular case studies are completed, Section IV of this essay undertakes a more general overview of the antidiscrimination laws, and

* My thanks to Uzair Kayani for his valuable research assistance on this paper.

doi:10.1017/S0265052508080217

attacks their positive self-description as "human rights" legislation. I contend that this label is more appropriately given to the earlier version of civil rights laws that guarantee full civil capacity to make contracts than to antidiscrimination rules that impose differential burdens on one side of such familiar relationships as employer/employee or landlord/tenant. I then document some of the unfortunate, and often overlooked, consequences of the modern version of human rights laws: their retreat from universal legal norms; their concealment of correlative duties; their unfortunate effect on affirmative action programs; and their systematic effect of reducing the information on and transparency of labor and other markets.

Section V discusses the relationship between law and popular opinion, and argues that in many cases a dominant social consensus counts as a good reason *not* to enact legislation.

Finally, Section VI closes with a much revamped human rights statute that better comports with classical liberal principles and offers the best of all possible worlds: greater levels of individual freedom; more equality among persons; higher levels of social productivity; less government intrusion; and lower administrative costs.

II. Preliminaries

A. Freedom of association as a species of freedom of contract

The principle of freedom of association has a long and storied history in both legal and political discourse. This principle holds that each person has the right to associate, or not to associate, with any other person or persons, for good reason, bad reason, or no reason at all. The major advantage of freedom of association is that the rule facilitates the creation of complex social institutions that are generated by the repeated application of the same generative principle.[1] Accordingly, once two or more individuals decide to associate with each other, they may exercise in combination the same right to do or not do business with any other person or group of persons. Small groups can thus form larger ones, just as larger ones can recognize special divisions within themselves. This traditional model still holds for all different types of contract: if two or more people contract to form a relationship (commercial or otherwise), an outsider may not deliberately interfere with their relationship. This simple contract model facilitates a variety of socially and

---

[1] See generally Robert Nozick, *Anarchy, State, and Utopia* (New York: Basic Books, 1974), 151. Nozick makes the point explicitly when he notes that his entitlement theory allows for claims to arise in accordance with (1) the principle of justice in acquisition and (2) the principle of justice in transfer, and "by (repeated) applications of 1 and 2." Nozick is wrong to conclude that these principles represent the only legitimate way to acquire entitlements, such that acquisition through forced exchanges is precluded. See Richard A. Epstein, "One Step Beyond Nozick's Minimal State: The Role of Forced Exchanges in Political Theory," *Social Philosophy and Policy* 22, no. 1 (2005): 286–313.

economically productive transactions. By definition, any voluntary trans-action excludes—or discriminates against—all nonparties to that trans-action. Under the standard legal theory, the secret to social welfare is to increase the velocity of transactions by reducing the transaction costs that stand in the way of mutual gain through voluntary association.[2]

B. The freedom of association in libertarian and classical liberal theories

The principle of freedom of association has been under heavy attack since the rise of the New Deal; critics view the principle as creating major opportunities for the illicit exclusion of some individuals from some vol-untary organizations. For the moment, I want to put aside this frontal assault on the principle of freedom of association to concentrate on two conflicting accounts of this principle, namely, the libertarian and classical liberal conceptions of freedom of association.[3] The difference here is impor-tant because the qualified classical liberal acceptance of freedom of asso-ciation is able to meet criticisms that look more plausible when leveled against the more uncompromising libertarian version.

Strong libertarian theory, such as that developed in Robert Nozick's *Anarchy, State, and Utopia*, does not allow for any use of forced exchanges via taxation or eminent domain. As such, it places few limitations on the application of the freedom of association principle. The most important limitation is that associations—now called conspiracies—that intend to use force or fraud against third persons can be punished in their own right, even if they have not achieved their goals. But that principle rests on the same narrow conception of a harmful externality that lies behind the basic libertarian theory, which places a prohibition on force and fraud because of the damage they do to other individuals.

Classical liberal theory also gives strong support to the principle of freedom of association, but hedges it in with two further exceptions, relating to the law of antitrust and common carriers—both of which pertain to the use of monopoly power. That focus should not be surpris-ing, since any theory of limited government starts with the objective of controlling the monopoly power that the state enjoys over the use of force within its territory.[4] The usual response to the monopoly problem is not to debar the state from acting at all, nor to prevent it from singling out individuals for punishment, fines, and prohibitions because they have committed a wrong involving force or fraud. Every coherent theory of government power accepts at least a version of the police power that

---

[2] See Ronald H. Coase, "The Problem of Social Cost," *Journal of Law and Economics* 3 (1960): 1–44.

[3] For further elaboration, see Richard A. Epstein, *Free Markets Under Siege: Cartels, Politics, and Social Welfare* (Stanford, CA: Hoover Institution Press, 2005), 12–16.

[4] See Max Weber, "Politics as a Vocation," in *Max Weber: Essays in Sociology* (New York: Oxford University Press, 1946), 77–128.

permits some state control over the use of property and the exercise of liberty in order to protect "safety, health, morals, and general welfare of the public."[5] But with respect to its general commands, the classical liberal position seeks to work its way between two extremes—the first a system that requires unanimous consent, and the second a system that relies solely on majority will. The first system creates the risk of political paralysis, and the second the risk of factional domination of minority interests.[6] One—I dare say the best—solution to this is to allow the majority to call the shots so long as it is bound, under a nondiscrimination principle, to the same obligations as the minority; this is a position that often expresses itself in the ideal of equal justice before the law.[7]

I will not attempt here to work out the implications of classical liberalism for the design of government on such vital issues as federalism and separation of powers. But I think the classical liberal view helps us understand why private monopolies will generate at least some concern, even if they cannot use force against other individuals. In this connection, the most sensible application of the antitrust laws forbids horizontal associations among competitors that are intended to restrict output and raise prices. Here the simplest remedy is to require each firm to act as a stand-alone competitor. The situation becomes cloudy, however, with firms in markets that are incapable of division, so that no competitive market solution is available. The key historical illustration of these "natural monopolies" was the common carrier, a large and important category, generally neglected in philosophical writings, which could include stagecoaches, inns, railroads, telecommunication networks, and internet operating systems. Although modern technology has reduced the number of settings in which firms can exert monopoly power,[8] in earlier eras the dominant position of inns, coaches, railroads, and telephone companies brought forth a legal regime that made refusals to deal prima facie unlawful, and imposed a duty on the common carrier to deal with all comers on reasonable and nondiscriminatory terms.

Yet beware of the crucial limitations. That duty never applied in simple two-party transactions. The common carrier rule only limited the refusal to deal in select cases. It never limited the ordinary rights of property

---

[5] For a narrow account of the police power, see, e.g., *Lochner v. New York*, 198 U.S. 45, 53 (1905). For the classic account, see Ernst Freund, *The Police Power: Public Policy and Constitutional Rights* (Chicago: Callaghan & Co., 1904), who defined the police power as "the power of promoting the public welfare by restraining and regulating the use of liberty and property."

[6] For a classic account of the problem of factions, see Publius, *The Federalist Papers*, ed. Jim Manis (Hazleton: Pennsylvania State University Electronic Classics Series, 2001), No. 10: 41–46.

[7] For a detailed defense of this position, see Richard A. Epstein, *Takings: Private Property and the Power of Eminent Domain* (Cambridge, MA: Harvard University Press, 1985), chap. 1 (working out the implications of a system that allows for takings with just compensation).

[8] For a discussion of the complex matters of remedy and liability, see Richard A. Epstein, *Why More Is Less: A Historical Study of Antitrust Consent Decrees* (Washington, DC: American Enterprise Institute, 2007).

owners to exclude others from their land, clubs, or vehicles. To warrant either forced association or forced entry—and the two are intimately linked—two conditions have to be satisfied simultaneously. First, the firm must enjoy some monopoly control, which derives either from a state franchise or some physical configuration that creates a natural monopoly, such as a harbor with room for only one dock company.[9] Second, the firm's activities must involve the dispensation of routine and fungible services that in no way turn on the distinctive characteristics of the party who receives them. Phone companies do not have professional or intimate relations with their individual customers. Any customer that follows the rules and pays the stipulated rates is entitled to service. The electric, water, and gas companies fall under the same basic regime. And in earlier days the same applied to innkeepers and railroads, neither of which holds monopoly power today, save perhaps in some niche markets.

The traditional common carrier rule on required service sought to steer a middle path between two extremes.[10] The first extreme was arbitrary price discrimination. The common carrier rule's prohibition against discrimination guarded against allowing firms to charge differential rates to two customers who received the same class of service. There is a spirited disagreement as to whether this principle is preferable to price discrimination, which has two advantages over uniform rates. In some cases at least, price discrimination allows back into the marketplace individuals who could afford to pay less than a uniform monopoly price for services, but only if high demanders are charged higher prices to pick up the shortfall in revenue. The overall mix of prices could be revenue-neutral to the firm. Or price discrimination could allow the firm to recover additional revenues and thereby encourage more rapid entry of new businesses into the market. This form of price discrimination, if left unregulated, allows firms to use their pricing power to achieve collateral "advantages," including discrimination on such questionable grounds as political affiliation, personal connections, and race. The strategy can work because the customer has no other provider to turn to for the same service. Thus, the usual compromise is to permit certain distinctions over *classes* of service (e.g., business and residential phone services), but not among individual customers within these categories.

The second extreme was arbitrary wealth redistribution. The classical regimes of public regulation were *not* redistribution schemes designed to make one class of customers richer at the expense of another. To prevent that redistribution from happening, the nondiscrimination principle, understood in economic terms, *requires* rate differentials to reflect differences in

---

[9] See, e.g., *Allnut v. Inglis,* 104 Eng. Rep. 206 (K.B. 1810) (recognizing the obligation to serve the "public interest" for both legal and situational monopolies). I discuss the case at length in Richard A. Epstein, *Principles of a Free Society: Reconciling Individual Liberty and the Common Good* (Boston, MA: Addison-Wesley, 1998), 279–86.

[10] *Western Union Telegraph Co. v. Call Publishing Co.,* 181 U.S. 92, 98 (1901).

the cost of providing services. That result always holds in competitive markets. No life insurance company, for example, can charge the same premium to two individuals in different risk categories. Faced with that strategy, the low-cost customer would go elsewhere: the insurer stands to lose money by selling insurance priced at some blended rate, but only to the high-risk customer. To prevent this adverse selection, the insurer charges different premiums to customers in different risk categories. That option is not available to regulated firms without any exit right because a firm requires the approval of some state commission before it is allowed to withdraw, either in whole or in part, from business. Accordingly, a regulator may easily require the firm to serve one class of customers at below cost, while charging higher rates to customers in other classes. Customers in the second group subsidize customers in the first group, as happens today routinely with the heavy business subsidies of residential phone service. The overall system therefore seeks to minimize the economic and political distortions that arise whenever individuals or firms are forced into win/lose arrangements. Sound forms of common carrier regulation work, over time, to avoid both monopoly profits and ruinous cross-subsidies. Associational interests (apart from lobbying organizations) among customers are nonexistent for most kinds of business—for example, power and communication—and have only limited resonance in such areas as transportation, where some voluntary sorting might take place. Even in the Old South, moreover, most firms resisted segregated facilities that government mandates forced upon them.[11]

But the common carrier rule never applied to intimate associations, clubs, businesses, or religious organizations. In these contexts, classical liberal theory collapses into libertarian theory, because both categorically reject any system of forced association that impairs the autonomy of group members and the efficiency of group operations when no monopoly problems are involved. By definition, some persons want to get into groups that wish to keep other individuals out. Transaction costs are typically low. If the group's enlargement were on net beneficial, then the membership would accept the outsiders wholly without regard to external coercion. But expanded membership hardly means a greater level of utility across the board. The gains to the outsiders are likely be smaller than the losses to the insiders, or otherwise the expansion of the group would have occurred by voluntary means. Wholly apart from issues of scale—that is, the case where the cost rises for additional individuals who are admitted as members[12]—it is easy to see why limiting membership

---

[11] On the policies of the Southern railroads, see Richard A. Epstein, *Forbidden Grounds: The Case Against Employment Discrimination Law* (Cambridge, MA: Harvard University Press, 1992), 93; and Jennifer Roback, "Southern Labor Law in the Jim Crow Era," *University of Chicago Law Review* 51 (1984): 1161–92.

[12] For the classic statement of this problem, see Garrett Hardin, "The Tragedy of the Commons," *Science* 162 (1968): 1243–48.

makes sense. The greater the diversity of views, the harder it is for any governance structure to overcome the bitter antagonisms that arise within the ranks. A religious organization cannot long survive if its members do not agree on mission, doctrine, or liturgy. That is why Protestants broke off from Catholics, Southern from Northern Baptists, and so forth.

The classical liberal position recognizes that these internal tensions impose real costs on the association and its members. If those tensions are perceived before organizations are formed, then any rule of universal inclusion could block the emergence of the organization in the first place. Rather than take inclusion as a strong presumptive norm, the classical liberal approach treats membership exclusivity as its prime objective. The aim is to make sure that all groups, regardless of their beliefs or membership requirements, can sprout up at will. In the long run, that approach will produce more vibrant organizations with a greater range of objectives and styles, all of which can survive because of their ability to cater to their members. The implicit assumption is that the expanded range of options works better than any legal regime that uses nondiscrimination rules to pry open membership. The desire to be inclusive at the back end creates a large, if invisible, barrier to entry at the front end. In sum, under classical liberalism, freedom of association becomes an inseparable and universalizable element of freedom, limited only by the concern with monopoly power. There are no efforts to limit the associational principle to certain subclasses of organizations, whether delineated by purpose, size, membership requirements, or anything else.

III. Antidiscrimination Laws as a Limitation on Freedom of Association

The classical liberal tradition ties the use of an antidiscrimination norm to the existence of monopoly power. The modern legal rules invent far broader justifications for the use of this norm. One potential application is in connection with "expressive" organizations. A second is with ordinary business relationships. The role of freedom of expression is best examined in connection with the asserted rights of the Boy Scouts to exclude gay individuals from their membership. The nonexpressive case is well illustrated by the restrictions that the Americans with Disabilities Act places on the right to exclude persons with disabilities. This section compares the classical and modern approaches in these two domains.

A. Expressive organizations: The Boy Scouts and the NAACP

The classical liberal resolution of the tension between regulation and freedom of association works as a convenient foil to the modern approach that limits freedom of association for reasons that have nothing to do with coercion, fraud, or monopoly. It is easy to identify two different attitudes toward this issue, one which is strongly sympathetic to the right of association, and another which is deeply suspicious of it. Oddly enough, these two different attitudes manifest themselves in connection with the role of discrimination in state power. To set the antidiscrimination principle in context for an extended discussion of gay rights, it is useful to see how the freedom of association principle evolved under the First Amendment before it came in conflict with the modern antidiscrimination laws.

In one sense, the common theme is the extent to which a principle of freedom of association deals with membership in voluntary organizations. The best introduction into this study is *NAACP v. Alabama* (1958),[13] which upheld on freedom of association grounds a First Amendment challenge to Alabama's efforts to gain the membership list of the local NAACP chapter during the height of the civil rights movement. Another important case is the Supreme Court's decision in *Boy Scouts of America v. Dale* (2000),[14] which upheld the right of the Boy Scouts to exclude gay members; this case raises an explicit challenge to the classical liberal principle of freedom of association because its facts are so stark and simple.

In the *NAACP* case, the Supreme Court had to decide whether the attorney general of Alabama could require the disclosure of the membership lists of the NAACP. The case itself was brought under the First Amendment, on the ground that the Alabama statute unconstitutionally burdened the freedom of association of the NAACP's members, by requiring the unwanted disclosure. Justice John M. Harlan recognized the close connection between the substantive right to freedom of speech and the related principle of freedom of association in a passage that requires close attention:

> Effective advocacy of both public and private points of view, particularly controversial ones, is undeniably enhanced by group association, as this Court has more than once recognized by remarking upon the close nexus between the freedoms of speech and assembly. It is beyond debate that freedom to engage in association for the advancement of beliefs and ideas is an inseparable aspect of the "liberty" assured by the Due Process Clause of the Fourteenth Amendment, which embraces freedom of speech. Of course, it is immaterial whether the beliefs sought to be advanced by association pertain to political, economic, religious or cultural matters, and state action which may

---

[13] *NAACP v. Alabama*, 357 U.S. 449, 460 (1958).
[14] *Boy Scouts of America v. Dale*, 530 U.S. 640 (2000). For an earlier statement of my views on the case, see Richard A. Epstein, "The Constitutional Perils of Moderation: The Case of the Boy Scouts," *Southern California Law Review* 74 (2000): 119–43.

have the effect of curtailing the freedom to associate is subject to the closest scrutiny.[15]

Justice Harlan's laudable argument rests on a conscious equivocation of terms. His use of "assembly" in the first sentence leaves the impression that the association right has an explicit textual foundation in the First Amendment. Instructively, the word "assembly" does not appear in the First Amendment, which references only "the right of the people peaceably to assemble, and to petition the Government for a redress of grievances." Even if the second clause is not a limitation on the first, the words "to assemble" in context read much more naturally as the ability to meet in public to discuss various issues. "To assemble" does not sound like the right to form associations that meet in private to plan and organize with respect to a full range of "political, economic, religious or cultural" issues. The transformation of the constitutional guarantee of a right "to assemble" is complete in Justice Harlan's second sentence, which substitutes the broader term "association" for the narrow term "assembly."

It is, however, worth stressing that Justice Harlan's conclusion would be correct even if the First Amendment stopped after the protection of "freedom of speech, and of the press." The basic classical liberal synthesis recognizes that individuals cannot work alone to achieve their ends, but must cooperate in order to obtain the benefit of gains from trade. It would be odd to read the First Amendment to say that any isolated individual could speak against government action, but two people could not pool their resources toward the same end. And once they do, the terms of partnership are theirs to decide; if the membership decides to specialize its functions to increase its output, those secondary decisions are protected as well. Nor should it make the slightest difference if some individuals contribute only cash to the joint venture while others contribute their time and imagination. To look at the speech of one person in isolation from that of others is to put on blinders. The right to engage in any form of productive labor directed toward any expressive end carries with it an associative right. The right of association toward the constitutionally protected ends follows by necessary implication from the basic constitutional text.

Harlan's reference to the due process clause of the Fourteenth Amendment is a bit of American constitutional law legerdemain, well established at the time, to the effect that the due process clause "incorporates" the First Amendment. This means that the clause applies the First Amendment against the state governments rather than just against the federal government.[16] And Harlan's final sentence notes, consistent with classical

---

[15] *NAACP,* 357 U.S. at 460–61.

[16] See *Gitlow v. New York,* 268 U.S. 652, 666 (1925). The *Gitlow* case announced a profound shift in constitutional jurisprudence in a most off-handed way: "For present purposes we may and do assume that freedom of speech and of the press—which are protected by the First Amendment from abridgment by Congress—are among the fundamental personal

liberal theory, that the rights of association for speech are not bounded by some specific subject matter but cover "political, economic, religious or cultural matters," uniformly. There is, accordingly, no need to decide which of these four ends the NAACP advanced, since all were equally protected. Harlan's last reference to "the closest scrutiny" meant that the Court would look on its own initiative to see whether the purported evil that the legislation addressed was in fact an evil. If so, the Court would then ask the question of whether the means chosen fit tightly with the ends, to guard against the potential overbreadth of the statute. The upshot was that the NAACP could claim the associational rights of its members and keep its membership lists from the prying eyes of Alabama state officials, at a time when segregation was still in its heyday. And it was critical, as Harlan noted, that the NAACP be able to assert this claim:

> If petitioner's rank-and-file members are constitutionally entitled to withhold their connection with the Association despite the production order, it is manifest that this right is properly assertable by the Association. To require that it be claimed by the members themselves would result in nullification of the right at the very moment of its assertion.[17]

In the end, therefore, the autonomous structure of the organization was protected against government intrusion on principles that are wholly consistent with the classical liberal view toward limited government. There was simply no justification for the desired state intrusion into the affairs of a private organization—all the more so because the organization was dedicated to undoing the political regime that sought to regulate its behavior. The NAACP was not engaged in plans for the violent overthrow of government, so it does not come close to falling under the force or fraud rationales for limiting associative freedom.

B. Boy Scouts of America v. Dale

The issue of freedom of expressive association raised itself in quite a different environment in *Boy Scouts of America v. Dale*, which puts the issue of gay rights front and center. James Dale entered the Boy Scouts at the age of eight in 1978 and rose to the level of Eagle Scout some ten years later. By all accounts, he excelled in his work. In 1989, he became an adult scout who was appointed an assistant scoutmaster of Troop 73, a position of trust within the organization. Shortly thereafter,

---

rights and 'liberties' protected by the due process clause of the Fourteenth Amendment from impairment by the States." The case then rejected the First Amendment defense against a criminal prosecution for publishing "The Left Wing Manifesto," a socialist tract, which issued a call to action that was widely ignored. *Gitlow* is not good law on this point today.

[17] *NAACP*, 357 U.S. at 459.

he acknowledged publicly that he was gay. In response, the Boy Scouts revoked his membership in the organization, explaining in response to his direct inquiry that the Boy Scouts "specifically forbid membership to homosexuals."

In one sense, the case looks different from *NAACP* because it does not involve government efforts to suppress political opposition. But the motivation for the government action is not the decisive question. What matters is the right of organizers to accept or refuse members as they see fit. The basic principle of freedom of association should allow the Boy Scouts to determine their own membership, unless it can be established that the Scouts had acted in breach of contract, or engaged in the threat or use of force or fraud, which they had not. For organizations of this type, the question of monopoly power is quite beside the point.

Nonetheless, New Jersey's Law Against Discrimination (LAD), which proceeds from very different assumptions, reached a very different conclusion. Similar to the Civil Rights Act of 1964,[18] but going far beyond it, New Jersey's Law Against Discrimination provides:

> N.J. STAT § 10:5-4. OBTAINING EMPLOYMENT, ACCOMMODATIONS AND PRIVILEGES WITHOUT DISCRIMINATION; CIVIL RIGHT. All persons shall have the opportunity to obtain employment, and to obtain all the accommodations, advantages, facilities, and privileges of any place of public accommodation, publicly assisted housing accommodation, and other real property without discrimination because of race, creed, color, national origin, ancestry, age, marital status, affectional or sexual orientation, familial status, disability, nationality, sex, gender identity or expression or source of lawful income used for rental or mortgage payments, subject only to conditions and limitations applicable alike to all persons. This opportunity is recognized as and declared to be a civil right.[19]

This statute is broader than the 1964 Civil Rights Act by virtue of a 1991 amendment, which added the phrase "affectional or sexual orientation" to the list of characteristics on the basis of which it is forbidden to discriminate.

There is only one applicable exception contained within the New Jersey statute, which reads:

> Nothing herein contained shall be construed to include or to apply to any institution, bona fide club, or place of accommodation, which is in its nature distinctly private; nor shall anything herein contained

---

[18] Civil Rights Act of 1964, Pub. L. No. 88-352, 78 Stat. 241 (1964).
[19] N.J. Stat. sec. 10:5-4 (2007).

apply to any educational facility operated or maintained by a bona fide religious or sectarian institution.[20]

Everyone agreed that the Boy Scouts could not be regarded as "distinctly private," with its membership of five million plus boys; and it was, quite by design, not affiliated with any religious institution. The classical liberal account I have outlined does not distinguish between religious and secular associations. It follows, therefore, that this statute limits freedom of association in ways that are unacceptable. Since the statute's language is clear, the only question of its legality was whether the prohibition it contained would fail a constitutional challenge under the First Amendment guarantees of freedom of speech and association. Within the framework of antidiscrimination law more generally, that had to be regarded as an uphill battle when the case was first brought, because of an unbroken line of Supreme Court and lower court cases that had rejected any and all challenges to the Civil Rights Act.

Just that fate befell the challenge to the Law Against Discrimination in the New Jersey Supreme Court. Chief Justice Deborah Poritz, writing for the unanimous New Jersey Supreme Court, held that the LAD survived the constitutional challenge. In reaching this decision, she noted that the state had offered a compelling justification for its antidiscrimination law by pointing out in its legislation the social evils that flowed from discrimination, including "economic loss; time loss; physical and emotional stress; and in some cases severe emotional trauma, illness, homelessness or other irreparable harm resulting from the strain of employment controversies; relocation, search and moving difficulties; anxiety caused by lack of information, uncertainty, and resultant planning difficulty; career, education, family and social disruption; and adjustment problems."[21] She then added a further commentary:

> The sad truth is that excluded groups and individuals have been prevented from full participation in the social, economic, and political life of our country. The human price of this bigotry has been enormous. At a most fundamental level, adherence to the principle of equality demands that our legal system protect the victims of invidious discrimination.[22]

There is much to disagree with in this defense of the LAD. At a social level, it is hard to credit various forms of discrimination with the potent consequences that the legislature attaches to them. To be sure, no one

---

[20] N.J. Stat. sec. 10:5-5 (2007).
[21] N.J. Stat. sec. 10:5-3 (2007).
[22] *Dale v. Boy Scouts of America*, 734 A.2d 1196, 1227 (N.J. 1999) (footnotes omitted).

disagrees that there are such consequences when private force is used to keep certain individuals out of gainful occupations or trades, a pattern and practice that characterized so much of the segregated South. But unless it could be shown that all individuals in concert engage in horrific behavior with respect to particular groups, the larger claim represents the worst kind of intellectual cherry-picking: Look at the bad outcomes in individual cases, but systematically ignore the gains from trade that are generated for all persons by competitive markets in all areas of life.

Nor is Poritz's grim account consistent with the enormous social transformation of attitudes toward gay and lesbian individuals over the past forty years. No longer do psychiatrists describe homosexuality as a clinical disease or disorder, and the expansion of gay and lesbian organizations—all rightly protected by the principle of freedom of association—has been remarkable and effective. It is simply a mistake to ignore the huge social transformation in attitudes and behaviors, which the principle of freedom of association has facilitated, so as to create a kind of supposed market failure to justify state intervention. The one real grievance of gay and lesbian individuals lies, ironically, in exactly the opposite direction, namely, in the continued state prohibition against same-sex marriages, a prohibition which regrettably has gained ground in recent years.

Yet the reason this prohibition really does harm is exactly the reason why the antidiscrimination law does little or no good. Dale, and others similarly situated, may be excluded from some organizations. But they are, by the same token, able to join or create thousands of others that welcome them into membership. Not so with the legal prohibition on same-sex marriages. The state has a monopoly position through its control over the licensing process, which is not limited by an antidiscrimination norm that would require treating gay couples by the same standards as straight couples. The upshot is that so long as democratic institutions bar gay marriages, the same-sex marriage option is effectively foreclosed because there is nowhere else to turn, even if a substantial minority of the state electorate disagrees with the legislative choices. We should never forget that this political minority is effectively silenced by legislation that enacts the dominant social opinion into law. Prohibitions on same-sex marriage belong, therefore, in the cross-hairs of any classical liberal theory, which must question why the state is in the business of issuing marriage licenses in the first place. The antidiscrimination norm in employment and public accommodations does not remove this barrier to voluntary arrangements.

Poritz's opinion falls prey to all these misunderstandings because it unthinkingly rejects outright the classical liberal distinction between state and private action, or, in the context of private actions, the distinction between monopoly and competitive situations. Instructively, Poritz uses the word "excluded" in the passive voice, and never bothers to mention which people were excluded by what groups, and what alternatives remained open to them. Her opinion just brands exclusion as an invidious social practice, with some consequences she does not like, without asking how the principle of freedom of association fares in the long run by giving other opportunities to people who have lost out in particular transactions. Nor does her opinion explain why full participation in social, economic, and political life is somehow not achieved via the civil capacity to vote, to enter into contracts, to join organizations, to give testimony in courts, and so on—rights that are fully consistent with the like liberties of all other individuals.[23] Her account simply speeds us along the path toward expanded state power.

When *Boy Scouts of America v. Dale* reached the U.S. Supreme Court,[24] the justices switched course by upholding the freedom of association claim on a narrow five-to-four vote for those expressive organizations protected by the First Amendment. The *Dale* majority, speaking through Chief Justice William Rehnquist, was not in the business of remaking American constitutional law so as to vindicate a neo-*Lochner* freedom of contract norm for all voluntary associations.[25] Thus, it faced a difficulty that does not trouble the defenders of the antidiscrimination law, which is how and why to draw the line between expressive and nonexpressive organizations. Perforce its discussion becomes murkier—just what is an expressive organization, and why should it matter? Of course, the Boy Scouts are concerned with inculcating moral values in the young. Does that make the organization expressive? Does it matter that its own code of conduct required young people to be "morally straight," but did not explicitly condemn homosexual conduct? How is that to be set off against the Scouts' consistent refusal to accept gay scout leaders?

To Justice John Paul Stevens, writing in dissent, this studied equivocation provided the wedge for sustaining the antidiscrimination law. He wrote as if large polyglot organizations were incapable of expressing unified positions. Yet the Boy Scouts' equivocation on moral questions forced them, in his view, to forfeit their associational freedoms: "In light of [the Scouts'] self-proclaimed ecumenism, furthermore, it is even more difficult to discern any shared goals or common moral stance on homosexuality."[26] Justice David Souter's brief opinion echoed the same theme: "no group can claim a right of expressive association without identifying a clear position to be advocated over time in an unequivocal way."[27] Unfortunately, the dissenting views leave it unclear whether organizations like the Boy Scouts have any associational freedoms that would

---

[23] I have defended this position in Richard A. Epstein, "Two Conceptions of Civil Rights," *Social Philosophy and Policy* 8, no. 2 (1991): 38–59.

[24] *Boy Scouts of America v. Dale*, 530 U.S. 640 (2000).

[25] *Lochner v. New York*, 198 U.S. 45 (1905).

[26] *Dale*, 530 U.S. at 670 (Stevens, J., dissenting).

[27] Id. at 701 (Souter, J., dissenting).

allow them to resist, for example, the disclosure of membership lists to the state.

The patchwork response of the two dissents fares poorly against the classical liberal alternative. That approach protects the freedom of association for all reasons, whether expressive or nonexpressive, and thus need not police a line that is not worth drawing in the first place. But even if the line between expressive and nonexpressive associations has to be drawn, as is the case in *Dale*, on which side of the line does any group like the Scouts that has multiple purposes fall? Certainly the insistence on a clear position makes little sense. Sprawling organizations like the Boy Scouts take evasive positions for a good reason. At over five million strong, the Scouts cannot please everyone.[28] Speak too loudly against gays, and they lose a large portion of their socially liberal membership base. Speak too softly, and a significant fraction of conservative parents might be unwilling to trust their sons to the Scouts. This fragile coalition can stay together only if internal dissent does not boil over into actual schism. With shades of Aristotle,[29] this equivocation is a form of moderation that allows individuals with divergent viewpoints to remain under the same tent, as part of a cohesive organization, instead of tenants in an office building who share utilities and common spaces. Associational freedom should never be reserved to those who take extreme positions. Just because the First Amendment protects the Ku Klux Klan[30] does not mean, as Chief Justice Rehnquist wrote, that it offers no protection to more popular groups.[31] Indeed, he hit the nail on the head when he wrote: "The fact that the organization does not trumpet its views from the housetops, or that it tolerates dissent within its ranks, does not mean that its views receive no First Amendment protection."[32] The unpopular Rehnquist decision does a far better job in balancing the equities than the more fashionable dissents of Justice Stevens and Justice Souter.

[28] Andrew Jacobs, "Victory Has Consequences of Its Own," *The New York Times*, June 29, 2000, at A28 (noting that the Boy Scouts organization risks a backlash for ousting Dale from its membership). For evidence of this prediction coming true, see, e.g., "Spielberg Unprepared," *The Chicago Tribune*, April 19, 2001 (reporting Steven Spielberg's resignation from the advisory board of the Boy Scouts of America given its policy of excluding homosexuals); Laurie Goldstein, "Jewish Group Recommends Cutting Ties to Boy Scouts," *The New York Times*, January 10, 2001 (reporting that Jewish religious leaders are asking Boy Scout troops to stop using synagogues due to the Scouts' policy on homosexuality); "Oak Park School Loses Scouts Over Gay Ban," *The Chicago Tribune*, December 7, 2000 (reporting that a Parent-Teacher Organization voted to prohibit a Boy Scout troop from meeting at the local elementary school given the Scouts' policy of excluding homosexuals); and "Evanston United Way Cuts Off Boy Scouts," *The Chicago Tribune*, September 22, 2000 (reporting a decision by a local division of the United Way to cease funding local Boy Scout troops given the Scouts' policy of excluding homosexuals).

[29] Aristotle's famous account of moderation (sometimes translated as "temperance") is in Book II of the *Nicomachean Ethics*, in *The Basic Works of Aristotle*, ed. Richard McKeon (New York: Random House, 1941).

[30] *Brandenburg v. Ohio*, 395 U.S. 444 (1969).

[31] *Dale*, 530 U.S. at 659–60.

[32] Id. at 656.

C. The Americans with Disabilities Act

The *Dale* case poses an interesting challenge to the modern liberal synthesis because it relies on the higher scrutiny of First Amendment law to return the law of free speech to the classical liberal synthesis. Many forms of regulation are not directed to matters of expression, but to other activities; and, regarding these ordinary activities, the level of constitutional scrutiny is so low that virtually no constitutional oversight is even attempted under current law. Thus, while the classical liberal principle of freedom of association goes beyond expressive cases, the protection of the First Amendment, no matter how broadly construed, does not. To see how this shift in orientation works, it is instructive to examine the vast legal apparatus against discrimination in public accommodations on various grounds. The public accommodations provisions on race under Title II of the 1964 Civil Rights Act were somewhat narrower than the analogous provisions of New Jersey's Law Against Discrimination. Insofar as they applied to race, they were implemented with barely a peep of protest, save from rabid segregationists who could never have imposed their will on established businesses solely by market pressures.[33] Segregation by race is a clunky way to do business in that it generates immense amounts of ill-will, so that most businesses affirmatively welcomed public accommodations regulation because it "forced" them to desegregate without having to face the wrath of local hoodlums who knew that they could burn down the premises without fearing any response by state police. These firms faced no expensive cost subsidies that desegregation would introduce.

The antidiscrimination norm in public accommodation generated a very different response under the 1990 Americans with Disabilities Act (ADA), which prohibits discrimination on grounds of disability both in employment and in access to a wide range of facilities. The statute starts with a definition of the general duty not to discriminate against disabled individuals either in employment or in the operation of various facilities.[34] The obligation to take into account the interests of handicapped persons is not absolute, but only requires (in a term of art) that "reasonable accommodations" be made, the account of which is governed by complex statutory provisions.[35] Thereafter, there is an offset with respect to those

---

[33] *Katzenbach v. McClung*, 379 U.S. 294 (1964).

[34] Americans with Disabilities Act, 42 U.S.C. 12112 (a): "General rule: No covered entity shall discriminate against a qualified individual with a disability because of the disability of such individual in regard to job application procedures, the hiring, advancement, or discharge of employees, employee compensation, job training, and other terms, conditions, and privileges of employment."

[35] 42 U.S.C. 12111 (9): "Reasonable accommodation. The term 'reasonable accommodation' may include (A) making existing facilities used by employees readily accessible to and usable by individuals with disabilities; and (B) job restructuring, part-time or modified work schedules, reassignment to a vacant position, acquisition or modification of equipment or

accommodations that create "undue hardship"—yet another term of art.[36] It is worth noting that no charitable interpretation can give either of these phrases a clear meaning. Both invoke a cluster of factors, expressed in vague terms, which necessarily speak about matters of degree, all of which are relevant and none of which are conclusive. No firm can get permits for new construction unless its operations are ADA-compliant under the most detailed and exhaustive of legal regimes.

The public accommodations requirements for disabled people present a wholly different landscape precisely because the cost of service to severely disabled persons can and does differ by orders of magnitude from the costs of equivalent service to other individuals. It is just those cost differentials that justify rate differentials under the classical liberal theory. To be sure, no firm is required to remove all cross-subsidies, and many would not choose to do so, within limits. Basic business sense and decency require ramps for wheelchairs in airports and hospitals, even if ramps for wheelchairs are also often used for baby strollers and luggage carts. The high density of use and the multiple classes of users overcome any hesitation about funding these expenditures from general revenues. Some steps toward improved handicap access would be routinely provided even in the absence of any disability statute. The measures taken would surely be less, however, than the champions of the disabled would like.

The battle in practice centers on the extent of the subsidy, and resistance to government-mandated subsidies is now on the rise, albeit covertly. Every community now contains a disability rights group that demands that every public or private bus or train be equipped with wheelchair hoists, or that every public toilet or remote rocky resort be made wheelchair accessible.[37] On this score, we would do well to remember the account that Philip K. Howard (founder and head of The Common Good)

---

devices, appropriate adjustment or modifications of examinations, training materials or policies, the provision of qualified readers or interpreters, and other similar accommodations for individuals with disabilities."

[36] 42 U.S.C. 12111 (10): "Undue hardship. (A) In general: The term 'undue hardship' means an action requiring significant difficulty or expense, when considered in light of the factors set forth in subparagraph (B).

"(B) Factors to be considered: In determining whether an accommodation would impose an undue hardship on a covered entity, factors to be considered include (i) the nature and cost of the accommodation needed under this chapter; (ii) the overall financial resources of the facility or facilities involved in the provision of the reasonable accommodation; the number of persons employed at such facility; the effect on expenses and resources, or the impact otherwise of such accommodation upon the operation of the facility; (iii) the overall financial resources of the covered entity; the overall size of the business of a covered entity with respect to the number of its employees; the number, type, and location of its facilities; and (iv) the type of operation or operations of the covered entity, including the composition, structure, and functions of the workforce of such entity; the geographic separateness, administrative, or fiscal relationship of the facility or facilities in question to the covered entity."

[37] For a general list of disability rights activists, see "List of Disability Rights Activists," *Wikipedia,* http://en.wikipedia.org/wiki/List_of_disability_rights_activists (accessed August 6, 2007).

has given of the human-rights-driven fiasco of trying to introduce public toilets into New York City. The only workable toilets were too small to accommodate wheelchairs. The larger toilets that could accommodate wheelchairs blocked public roads and also had to remain locked so that they could not be used for prostitution and other illicit sexual activities. A new institution that provided benefits for most but not for all was dutifully blocked, even though more public toilets reduced unwanted odors in public places—a classic public good.[38]

Unfortunately, disability groups typically object to all measures of interest to them that make some people better off if they do not make their members better off as well. Across-the-board improvements that lead to greater inequality of fortune are somehow out of bounds. Recall that traditional rules on common carriers only required equal charges for persons for whom the cost of service was, roughly speaking, identical. The new version of public accommodations ignores that equal-cost constraint and thus spawns huge subsidies that deter sensible innovation in the absence of any monopoly power. Here is one easy test of why the subsidies induced by the ADA make little sense: Suppose that disabled individuals could receive in cash, pro rata, the extra money needed to make the new public toilets accessible to them and safe for everyone else—say, by posting a twenty-four-hour guard at each facility. Then ask how these individuals would vote in an election in which they would all be bound by the consensus outcome, so that all free-riding problems would be eliminated. Would most individuals vote to spend the money on those collective improvements, or would they choose to spend it in other ways? The betting here is that they would find better uses of the money, which is a good reason not to make this particular expenditure. Better to do without the accessible toilets and, if need be, make a more sensible public expenditure from which disabled individuals could derive either exclusive or disproportionate benefits.

At this point, the dangers of myopic antidiscrimination legislation exceed the dangers of exclusion by private parties. The insistence on the modern mandate that requires private firms to provide reasonable accommodations for handicapped individuals that do not impose "undue hardship," for which no clear standard can be articulated, should be abandoned as unworkable.[39] In a world in which no requirements were

---

[38] See Philip K. Howard, *The Death of Common Sense: How Law Is Suffocating America* (New York: Grand Central Publishing, 1996), 113–18.

[39] "No individual shall be discriminated against on the basis of disability in the full and equal enjoyment of the goods, services, facilities, privileges, advantages, or accommodations of any place of public accommodation by any person who owns, leases (or leases to), or operates a place of public accommodation." 42 U.S.C. sec. 12182(a).

Unlawful discrimination includes "a failure to take such steps as may be necessary to ensure that no individual with a disability is excluded, denied services, segregated or otherwise treated differently than other individuals because of the absence of auxiliary aids and services, unless the entity can demonstrate that taking such steps would

imposed, some accommodations would still be made, and most of these would be reasonable even if they involved some net cost to the firm. But in a world in which public enforcement agencies and laws define what counts as "reasonable accommodations" and "undue hardship," the natural equilibrium shifts. All too many concessions are made when benefits are printed in bold, large type and burdens in regular, small type. The University of Chicago Law School has its own monument to the folly of the current disability regime in the form of an expensive and ugly five-stop elevator that is virtually never used to move wheelchairs from one level of the school's auditorium space to another. It is not an isolated example. The costs for handicap compliance are large, with the common estimates from architectural and construction firms usually running between 20 and 25 percent of project costs, often to satisfy the needs of at most one or two users.[40] We are not speaking of small effects from the aggressive enforcement of the antidiscrimination laws.

IV. Antidiscrimination Laws as Human Rights Laws

A. Their basic structure

The current antidiscrimination norms exert a powerful hold over all forms of business and social arrangements, subject only to a modest, and vulnerable, exception for expressive organizations. It is critical to understand, therefore, how the antidiscrimination requirement should be applied to private associations and public accommodations. The risk that these laws can go off the rails, as it were, should caution us against their application to routine businesses, churches, schools, universities, charities, and voluntary associations. Unfortunately, the ambition of the civil rights movement is not constrained by these niceties. Rather, it is premised on the resolute insistence that private and public discrimination are morally objectionable in a broad range of social institutions.

One effort to make the modern antidiscrimination laws more palatable is to call them "human rights laws," in the hopes that this new label can give them a degree of universality that helps legitimate them in the eyes of the world at large. That is the verbal strategy of the New York Human Rights Act (1945), whose substantive provisions track those of New Jersey's LAD, in the broad definition of public accommodations and the

---

fundamentally alter the nature of the good, service, facility, privilege, advantage, or accommodation being offered or would result in an undue burden." 42 U.S.C. sec. 12182(b)(2)(A)(iii).

[40] For examples of the high costs of making buildings accessible, see the Florida Building Commission Accessibility Advisory Council, Minutes, August 25, 2003, http://www.dca. state.fl.us/fbc/committees/accessibility/aac/aacmin0803.pdf (accessed August 6, 2007) (granting waivers to several builders when more than 20 percent of the project costs would be spent on accessibility).

narrow exclusions from the basic antidiscrimination command for distinctively private organizations.[41]

My point here is not to quarrel with the details of coverage. Within their chosen sphere, the drafters of the human rights statutes have *not* misconstrued their own mission. No analyst may know the exact intensity that people attach to choosing their social groupings, but we do have a strong intuitive sense of their implicit orderings, which helps explain the exceptions found in the human rights acts. It would be odd to allow a facility manager to keep healthy people from working in his restaurant. But it would be equally odd to say that he is bound not to discriminate against infected food-handlers who could spread diseases to innocent customers. Likewise, it would be an odd human rights statute that allowed people to take sex into account in providing financial advice, but not in counseling for victims of rape or sexual harassment. The law to one side, we all share some general sense of the social differences between general business friendships and intimate personal relations. From a public choice perspective,[42] it is quite inconceivable that any winning coalition could reverse the widespread agreement over these implicit orderings by requiring that individuals in the marriage market not discriminate on the grounds of race, age, sex, or sexual orientation.

B. Why these human rights?

Why does any government get into the "human rights" business at all? To be sure, the phrase "human rights" is a masterstroke of political rhetoric: Who can oppose a statute that protects "human rights," especially if it contains no mention of human duties? Each of us is human, and thus the rights we seek to protect are only those belonging to ourselves. No one would argue that the human rights laws are fundamentally misconceived by denying, perversely, all possibility of human rights as such. Yet the choice of *these* human rights raises deeply troublesome questions about these statutes. These questions go to the universality of the purported rights, the specification of their correlative duties, their impact on affirmative action programs, and their effect on the production of useful information.

Universality. Although human rights acts establish many rights, nobody claims that they contain the entire corpus of individual rights conferred

---

[41] N.Y. Exec. sec. 296 (2005). Recent proposed amendments to the New York Human Rights Act seek to ensure that firms will not be required to provide accessibility that is not "readily achievable" in financial terms, subject to the usual multifactor determinations on costs, benefits, overall resources, type of operations, and the like. See, e.g., 2007 N.Y.A.B. 4932 (2007).

[42] Public choice theory analyzes the behavior of individuals in various political settings, as self-interested actors who respond to the incentives created by the political system. For an introduction to the theory, see James M. Buchanan and Gordon Tullock, *The Calculus of Consent: Logical Foundations of Constitutional Democracy* (Indianapolis, IN: Liberty Fund, 1999).

by any legal system, ancient or modern. People possess many other rights, such as rights of personal autonomy and conscience, rights of religion, rights of free speech, rights to contract, and rights over their own persons and property. Some of these rights relate to economic liberties; others are critical to political participation; some matter for individual self-realization; some play into all three. All of these rights generally are highly important. Yet it is never quite explained why these rights fail to qualify for inclusion in human rights statutes. If we do not regard these traditional liberties as human rights, then how should we classify them? Are they second-class rights? Rights that only exist at the whim of the legislature, which may revise or redefine them at will?

The lack of universality in modern human rights laws is also evident by the incompleteness in the list of covered organizations. The classical liberal position draws no distinctions among lawful organizations with respect to their size, their membership, or their ends. All lawful organizations are protected against forced association, on the ground that those who are excluded from one organization continue to have a wide range of other organizations to choose from. But the modern position is much less sure of its grounds. As noted, the New York and New Jersey antidiscrimination statutes say that distinctly private organizations are not covered: clearly, the law is not intended to prevent people from discriminating on the grounds of sex, race, or religion in choosing marriage partners. All this is sensible enough. But the narrow exceptions do not make the case for the basic prohibition. As we move from groups of two in intimate settings to larger groups in various relationships, just where should the principle of freedom of association give way to the nondiscrimination principle? The allowance for expressive organizations, discussed in Section III above, raises the simple question of whether businesses with distinct credos should be regarded as expressive or whether they should fall into some other category reserved for ordinary businesses. It is hard to draw any line or to justify any line once drawn.

To see the gap between contemporary human rights statutes and earlier visions of human rights, compare the modern statutes with one key civil rights statute. I refer here not to the Civil Rights Act of 1964, but to the earlier and wiser human rights statute, the 1866 Civil Rights Act,[43] passed by a Reconstruction Congress in the aftermath of the Civil War. There is *no overlap* in the civil rights protected by the 1866 act and the modern human rights acts. The 1866 statute gave to *all* citizens rights such as the right to contract, to hold property, to convey real estate, to testify in court, and to sue or be sued.[44] It essentially guaranteed civil capacity—the right

[43] Civil Rights Act of 1866, 14 Stat. 27.
[44] Civil Rights Act of 1866, chap. 31, 14 Stat. 27. Section 1 states that "all persons born in the United States ... shall have the same right, in every State and Territory in the United States, to make and enforce contracts, to sue, be parties, and give evidence, to inherit, purchase, lease, sell, hold, and convey real and personal property, and to full and

to participate in a social order organized under the law of property, contract, and tort. The 1866 Civil Rights Act primarily dealt with economic rights and liberties. It is also possible to clearly delineate the correlative duties to these enumerated rights. If *A* and *B* have the right to contract, then *C* is duty-bound not to block their joint endeavors with the use of force or fraud; if *A* is competent to give testimony in court, then no one can prevent his appearance; and so on down the line.

None of these rights is mentioned, let alone affirmed, in modern civil rights legislation. Certainly no one holds that the Bill of Rights has depreciated over time, even though most of its liberty-based claims are in tension with modern human rights laws. To put this another way, if the rights specified in human rights acts are truly fundamental, why historically have they taken so long to surge to the forefront of anyone's legislative agenda? In the United States, their influence dates only from the 1960s. The same pattern holds around the world.

I think that their delayed introduction stems from the simple fact that no one regards any right to be free of discrimination in ordinary social or business transactions as truly fundamental for his or her own well-being and security. Consider this question: On an all-or-nothing basis, how would you choose between having only the protection of a human rights act, with its various prohibitions on discrimination, or the common law prohibition against the use of force? I know exactly which rights I would disregard. I would allow people to refuse to hire me for any reason at all, so long as the state protected my bodily integrity. I doubt that in any real-world setting a single person would choose differently. Nobody would prefer the risk of being killed by a "nondiscriminatory" murderer to a flat prohibition against the use or threat of force. The result does not change if we compare the modern statutory guarantees against discrimination to the classical liberal right to make contracts to dispose of one's labor or property. Once again, the basic right to trade occupies the more fundamental niche, no matter what the structure of the marketplace. To deny people the right to trade forces them to rely exclusively on their own resources and negates the enormous gains from the division of labor. Any antidiscrimination norm is therefore heavily parasitic on the basic right to trade, which it seeks to limit in unproductive ways, and largely for misguided reasons. The antidiscrimination norm cannot survive as a standalone principle.

The lack of universality in modern human rights laws is further revealed by the limited class of persons to whom they apply. The older civil rights statutes applied to all citizens regardless of the role that they occupied in some particular relationship. The 1866 statute, for example, sought to end

---

equal benefit of all laws and proceedings for the security of person and property, as is enjoyed by white citizens, and shall be subject to like punishment, pains, and penalties, and to none other, any law, statute, ordinance, regulation, or custom, to the contrary notwithstanding."

discrimination on the grounds of race by guaranteeing to "citizens, of every race and color" the same right "to make and enforce contracts, to sue, be parties, and give evidence, to inherit, purchase, lease, sell, hold, and convey real and personal property, to full and equal benefit of all laws and proceedings for the security of person and property, as is enjoyed by white citizens."[45] In one sense, this provision is not universal because it does not extend its protection to aliens, which is in line with the uneasy tradition that, within each nation, citizenship gives advantages in the economic realm that can be denied to foreigners. That is certainly the case with respect to the United States Constitution, where the privileges or immunities clause of the Fourteenth Amendment, adopted two years after the 1866 Civil Rights Act, provides that "No State shall make or enforce any law which shall abridge the privileges or immunities of citizens of the United States."[46] The 1866 act is, in one sense, a nondiscrimination provision because it refers to the various rights that are protected under the classical liberal framework, but only protects them to the extent that they are enjoyed by white persons. The purpose of that limitation is to make sure that various limitations on these rights can be imposed so long as it is done in an even-handed fashion with respect to race. Yet, at the same time, the one result that the Fourteenth Amendment does *not* bring about is to override the key notion of freedom of association by denying to all private persons the right to choose whom they wish to contract with in the first place.

The dominance of the antidiscrimination norm makes it easy for courts to convert the classical liberal conceptions that animated the 1866 Civil Rights Act into a robust version of the antidiscrimination principle. The Warren Court adopted this interpretation of Section 1982,[47] the modern statutory successor to the 1866 act, in *Jones v. Alfred H. Mayer Co.* (1968).[48] The *Jones* decision held that Section 1982 barred all forms of private discrimination in the sale or renting of real estate on the grounds of race, by virtue of its plain meaning. Yet the decision never acknowledged the sensible reading of Section 1982, namely, that if white persons could sell, or refuse to sell, to white or black persons, then black persons could

---

[45] Civil Rights Act of 1866, chap. 31, 14 Stat. 27, 27–30 (codified as amendments at 42 U.S.C. secs. 1981, 1982 [2005]).

[46] U.S. Constitution, Fourteenth Amendment, Section 1. For an analysis of the relationship between the citizens protected under the privileges or immunities clause of the Fourteenth Amendment and the persons protected under the due process and equal protection clauses, see Richard A. Epstein, "Of Citizens and Persons: Reconstructing the Privileges or Immunities Clause of the Fourteenth Amendment," *New York University Journal of Law and Liberty* 1 (2005): 334–54; Richard A. Epstein, "Further Thoughts on the Privileges or Immunities Clause of the Fourteenth Amendment," *New York University Journal of Law and Liberty* 1 (2005): 1095.

[47] 42 U.S.C. section 1982: "Property rights of citizens: All citizens of the United States shall have the same right, in every State and Territory, as is enjoyed by white citizens thereof to inherit, purchase, lease, sell, hold, and convey real and personal property."

[48] *Jones v. Alfred H. Mayer Co.*, 390 U.S. 409 (1968).

sell, or refuse to sell, to white or black persons. Far from imposing a non-discrimination obligation on persons of all races, Section 1982 expressly negates that obligation.[49] Yet once the error in *Jones* is put aside, nothing in the 1866 Civil Rights Act or any of its successors has the built-in role-specific characteristic of modern human rights statutes. The modern human rights statutes all protect, for example, tenants against landlords, or employees against employers. The 1866 act and its successor did not favor one side of the relationship. Rather, they allowed any person to decide whether to become a landlord or a tenant, an employer or an employee, with the same level of contractual protection always enjoyed by whites.

Correlative duties. The modern human rights laws are also deficient by being inattentive to the duties that are correlative to the rights created. Rights are claims over scarce resources—human, physical, or intangible. Any claim only makes sense if the assignment of a right to *A* necessarily imposes duties on at least some *B*.[50] A mature system of rights thus requires, at a minimum, internal coherence. It is not sufficient to identify the holder and the object of the right; it is also necessary to specify who is bound and to what correlative duties. Accordingly, classical jurisprudence always paired human rights with correlative human duties. To the extent that one person's sphere of action is expanded, the liberty of action of all other individuals is *necessarily* contracted. In designing a system of rights, the advantages that we conceive of and create for certain individuals should more than offset the disadvantages thereby imposed upon others. Today's mantra of human rights refuses, rhetorically, to acknowledge the existence, and certainly the weight, of these correlative duties. No one wants to defend the "Reconfigured Human Rights and Duties Act," much less the "Human Duties Act." Yet why the lack of candor?

The answer is simple. It is much easier to forge winning coalitions by accentuating the positive. The strong constraints of scarcity are ignored, so it looks as though the new legal reform does create free lunches for all. To be sure, the classical liberal position also has explicit correlative duties, namely, those universal duties of noninterference in the state of nature, and those specific duties of compliance with voluntary obligations. But these rules have powerful efficiency properties. The primary duties among strangers are relatively easy to state, and, most critically, are scalable, so that the content of these duties is the same whether we work in a society of thousands or millions. The gains from noninterference dwarf the losses. And for particular obligations, the ability to pick trading partners helps assure joint gains. Disappointed competitors may lose, as they always do, but the increased wealth and opportunities for all enhance the overall size of the pie, creating positive externalities, which should not be ignored in

---

[49] For my further defense of this position, see Epstein, "Two Conceptions of Civil Rights."

[50] Wesley Newcomb Hohfeld, *Fundamental Legal Conceptions, As Applied in Judicial Reasoning and Other Legal Essays* (New Haven, CT: Yale University Press, 1919).

the social calculus even if they are (unlike nuisances) rarely the subject of legal action.

Affirmative action. The classical liberal position and the modern human rights acts also take radically different approaches to the recurrent question of affirmative action programs, which are intended to give some individuals preferences for jobs or positions in universities, say, on the grounds of race or sex. The classical liberal view, of course, does not care why people choose to associate with others. So it does not demand any special public justification by private organizations for preferring women or minority members. Just do it, is the answer. But the flipside is that other groups, be they many or few, may favor men or members of some privileged white elite if they so choose. In practice, voluntary organizations tend to follow the patterns preferred by the defenders of affirmative action, but that hardly provides a reason for exempting only these preferred patterns from the antidiscrimination principle under some ad hoc exception that stresses the historical differences in the treatment of, say, minority groups and women. All that historical information is public, and, if they choose, private organizations can take it into account in fashioning their rules of admission. If women's clubs are permissible, then why not men's? The historical record does not go to general unique entitlements. It only influences the likelihood that men's or women's clubs will form. More specifically, there is no reason to condition the ability of women to form private associations on some proof of past discrimination against women or on some supposed social consensus that bias, either overt or subconscious, persists against members of certain groups.

Nor should we like the current system that justifies some forms of discrimination by consulting the historical record. Using past discrimination to justify the exemption of some forms of discrimination from modern human rights laws creates a real moral hazard: it leads both government and private parties to exaggerate their own past injustices against their favored groups in order to sustain preferential treatment in those groups' favor. That effort to skew the political dialog is both mischievous and unnecessary. Let any group form along any lines, and the pattern of preference gives a good sense of the social response without forcing dissenters to hew to the majority will. There is, in fact, no need for any private group to offer some special justification for its own affirmative action programs.

The situation with public institutions is somewhat more complex, for here state agencies tend to be fiduciaries of the public at large, and these agencies neither do nor should have the same freedom of action as private parties.[51] That point carries with it special power in connection with the enforcement of the basic rights to bodily integrity and private

---

[51] For a more detailed statement of my views, see Richard A. Epstein, "A Rational Basis for Affirmative Action: A Shaky but Classical Liberal Defense," *Michigan Law Review* 100 (2002): 2036–61. For the mainstream position, see, e.g., Erwin Chemerinsky, "A Grand Theory of Constitutional Law?" *Michigan Law Review* 100 (2002): 1249–64.

property. There can be no system of affirmative action in dealing with criminal situations, with one law of murder for whites and another for blacks. But the modern state also deals heavily in the provision of key goods, such as education, which in an ideal world should be left to private actors. And once the government is in the management business, it has to have some greater degree of discretion than it does with the enforcement of the criminal law, or other functions of the minimal state. At this juncture, I think that the distribution of popular sentiment should help influence what the state can do. So long as there is—and there is—extensive support for affirmative action programs at all kinds of private universities, there is a presumption that these programs should be allowed for their public competitors. I would not apply this test to the Jim Crow era, where all public and private decisions were governed by corrupt political institutions. But I think the relative openness of modern political choices makes it defensible to allow affirmative action programs to function in the public setting—as a second-best solution when there is no realistic way to eliminate state institutions of higher education.

Information destruction. Yet another unfortunate feature of modern human rights laws stems from their adverse impact on one of the most essential ingredients of well-functioning markets: a high level of information flow among parties to voluntary transactions. Once a human rights law designates certain characteristics as "off limits," that law must implement ways to keep the parties subject to it—landlords, proprietors, and especially employers—from using information about those characteristics for improper purposes. In multiple ways, therefore, the task of the legal system is to keep regulated parties in the dark. Two illustrations make this basic point: one deals with testing and the other with medical records.

First, the prohibition against discrimination in employment quickly led, in the important case of *Griggs v. Duke Power Co.* (1971),[52] to an explicit limitation on systematic standardized testing by employers of their prospective and actual employees. The disparate impact, whereby black applicants systematically perform worse than white applicants, counts as a form of discrimination that can only be justified by business necessity.[53] No longer can private employers rely on standardized tests, such as

---

[52] *Griggs v. Duke Power Co.*, 401 U.S. 424 (1971).

[53] For my views, see Epstein, *Forbidden Grounds*, 159–266. For earlier work in this vein, see Harold Demsetz, "Minorities in the Market Place," *North Carolina Law Review* 43 (1965): 271–97; Alfred Avins, "Anti-Discrimination Legislation as an Infringement on Freedom of Choice," *New York Law Forum* 6 (1960): 13–37; Milton Friedman, *Capitalism and Freedom* (Chicago: University of Chicago Press, 1962), 108–18 (noting the relationship between economic freedom and the absence of discrimination, and criticizing antidiscrimination laws as ineffective and costly); and Richard Posner, "The Efficiency and the Efficacy of Title VII," *University of Pennsylvania Law Review* 136 (1987): 513–21 (assessing the costs that are either ignored or imposed by Title VII).

the Wonderlic test,[54] which have proved valuable in a wide range of contexts. Instead, the statutory approach kills the messenger by barring the use of any standardized test in which minority employees are underrepresented unless it passes a tight definition of job-relatedness.[55]

No one claims that these tests are perfect, or that other forms of employer evaluation don't count. The only question is whether the hiring process can be made more rational with this information than without it. The current rule states that testing cannot be used even if it improves prediction of successful job performance, unless it has a virtually perfect correlation with success, which no test has. The costs of this approach are quite large because it forces the preparation, at great expense, of particularized tests that must focus narrowly on certain defined tasks. Such job-specific tests are of little value in identifying the long-term career paths of job candidates and employees. The consequence is that employers have less information to make decisions, and workers have a reduced incentive to acquire those forms of information that are not tested.

Second, with respect to medical records, the tendency toward disinformation also arises under the Americans with Disabilities Act. Information about potential disabilities generally cannot be taken into account in making decisions on hiring or promotion,[56] but the ADA permits employers to collect the same information for medical purposes.[57] The entire system thus requires deliberate concealment and material nondisclosure that would, if not government sanctioned, be branded as a serious form of fraud (say, for example, under the 1933 Securities Act).[58] The consequence, of course, is the creation of large, concealed cross-subsidies, as healthier workers are forced to bear some fraction of the medical costs of

---

For defenses of the modern view, see Steven L. Willborn, "The Disparate Impact of Discrimination: Theory and Limits," *American University Law Review* 34 (1985): 799–837 (defending the disparate-impact test, using economic analysis); and George Rutherglen, "Disparate Impact Under Title VII: An Objective Theory of Discrimination," *Virginia Law Review* 73 (1987): 1297–1345 (defending the *Griggs* disparate-impact test as a logical judicial application of the 1964 Civil Rights Act).

[54] For details on the Wonderlic test, which is a twelve-minute, fifty-question exam meant to test employees' acuity, see "Wonderlic Test," *Wikipedia,* http://en.wikipedia.org/wiki/Wonderlic_Test (accessed August 8, 2007).

[55] A plaintiff may demonstrate that use of a test is an unlawful business practice if he demonstrates that the testing "causes a disparate impact on the basis of race, color, religion, sex, or national origin and the respondent fails to demonstrate that the challenged practice is job related for the position in question and consistent with business necessity." 42 U.S.C. sec. 2000e-2(k)(1)(A)(i). Even if the plaintiff cannot meet this burden, "the plaintiff can still prevail if he can show that there is an alternative selection method that has substantial validity and a less disparate impact." *Firefighter's Institute for Racial Equality v. City of St. Louis,* 220 F.3d 898 (8th Cir. 2000), citing 42 U.S.C. sec. 2000e-2(k)(1)(A)(ii).

[56] 42 U.S.C. sec. 12112(a).

[57] 42 U.S.C. sec. 12112(d)(3).

[58] For an example of the high level of disclosures required in the securities context to avoid liability for tortious misrepresentation, see *TSC Industries Inc. v. Northway Inc.,* 426 U.S. 438, 449 (1976): "An omitted fact is material [and therefore requires disclosure] if there is a substantial likelihood that a reasonable shareholder would consider it important in deciding how to vote."

their less fortunate colleagues. It may well be that some public support should be provided to workers who are unable to obtain insurance through their employers. But the current situation is highly unstable.

To be sure, it is easy to make arguments that the gain to a worker from additional medical insurance produces a greater social benefit than the financial loss sustained by the employer. Cass Sunstein offers the hypothetical case of a poor disabled worker who is only willing to pay $20 more for an accommodation that it costs an employer $150 to supply; he reasons that the employer should bear the $150 cost, since the gain in social welfare would be greater than the cost as measured by some impoverished standard of willingness-to-pay.[59] Everyone likes to make interpersonal comparisons of utility in the abstract. But this ostensible appeal to a social-welfare standard is wholly myopic because it ignores the full institutional setting. It does not ask whether, for example, separate facilities for disabled workers should be encouraged because they reduce the employer's average costs so as to make the alteration feasible. Build a facility for ten disabled workers, and its benefits could exceed the cost to the employer, such that in a low-transaction-cost environment, the improvement can take place. But if it cannot, then announcing that we should force the exchange has profound negative consequences. First of all, without a willingness-to-pay criterion, no one knows how real these numbers are. It is easy to inflate preferences when they need not be backed by dollars. Nor do those simple numbers take into account the effect of the change in amenities for other workers or customers—an effect which could, depending on circumstances, be either positive or negative. Nor does any simple effort to get to overall welfare without going through market transactions take into account the profound incentive effects that the systematic coercion has on employers, who will flee from hiring, especially in large numbers, disabled workers who cost them more in total compensation than they bring in return benefits.[60]

The mistake here lies in thinking that any long-term social improvement can come by using the coercive power of the state to force win/lose relationships on employers, or for that matter, on anyone else. The program is too reminiscent of the general socialist mind-set that central planning can do a better job with social welfare than individual choice. But it always backfires. Universalize this social-welfare norm and every firm could be bankrupted by constant demands to supply benefits that cost the firm more than it generates in revenue. With bankruptcy looming, employers will evolve to minimize the legal pressure, by reconfiguring their

---

[59] See Cass Sunstein, "Willingness to Pay vs. Welfare," *Harvard Law and Policy Review* 1 (2007): 303. The use of contingent valuation in environmental contexts on issues relating to pollution is always more defensible, because some collective judgment is necessarily required, and there is no disruption of voluntary transactions.

[60] Thomas DeLeire, "The Wage and Employment Effects of the Americans with Disabilities Act," *Journal of Human Resources* 35 (2000): 693–715.

operations in ways that make them less dependent on the labor of disabled persons.

Ironically, one point that we can be confident of is that the introduction of any antidiscrimination law will introduce covert discrimination. In open markets, the ability to adjust wage and other terms allows all sorts of persons to compete by accepting lower wages, if need be. But once those wage adjustments are ruled out, we should expect employers to take, covertly to be sure, avoidance measures to minimize their exposure. We cannot improve welfare by destroying markets.

The message is therefore cautionary. If some government intervention is appropriate to deal with the additional health-care costs of disabled individuals, an explicit government subsidy is a more transparent and efficient way to handle this problem. Unfortunately, the current appetite for hidden cross-subsidies has the predicted effect. It tends to discourage firms from hiring disabled employees in the first place.

Explicit state discrimination. The aggressive enforcement of human rights laws does more than increase the levels of private discrimination. In the public sphere as well, it can create the very abuses that these laws were intended to guard against. As with affirmative action, it is critical to distinguish between the government as an enforcer of rights and the government as a manager of its own businesses. As to state regulation, the key element to success is to reduce the level of discretion in the enforcement of law. The multifactor tests under all the antidiscrimination laws necessarily increase the scope of government power to regulate private firms. State officials have to collect evidence to establish certain violations and determine remedies. They have to decide whom to sue and with whom to settle. They know that bringing any enforcement action can impose real costs on private parties, even those that prevail after painful litigation, with the attendant loss of reputation.

So who are the officials who carry out these sensitive roles? People who tend to be supporters of the human rights statutes. They, in turn, erect questionable presumptions of wrongdoing that bear little relationship to fact, or impose race- or sex-specific remedies in order to correct what they regard as unconscious forms of discrimination. There is little, however, that anyone can do to restrain the vast reservoirs of state discretion, which pose a serious threat to the rule of law.

The situation is grim on the other side as well. State agencies have to make their own hiring decisions. Yet under the current law they are vulnerable to disparate impact cases even when they have introduced affirmative action programs that parallel those in private businesses. The most perverse upending of these programs arose in *Connecticut v. Teal* (1982),[61] still good law, where the state agency both ran an aggressive affirmative action program (on the one hand), and conducted extensive

---

[61] *Connecticut v. Teal*, 457 U.S. 440 (1982).

standardized testing, with the usual black/white disparities (on the other). The logic of the Connecticut program was first to set an appropriate ratio between white and black employees, and then to select the strongest candidates from each group. One can easily quarrel with the use of explicit race-based criteria for government employment. But so long as affirmative action programs are a part of public and private life, the key question is how to maximize the efficiency of the workforce subject to that constraint, which the Connecticut program did.

In the *Teal* decision, however, Justice William Brennan struck down the use of the test in the case of a black applicant who fell below the cut-off line for the black group on the ground that the test did not meet the rigorous job-related standards established in *Griggs*. But Brennan's decision was wholly context-blind. The attack on testing in *Griggs* was motivated by the (not-unjustified) fear that some employers might seek to introduce race classifications through the back door under the guise of testing. But that fear was wholly negated by the unquestioned implementation of Connecticut's extensive affirmative action program. The effect of *Teal* was to knock out the testing that allowed for efficient sorting of job candidates. With the decline of testing, subjective factors come back into the equation, leading to various forms of intrigue in public and private workplaces, even those committed to affirmative action. It is important to recall that the key function of the antidiscrimination principle is to operate as a brake against the monopoly power of the state. Those concerns are not present in labor markets, where the government as employer is in competition with private employers. Without question, these private employers would resort to testing to get better information about their workers if left free to do so by the state. There is no reason why the state should not be allowed to operate in the same fashion as its private competitors.

The illusion of abundance. The failure to recognize the exaggerated claims about the benefits of human rights laws has the unfortunate consequence of ignoring or understating their associated costs. As long as this is the case, we will live, and suffer, under the happy illusion that the constraints of scarcity do not really matter—that we will be able to magnify certain rights without limitation, while nobody need pay the cost either directly or indirectly. That is, of course, a fantasy. How, then, does this fantasy take hold? It does so partly, I believe, through employing the following technique. Instead of talking in terms of human beings on both sides of the rights/duties divide, we depersonalize the entities on whom the duties are imposed. Individual people receive the benefits created by human rights laws, but the burdens of the laws are imposed on abstract entities such as corporations, unions, universities, and other organizations.

This mental conjuring trick rests on illusory foundations. The collectives on which we impose duties are comprised of individuals as shareholders and members. Organizations do not act themselves; they act through individuals and for individuals, be they shareholders, union members, or faculty and students. Consequently, in analyzing the impact of a statute, we must return to the postulate of methodological individualism, so congenial to the classical liberal tradition. We cannot simply match human rights to a set of correlative duties on abstract bodies. We cannot just appeal to notions of community to impose obligations on individuals and the groups they form. We must trace the implications of the statute through the entity to the particular individuals on whom those duties will be imposed.

In politics the same principle applies. It is incorrect to say that the government has a "duty" to supply benefits to its citizens. Any benefits created by the government must necessarily be backed by regulation, taxation, or the imposition of liability on other individuals. Those burdens must be recognized and weighed against the benefits, if an appropriate balance is to be obtained. Unfortunately, this balance will *not* be obtained if public rhetoric conceals the relevant trade-offs.

Moreover, even when the cost elements of a modern human rights statute are allowed to enter into the equation, they are never placed on the same footing as the rights side. Characteristically, in these statutes the rights are put, so to speak, in bold sixteen-point type at the top of the page while underneath, in a corner, the costs are set out in barely legible eight-point type.[62] If the costs turn out to be too great, they may not even feature in the discussion at all.

V. Law and Popular Opinion

The modern conception of human rights is on a collision course with the rival norm of freedom of contract and association. But why worry? In many cases, the legal conflict is submerged because the relevant actors choose voluntarily to adopt social or trading norms that track those embodied in the human rights laws. Why fight, the argument goes, the passage and enforcement of laws with which you willingly comply? After all, even in the absence of antidiscrimination laws, it is rarely a winning strategy for any large firm or institution to state publicly that it will not trade with women or racial minorities. Everyone else has the parallel

---

[62] At the very beginning of the text of the Americans with Disabilities Act, Congress loudly proclaims the benefits created by the statute: "(1) to provide a clear and comprehensive national mandate for the elimination of discrimination against individuals with disabilities; (2) to provide clear, strong, consistent, enforceable standards addressing discrimination against individuals with disabilities; (3) to ensure that the Federal Government plays a central role in enforcing the standards established in this Act on behalf of individuals with disabilities; and (4) to invoke the sweep of congressional authority, including the power to enforce the fourteenth amendment and to regulate commerce, in order to address the major areas of discrimination faced day-to-day by people with disabilities." Pub. L. No. 101-336, sec. 2, 104 Stat. 327 (1990). It is not until much later, hidden in the "definitions" section, that Congress hints that there might be costs associated with the creation of these benefits. See sec. 101(10) (defining undue hardship).

right to refuse to do business with that firm, and to urge like-minded individuals to take the same course. The reputational constraints are so powerful that many firms would voluntarily adopt the mantle of equal opportunity employers. Indeed, many of these firms would, and now do, adopt some affirmative action programs to improve their position in key markets. It would be wholly cynical to dismiss all these programs merely as clumsy efforts to ward off liability under the antidiscrimination laws. Much of the problem of discrimination would take care of itself.

With that said, why object to a legal rule that only requires those practices that enjoy widespread social compliance? The best answer puts that query in reverse. If the social sanctions against egregious behavior are strong, as they are, then why resort to law? There is no need for all firms in any given market niche to toe the same line. It is far better to encourage some sensible sorting of institutions. Organizations with mainstream beliefs will adopt mainstream behaviors. The strong popular sentiment that crystallizes behind human rights statutes will influence the choices in most private institutions even if those statutes are repealed tomorrow. But that general pattern still leaves dissenters the option to go to niche organizations that satisfy their idiosyncratic preferences. Women who want to associate with men on the job can also choose, no questions asked, a female obstetrician, even if the extensive (if diminishing) presence of male obstetricians proves that the sex of physicians is not what our antidiscrimination laws call a "bona fide occupational qualification."[63] Ostensibly, a hospital or physician group must choose male doctors on a par with female doctors or face charges of sex discrimination. Patient preferences do not count unless we create an exception for physicians. (Would this exception cover all physicians? Some? Which?) Many women ski students prefer women instructors as well, so now we have a second exception.

Unfortunately, however, the relevant human rights statutes make categorical determinations about individual preferences that map poorly onto the tastes of ordinary people, for whom sex (and race) matters in some but not all contexts. Human rights law has only two choices: ignore the variations or become so complex that no one can administer it. But why try to refine the classifications? Relaxing the human rights rule does not confer an advantage on one sex over the other. Male patients may well prefer male urologists and female dermatologists. Or perhaps not. But who cares? The classical liberal principle of freedom of association does not require us to gather the refined information that would be needed to sort out these various exceptions. It just lets people do so themselves. Where race and sex don't matter, this will be reflected in personal choices, which generate powerful market dynamics. Where they do matter, that will be taken into account as well. Just go with the flow, and the problem

---

[63] Civil Rights Act of 1964, 42 U.S.C. sec. 2000e-2(e).

will solve itself, without the discontinuous bumps and starts so characteristic of legislative intervention and private litigation, both of which can
make demands that move far beyond the underlying social consensus.

VI. A New Human Rights Act

The dangers of human rights legislation should induce us to return to
the classical liberal conception of human rights, with its emphasis on
self-determination, private property, and voluntary exchange, subject only
to the monopoly constraint (discussed above in Section II.B). Here is a
short, snappy, and comprehensive human rights statute that implements
the classical liberal program on a universal basis. It is indifferent to status
or role, and requires no elaborate administrative apparatus. Its purpose
here is facilitative, not restrictive. The contrast with the New Jersey LAD
and the New York Human Rights Law should be evident.

Human Rights Act, Revised

§1. Every individual and group shall, in the use and disposition of
property or labor, have the right to contract, associate, or otherwise transact or do business with any other individual or group
whom they choose on whatever terms and conditions they see fit,
and for whatever purposes they see fit, be they commercial, social,
or religious.

§2. Every individual and group may refuse to contract or associate
with, or otherwise discriminate for or against, any other group or
individual for whatever reasons they see fit, including, without
limitation, decisions based in whole or in part on race, creed, sex,
religion, age, disability, marital status, or sexual orientation.

§3. (a) Every individual or group may ask of any other individual or
group any question they see fit, no matter how offensive, imper-
tinent, intrusive, superficial, or irrelevant. (b) Every individual or
group may refuse to answer any question, however tactful, pertinent, respectful, insightful, or relevant.

§4. (a) Every agreement, contract, or association shall be construed in
accordance with the ordinary meanings of its terms, as informed
by custom and common usage within the relevant trade, industry, or social or religious grouping. (b) No construction or interpretation of any agreement, contract, or articles of association
shall be made or influenced by principles of unconscionability,
adhesion, inequality of bargaining power, *contra proferentem*, or
any other rule that presumes one party to the agreement or contract enjoys a protected or preferred social status relative to the
other.

§5. Every individual or group shall have the right to offer transportation or other services for hire on the public highways or

waterways, or in the public airspace, subject only to reasonable and nondiscriminatory regulations imposed in the interest of public safety.

§6. All actions brought to enforce rights under any contract, agreement, or association shall be commenced in the trial court of general jurisdiction. The Human Rights Commission, the Equal Opportunity Employment Commission, the Employment Court, and all other specialized courts are hereby abolished.

This modest reform eliminates thousands of pages of regulation and thousands of government administrative positions. It will save, annually, billions of dollars in administrative and compliance costs. What's not to like?

Law, The University of Chicago

FREEDOM OF ASSOCIATION IN HISTORICAL PERSPECTIVE*

By Stephen B. Presser

I. The Way It Once Was: Encouraging Laudable Associations

This essay is about some American conceptions of freedom of association, and it is helpful, in order to determine how we ought to think about that freedom of association, to begin by exploring the purposes for which Americans have sought to associate. This requires considering shared conceptions of American society, if not, indeed, the most basic questions about humanity, morality, religion, philosophy, and politics in their historical American context. Keeping things very simple, let's begin by asking, "What was the original understanding of the purpose of American society?" A good historical starting point is the Declaration of Independence, which set out the reasons Americans sought to break with their mother country. The Declaration notes that governments exist in order to preserve and protect "inalienable rights" to life, liberty, and the pursuit of happiness, and it tracks John Locke's similar assertion (in his *Second Treatise*) of government's job as the protector of life, liberty, and property.[1] This suggests the enduring importance of individual rights in American society, since the preservation of these rights is viewed as the job of the American governments, but while the Declaration of Independence makes clear the importance of individual rights to Americans, the Declaration itself tells us little about what we are supposed to do with these individual rights, and indeed, how, precisely, they are supposed to aid us in interacting with each other—or, to put the problem in more general terms, why these rights (and possibly others) are necessary for human flourishing.

Not so very long ago, it used to be said, by undergraduates at one Connecticut institution of higher learning, that one ought to be "for God,

* I wish to thank Andrew Koppelman for helpful discussions on this topic, though he bears no responsibility for the conclusions reached here, and, indeed, vehemently disagrees with many of them. I have no claims to be regarded as an experienced freedom of association doctrinal scholar. I seek only to examine what look to a nonspecialist to be some fundamental discontinuities in the judicial treatment of freedom of association.

[1] See generally, e.g., Carl Becker, *The Declaration of Independence: A Study in the History of Political Ideas* (New York: Vintage Books, 1958); and Pauline Maier, *American Scripture: Making the Declaration of Independence* (New York: Knopf, 1997). For Locke's *Second Treatise*, see John Locke, *Two Treatises of Government*, ed. Peter Laslett (Cambridge: Cambridge University Press, 1988).

doi:10.1017/S0265052508080229

for Country, and for Yale."[2] If we can generalize, perhaps this means that there was an ethos, pervasive and dominant until very recently, that it was the divinely sanctioned task of humans to glorify God, to serve their country, and to demonstrate loyalty to certain of what we now call intermediate institutions,[3] such as universities, churches, fraternal organizations, unions, trade organizations, and families. Put even more simply, in America the purpose of human life on earth, guided by Christian morals and a belief in a God who rewarded the good and punished the wicked,[4] was to ensure one's place in the afterlife through altruistic service to one's fellows, one's country, and one's God. Such altruism was, of course, impossible unless one were in a position to associate with other members in society; and, thus, freedom of association, as a means to religiously inspired altruistic service to others, could be conceived as indispensable to human flourishing.

Societally coerced association, in most quarters, was believed to be anathema, in no small part because Christian concepts of salvation, at least the dominant ones in eighteenth- and nineteenth-century America, required the exercise of free choice. This explains the American penchant for freedom to seek God's grace in one's own fashion—in short, for freedom of religion. Two contemporary expressions limn that freedom of religion and are worth quoting here. These are the First Amendment to the United States Constitution (1791) and the 1786 Virginia Statute for Religious Freedom.

The First Amendment was passed because of a fear that the newly established federal government might unduly interfere with Americans' exercise of important social activities,[5] and provides that "Congress shall make no law respecting an establishment of religion, or prohibiting the free exercise thereof; or abridging the freedom of speech, or of the press;

---

[2] See, e.g., Kristen Thompson, "Yale's Response Through a Century of War: What 'For God, for Country, and for Yale' Has Meant to Generations of Yalies," *The Yale Herald* 35, no. 10 (April 4, 2003), available at http://www.yaleherald.com/article.php?Article=1995.

[3] The importance of intermediate institutions—institutions occupying a social space between the individual and the government—was one of the central insights not only of conservatives such as Edmund Burke, but also of the left in the American legal academy. See, e.g., Roberto M. Unger, *Knowledge and Politics* (New York: The Free Press, 1975), 236–95 (setting forth Unger's theory of "organic groups," intermediate associations which he recommends for a just society).

[4] See, e.g., the Pennsylvania Constitution of 1776, chapter II, section 10, requiring each member of the legislature to make the following "declaration": "I do believe in one God, the creator and governor of the universe, the rewarder of the good and punisher of the wicked, and I do acknowledge the scriptures of the Old and New Testament to be given by Divine Inspiration." Reproduced in Stephen B. Presser and Jamil S. Zainaldin, *Law and Jurisprudence in American History*, 6th ed. (Minneapolis, MN: Thomson/West, 2006), 120.

[5] For a work exploring the original purposes of the First Amendment's religion clauses and subsequent misunderstandings of those purposes, see Steven D. Smith, *Foreordained Failure: The Quest for a Constitutional Principle of Religious Freedom* (New York and Oxford: Oxford University Press, 1997). On this point, see also Stephen B. Presser, "Some Realism about Atheism: Responses to the Godless Constitution," *Texas Review of Law and Politics* 1, no. 1 (Spring 1997): 87–121.

or the right of the people peaceably to assemble, and to petition the government for a redress of grievances." [6]

The 1786 Virginia Statute for Religious Freedom, while not widely known today, was one of the most important documents of the early republic, and was apparently one of the three proudest accomplishments of Thomas Jefferson, its principal draftsman.[7] It is worth lingering with the statute for a while for the sense that it gives us, similar to that provided by the First Amendment to the U.S. Constitution, of the primary importance of religion in general and religious freedom in particular. Thus, in the first section of the statute, Jefferson sets out the place of religious freedom in a sensible society, and his basic beliefs regarding what that freedom is to accomplish:

> Whereas Almighty God hath created the mind free; that all attempts to influence it by temporal punishments or burthens, or by civil incapacitations, tend only to beget habits of hypocrisy and meanness, and are a departure from the plan of the Holy author of our religion, who being Lord both of body and mind, yet chose not to propagate it by coercions on either, as it was in his Almighty power to do; that the impious presumption of legislators and rulers, civil as well as ecclesiastical, who being themselves but fallible and uninspired men, have assumed dominion over the faith of others, setting up their own opinions and modes of thinking as the only true and infallible, and as such endeavouring to impose them on others, hath established and maintained false religions over the greatest part of the world, and through all time; that to compel a man to furnish contributions of money for the propagation of opinions which he disbelieves, is sinful and tyrannical; that even the forcing him to support this or that teacher of his own religious persuasion, is depriving him of the comfortable liberty of giving his contributions to the particular pastor, whose morals he would make his pattern ... ; that our civil rights have no dependence on our religious opinions, any more than our opinions in physics or geometry; that therefore the proscribing any citizen as unworthy the public confidence by laying upon him an incapacity of being called to offices of trust and emolument, unless he profess or renounce this or that religious opinion, is depriving him injuriously of those privileges and advantages to which in common with his fellow-citizens he has a natural right; that it tends only to

---

[6] United States Constitution, Amendment I (1791).

[7] Jefferson was the third president of the United States, the second vice president, and the first secretary of state. Nevertheless, pursuant to his directions, the only three accomplishments noted on his tombstone were that he was the author of the Declaration of Independence, the author of the Virginia Statute for Religious Freedom, and the founder of the University of Virginia. See, e.g., U.S. Presidents, Profiles: Thomas Jefferson," http://www.exploredc.org/index.php?id=72.

corrupt the principles of that religion it is meant to encourage, by bribing with a monopoly of worldly honours and emoluments, those who will externally profess and conform to it; that though indeed these are criminal who do not withstand such temptation, yet neither are those innocent who lay the bait in their way; that to suffer the civil magistrate to intrude his powers into the field of opinion, and to restrain the profession or propagation of principles on supposition of their ill tendency, is a dangerous fallacy, which at once destroys all religious liberty, because he being of course judge of that tendency will make his opinions the rule of judgment, and approve or condemn the sentiments of others only as they shall square with or differ from his own; that it is time enough for the rightful purposes of civil government, for its officers to interfere when principles break out into overt acts against peace and good order; and finally, that truth is great and will prevail if left to herself, that she is the proper and sufficient antagonist to error, and has nothing to fear from the conflict, unless by human interposition disarmed of her natural weapons, free argument and debate, errors ceasing to be dangerous when it is permitted freely to contradict them . . .

Given, then, Jefferson's belief that if matters of religion were to be able to be freely debated, religious truth (the existence of which was assumed) would be able to prevail, the second section of the statute provided that no Virginian

shall be compelled to frequent or support any religious worship, place, or ministry whatsoever, nor shall be enforced, restrained, molested, or burthened in his body or goods, nor shall otherwise suffer on account of his religious opinions or belief; but that all men shall be free to profess, and by argument to maintain, their opinion in matters of religion, and that the same shall in no wise diminish, enlarge, or affect their civil capacities.

In quite an extraordinary underscoring of the importance of these first two sections of the statute, Jefferson added a third, designed for the ages. Referring to what everyone then understood to be the plenary power of the Virginia legislature (since no Virginia Constitution restricting it on religious matters then existed), Jefferson concluded:

[T]hough we well know that this assembly elected by the people for the ordinary purposes of legislation only, have no power to restrain the acts of succeeding assemblies, constituted with powers equal to our own, and that therefore to declare this act to be irrevocable would be of no effect in law; yet we are free to declare, and do declare, that the rights hereby asserted are of the natural rights of mankind, and that if any act shall be hereafter passed to repeal the present, or to narrow its operation, such act shall be an infringement of natural right.[8]

The meaning of this rather remarkable statement—the linkage of religious freedom with the "natural rights of mankind"—made it as clear as possible that this was fundamental stuff, and of the essence of American life. Still, it is worth understanding, as Jefferson suggests, that freedom of religion and freedom of association had to allow for improper choices as well as proper ones, if the responsibility for one's immortal soul rested, after all, on one's own shoulders. Religious choices, for Jefferson, were not something the state should coerce, because this was contrary to the plan of God himself.

Still, among most of the Framers of the U.S. Constitution, there appears to have been a shared belief that it was the duty of the state not only to provide freedom of religion and freedom of association, but also to provide support for the encouragement of religion, and probably specifically for the Protestant Christian variety. Even though Jefferson is generally regarded as a firm proponent of the separation of church and state, the most recent scholarship on Jefferson suggests that he, too, was, to a certain extent, a proponent of using the power of the state to support religion:

Too many acts and writings of Thomas Jefferson contradict the image of him as a strict separationist to allow us to conclude that he sought to build a high and impregnable wall of separation between church and state. As President he attended religious services in the halls of Congress and allowed others to engage in such services in federal buildings. While it is true that he refused to proclaim official days of thanksgiving, he frequently made official public announcements that accomplished the same thing. Indeed he went so far as to use religion for explicitly political purposes as President, particularly in his dealing with Native Americans. He gave his approval to both the use of public tax dollars for the purpose of promoting Christianity among Native Americans and to the teaching of religion in public schools in Virginia. None of these acts demonstrate that Jefferson was not serious about allowing individuals freedom of conscience when it came to religious matters because none of them interfered with such freedom. But almost all of these activities suggest that Jefferson was willing to allow a certain level of interplay between religion and the state where such interplay did not infringe upon individual religious freedom.[9]

---

[8] W. W. Hening, ed., *Statutes at Large of Virginia*, vol. 12 (1823), 84–86.
[9] Mark J. Chadsey, "Thomas Jefferson and the Establishment Clause," *Akron Law Review* 40 (2007): 623, 645 (footnotes omitted).

Moreover, there were at the time of the American Revolution at least three established state churches: the Church of England (Anglican) in Virginia, and the Congregational Church in Connecticut and Massachusetts. And one can find, in the courts, explicit examples of judges seeking, in an appropriate Christian manner, the salvation of the souls of Christian defendants condemned to the gallows. The best example I have found was an admonition from the bench to John Fries, convicted of treason for participating in an armed rebellion in 1799 against federal tax collectors in eastern Pennsylvania. Fries and his co-participants in what came to be called the "Fries Rebellion" or the "Hot Water War" (because some of the Pennsylvanians had sought to douse the tax collectors with scalding water) had virtually shut down the federal government in general and the collection of taxes in particular in that part of the state. As the ringleaders, Fries and a few of his fellows were convicted by a Philadelphia jury presided over by Samuel Chase, an associate justice of the United States Supreme Court. As Fries stood condemned to hang, Chase stated to Fries:

> You have forfeited your life to justice. Let me, therefore, earnestly recommend to you most seriously to consider your situation—to take a review of your past life, and to employ the very little time you are to continue in this world in endeavors to make your peace with that God whose mercy is equal to his justice. I suppose that you are a Christian; and as such I address you. Be assured my guilty and unhappy fellow-citizen, that without serious repentance of all your sins, you cannot expect happiness in the world to come.... Your day of life is almost spent; and the night of death fast approaches. Look up to the Father of mercies, and God of comfort. You have a great and immense work to perform, and but little time in which you must finish it. There is no repentance in the grave, for after death comes judgment; and as you die, so you must be judged.... If you will sincerely repent and believe, God has pronounced his forgiveness; and there is no crime too great for his mercy and pardon.[10]

In the leading case proclaiming the United States "a religious people," the United States Supreme Court observed in *Holy Trinity Church v. U.S.* (1892) that "From the discovery of this continent to the present hour, there is a single voice making this affirmation." [11] When Queen Elizabeth authorized Sir Walter Raleigh to enact statutes for the Virginia colony, it was provided that "they be not against the true Christian faith nowe professed in the Church of England," and King James I's charter, granted to Virginia in 1606, provided that Virginia "may, by the Providence of Almighty God,

---

[10] See the words of United States Supreme Court Associate Justice Samuel Chase to John Fries, the defendant in *United States v. Fries*, 9 Fed. Cas. 826, 934 (1800).

[11] *Holy Trinity Church v. U.S.*, 143 U.S. 457, 465 (1892).

hereafter tend to the Glory of His Divine Majesty, in propagating of Christian Religion to such People, as yet live in Darkness and miserable Ignorance of the true Knowledge and Worship of God."[12] Similar language was to be found in other charters granted to Virginia and other of the American colonies. Thus, for example, the Mayflower Compact of 1620 declared:

> Having undertaken for the Glory of God, and Advancement of the Christian Faith, and the Honour of our King and Country, a Voyage to plant the first Colony in the northern Parts of Virginia [what was later to be Plymouth, Massachusetts]; [We] Do by these Presents, solemnly and mutually, in the Presence of God and one another, covenant and combine ourselves together into a civil Body Politick, for our better Ordering and Preservation, and Furtherance of the Ends aforesaid.[13]

Similarly, the "fundamental orders of Connecticut" (1638–1639), in effect a constitution for the colony's government, observed:

> [W]ell knowing where a people are gathered together the word of God requires that to mayntayne the peace and union of such a people there should be an orderly and decent Gouerment established according to God, to order and dispose of the affayres of the people at all seasons as occation shall require; [we] doe therefore ... enter into Combination and Confederation together, to mayntayne and [preserve] the liberty and purity of the gospell of our Lord Jesus w[hi]ch we now pr[o]fesse, as also the disciplyne of the Churches, w[hi]ch according to the truth of the said gospell is now practised amongst us.[14]

To the same effect, the charter of privileges granted by William Penn to the province of Pennsylvania in 1701 provided that "Because no People can be truly happy, though under the greatest Enjoyment of Civil Liberties, if abridged of the Freedom of their Consciences, as to their Religious Profession and Worship; And Almighty God being the only Lord of Conscience, Father of Lights and Spirits; and the Author as well as Object of all divine Knowledge, Faith, and Worship,"[15] freedom of religion was secured.

Coming closer to the present, the Supreme Court in *Holy Trinity* observed: "Every constitution of every one of the [then] 44 states [existing in 1892]

---

[12] Id. at 466.
[13] Id.
[14] Id. at 467.
[15] Id.

contains language which, either directly or by clear implication, recognizes a profound reverence for religion, and an assumption that its influence in all human affairs is essential to the well-being of the community."[16] Typical among many such constitutional provisions were those from articles 2 and 3 of part 1 of the constitution of Massachusetts (1780):

> It is the right as well as the duty of all men in society publicly, and at stated seasons, to worship the Supreme Being, the Great Creator and Preserver of the universe. * * * As the happiness of a people and the good order and preservation of civil government essentially depend upon piety, religion, and morality, and as these cannot be generally diffused through a community but by the institution of the public worship of God and of public instructions in piety, religion, and morality: Therefore, to promote their happiness, and to secure the good order and preservation of their government, the people of this commonwealth have a right to invest their legislature with power to authorize and require, and the legislature shall, from time to time, authorize and require, the several towns, parishes, precincts, and other bodies politic or religious societies to make suitable provision, at their own expense, for the institution of the public worship of God and for the support and maintenance of public Protestant teachers of piety, religion and morality, in all cases where such provisions shall not be made voluntarily.[17]

Referring to these and other provisions, the Court states: "These are not individual sayings, declarations of private persons. They are organic utterances. They speak the voice of the entire people."[18]

To substantiate this assertion, that the United States was a Christian nation, the U.S. Supreme Court turned to state court precedent in order to observe that

> in Updegraph v. Comm., 11 Serg. & R. 394, 400, it was decided that, "Christianity, general Christianity, is, and always has been, a part of the common law of Pennsylvania; . . ." And in People v. Ruggles, 8 Johns. 290, 294, 295, Chancellor KENT, the great commentator on American law, speaking as chief justice of the supreme court of New York, said: "The people of this state, in common with the people of this country, profess the general doctrines of Christianity as the rule of their faith and practice . . . but to revile, with malicious and blasphemous contempt, the religion professed by almost the whole community is an abuse of that right. Nor are we bound by any expressions

[16] Id. at 468.
[17] Id. at 469.
[18] Id. at 470.

in the constitution, as some have strangely supposed, either not to punish at all, or to punish indiscriminately the like attacks upon the religion of Mahomet or of the Grand Lama; and for this plain reason that the case assumes that we are a Christian people, and the morality of the country is deeply ingrafted upon Christianity, and not upon the doctrines or worship of those impostors." [19]

Further indicating the pervasive and favored status of religion in American life, the *Holy Trinity* Court noted:

The form of oath [to tell the truth, the whole truth and nothing but the truth] universally prevailing, concluding with an appeal to the Almighty; the custom of opening sessions of all deliberative bodies and most conventions with prayer; the prefatory words of all wills, "In the name of God, amen"; the laws respecting the observance of the Sabbath, with the general cessation of all secular business, and the closing of courts, legislatures, and other similar public assemblies on that day; the churches and church organizations which abound in every city, town, and hamlet; the multitude of charitable organizations existing everywhere under Christian auspices; the gigantic missionary associations, with general support, and aiming to establish Christian missions in every quarter of the globe. [20]

"These and many other matters which might be noticed," concluded the Supreme Court, "add a volume of unofficial declarations to the mass of organic utterances that this is a Christian nation." [21]

Adding all of this up suggests that, in the early years of our republic, freedom of association carried with it an understanding that it was the job of the government to further associations for laudable purposes, and to discourage or condemn those associations whose purposes were not so desirable. Hence the early notion borrowed from the English common law, for example, that an association of journeymen bootmakers formed to raise their wages and to further closed shops ought to be viewed as an unlawful conspiracy rather than a laudable association. [22] By 1842, this particular type of intermediate association (a prototypical labor union) was gaining some legal support, but only because of a recognition that workers might associate for benevolent purposes (such as furthering temperance), rather than malevolent ones (such as driving away scabs or

---

[19] Id. at 470–71.

[20] Id. at 471.

[21] Id.

[22] On this point, see the cases and discussion in Presser and Zainaldin, *Law and Jurisprudence in American History*, 689–726.

extorting undue sums from employers).[23] In the past, then, it was governmental policy to promote laudable associations, and particularly religious and moral ones.

II. THE WAY IT IS NOW: FURTHERING RADICAL INDIVIDUALISM

Nowadays, however, when one can get oneself pilloried if one seeks to argue that ours is a "Christian country,"[24] things have changed; and, not surprisingly, the concept of freedom of association has most likely changed as well. Instead of serving God, Country, and Yale, it looks as if the purpose of freedom of association, insofar as it is to further the more general modern purposes of American society, is to further what we used to call "self-actualization," or perhaps, in its current form, the encouragement of self-gratification. We are now, as a culture, at least among the chattering classes, more committed to radical individualism than we are to altruism. For me, at least, this is summed up in the famous "mystery passage" (or, as it was called by Justice Antonin Scalia, "the sweet mystery of life passage")[25] written by Justice Anthony Kennedy[26] and first announced in the important plurality opinion in the United States Supreme Court case of *Planned Parenthood v. Casey* (1992):

[23] Thus, in *Commonwealth v. Pullis*, decided by the Mayor's Court of Philadelphia in 1806, the court held, following English law, that any labor union which sought to raise wages above the prevailing level was a criminal conspiracy, and the court appeared to suggest that any agreement among workers to refuse to work for an employer who hired nonunion labor might also be such a criminal conspiracy. However, in *Commonwealth v. Hunt*, 45 Mass. (4 Metc.) 111 (1842), a Massachusetts case decided by the renowned Chief Justice Lemuel Shaw, it was held that it was permissible for union members to insist on a closed shop, because they might be attempting to further laudable endeavors, such as maintaining an alcohol-free workplace. These two cases are reprinted and discussed in Presser and Zainaldin, *Law and Jurisprudence in American History*, 689–726.

[24] As indicated earlier, the United States Supreme Court once noted, after reviewing a plethora of official statements to that effect, that this country was "a Christian nation." See *Holy Trinity Church v. United States*, 143 U.S. 457, 471 (1892). But a little more than a century later, when Mississippi governor Kirk Fordice made the same assertion at a Republican governors' conference, there was an immediate negative reaction from B'nai B'rith. "South Carolina governor Carroll Campbell quickly offered a correction, adding 'Judeo-' as a prefix to Christian, but Fordice snapped back that he meant what he said. Fordice later apologized for any offense." See "Kirk Fordice," *Wikipedia*, http://en. wikipedia.org/wiki/Kirk_Fordice (accessed November 19, 2007). See also "An Apology for 'Christian Nation' Remark," *New York Times*, November 21, 1992, late edition–final, section 1, page 9: "Gov. Kirk Fordice apologized today for comments in which he pointedly referred to the United States as 'a Christian nation,' and the head of the state's largest Jewish congregation said he was satisfied. A number of Jewish organizations had protested the Governor's remarks. . . ."

[25] For Scalia's appellation of the plurality's words as the "sweet-mystery-of-life" passage, see *Lawrence v. Texas*, 539 U.S. 558, 588 (2003) (Scalia, J., dissenting).

[26] For the assertion that Justice Kennedy is the author of the passage, see, e.g., John Leo, "The Supremes' Sophistry," originally published in *U.S. News* on July 14, 2003, and available at http://www.usnews.com/usnews/opinion/articles/030714/14john.htm (accessed November 19, 2007). Leo refers to the passage as the "much-mocked, anything-goes 'mystery passage.'"

At the heart of liberty is the right to define one's own concept of existence, of the universe, and of the mystery of human life. Beliefs about these matters could not define the attributes of personhood were they formed under the compulsion of the state.[27]

There is more than a little obscurity in the meaning of this passage, but whatever it means, it seems to suggest that the government should get itself out of the business of morals or religion, and leave these things to individuals. As Notre Dame University law professor Gerard Bradley, one of the most sensitive critics of the passage, has observed, "the Justices wish to be seen as affirming the right of each person to make up his own moral universe, but to affirm it without making any moral commitments of their own. As if taking the view that everybody can, or should, or should be thought to, inhabit his own world were all 'neutral' propositions."[28]

There are, of course, grave problems with the mystery passage, and, in particular, with its assumption that one can "define one's own concept of existence, of the universe, and of the mystery of human life," since all of these probably can only be worked out through the aid of others, living or dead; these are things that come from one's fellows or one's culture, not from within oneself. As Bradley puts it, "Making up one's world is existentially impossible, no more empirically available than a unicorn." "Of course," he adds, thinking perhaps of Justices Kennedy, Souter, and O'Connor, the named authors of the plurality opinion in which the mystery passage first appeared, "some people believe in unicorns." To similar effect, John Leo writes that if the passage were "rigorously applied," it "would justify suicide clinics, prostitution, bestiality, polygamy, and maybe interspecies marriage. The passage elevates individual desire over all known law on any issue any court might deem 'central to personal dignity or autonomy.' It's also a charter for resolving all issues of the culture war by removing them from normal democratic politics and handing victory to the liberationist side of the battle."[29]

With the "mystery passage," then, we have the antithesis of altruism, and the apotheosis of individualism. By this I mean that the "mystery passage" seems to be all about individual self-gratification, but our older notions of altruism, religion, and association seem to be about meeting the needs of others, about meeting the responsibilities of our social duties rather than fulfilling our individual desires. This simplistic analysis—an American past of altruism and an American present of individualism—undoubtedly fails to capture a much subtler reality. As Duncan Kennedy

---

[27] *Planned Parenthood v. Casey*, 505 U.S. 833, 851 (1992).

[28] Gerard V. Bradley, "Mighty Casey at the Bat," available at http://www.catholic.net/RCC/Periodicals/Dossier/MAYJUN99/Casey.html (accessed November 19, 2007).

[29] Leo, "The Supremes' Sophistry."

suggested in his seminal work on contract law, our law is simultaneously shot through with both individualism and altruism;[30] but surely it does not go too far to suggest that, at any given time, one strand might dominate over the other—and then, perhaps later, that ascendance might be reversed.

III. Two Models of Freedom of Association

For the purposes of trying to understand some of the inconsistencies in freedom of association doctrine—and, in particular, to try to understand why courts have recently upheld some claims to freedom of association and rejected others—it might help to posit the existence of different cultural conceptions and see where this leads us in understanding the law. I am actually going to contrast only two conceptions of freedom of association, one that I will call the "traditional" model and another that I will designate as the "modern" model. As an example of my "traditional" model, I will present the conception articulated by Herbert Wechsler in his famous article on "neutral principles" in constitutional law. As my "modern" example, I will present the conception articulated by Andrew Koppelman, which he has sketched in two provocative law review articles. I will supplement Koppelman's model of freedom of association with a take on constitutional jurisprudence provided by Cass Sunstein, in his recent blast at conservative judges, *Radicals in Robes* (2005).[31] I am going to argue that these two conceptions, Wechsler's on the one hand and Koppelman's and Sunstein's on the other, reflect different cultural moments or different strains in American society, and that one way of explaining American constitutional law's confusion over the issue of freedom of association is to suggest that constitutional law, in seeking continuity in the doctrinal treatment of freedom of association, has failed to acknowledge a fundamental cultural discontinuity.

While the fit may not be exact, I argue here that the Framers' and Wechsler's conceptions of freedom of association share at least some attributes, and that this "traditional" conception has been, for at least the last few decades, engaged in a clash with a different view, the view articulated by Koppelman and Sunstein. I will seek to show that Supreme Court decisions in this and related areas come out differently in different cases because various justices subscribe to either the traditional view or the newer view. To put this at its simplest, my effort here is simply to compare and contrast some older, traditional ideas about freedom of association with some newer, more individualistic ones.

[30] Duncan Kennedy, "Form and Substance in Private Law Adjudication," *Harvard Law Review* 89 (1976): 1685, passim.

[31] Cass R. Sunstein, *Radicals in Robes: Why Extreme Right-Wing Courts Are Wrong for America* (New York: Basic Books, 2005).

IV. Herbert Wechsler on Freedom of Association

Let us begin, then, with Wechsler. Wechsler's article, "Toward Neutral Principles of Constitutional Law" (1959),[32] one of the most frequently cited in the entire law review canon,[33] was an attack on the Warren Court for what Wechsler regarded as its unseemly failure (in cases regarding, in particular, race in American life) to articulate constitutional principles that were something other than purely result-oriented. Wechsler labeled his sought-after principles as "neutral" (meaning not simply determined by the preferred outcome) and described them as applicable not just to the case at hand, but to future cases involving similar issues (he labeled principles with this quality as "general"). Wechsler's notion (in one way, at least, a very traditional one) was that a court which was merely "result-oriented," and which produced results that could not serve as precedents for future cases, was not engaging in the appropriate behavior we expect of courts.[34]

The rule of law, for Wechsler, demanded activities different from the essentially legislative efforts that he saw the Warren Court engaged in. Given that we are all now "legal realists," and that we all now pretty much accept the insights of the precursor of legal realism, Oliver Wendell Holmes, Jr., and his latter-day acolytes such as Jerome Frank[35] and Karl Llewellyn,[36] who held that the judicial task is inevitably legislative in nature, it is not surprising that Wechsler's search for "neutral" and "general" principles has been labeled as naïve and possibly reactionary.[37] Still, unless we are prepared simply to throw in our lot with the political scientists, to give up any pretense that the rule of law is a meaningful concept, and to cashier the notion that adjudication is different from legislation, there is much to admire in Wechsler's enterprise.

Wechsler was not only seeking to criticize the Warren Court, he was also trying to find a method of constitutional hermeneutics that would be

[32] Herbert Wechsler, "Toward Neutral Principles of Constitutional Law," *Harvard Law Review* 73 (1959): 1–35.

[33] In a study of law review article citations from 1947 to 1984, Wechsler's piece was found to be the second most frequently cited law review article ever written. See Fred R. Shapiro, "The Most-Cited Law Review Articles," *California Law Review* 73 (1985): 1540, 1549. Wechsler's article is also one of the pieces chosen for the recent twenty-article *Canon of American Legal Thought* by Harvard law professors David Kennedy and William Fisher III. See David Kennedy and William Fisher III, eds., *The Canon of American Legal Thought* (Princeton, NJ: Princeton University Press, 2006).

[34] Wechsler, "Toward Neutral Principles," 15: "I put it to you that the main constituent of the judicial process is precisely that it must be genuinely principled, resting with respect to every step that is involved in reaching judgment on analysis and reasons quite transcending the immediate result that is achieved."

[35] See, in particular, Jerome Frank, *Law and the Modern Mind* (New York: Brentano's, 1930).

[36] See, e.g., Karl N. Llewellyn, *The Common Law Tradition: Deciding Appeals* (Boston: Little, Brown & Co., 1960).

[37] See, e.g., J. Skelly Wright, "Professor Bickel, the Scholarly Tradition, and the Supreme Court," *Harvard Law Review* 84 (1971): 769.

different from the orthodoxy suggested by his predecessor at the Oliver Wendell Holmes, Jr. lecture podium at Harvard, Judge Learned Hand.[38] Hand had also lambasted the Warren Court for its failure to follow precedent and for its blatant result-orientation. Hand had further maintained that the Warren Court's error was in failing to interpret the Constitution according to the understanding of the Constitution's text when it was originally ratified. This method, "originalism," is still honored, even in the breach, and is best exemplified today by Justices Antonin Scalia, and Clarence Thomas.[39] Wechsler believed that the Constitution was drafted to embody certain values, and that the application of these values changed over time, so that it was the task of the Court to apply these values to changed social circumstances. For Wechsler, then, we had a "living Constitution,"[40] one whose application would change over time, though Wechsler did not believe that the fact that the specific application of constitutional values or "principles" might change meant that the judicial task was a legislative one. Instead, Wechsler thought that for any given constitutional question, its neutral and general resolution could be determined simply by objective reference to the preexisting principles already embedded in the document.

Unfortunately, Wechsler himself proved unable to reconcile these purported constitutional principles in order to resolve the issues concerning race that confronted the Warren Court and its predecessors. Wechsler conceded that *Brown v. Board of Education* (1954),[41] which ruled that racially segregated public schools were unconstitutional, *Smith v. Allwright* (1944),[42] which held that a private "whites-only" political party primary election violated the Constitution, and *Shelley v. Kraemer* (1948),[43] which held that racially restrictive covenants were impermissible, were laudable insofar as these practices did violate the great constitutional principle embedded in the Fourteenth Amendment (requiring that no state deny any citizen "the equal protection of the laws"). While Wechsler was not completely clear on this, we could also label this principle the principle of a "color-blind" Constitution. But even if the principle of "color-blindness" was in the Constitution, Wechsler maintained that the Warren Court failed in its

---

[38] These lectures of Hand's were published as Learned Hand, *The Bill of Rights* (Cambridge, MA: Harvard University Press, 1958).

[39] See ibid. On the continuing importance of originalism, see, e.g., Stephen B. Presser, "Reading the Constitution Right: Clarence Thomas's Fidelity to Our Founding Documents Is Making Its Mark on the Supreme Court," *City Journal* 17, no. 2 (Spring 2007): 90–97.

[40] On the "living Constitution," see, e.g., William H. Rehnquist, "The Notion of a Living Constitution," *Texas Law Review* 54 (1976): 693.

[41] *Brown v. Board of Education of Topeka*, 347 U.S. 483 (1954).

[42] *Smith v. Allwright*, 321 U.S. 649 (1944). *Smith* involved a primary which was not conducted by the state, but by private persons. Three years earlier, in *U.S. v. Classic*, 313 U.S. 299 (1941), the Supreme Court had held that racial discrimination was impermissible in a primary conducted by the state, but *Smith* overruled earlier judicial precedent that such discrimination was permissible for a primary not conducted by state officials.

[43] *Shelley v. Kraemer*, 334 U.S. 1 (1948).

task of "neutrality" because it failed to take account of a competing constitutional principle, that of freedom of association. Wechsler appeared to suggest that he, personally, favored the principle of a color-blind Constitution over the principle of freedom of association, but he could not defend his personal preference as a matter of constitutional law, because he was able to offer no constitutional standard for preferring one competing constitutional principle over another.

Precisely what Wechsler understood by freedom of association was something he never defined, but, curiously, it appears to be similar to (if not the same as) the earliest view of freedom of association that I have set forth above. Thus, for Wechsler, freedom of association implied the freedom to discriminate,[44] and, in this context, the freedom to choose not to associate with persons of a race different from one's own. This appeared most clearly in Wechsler's criticism of the *Shelley v. Kraemer* decision, which had held that the use of state courts to enforce racially restrictive covenants was "state action" which violated the Fourteenth Amendment's prohibition against any state denying any of its citizens "the equal protection of the laws." Nonetheless, Wechsler explained that one ought to understand the Fourteenth Amendment's prohibition against "*state* action" to imply that individuals were free to engage in the very discrimination prohibited to the state, so that if individuals wished to discriminate on the basis of race, the Fourteenth Amendment presumably secured this "right" for them. And if they had this right, he continued, this meant that the state was required to enforce the right in its courts.[45] Racially restrictive covenants, then, should have been enforceable in courts because enforcement in courts is the traditional means of securing rights. The courts should have been required to enforce the individual right to discriminate. Such action ought not properly to be viewed as state action, but ought to be understood as merely permissible acts of individuals, individuals who wished to exercise their constitutional rights to freedom of association, or, more precisely, freedom from association with those with whom they did not choose to associate.

For Wechsler, this freedom of association, or freedom from forced association, extended also to the formation of racially restricted political parties,[46] and, it would seem, to racially segregated schools (at least where the "separate but equal" mandate of *Plessy v. Ferguson* was actually followed).

---

[44] For the early view on religion that implied a freedom to discriminate, see, e.g., the Massachusetts Constitution of 1780, supra note 17, which authorized the use of public funds for "public *Protestant* teachers of piety, religion and morality" (emphasis added), and Chancellor Kent's suggestion, supra note 19, that though the state could punish as blasphemy statements made against Christianity (as Christianity was a part of the common law of New York), this implied no obligation to punish as blasphemy attacks on "those impostors," "the religion of Mahomet or of the Grand Lama."

[45] Wechsler, "Toward Neutral Principles," 29–30.

[46] Wechsler indicated that he did not favor such parties, but that he could find no constitutional bar to them. Ibid., 29.

Thus, for Wechsler, freedom of association, simply stated, included the free-dom from purportedly odious personal contact with persons of different races. This conception of freedom of association as a license for individ-uals racially to discriminate is probably unpalatable to most of us, and Wechsler's critics, such as Judge J. Skelly Wright, simply dismissed Wechsler's purported manufacturing of a constitutionally protected right to discriminate based on race.[47] For Wright, the Fourteenth Amendment's equal-protection value of "color-blindness," or at least the value of remain-ing free from state-imposed racially discriminatory actions, clearly trumped any purported freedom of association. Wright did not exactly completely dismiss freedom of association, but he had no difficulty in deciding that the purportedly constitutionally mandated freedom from racial discrim-ination was more important. Wright suggested that it was the job of Supreme Court justices (and lower-court judges) to create a hierarchy of constitutional values and then apply the appropriately ordered principles to resolve particular cases, but other than suggesting that this had been the task in which the Warren Court had been engaged (and the heavens didn't fall), and that one could establish such an ordering pursuant to a juris-prudence of "goodness," Wright never explained how such a hierarchy of values could be derived.

Setting aside these probably insoluble questions of constitutional inter-pretation, what is most interesting for our purposes is Wechsler's concep-tion of freedom of association as freedom to discriminate.[48] Discrimination on the basis of race could conceivably be driven by observations about actual physical, intellectual, or cultural differences between ethnic or racial groups, but there is certainly a strong possibility that it is undertaken as a result of personal prejudice, or idiosyncratic personal preference, or maybe even utter irrationality or hatred. This was perhaps why Judge Wright, who believed passionately in the equality of the races, found it so easy to con-demn Wechsler's views, but perhaps Wechsler was, nevertheless, on to something. As the Greeks understood, as Sigmund Freud perceived, and as anyone who has ever been in love knows, humans are, at bottom, not particularly rational creatures. They are, one suspects, as often guided by their emotions as they are by their intellect. Religion, still a great driving force in American society, is not, despite the best efforts of religious lead-ers, philosophers, and writers for thousands of years, something that is easily subject to rational analysis; instead, it draws its strength from the

---

[47] Wright, "Professor Bickel, the Scholarly Tradition, and the Supreme Court."

[48] The United States Supreme Court, even in the case that compelled the Jaycees to admit women, *Roberts v. United States Jaycees*, 468 U.S. 609 (1984), has actually recognized that freedom of association, to a certain extent, carries with it freedom to discriminate: "There can be no clearer example of an intrusion into the internal structure or affairs of an asso-ciation than a regulation that forces the group to accept members it does not desire. Such a regulation may impair the ability of the original members to express only those views that brought them together. Freedom of association therefore plainly presupposes a freedom not to associate" (id. at 623).

irrational, from the emotions, whether they are emotions of love or fear. It is undoubtedly significant that alongside Wechsler's defense of racially discriminatory political parties was his defense of political parties organized by religion.

Wechsler did not put it in so many words, but perhaps, given his express advocacy of the legitimacy of political parties based on religion,[49] we might be able to impute to Wechsler an understanding that freedom of association was a value secured by the First Amendment's "free exercise" of religion clause as well as the "freedom of speech" clause, and, indeed, that it was a value designed, at least in part, to further the flourishing of religion. I think it does not go too far to suggest, then, that Wechsler might have understood freedom of association as a means of meeting human needs that were more emotional (perhaps even irrational) than intellectual.[50] In any event, I think Wechsler's conception of freedom of association, insofar as it may have acknowledged special protection for religion, was of a piece with the traditional common law view, understood by the Framers, that religion was an indispensable prop for civilized society, and that a religiously-discriminatory concept of freedom of association furthered that goal. Religious discrimination in the exercise of freedom of association might be perceived as being just as emotional or as irrational as racial discrimination, but it was the protection of that irrationality (for lack of a better word) as a basic human quality that enabled freedom of association to do its job in allowing us freely to form intermediate associations that would be meaningful to us, and that, presumably, would altruistically benefit at least some of our fellows.

V. *Dale* and *Jaycees* as Adhering to Different Forms of Freedom of Association

Wechsler's concept of freedom of association—a freedom to discriminate (even irrationally) against those one does not wish to have as co-members of one's intermediate associations—appears to be the same concept involved in *Boy Scouts of America v. Dale* (2000),[51] the most recent important freedom of association case.[52] In that case, the right of the Boy

---

[49] Again, Wechsler suggested that barring political parties based on religion was a result "plainly to be desired," but not one that he could find support for in neutral principles derived from the Constitution. Indeed, Wechsler stated that it was "easier to project an analysis establishing that such a proscription would infringe rights protected by the first amendment." Wechsler, "Toward Neutral Principles," 29.

[50] Thus Wechsler defends his argument that freedom of association ought to protect members of one race from associating with members of another simply because they might find such an association "unpleasant or repugnant." Ibid., 34.

[51] *Boy Scouts of America v. Dale*, 530 U.S. 640 (2000).

[52] For *Dale*'s importance and a liberal-oriented critique of the decision, see two pieces by Andrew Koppelman: "Should Noncommercial Associations Have an Absolute Right to Discriminate?" *Law and Contemporary Problems* 67 (2004): 27; and "Signs of the Times: *Dale v.*

Scouts to forbid an openly gay scout leader was upheld by the United States Supreme Court. This policy of the Boy Scouts seems to be tremendously unpopular, and has resulted in the Scouts being barred from participating in some forms of fund-raising, such as many local United Way appeals.[53] The Supreme Court's decision in *Dale* has also come in for some blistering scholarly criticism, apparently on the grounds that important national associations should simply not be permitted to discriminate in what is now generally regarded as a politically incorrect manner. Among the intelligentsia, it would seem, just as it was true for Wright's critique of Wechsler,[54] there is a hierarchy of constitutional values, and freedom of association (at least to the extent that it includes a freedom from unwanted association) simply ranks lower than freedom from discrimination, at least for racial discrimination, sexual discrimination, or discrimination against particular sexual orientations.

Something like this feeling also seems to have motivated the Supreme Court in rendering its decision in *Roberts v. United States Jaycees* (1984), where it ruled that the Jaycees could not discriminate on the basis of sex.[55] Given the Court's holding in the *Jaycees* case, it is surprising that the Court proceeded to allow discrimination against gays in *Dale*, but perhaps the Court is here reflecting American society's somewhat deeper-seated traditional aversion to homosexual behavior than to equality for women. The usual reason supporting anti-gay discrimination is purported religious hostility, and it is interesting to speculate as to whether, if the *Jaycees* case had come up a hundred years ago, it would not have gone the other way based on the then-popular conception (rooted in biblical teachings) that women were meant for a subordinate role to men. Had it come up at the time of *Bradwell v. Illinois* (1873),[56] of course, Justice Joseph Bradley's observation in his concurring opinion that it was the "law of the Creator" that the "paramount destiny" of women was to "fulfill the noble and benign offices of wife and mother,"[57] would have carried the day, and just as Myra Bradwell was not permitted to practice law in Illinois, so women would not have been permitted to join the Jaycees.

VI. CASS SUNSTEIN, ARBITRARINESS, AND EDMUND BURKE

How, then, do we distinguish between different forms of religiously motivated discrimination, supporting some forms on the basis of "free-

---

Boy Scouts of America and the Changing Meaning of Nondiscrimination," *Cardozo Law Review* 23 (2001–2002): 1819.

[53] For a listing of many local United Way appeals which have barred the Boy Scouts from participating, see http://grassfire.net/factbox.htm (accessed November 19, 2007).

[54] See Wright, "Professor Bickel, the Scholarly Tradition, and the Supreme Court."

[55] *Roberts v. United States Jaycees*, 468 U.S. 609 (1984).

[56] *Bradwell v. State of Illinois*, 83 U.S. 130 (1873).

[57] Id. at 140 (Bradley, J., concurring).

dom of association," and not permitting others, even if "freedom of association" is invoked? Are there clear constitutional doctrinal guidelines? The intractability of the effort to draw such clear guidelines might well be the central problem in modern constitutional theory. This difficulty has led some, perhaps most notably University of Chicago law professor Cass Sunstein, to opt out of high theory altogether. Thus, Sunstein has embraced what seems to be a shamelessly pragmatic case-by-case approach, taking as his ideal the method of constitutional exegesis practiced by Justices Anthony Kennedy and Sandra Day O'Connor, who have rather notoriously been proceeding on a case-by-case basis. O'Connor was the most egregious in this regard, with her jurisprudence differing little in kind from her actions taken earlier as a state legislator. In other words, Justice O'Connor's constitutional jurisprudence was not all about following precedent, it was all about making prudential, or, more precisely, legislative judgments.[58] Sunstein, who believes that in advocating this sort of jurisprudence he is emulating the great conservative Edmund Burke (who purportedly eschewed abstract theories in favor of a prudential approach to political problems), appears to be certain about what the substance of such a prudential approach would be.

Sunstein has made it clear, for example, that he thinks no sensible person could dispute the correctness of certain Supreme Court decisions that he favors. He believes that it would endanger "democracy and our rights," for example, if the Court were to abolish the "right to privacy" first discovered in penumbras and emanations of the Constitution in the 1965 *Griswold*[59] case (which prevented states from prohibiting the sale of contraceptives to married adults) and then extended in 1973 in *Roe v. Wade*[60] to include a constitutional right to terminate pregnancies. Similarly, Sunstein believes that the New Deal Court's expansive readings of the federal government's power to regulate commerce were correct. He fears that a conservative Supreme Court, seeking perhaps to recapture the "Constitution in Exile,"[61] would be wrong narrowly to construe the commerce clause and thus endanger the federal Clean Air Act, the Federal Communications Commission and the Occupational Safety and Health

---

[58] For criticism of the idiosyncratic nature of O'Connor's jurisprudence, see, e.g., Stephen B. Presser, "A Conservative Comment on Professor Crump," *Florida Law Review* 56 (2004): 789; or Stephen B. Presser, *Recapturing the Constitution: Race, Religion, and Abortion Reconsidered* (Washington, DC: Regnery Publishing Co., 1994), and sources cited there.

[59] *Griswold v. Connecticut*, 381 U.S. 479 (1965).

[60] *Roe v. Wade*, 410 U.S. 113 (1973).

[61] "Constitution in Exile" is a term current among constitutional theorists that refers to the U.S. Constitution as construed before 1937, that is, before the United States Supreme Court began much more broadly to construe the commerce clause to permit Congress to legislate in areas of economic regulation which had formerly been reserved to the state and local governments. For descriptions of the "Constitution in Exile" movement, see, e.g., William W. Van Alstyne, "The Constitution in Exile: Is It Time to Bring It in from the Cold?" *Duke Law Journal* 51, no. 1 (2001); and "Constitution in Exile," *Wikipedia*, http://en.wikipedia.org/wiki/Constitution_in_exile (accessed November 19, 2007), and sources cited there.

Administration, all of which Sunstein seems to regard as laudable purveyors of sensible public policy. Sunstein favors a broad interpretation of the equal protection clause of the Fourteenth Amendment, which he believes would not permit the federal government to use racial profiling in the war on terror, or permit the states to discriminate on the basis of sex (say, to operate single-sex military academies) or race (say, to set up "separate but equal" racially discriminatory academies).

Sunstein, like virtually every legal academic practicing today, and like the vast majority of recent members of the United States Supreme Court, believes that the First Amendment ought to be incorporated into the Fourteenth, and thus that the Court has been correct to bar mandatory prayer and Bible reading in the public schools; and he condemns conservatives, such as Justice Thomas, who understand the First Amendment to have been a federalism measure, so that the states should still be able to decide for themselves how properly to encourage religion, if they so choose.[62] Sunstein has a limited view of executive power, and fears that a conservative Supreme Court could give the president the power without warrants or other judicial supervision to detain suspected terrorists or those who are alleged to have assisted them. Sunstein even goes so far as to suggest that civil rights laws might be found unconstitutional by conservative justices holding a narrow conception of the interstate commerce power, that gun control laws might all be found unconstitutional because of conservatives' understanding of the Second Amendment, and that all campaign finance reform legislation might be thrown out because of conservatives' view that such legislation prevents political speech protected by the First Amendment. The civil rights laws, the gun control laws, and the campaign finance measures are all legislation that Sunstein favors, and he implicitly suggests that no sensible person ought to disagree. Sunstein also believes in affirmative action and condemns the possibility that conservative justices might reject it because of their belief in a color-blind Constitution. Finally, Sunstein suggests that because of conservatives' strong belief in the primacy of private property rights, those rights might be expanded to compensate for more regulatory takings, forbidding the government from carrying out policies, such as protection of the environment, that Sunstein favors.[63]

[62] For Justice Thomas's view on this issue, see, e.g., *Elk Grove Unified School District v. Newdow*, 542 U.S. 1, 19 (2004) (Thomas, J., concurring, and indicating that the First Amendment's establishment clause should not be incorporated into the Fourteenth Amendment). For a brief introduction to the debate over incorporation, see, e.g., Michael Kent Curtis, "Incorporation Doctrine," in Kermit Hall, ed., *The Oxford Companion to the United States Supreme Court* (New York and Oxford: Oxford University Press, 1992), 426–27. One of the best known (although also one of the most controversial) scholarly attacks on the incorporation doctrine is Raoul Berger, *Government by Judiciary: The Transformation of the Fourteenth Amendment*, 2d ed. (Indianapolis, IN: Liberty Fund, 1997).

[63] This section of the essay is based in part on Stephen B. Presser, "Was Ann Coulter Right? Some Realism about 'Minimalism'," *Ave Maria Law Review* 5 (2007): 23–46. Sunstein's ideas referred to in the text are developed in Sunstein, *Radicals in Robes;* and Cass R. Sunstein, "Burkean Minimalism," *Michigan Law Review* 105 (2006): 353.

The burden of Sunstein's argument in his polemical book *Radicals in Robes: Why Extreme Right-Wing Courts Are Wrong for America* (2005) is that conservative justices such as Scalia and Thomas are as far out of the mainstream as religious fundamentalists such as Jerry Falwell and Osama Bin Laden, and that Falwell's and Bin Laden's superstitious reverence for a sacred text is a good analogy for Scalia's and Thomas's penchant for interpreting the Constitution according to its original understanding. Just as Falwell and Bin Laden's fundamentalism is a threat to America, so, Sunstein claims, are the conservative judges Sunstein labels as "fundamentalists."

The "fundamentalist," "extreme right-wing," or "conservative" judges whom Sunstein believes are combining in a project to take away rights from Americans and destroy democracy would not, of course, view themselves as engaged in any such efforts. Indeed, their goal (one I tend to share) is simply to reverse the undemocratically-imposed rulings of the Supreme Court on issues such as race, religion, abortion, and federalism and to restore the right to settle these issues of public policy to the American people, acting through their local governments. Sunstein's name-calling here is of a piece with modern American politics, where one labels those one likes "moderates," and one's foes "extremists." This isn't jurisprudence, really; it's mud-slinging.[64]

It is not at all clear that most Americans would condemn the same jurisprudential results that Sunstein does, and his pragmatism may be designed to preserve the achievements of the late-twentieth-century Supreme Court which liberals favor and which are anathema to conservatives. Again, of course, this is not constitutional jurisprudence; it is the securing of politically favored results disguised as what Sunstein calls a theory of "constitutional minimalism." It masks a series of debatable political choices, and boldly asserts that to change these undemocratically-imposed choices would be to threaten "democracy and our rights." The point that is relevant to us, of course, is that Sunstein offers no principled basis to defend the constitutional results he favors, and if a scholar who is regarded as one of the very best in his field sees no need to do that, then perhaps to attempt to fashion a theoretically coherent approach to freedom of association is to engage in folly.

Sunstein, by the way, may believe that he is being a good Burkean, but Burke was a great believer in the wisdom of the collective people, in tradition, in religion, in morals, and in the rule of law; and insofar as the Supreme Court holdings that Sunstein embraces are arbitrary innovations and rejections of our traditions, it is difficult to believe that Burke would embrace Sunstein as a philosophical colleague. Are there, then, approaches to freedom of association that amount to more than embracing the results

---

[64] See generally Presser, "Was Ann Coulter Right?"; and Ann Coulter, *Slander: Liberal Lies about the American Right* (New York: Crown Publishing Group, 2002).

one favors? Are there any approaches that really do reflect our traditions, and that one could actually endorse while being a true Burkean?

VII. Andrew Koppelman on Freedom of Association

Let us consider the approach of Andrew Koppelman. Koppelman has written two provocative pieces critical of the United States Supreme Court's decision in *Boy Scouts of America v. Dale* (2000),[65] the case that I have hinted looks back toward the traditional American conception of freedom of association. In *Dale*, the Boy Scouts sought to expel an assistant scout-master, James Dale, on the grounds that he was gay and a gay-rights activist, and that allowing such a gay young man in the Scouts would send a message of approval of his lifestyle that would purportedly be inconsistent, inter alia, with "the values embodied in the Scout Oath and Law, particularly those represented by the requirement that Scouts be 'morally straight' and 'clean.' "[66] Dale then sought the aid of the New Jersey courts to reinstate him in the Scouts on the grounds that the Scouts were a "public accommodation" and New Jersey law forbade discrimination on the basis of sexual orientation.

Dale won with that argument in the New Jersey Supreme Court, but the United States Supreme Court reversed the New Jersey decision and held that the application of the state's "public accommodation" antidiscrimination law to the Scouts violated the Scouts' freedom of association rights. In Koppelman's simply stated view, commendably pulling no punches, the United States Supreme Court's opinion in *Dale* was "disastrous"[67] and "sheer lunacy."[68] This was because, for Koppelman, the Supreme Court in *Dale* was either saying, "All antidiscrimination laws are unconstitutional in all their applications," or "Citizens are allowed to disobey laws whenever obedience would be perceived as endorsing some message," or both.[69] Koppelman states that "[b]oth of these propositions are absurd," so we can add "absurd" to the catalogue of epithets that Koppelman bestows on the Court.

One gets the strong feeling that Koppelman doesn't like the *Dale* decision. He has many reasons to criticize the Court and its idea that freedom of association forbids compelled speech of the kind that would

---

[65] *Boy Scouts of America v. Dale,* 530 U.S. 640 (2000). For Koppelman's most recent piece on *Dale,* see Koppelman, "Should Noncommercial Associations Have an Absolute Right to Discriminate?" For his earlier, more pungent piece, see Koppelman, "Signs of the Times."
[66] *Dale,* 530 U.S. at 653.
[67] Koppelman, "Signs of the Times," 1820.
[68] Ibid., 1819. Contrast with Koppelman's views the view of Northwestern University law professor Martin Redish, in a coauthored piece in which it is argued that the *Dale* decision was not only right, but didn't go far enough. See Martin H. Redish and Christopher R. McFadden, "Symposium on the Freedom of Expressive Association: HUAC, the Hollywood Ten, and the First Amendment Right of Non-Association," *Minnesota Law Review* 85 (2001): 1669.
[69] Koppelman, "Signs of the Times," 1819.

purportedly be transmitted if the Boy Scouts allowed gay members, but what I think is most interesting about Koppelman's ire is that he is probably illustrating the same kind of hierarchical ordering of constitutional values as did Skelly Wright, and almost the same sort of intuitive sense of what political choices are correct as Cass Sunstein. I do not mean to belittle Koppelman's considerable abilities as a doctrinal analyst. I think he is right, for example, in his implicit suggestion that if *Dale* is right then *Jaycees* is wrong, because the Jaycees probably had an argument to make that admitting a woman sends a message they did not wish to send—although it is possible that one could say, as Justice O'Connor might have believed (and Koppelman acknowledges), that *Jaycees* still stands even if *Dale* is correct, because the Jaycees were a commercial organization not primarily concerned with sending expressive messages, while the Boy Scouts are a noncommercial organization more openly committed "to develop[ing] good morals, reverence, patriotism, and a desire for self-improvement."[70]

For Koppelman, what is really galling about *Dale*, it would seem, is its embracing of the "pariah status of gays,"[71] its apparent acquiescence in the notion that gay people lack "emotional stability," its implicit suggestion that their "indulgence in acts of sex perversion weakens the moral fiber of an individual to a degree that he is not suitable for a position of responsibility," and its implicit acceptance of the notion that gay people are prone to "entice normal individuals to engage in perverted practices."[72] By allowing this sort of prejudice, this sort of irrational thinking, Koppelman appears to be saying, the *Dale* Court's decision will result in a situation where "[p]rejudices will be insulated from the law precisely to the extent that they are widespread."[73] Koppelman acknowledges the widespread nature of prejudices against gay people, and argues that the "compelled speech doctrine" as understood by the Court in *Dale* "unjustifiably privileges the status quo."[74] Koppelman appears to argue that, instead of favoring the values of pluralism and the autonomy of diverse groups, the *Dale* Court should have recognized that "it doesn't follow that these values should always take priority over the effort to break up entrenched patterns of discrimination and include, in socially valued activities, people who have traditionally been outcasts."[75]

Koppelman concludes that "[i]t was a mistake to grant certiorari in *Dale*," and that "[i]f the courts have nothing useful to say, then they ought to shut up."[76] He suggests that the Supreme Court was making

---

[70] Ibid., 1824–25.
[71] Ibid., 1830.
[72] Ibid., 1831, quoting from a 1950 Senate Report making these points.
[73] Ibid., 1832.
[74] Ibid., 1833.
[75] Ibid., 1835.
[76] Ibid., 1838.

an "implicit judgment that the Boy Scouts are especially worthy of judicial protection, or that gay people are especially unworthy of legislative protection, or both."[77] For Koppelman, then, freedom of association, or the Court's version of it in *Dale*, is less important than ending irrational prejudices, old stereotypes, and, in short, discrimination against homosexuals.

Koppelman's values are clear: he is against discrimination; he believes that one's sexual orientation should not be viewed as a danger to one's fellows; and he believes that the enforcement of such nondiscrimination by society is appropriate. Because Koppelman appears to have some difficulty with noncommercial associations having the freedom to discriminate among members, perhaps it is fair to say that Koppelman believes that individuals must have the freedom to work out their own lifestyles and not be penalized for the choices they make (or feel compelled to make) with regard to their intimate behavior toward others. Koppelman has not said this explicitly, but perhaps it does not go too far to suggest that Koppelman's critique of the *Dale* Court flows from his adherence to the views of the "mystery passage,"[78] and its reluctance to permit the government to be involved in dictating moral choices, especially those based on religion. While the Boy Scouts claimed that their decision to exclude homosexuals from their membership flowed from their religious and moral views, and while Koppelman does not contest that those views might well be sincerely held (though there was some debate about that in the *Dale* case), he would still let state antidiscrimination laws trump those religious and moral views. Curiously, while the Supreme Court appears to have shared Koppelman's reluctance to allow tradition and prejudice to trump antidiscrimination in the *Jaycees* case, in *Dale* the Court returned to the traditionalist view.

VIII. CONCLUSION: WHAT'S REALLY GOING ON IN THE FREEDOM OF ASSOCIATION CASES

The *Dale* case (and Koppelman gets this one right, I think) stands for the proposition that some forms of discrimination, at least, must be permitted in furthering freedom of association. While the Supreme Court tends to ground its view in the transmission of messages, so that the Court appears to link freedom of association with the First Amendment's free speech clause, it might be more appropriate, in the *Dale* case at least, to see freedom of association in a context in which it is anchored in the First Amendment's "free exercise" of religion clause, since the Boy Scouts were essentially making a religious point. *Dale* might thus be recognized as perhaps an anachronistic case in which

---

[77] Ibid.
[78] See Section II above.

the Court recognizes the historic role of religious intermediate associations in promoting the good life, as described earlier in this essay.

Koppelman, with the same assurance as Sunstein, believes in the civil rights laws, and believes that the antidiscrimination norm ought to take precedence over a religiously-based purported freedom of association. Like Sunstein, Koppelman has no difficulty in understanding what is rational and right, and thus his conclusion that *Dale* is an exercise in "lunacy." The views of Koppelman and Sunstein, and Justice Kennedy, are the more modern views, and purport to reflect advanced and more civilized values. But Burkeans favor following well-established traditions, on the theory that the individual may be foolish, but the species is wise. Could it be that a Burkean would embrace *Dale*, and reject *Jaycees*?

The conception of human flourishing advanced by Sunstein and Koppelman demands adherence (at least in Sunstein's case, and quite possibly in Koppelman's as well) to a certain set of political choices, including the legality of a right to privacy, the possibility of affirmative action, campaign finance reform, a secular public square, an expanded role for the federal government, and, generally speaking, restrictions on the exercise of the state police power, while aggrandizing the reach of the federal government. All of this is to favor weakening the authority of tradition, religion, and maybe even private property, in the service perhaps of the kind of redistribution and reallocation of power that has tended to characterize American politics since the New Deal. But what if the Framers got it right with regard to the inevitable nexus between law and morals, and morals and religion? What if freedom of association, as a concept, ought properly to be infused with these views of the Framers? Then, it would seem, the *Dale* decision was anything but lunacy; it was, instead, a reflection of a traditional Burkean deference to long-standing beliefs where matters of religion and morals are concerned. The *Dale* decision, then, may have been right, and, if it was, then perhaps the *Jaycees* decision was wrong.

Legal History, Northwestern University School of Law

THE PARADOX OF ASSOCIATION

By Loren E. Lomasky

I. Introduction

Civil societies are nourished not by one but by two freedoms of association. The first is positive freedom of association, a power to combine with some other party or parties in a shared activity or status. Positive freedom of association admits of varying degrees of attractive force. The weakest is an association constituted by the consent of all parties. Stronger is an association one is empowered to join even if some other party or parties prefer not to be so associated, while others desire association. Strongest is where one's membership in the association is guaranteed, not requiring the consent of any other. The second freedom is negative freedom of association, a liberty to dissociate from unwanted relationships. The strongest version of negative freedom of association is the power to withdraw regardless of the assent of others. Less strong forms of negative freedom permit withdrawal subject to the concurrence of certain others. So, for example, in certain traditional marriage practices, a husband enjoys a very strong freedom to dissociate; he is empowered to dissolve the marriage on his own volition. A wife, however, may dissociate only with the concurrence of her husband and therefore enjoys only a weak negative freedom. (If divorce is not permitted under any conditions, then the parties altogether lack the freedom to dissociate.)

I characterize these as two distinct freedoms of association because, although complementary, they stand in potential tension. The former is centripetal, the latter centrifugal, and imperatives to draw together are weakened or negated by permissions to withdraw. This tension is especially acute within a liberal order. Because such an order vests primary authority in the decisions of individuals, it must afford them great latitude to go their own way as they see fit. But because it is indeed a *social* order, it is charged to uphold a standard of general inclusiveness. The freedom to associate is checked by a freedom to withhold unwanted association, and vice versa. What may be called the Paradox of Association was most memorably stated by Marx when he announced, "I refuse to join any club that would have me as a member." [1] The task of this essay is to examine the plausibility of some proposed rules of club membership.

---

[1] See Groucho Marx, *Groucho and Me* (New York: Da Capo Press, 1995). I have been unable to find any evidence that Marx was an influence for Yogi Berra's assertion, "No one goes there nowadays, it's too crowded."

doi:10.1017/S0265052508080230

Section II sketches various bases of the negative freedom of association. These are seen to be manifold and indispensable to the liberal enterprise. Section III presents positive association both as liberty and as ideal. Section IV takes up a handful of potential conflicts between the two freedoms of association. Section V sums up with a program for not quite resolving but at least living with the Paradox of Association.

II. Freedom of Dissociation

The absence of liberty to go one's own way is subjugation. Consequently, any regime other than a slave society countenances in some measure that liberty—and even slave societies are unable to extinguish the primordial human desire to live freely. It is the particular distinction of liberalism, however, to put expansion of the domain of protected choice front and center as a regulative political principle. The early liberal campaign was waged along a number of dimensions in which freedom to dissociate is paramount.

Freedom of conscience, especially as related to religious practice, was an early outpost of the struggle. Insofar as it is understood as the struggle of individuals to secure adequate scope to practice their faith alongside others who espouse similar convictions, this is a mode of positive freedom of association. However, these confessional congregations cannot begin to get underway until there is acknowledged a negative freedom to dissociate from the established church. In the early modern period, conscience was understood to be a jealous mistress who does not brook any sharing of favors with competitors. To follow a preferred path to salvation was to eschew incompatible routes. Thus, freedom of religion is, in the first instance, a negative entitlement.

Freedom of speech is similar. Although it is not in any obvious way a mode (either positive or negative) of association, it displays aspects of both. Other than the limiting case of soliloquy, speech is an act of interpersonally shared communication that unites speaker with listener. *Sotto voce* free speech doesn't count for much. Therefore, the realization of freedom of speech incorporates some form or other of semantic association. But prior to a liberty to speak one's mind is a permission to desist from echoing the words that issue from the commanding heights of pulpit or palace. That is, freedom of speech is no less fundamentally a freedom not to give utterance to objectionable phrases than it is to give declaration to one's own beliefs and attitudes. Speech rights are, then, associational and, in the first instance, negative.[2]

Occupational and *residential mobility* emerged with the waning of a feudalism that tied individuals to land and labor. Entitlement to take up

---

[2] The Fifth Amendment protection against compelled self-incrimination is a related species of the liberty to withhold speech.

whatever employment may be on offer presupposes a liberty to divest oneself of prior jobs; moving to a new address presupposes a right to leave the old address. Both liberties were planks of early liberal platforms.[3] At a somewhat later date, the liberation of women from paternal or spousal control moved to the center of liberal concern.[4] Classical feminism displayed various interrelated facets, but integral to many was an underlying freedom to dissociate.

Private property rights are not usually thought of in terms of freedom of association. However, insofar as ownership establishes against all others a duty to refrain from access to the object in question absent the owner's assent, it is a strong barrier against unwanted intrusions. Property affords one a say concerning with whom one will associate and on what terms. If a man's home is his castle, that is not in virtue of sumptuous interiors or lofty towers but rather because of a figurative moat around the perimeter that excludes unwanted entry. What one owns is that from which one is at liberty to exclude others for good reasons, bad reasons, or no reasons at all. The other side of the property coin is that it affords individuals means to induce others to undertake positive associational relations. The home/castle is not usually a hermit's cell; more often, it is a site for raising families and hosting friends. Personal property is that with which people truck, barter, and exchange.[5] If it is only through the ongoing concurrence of others that one holds land or chattels, one's life is only in a diminished sense one's own. Property is the fount of independence.[6]

For early modern political theory, no imperative sounds more emphatically than the need to establish conditions of *peace*. Thomas Hobbes famously identifies the state of nature with the state of war,[7] and although John Locke resists that equation, he is under no illusion that people in anarchy will be able to avoid the "inconveniences" consequent on lacking a common judge to resolve disputes.[8] It is worth noting that freedom to dissociate is a crucial element of the quest for social peace. If individuals'

---

[3] See, for example, Adam Smith's denunciation of the law of settlements that restricted the occupational mobility of would-be workers: "To remove a man who has committed no misdemeanour from the parish where he chuses to reside, is an evident violation of natural liberty and justice.... There is scarce a poor man in England of forty years of age, I will venture to say, who has not in some part of his life felt himself most cruelly oppressed by this ill-contrived law of settlements." Smith, *The Wealth of Nations* I.x.c (Indianapolis, IN: Liberty Press, 1981), 157.

[4] Among the many pleas on behalf of women's liberty to dissociate, see Mary Wollstonecraft, *A Vindication of the Rights of Woman* (New York: Penguin Classics, 2004); and John Stuart Mill, *The Subjection of Women* (New York: Dover, 1997).

[5] The phrase is Adam Smith's. See *The Wealth of Nations* I.ii, p. 25.

[6] Secure control over one's body and labor are also requisite for independence. John Locke and other classical liberal theorists tend to amalgamate these as forms of property.

[7] Thomas Hobbes, *Leviathan*, chap. XIII, "Of the Naturall Condition of Mankind as concerning their Felicity, and Misery."

[8] John Locke, *Second Treatise*, in Locke, *Two Treatises of Government*, ed. Peter Laslett (Cambridge: Cambridge University Press, 1988), sec. 13.

only recourse for avoiding unwanted association is to fight, then fight they will. Far better for purposes of general comity is the extension of a robust liberty to go one's own way. To be obliged to act in concert with those whose ends or attributes one disdains is costly to one's integrity. When that disdain is intense enough, the cost may well be deemed not worth paying. If not altogether eliminated, the cost is at least reduced when the disfavored enterprise can be viewed as *theirs* rather than *ours*. Insofar as a freedom to dissociate empowers individuals to avoid involuntary implication in disfavored designs of others, it conspicuously promotes the quest for peace.

If peace is the *sine qua non* of early liberalism, the leading player in more recent incarnations of the theory is *autonomy*. An autonomy-centered liberalism holds that conceptions of the good are not to be imposed from above (or below, or sideways) on individuals, but rather are to be self-determined. Autonomy rejects all ideologies of one-size-fits-all. There is, to be sure, a significant role for the state in promoting values, but it is the indirect and derivative role of affording to individuals conditions conducive to independence of thought and deed. Just what those conditions are is the subject of ample philosophical debate. For modern welfare liberals, the extent of these conditions goes well beyond noninterference to include positive provision of items such as education, health care, and wealth redistribution. These are to be afforded not because the state officially ranks them above other goods, but because they enable individuals to achieve autonomy. Whatever one thinks of these additions to the traditional package of state responsibilities, they augment but do not replace the primacy of freedom of dissociation. A person who is constrained to run with the herd may travel in a propitious direction, but it will not be her direction. Only when people are free to detach themselves from other values, modes of life that are not their own, are they able to act autonomously. This is arguably not a sufficient condition for the autonomous life—one may perhaps, with Jean-Jacques Rousseau, hold it necessary from time to time to force individuals to be genuinely free—but it is necessary.

If autonomy was the liberal ideal of the twentieth century, it is conceivable that *diversity* will assume that status in the twenty-first. There may not be much of Mao's legacy preserved in contemporary China, but his injunction to let a thousand flowers bloom is treasured on every American college campus and by every governmental bureau. To be sure, general declarations of praise for diversity are often best interpreted as coded messages in support of some particular favored pattern of representation, but these invocations could not succeed even as euphemism were it not the case that "diversity" in its primary, uncontaminated sense carries positive connotations. Nothing is more necessary for genuine diversity to flourish than a protected freedom for individuals and groups to separate from and act independently of dominant social entities. A minority culture that is forcibly subsumed within some larger collectivity has its own distinctive identity thereby besmeared. In principle, this applies all the way down to the level of individuals and to novel associational linkages; I do not deny that the practice of the diversity industry often operates otherwise.

Dissociation serves other aspects of a free and prosperous society. *Innovation*, almost by definition, requires detachment from traditional patterns of personal interaction and productive practices. That is not to maintain that all innovation constitutes improvement, but its absence is economic and cultural stagnation.[9] Since selection through comparative fitness operates on products of invention much as it does in the realm of biological evolution, there exists an asymmetry in favor of innovation even if its fruits are randomly distributed between useful and useless. Because intention and deliberation guide the process, better than Darwinian outcomes are to be expected. What Joseph Schumpeter calls "creative destruction"[10] is often unsettling, but it is the antidote to stasis and stultification.

Dissociation also serves to foster the proliferation of *positional goods*. If there exists a common metric for an entire collectivity, the top will be lonely; only in Lake Wobegon can *all* the children be above average. However, if people separate themselves out in a multitude of ways, endlessly creating activities to which they can lend their efforts, the likelihood that a representative individual will discover some avenue along which he can be the best (or excel somewhat, or at least be above average) increases. The economist Tyler Cowen notes that there are in America over three thousand Halls of Fame (an improbably large number of them devoted to bowling).[11] It is arguable whether comparing one's own accomplishments to those of deficient others is an altogether morally savory practice, but it seems clear that individuals' self-esteem is in large measure a function of their positional standing. (Crowds in stadiums declaim "We're Number 1! We're Number 1!" not "We lose a lot of games but play pretty darn hard!") Enhanced access to positional goods not only massages individual psyches but also serves other political ends noted above, including especially the maintenance of civic peace.

This is not meant to be an exhaustive accounting of the merits of negative freedom of association, the liberty to dissociate. The aim has been to say enough to establish the following two points: (1) freedom of dissociation is a major element of many political desiderata; and (2) positive freedoms of association often presuppose the corresponding negative freedom. It is to the positive freedom that I now turn.

[9] Both Adam Smith in *The Wealth of Nations* and J. S. Mill in *On Liberty* are insistent on this point.
[10] Joseph Schumpeter, *Capitalism, Socialism, and Democracy* (New York: Harper, 1975), 82.
[11] Tyler Cowen, *What Price Fame?* (Cambridge, MA: Harvard University Press, 2000).

III. Positive Freedom of Association

Should it be concluded that a liberal political order can dispense with any independent concern for a centripetal positive freedom of association? In a word, no. At least one association is mandatory for those within civil society: the universal association that is the political order itself.[12] For all those located within borders, aliens as well as citizens, obeisance to the social contract is not open for negotiation.

Both Hobbes and Locke officially depict the state as generated by the consent of sovereign individuals, although in Hobbes's case the voluntariness of that consent may be impugned by his insistence that even when extracted at the point of a sword, it remains valid.[13] For both, however, that consent once given is irrevocable. The only way to withdraw from duties of obedience to the state is physical relocation. Neither secession of a territory over which one holds ownership nor declared intent to resume the status of an independent is permissible. Immanuel Kant's insistence on the necessity of incorporation within the political association is even less compromising. No initial voluntary declaration of allegiance is required:

> [T]he first decision the individual is obliged to make, if he does not wish to renounce all concepts of right, will be to adopt the principle that *one must abandon the state of nature* in which everyone follows his own desires, and unite with everyone else (with whom he cannot avoid having intercourse) in order to submit to external, public and lawful coercion. . . . In other words, he should at all costs enter into a state of civil society. . . . Anyone may thus use force to impel the others to abandon this state for a state of right.[14]

Liberals may differ among themselves concerning whether secession is justified *in extremis* (and how dire circumstances must be to lie on the far side of *extremis*), but the essential point is that over a very wide range of political practice, there is one association that is not optional, not dispensable.

Mandatory membership promotes peace. It is also conducive to the cultivation of autonomy. Kant argues that autonomy is expressed by

---

[12] Universal, that is, relative to the civil order in question. Pending the success of cosmopolitanism, multiple universalisms are the only ones on political offer.

[13] "When the Vanquished, to avoyd the present stroke of death, covenanteth either in expresse words, or by other sufficient signes of the Will, that so long as his life, and the liberty of his body is allowed him, the Victor shall have the use thereof, at his pleasure." Hobbes, *Leviathan*, chap. XX, "Of Dominion Paternall and Despoticall." Locke also extends the bounds of consent by an expansive understanding of what constitutes an act of tacit consent.

[14] Immanuel Kant, *Metaphysics of Morals*, in *Kant: Political Writings*, ed. Hans Reiss (Cambridge: Cambridge University Press, 1970), 137–38; emphasis added.

directing one's conduct in accord with practical reason's moral law. If individuals are to engage in genuinely moral relations with others as governed by the categorical imperative, there must exist a standard that all parties have reason to acknowledge as rationally authoritative over their wills. That is impossible in a state of nature. Autonomy and the establishment of property rights travel together. In order to respect the distinction between *mine* and *thine,* ownership must be interpersonally grounded via impersonal principles of right. Only civil law can provide those principles, and only a state can generate civil law. Positive freedom of association, then, is arguably no less essential for the realization of liberal ideals than is freedom of dissociation.

For many theorists, however, one inescapable association defined simply in terms of law-abidingness is too thin a gruel. They maintain that more is needed to ground an adequately humane society. That criticism of ancestral liberalism is manifest in the French Revolution's replacement of Locke's triad of "life, liberty, and property" (and Thomas Jefferson's "life, liberty, and the pursuit of happiness") with "Liberty, Equality, Fraternity." Citizens—and this was by a wide margin the preferred term for co-nationals—should be drawn together by more than an arbitrary shared geography and legal duties. As partners in an exercise of political self-determination,[15] they are united at a portentous level by a project that unifies and confers meaning on their efforts. According to Rousseau, they transcend the condition of discrete centers of desire and come to partake of a "general will." As "patriots," they are the progeny of a fatherland that renders them all brothers and sisters. The conception at work here is premodern, hearkening back to Aristotle's understanding of "civic friendship" and to Plato's Myth of the Metals in the *Republic,* in which a story of radical political consanguinity is proffered. But although ancient, it surfaces in an important strand of modern liberal democratic thought.

Fraternity, almost by definition, privileges the centripetal over the centrifugal. The good life is not well-lived by the "solitary rights-bearer";[16] rather, it is social. Classical liberalism's focus on staying out of each other's way is criticized as generating a desiccated politics, an "atomistic individualism."[17] The state is not, of course, the only society that affords sustenance to individuals, but it is preeminent in virtue of being comprehensive in its makeup and requisite for the flourishing of all lesser associations. Therefore, a proper function of government is to

[15] The nature of the "self" in question, and its determinations, are admittedly among the more opaque subjects in all of political philosophy.

[16] The term is Mary Ann Glendon's from her book *Rights Talk: The Impoverishment of Political Discourse* (New York: Free Press, 2004).

[17] See, for example, Charles Taylor, "Atomism," in Shlomo Avineri and Avner de-Shalit, eds., *Communitarianism and Individualism* (New York: Oxford University Press, 1992), 29–50; and C. B. Macpherson, *The Political Theory of Possessive Individualism* (Oxford: Clarendon Press, 1962).

provide institutional structures that draw persons together, most especially with regard to activity on behalf of the commonwealth itself. For
those who take fraternity seriously, laissez-faire is not nearly good
enough.

Opponents of an austere classical liberalism typically fault its excessive
devotion to freedom of dissociation. Such is the nub of the *communitarian*
critique.[18] We do not form conceptions of the good adequate to nourish a
meaningful life in a normative vacuum. Rather, says the communitarian,
our valuational inclinations are no less the product of a formative social
environment than is the language we speak. It is, then, a matter of some
urgency for a political order intent on sustaining itself and its members in
full civic health to promote meaning-conferring associations. Indiscrimi-
nate exercise of the exit option is inimical to the vitality of the body
politic. Therefore, communities are to be afforded considerable latitude,
including well-aimed applications of coercion, to give effect to their constitutive values and thereby hold themselves together against the corro-
sive forces of untrammeled dissociation.

Although John Rawls is usually the communitarians' preferred foil in
virtue of his emphasis on the importance for moral theory of the separateness of persons, he is not altogether immune to the attractions of
extended association. In a striking characterization of his own theory, he
declares: "In justice as fairness men agree to share one another's fate."[19]
Being bound to one another's fate is an extraordinarily powerful form of
association. It is a melding of the good of one with the good of all. Rawls
does not present sharing of fate as an exclusive attribute of relations of
deep friendship or familial solidarity; to the contrary, it is a precept of
justice. Thus, it establishes an associative nexus both general and mandatory. Implications within his theory are sweeping, including a strongly
egalitarian difference principle from which individuals are not at liberty
to dissociate.

Socialism similarly configures the polity as an economic association
within which, by default, all individuals are shareholders. Unlike the
investors in a capitalistic enterprise, however, their holdings are quanti-
tatively identical and not alienable. If private ownership separates individuals and confers on them independence one from another, public
ownership of the means of production renders them mutually interdepen-
dent. It would be a mistake to view socialist theory merely as a hypothesis
about how to secure efficient and equitable economic production—which,
in any case, has never been a locus of conspicuous achievement for the

---

[18] See, for example, Michael Sandel's critique of liberalism's "unencumbered selves" in
Liberalism and the Limits of Justice (Cambridge: Cambridge University Press, 1982), and
Alasdair MacIntyre's invocation of communal norms in *After Virtue* (Notre Dame, IN: Uni-
versity of Notre Dame Press, 1981).
[19] John Rawls, *A Theory of Justice* (Cambridge, MA: Harvard University Press, 1971), 102.
It is worth observing that in the revised edition of the book, this sentence is excised.

theory. It also, and more centrally, incorporates an ideal of shared fates, perhaps in a sense even stronger than that intended by Rawls.

If social contract is the birth of a state, secession and civil war are its death. Cohesiveness combats dissolution, and strong association promotes cohesiveness. The ideal of the *melting pot,* although drastically out of favor in an age of enthusiastic paeans to diversity, directly addresses the cohesion problem. Cooperation with those one finds disconcertingly different is problematic. They are instead likely to be perceived as threats eliciting either avoidance or confrontation. But if that which divides potentially antagonistic parties is burned off in the political smelter, then passions that commonly set individuals and groups in opposition will be defused. People who are rendered more similar will dissociate less often and less intensely. That's good for social harmony.

If "melting" is deemed an improbable (or potentially tyrannous) goal, applying layers of "social glue" to hold together disparate segments can present itself as a more moderate means to a similar peace-preserving end. A currently fashionable brand of this glue goes by the name *social capital.*[20] It is formulated through associations in which people who know each other on a face-to-face basis come to develop dispositions to trust and to cooperate. Social capital cements a wide range of relationships, including especially those bound up with peaceful coexistence. Even such seemingly apolitical entities as bowling leagues, book discussion groups, and the Loyal Order of Moose have strongly positive effects on general comity. Therefore, governments are well-advised to adopt measures friendly to the formation of social capital. At the very least, governments are most emphatically not to be neutral between civic association and dissociation.

The moral to be drawn from this and the preceding section is that there are powerful currents within modern political philosophy supporting strong freedom of dissociation, and there are comparably powerful currents that favor active promotion through governmental means of positive association. As morals go, this one is feeble, reminiscent of the old joke about the rabbi and the disputing congregants.[21] The interesting question is not whether there might be something to be said on behalf of both positive and negative association, but rather which ought to take pride of place when they conflict. It is to this inquiry that the discussion now turns.

---

[20] The most noteworthy social capital evangelist is Robert Putnam. See Putnam, *Making Democracy Work: Civic Traditions in Modern Italy* (Princeton, NJ: Princeton University Press, 1993), and, especially, Putnam, *Bowling Alone* (New York: Simon and Schuster, 2000).

[21] Rabbi Schwartz is listening to the complaints of two feuding congregants. The first man explains why the other guy is in the wrong, and the rabbi responds, "You're right!" Then the second man presents his case and the rabbi says, "You're right!" Then a third man who was standing nearby asks, "Rabbi, they're at odds, so how can they both be right?" Rabbi Schwartz scratches his chin, thinks for a while, and then turns to the third man and says, "Yes, you're right, too!"

IV. A HANDFUL OF APPLICATIONS

Consider the following two-part principle: (1) Preservation of the universal association constituted by the political order itself trumps all exercises of freedom of dissociation. (2) Nothing else does. It is as invigoratingly bold as the conclusion of the preceding section was timid. Unfortunately, it is too uncompromising to be supportable. If a regime is sufficiently vile, then its destruction through forceful exit is justified. (The breakup of the Soviet Union presaged by the departure of the Baltic nations is an instance of salutary dissociation.) Also, acts of dissociation which do not seriously threaten the continued existence of the state but which contribute to friction in its internal operations may permissibly be stymied, either through outright prohibition or via more subtle means of discouragement. Therefore, it is necessary to preface the principle with "For the most part." So qualified, it is defensible but too noncommittal to be very helpful.

One way to lend more substance to the (qualified) principle is to apply it to selected cases and observe how they fare as instances of the Paradox of Association. A trade-off between breadth and depth is operative here. Multiplying cases affords more data points against which the theory can be assessed, but each case will be presented more superficially. Because the aim of this section is not so much to adjudicate particular policy disputes by analyzing them all the way down to the ground as it is to exhibit the sorts of considerations that can be brought to bear on a wide range of questions, the superficiality concern is less worrisome. I display in the remainder of this section a handful of illustrative cases, one of mostly historical interest, the others currently disputed. Readers are invited to develop other instances of negative and positive association in tension.

A. "Separate but equal"

In the United States prior to the pivotal 1954 *Brown v. Board of Education* case,[22] coercively imposed separation of the races with regard to the enjoyment of state services was countenanced subject to the condition that the quality of provision be equal. There are numerous grounds on which this policy could be (and was) challenged: equal quality was not, in fact, achieved (or even seriously intended); racial discrimination is inherently invidious and thus unequal; the Constitution is color-blind. This is not the occasion for entry into the realm of jurisprudence. Rather, the point of revisiting the distant world of *Plessy v. Ferguson* (1896)[23] is to observe that as a matter of pure political philosophy, state enforcement of the "separate but equal" doctrine is dubious. That is because it impugns

---

[22] *Brown v. Board of Education of Topeka*, 347 U.S. 483 (1954).
[23] *Plessy v. Ferguson*, 163 U.S. 537 (1896).

the integrity of the universal positive association. Forcible exclusion of some citizens from the terrain of others creates the shadow of a state within the state, a house divided against itself. A social contract that systematically differentiates between subpopulations might better be characterized as an antisocial contract.

Suppose, counterfactually, that racial discrimination had been instituted as the expressed preference of majorities within the entire citizenry. Does that afford democratic legitimacy to segregation? Not if the minority reasonably takes itself to be thereby disadvantaged. Suppose (further out on the counterfactual curve) that majorities within both races favored separation. Is it then justifiable policy? The answer is not entirely clear-cut. One theory of peaceful coexistence maintains that good fences make good neighbors. If segregation alleviates frictions that might otherwise be inimical to civic peace, then it could be justified in the name of ensuring the stability of the universal association. In effect, "separate but equal" amounts to a sort of tension-reducing racial federalism. This is, of course, far-fetched. More plausibly, enforced separation is a step in the direction of internal division and disrepair. Unless the avowed interest of all groups is to divide—in which case we would wonder why they wish to remain in political association at all—even scrupulously equal separation policies are contraindicated.

B. Affirmative action

The term "affirmative action" is fuzzy, covering a range of policies from the innocuous to the controversial. I am not concerned here with activities designed to transmit knowledge of employment or admissions openings to classes of people who might otherwise lack awareness of their availability. Instead, I confine my attention to application of differential selection standards predicated on group membership. These include adding some specified weight to applications of favored candidates, affording them an indeterminate preference when qualifications are close, or imposing fixed selection quotas. Although affirmative action so specified can be applied to any (dis)favored group, the paradigmatic context of categorization in the United States is racial. Because the goal is enhanced inclusion of previously excluded parties, affirmative action policies fall under positive freedom of association. Are they justifiable?

If affirmative action is voluntarily practiced by a nongovernmental entity in service of its own values, then it is relatively unproblematic.[24] Company X or University Y is at liberty to extend its own preferred terms of association to willing others just as you and I are at liberty with regard to with whom we will pass our convivial hours. The two more complicated cases are (i) affirmative action practiced by organs of the state in the

[24] But see note 25.

conduct of their own operations, and (ii) governmentally-mandated affirmative action requirements that fall on nonstate actors. I take these two cases up in turn.

Considerations adduced in the previous subsection speak against state-practiced affirmative action. Although it aims not to separate races but rather to bring them into more extensive association, the method of doing so is to apply different standards to subpopulations. No one is excluded from the universal association, but terms of membership are to the advantage of some against others. This is inherently inimical to the primary desideratum of the social contract: peace. All else equal, state-sponsored affirmative action is an inferior form of positive association.

All else, however, is far from equal. The great enduring rip in the social fabric of the United States is slavery and its aftermath. Neither the Civil War nor civil rights initiatives a century on succeeded in establishing an adequately inclusive social order. Thus, derivation of recommended principles of political association is a task of non-ideal theory, what the economists call the realm of "second-best." A history of flawed policy can render acceptable or even mandatory responses that would otherwise be unacceptable. (Compare with the practice of punishing people who have been found guilty of offenses by forcibly depriving them of life, liberty, or property.) Racial frictions are the single ugliest blotch on the canvas of U.S. domestic relations. A significant prospect of substantial melioration might, then, outweigh the presumption against applying differential criteria. This is especially the case if those who bear the burden of these policies are, in other precincts of civic life, beneficiaries of differential standards that work to their own favor. To extend dissimilar treatment to different subpopulations is to infringe standards of association for the sake of promoting association. A separate matter is whether affirmative action as practiced by organs of the state does, in fact, tend to promote harmonious interracial association. That is a question not best answered from the comfort of an armchair. As a matter of theory, though, there is room from a liberal free association perspective for a coherent case on behalf of state-sponsored affirmative action.

Imposition of affirmative action requirements on private parties blocks otherwise available dissociation prerogatives and thus confronts a yet steeper justificatory hurdle. The criteria one employs for undertaking relations with willing others are important components of one's conception of how best to lead one's life. To be subject to external direction in these matters is a significant imposition. That it is within the purview of the liberal state to impose such requirements for broadly utilitarian or egalitarian reasons is highly disputable. If, however, the rationale is enhancement of civic peace, then the case becomes more difficult to adjudicate. In effect, some measure of the negative freedom of dissociation is being traded off for augmentation of positive association. Both freedoms are integral to a decent political order, and, therefore, it is at least an open question whether an exchange of one for the other is well-undertaken. And because the stability of the universal association is a prerequisite for all other associational and dissociational liberties, its maintenance is a trump. Three centuries of racial hostility constitute a prima facie plausible rationale for strong meliorative intervention. Peace is worth some constraint, especially if that constraint is of limited duration such that it will more or less automatically expire when the end for which it was inaugurated is achieved. If duration and scope of application are open-ended, then the onus against restriction is heavier. Again, whether the policy tends more to soothe or to exacerbate conflict cannot be settled as a matter of pure theory.[25]

C. Public schools

Let it be granted for the sake of argument that children possess a welfare right to be educated, and that the duty correlative to this right is lodged against the general public rather than the child's parents. It does not follow that the state is justified in establishing a privileged system of free (to the user, not, of course, to taxpayers) public schools. Governmental support of primary education could instead be decentralized to the household level via cash payments or vouchers for the parents/guardians of school-age children. Nonetheless, in the U.S. each of the fifty states funds a monolithic public school system; not one state offers more than a nugatory amount of decentralization through parental choice.[26] Why?

This could be interpreted as a question about the balance of political forces, in which case extended reference to the strength of teachers' unions and other battalions making up the educational juggernaut would be to the point. Take it instead as a request for justification. Then answers are not so readily forthcoming. Or, rather, *credible* answers are elusive. For example, if it is claimed that state schooling is necessary to promote equality, that otherwise the poor would suffer inferior educational services, the obvious retort is that despite—or because of?—state schooling, the poor fare much worse than do the rich. A claim that kids will learn

[25] These points apply equally to statutes (such as the Civil Rights Act of 1964) outlawing discrimination by private parties with regard to hiring, access to hotels, restaurants, and other public accommodations, and so on. It is very difficult to justify these as applications of compensatory justice because the parties on whom the associational constraints fall are typically not those responsible for prior patterns of injustice. However, insofar as these mandates are reasonable prescriptions for addressing the kinds of social distemper that jeopardize civic peace, they may be justified.

[26] A partial exception to this generalization is the passage in 2007 by Utah's legislature of a means-adjusted universal voucher program. As this essay is being written, implementation of the program remains blocked by opponents who have gathered signatures sufficient to force a referendum. See Martin Stoltz, "Voters Will Decide on Voucher Program," *New York Times*, May 15, 2007, http://query.nytimes.com/gst/fullpage.html?res=9B00EEDE1331F936A25756 C0A9619C8B63 (accessed August 15, 2007).

well if and only if the state is directly involved in the provision of schooling will not survive a cursory glance at standardized test scores. The argument that parents in general and uneducated ones in particular will do an inferior job of selection in an open market generates in response the question "Compared to what?" If the relevant comparison class is the schooling currently provided by the public education cartel,[27] then it is questionable whether parents are liable to do worse. The argument that under a scheme of vouchers the most able and ambitious will exit the public system, leaving only the hard cases behind, is morally disgraceful insofar as it regards holding children hostage as acceptable social policy. The list of defective rationales could easily be extended.

The interesting puzzle for political theory is why, despite such palpably inferior arguments, public schooling remains popular.[28] Ignorance and differential concern might provide part of the answer: parents estimate more highly the quality of their own children's schools than those attended by other children. In addition, though, associational considerations bear significantly on the continuing strength of affection for public schooling. A Great American Myth presents the public schools as heroic agents of socialization, the indispensable institution that unites children of plenty with children of want, newly arrived immigrant populations with long-time residents, kids of all different ability levels. Whether in the one-room schoolhouse of the prairie or the urban repositories of the children of tenements, public schools were instrumental in turning a diverse population of boys and girls into . . . Americans. To be sure, the myth never applied very plausibly to substantial segments of the population, most notably those separate but allegedly equal black children and those who assumed the financial burden of funding parochial education. Nonetheless, it is evocative. The ideal it serves is that of a population of diverse citizens united by allegiance to a distinctively public weal. However much they ultimately go their separate ways with regard to religion, economic

---

[27] I speak of *cartel* rather than *monopoly* because there is significant diversity among K through 12 educational services providers. Both within and among states, there exists a plethora of more or less independent school districts that parents "buy" via their residential choices. Private and parochial schools are also at liberty to compete for patrons, but they do so from a position of acute disadvantage against state-supported competitors that price their services at a marginal cost of zero to the consumer. Parents are not forbidden to exit, but they must pay a steep price to do so. Many who might wish to opt out of the public schools lack the financial means to do so. Moreover, ubiquitous governmental regulation imposes further constraints on alternative providers and on parents. Positive freedom of classroom association in state schools is, then, not mandatory, but people's choices are very much tipped in that direction by current educational policy.

[28] A typical statement: "The American public still stands behind their public schools and their local school board according to the *39th Annual Phi Delta Kappa/Gallup Poll of the Public's Attitudes Toward Public Schools*. The majority of the public rate their local public school with an A or B. They also prefer that local school boards have the greatest influence in deciding what is taught in public schools." See http://www.centerforpubliceducation.org/site/c.kjJXJ5MPIwE/b.1427855/k.FAA3/Welcome_to_the_Center_for_Public_Education.htm (accessed August 15, 2007).

status, and culture, they nonetheless remain linked by a shared commitment to the universal association. Public schools, on this conception, are
validated less by what students learn than by the fact that they are learning together—and that they are thereby learning how to do yet other
things together.

I am agnostic concerning how accurately the myth applies to public
schooling during its 1850–1950 heyday, and considerably more skeptical
with regard to current applicability. If it was/is the case, however, that
state schooling supplies public cohesion that would otherwise be absent,
and if that cohesion is a significant contributor to civic peace, then restrictions on the liberty of parents to go their own way with regard to educational choices might be defended. I speculate that the continuing
popularity of public schooling rests on some such belief. Or if not belief,
then pious hope: In an age of fragmentation where along numerous dimensions the center appears not to be holding, it might seem too risky to
disestablish the institution with the myth behind it. In the calculations of
state schooling cartel advocates, positive association defeats negative.
One may have reason to suspect that these calculations incorporate erro-
neous estimations, but the underlying theme of the need to safeguard
crucial positive associations is worthy of respect.

D. Immigration

When individuals who hold foreign passports are interdicted at borders, their freedom of mobility is obviously impaired. Somewhat less
obvious is that immigration restrictions thwart association. Very few people cross the Rio Grande or the Pacific into the United States with the
intention of establishing themselves as hermits. Rather, they aspire to
secure work with willing employers, to obtain residences through mutually acceptable transactions with landlords, and to purchase the necessi-
ties and a few of the superfluities of life from eager merchants. They also
will tend to establish consensual relationships with their new neighbors
in matters religious, cultural, and social. Blocking immigration is not
merely an imposition on those left outside of borders looking in; it limits
valued associational opportunities for those already here.[29]

There are any number of reasons that can be given on behalf of restricting foreign access. It is my opinion that these mostly fail. Those considerations that do have some merit support less draconian measures than
exclusion. I have examined these arguments elsewhere and will not repeat
them here.[30] I here acknowledge, though, that the severe impediments to

---

[29] So also do constraints on trade. I discuss these matters at greater length in "Toward a
Liberal Theory of National Boundaries," in David Miller and Sohail Hashmi, eds., *Boundaries and Justice* (Princeton, NJ: Princeton University Press, 2001), 55–78.
[30] See my essay "Liberalism Beyond Borders," *Social Philosophy and Policy* 24, no. 1 (Winter
2007): 206–33.

free association created by tight border control can be countered, not entirely implausibly, with an argument also predicated on the importance of free association.

From the birth of the United States as a land with open borders that seekers of liberty were invited to cross, there have always been nay-sayers who warned that the cohesion of the republic was gravely imperiled by the influx of waves of people ignorant of our traditions and temperamentally unsuited to our way of life.[31] Although these alarums have always been belied (*pace* hard-line nativists), this does not clinch the case that they will continue to be inaccurate. Inductions in the service of political prediction are notoriously perilous, especially when salient conditions have undergone transformation. One such condition might be the burgeoning of the welfare state; another is the waning of the melting-pot ideal and the concomitant waxing of cultural pluralism. The nativist contention, then, deserves to be taken seriously, both with regard to the merits of its empirical foundations and also its moral standing. That is, there are possible worlds in which it would be efficacious and morally appropriate to harden borders. Is one of them the actual world?

I do not find plausible the suggestion that even a very large intake of foreign nationals seeking to better their lot and to enjoy the perquisites of residence in an advanced liberal democracy threatens national cohesion. The contrary seems to be more indicated; those who display their values by voting with their feet for this way of life thereby endorse the universal positive association. Their accession can be expected to afford it strength. But immigrants who establish residence in democratic societies while rejecting the liberal values on which those societies are founded, and who seek to form insular oppositional enclaves apart from the host civilization, may indeed be exercising liberties of dissociation inimical to the common good. It is one thing to defend cultural pluralism within the ambit of an overarching universal association that enjoys the support of the various different factions, and quite another to countenance those who would subvert the underpinnings on which that association is sustained. A free society is not obliged to welcome into its midst those who espouse a rejectionist ideology. In the wake of September 11, 2001, the obvious candidate for such designation is revanchist Islam. No great prophetic facility is needed to predict that over the next decade and beyond this will be the locus of a major debate in the United States and, especially, Western Europe about appropriate terms for sustainable civil association.

E. Health-care policy

There are innumerable reasons to believe that the U.S. system of delivering health care is gravely flawed. Many people lack regular access to

---

[31] One such force was the "Know Nothing" movement of the 1850s, notable among other things for being the most aptly named political party in American history.

routine health services; care is inordinately expensive both in absolute terms and as a percentage of national GDP; perverse incentives and cross-subsidies abound. All of these are reasons to support some form of universal health care such as that on offer in Canada or the UK. There are, however, reasons to be very wary of these alternatives, including limitations on choice, shortages of materiel and personnel, and protracted wait times for noncritical (and, occasionally, critical) procedures. Reasonable people can differ concerning what would and would not count as an improvement. Here I confine my attention to one less frequently observed motif underlying the health-care debate: implications for the universal association.

In a society fractured along virtually every conceivable dimension, the cords that hold a citizenry together become increasingly tenuous and frayed. One need not be a communitarian enthusiast to be apprehensive about the staying power of a society that has a shrinking store of shared commitments and experiences. A large part of the attractiveness of universal health care is that it answers to the demand for an important common enterprise in which all have an equal stake. National health care serves something of the same functions that an established church did in premodern times. It addresses itself to our deepest concerns about human fragility and mortality, concerns that are no respecters of wealth or power. Its practice is mostly carried out in imposing edifices served by specially anointed, distinctively garbed professionals who are initiated in mysteries not vouchsafed to the common run of men and who, in keeping with their lofty status, are addressed in deferential terms of respect. Denial of access to their ministrations is an especially cruel form of excommunication. They carry the keys to the kingdom, albeit a thoroughly secular one. In a word, health care in the contemporary world is sacramental. (Or if it isn't, nothing else serves as half so plausible a simulation.) To withhold it from some while affording it in abundance to others may seem indecent, to be in flagrant violation of the terms of a minimally acceptable social contract.[32]

The preceding is admittedly speculative. And it may have less applicability to the United States than to countries that place a higher premium on solidarity. It does, though, go some distance toward explaining why even in the allegedly market-based system of health-care delivery in this

---

[32] In response to an earlier draft of this essay, one reader protested: "Isn't the Post Office sufficient? We need to all share a loathing of an inefficient and uncaring national health system, like Britain's, to solidify waning solidarity? That doesn't make a whole lot of sense to me. . . . Everyone needs to be equally mistreated, subjected to endless waits, and denials of expensive or 'experimental' care?"

I confess to some sympathy with this denunciation. But the more accurate its depiction of the warts of national health care, the more puzzling becomes the overwhelming support in countries such as Canada and Great Britain for their systems of universal provision. Reforms are proposed from time to time, but fundamental revision or replacement is politically unthinkable. Why? The conjecture on offer here is that the perceived attractiveness of positive freedom of association possesses some measure of explanatory force.

country, there exist innumerable mandates governing provision which, taken *in toto*, render American health care expensive, ponderous, and inflexible. The "free market" is not supposed to operate that way!

Health care is almost universally regarded on both the left and the right as what the economists call a "merit good," that is, an item that will be underprovided by ordinary market mechanisms even under conditions of perfect competition.[33] Thus the opposition even in the United States to a truly market-based system. (Republican politicians who made hay with derisive excoriations of "Hillarycare" nonetheless presided over the 2003 Medicare prescription drug benefit legislation that added a trillion dollars, give or take, over the next decade to the already massive socialized component of American health-care spending.) This opposition to a market-based system is not, I believe, a function simply of medicine's role in addressing basic human needs. Food and housing are no less essential, yet they do not seem to generate so strong a demand for uniform provision. If the preceding suggestions are on the mark, health-care delivery is special because of its implications for positive association.

V. Conclusion

The policy examinations of the preceding section yield no algorithm for resolving eruptions of the Paradox of Association but nonetheless may be usefully illustrative. Let me offer a tentative summing-up. A protected freedom to dissociate merits wide scope within a liberal order. Successful pursuit of those personal projects that confer value on individual lives requires that individuals be at liberty to disengage from relationships they take to be unpromising so that they may instead seek elsewhere for meaningful activity. Their choices are not to be held hostage either to ancestral precedents or to other people's uncongenial aspirations. This liberty to disengage has to be of wide scope because a pursuit that is central to one person's conception of a life well-lived may be peripheral to the concerns of others. Free exercise of religion doesn't matter a great deal to me; I don't care very much about which house of worship it is that I'm going to be staying away from tomorrow. But millions of other people who take no interest whatsoever in a liberty to generate philosophical scribblings place a life of fidelity to their god at the pinnacle of their valuations. You may not care to mount a Harley Davidson at all, but others find it insufferable not to be allowed to do so sans helmet. There are, according to some respected accounts, even people devoted to the practice of grass counting. It is not within the legitimate purview of state officials to declare which pursuits are sufficiently meritorious to be protected by associational rights and which are not. Rather, those officials are

---

[33] See Richard Musgrave's entry "merit goods" in *The New Palgrave: A Dictionary of Economics* (New York: Macmillan, 1987), 3:452–53.

to take their bearings from the decentralized decisions of the populace they serve. An adequate negative freedom of association must, therefore, be capacious.

Positive freedom of association in all but its weakest version binds individuals even when one or more parties wants out of that relationship. It must, therefore, confront a strong presumption in favor of the right of individuals to dissociate. Serious threats to the maintenance of the political order typically overcome that presumption. The conclusion suggested by the preceding discussion is that, under tolerable conditions of political life, nothing else does. Paternalistic concerns for health or morals do not suffice. Nor do vague aspirations toward community, programmatic models for implementing particular patterns of diversity, or a fondness for income equality. Or rather, none of these suffice until and unless they jeopardize the stability of the universal association. Claims derived from positive association, then, are maximally deep but very narrow.

Advocates of the various positions examined in Section III will argue that this is to be insufficiently generous to positive association. Those who are more enamored of the points raised in Section II will claim, to the contrary, that it concedes too much. They will maintain that would-be constrictors of freedom routinely claim to discern some peril to the integrity of the polity. If no direct chain of causation can be adduced, then some stunningly subtle path to possible social breakdown will be discerned. The goal, of course, is to justify intrusions on individuals' capacity to reject the club that will have them for a member.

I concede the point. Of political inventiveness there is no limit. Has anybody succeeded in keeping count of the many and varied justifications of the Iraq incursion proffered by President George W. Bush (or for the previous Iraq war by the previous President Bush)? Even if most such invocations of necessity are bogus, they could not do useful work as pretexts unless the rationale to which they appeal had genuine instances. It is the task of political wisdom, not political philosophy, to distinguish genuine from bogus.

Philosophy, University of Virginia

THE PRIVATE SOCIETY AND THE LIBERAL PUBLIC GOOD IN JOHN LOCKE'S THOUGHT

By Eric R. Claeys

I. Introduction

John Locke may have done more than any other individual to shape Anglo-American attitudes toward constitutionalism. Throughout the English-speaking world, a Lockean theory of rights informs "social and political practices and institutions" and "many . . . commonsense judgments about right and wrong, just and unjust." When academic commentators defend constitutional freedom of association, they suggest that it is integral to a system in which "the purpose of government is" Lockean: "to secure the natural rights of the citizenry—life, liberty, and property." Similarly, some United States Supreme Court cases invalidate laws restraining freedom of association because they threaten to "emasculate" a foundational Lockean principle—"the distinction between private as distinguished from state conduct."[1]

It is thus a surprise to see that, in normative scholarship on associational freedom, Locke is treated as a bit player. In legal scholarship, Locke is commonly assumed (in Robert Horn's description) not to have "express[ed] his thought about associations in general terms" but rather to have focused his "concern [on] freedom for one kind of association, the church."[2] In Horn's reading, because Locke treats the problems of free association most extensively in his *Letter Concerning Toleration*,[3]

---

[1] A. John Simmons, *The Lockean Theory of Rights* (Princeton, NJ: Princeton University Press, 1992), 14; David E. Bernstein, "Antidiscrimination Laws and the First Amendment," *Missouri Law Review* 66 (2001): 83, 105 n. 109; *Moose Lodge No. 107 v. Irvis*, 407 U.S. 163, 173 (1972).

[2] Robert A. Horn, *Groups and the Constitution* (Stanford, CA: Stanford University Press, 1956), 7; see also John Dunn, "The Claim to Freedom of Conscience: Freedom of Speech, Freedom of Thought, Freedom of Worship?" in Ole Peter Grell, Jonathan I. Israel, and Nicholas Tyacke, eds., *From Persecution to Toleration: The Glorious Revolution and Religion in England* (Oxford: Oxford University Press, 1991), 170–93.

[3] References to Locke's *Letter Concerning Toleration* are made not in the notes but parenthetically in the text, with the following conventions. "*LT* 32" refers to William Popple's translation of *A Letter Concerning Toleration* (London: Printed for Awnsham Churchill, 1689), page 32. I thank Tom West for pointing out to me several discrepancies between Popple's translation and Locke's original Latin. In cases involving those discrepancies, I translate Locke's Latin myself, citing John Locke, *Epistola de Tolerantia: A Letter on Toleration*, ed. Raymond Klibansky, trans. J. W. Gough (Oxford: Clarendon Press, 1968).

References to Locke's other major, mature writings are also made in the text, with the following conventions: "*TT* I.86" refers to John Locke, *Two Treatises of Government*, student edition, ed. Peter Laslett (Cambridge: Cambridge University Press, 1988), treatise 1, section

doi:10.1017/S0265052508080242

Locke's theory of associational freedom is really only a theory of religious freedom, not to be extended to "other kinds of [i.e., nonreligious] associations which, like the state, are concerned with man's material welfare here on earth."[4] Similarly, in his essay "The Madisonian Paradox of Freedom of Association," Richard Boyd illustrates a tendency in normative political theory to portray Locke as defending associational freedom in terms too qualified and prudential to teach general lessons. In historical and hermeneutical scholarship about Locke, interpreters also tend to focus on Locke's theory of religious toleration and not on his views on associational freedom generally.[5]

It is easy to understand why these tendencies have developed. Locke's theory of associational freedom does not jump out at readers of Locke's corpus. For example, in the *Letter Concerning Toleration*, Locke frequently refers to a denominational sect as "a free and voluntary Society" (*LT* 9, 15). If one focuses on the occasional purpose of the *Letter*, Locke seems to be making a strong normative claim specifically about religious freedom. But Locke has a broad view of associational freedom. If one reads the same passage from the *Letter* with an eye toward issues about associational freedom, Locke is making a far more radical point: *All* private societies, churches and otherwise, deserve a presumption of associational freedom. While Locke does not focus on this claim specifically in any single writing, he does substantiate it with consistent insights and arguments across all his mature writings. Readers deserve to consider Locke's various treatments of human society in one space, as parts of a single, integrated argument.

To help readers appreciate the sweep of Locke's critique, this essay interprets and expounds Locke's theory of the private society. Practically, Locke entitles citizens to associate with the widest domain of freedom consistent with the like rights of fellow citizens and the needs of the public. The crucial qualification comes in how Locke understands the

---

86. "*ECHU* II.21.51" refers to John Locke, *An Essay Concerning Human Understanding*, ed. Peter H. Nidditch (Oxford: Oxford University Press, 1979), book 2, chapter 21, paragraph 51. "*RC* 235" refers to John Locke, *The Reasonableness of Christianity*, ed. George W. Ewing (Washington, DC: Regnery Gateway, 1965), paragraph 235. "*STCE* 70" refers to John Locke, *Some Thoughts Concerning Education*, in Locke, *Some Thoughts Concerning Education and Of the Conduct of the Understanding*, ed. Ruth W. Grant and Nathan Tarcov (Indianapolis, IN: Hackett Publishing Co., 1996), paragraph 70.

In quoted passages, all italics are in the original unless otherwise noted.

[4] Horn, *Groups and the Constitution*, 8. See also Peter Laslett, "Introduction," in *Locke, Two Treatises of Government*, 3, 86; Maurice Cranston, "John Locke and the Case for Toleration," in Susan Mendus and David Edwards, eds., *On Toleration* (New York: Oxford University Press, 1987), 101–21, 119 and passim. Similarly, while Ingrid Creppell treats Locke's *Letter Concerning Toleration* as justifying a broader theory of liberalism, she works with Locke's observations on religion and not with his observations on private associations generally. See Ingrid Creppell, "Locke on Toleration: The Transformation of Constraint," *Political Theory* 24, no. 2 (1996): 200, 226, 228–29.

[5] See Richard Boyd, "The Madisonian Paradox of Freedom of Association" (elsewhere in this volume); and A. John Simmons, *On the Edge of Anarchy: Locke, Consent, and the Limits of Society* (Princeton, NJ: Princeton University Press, 1993), 135–36.

needs of the public. One such need covers the minimal moral conditions by which the society promotes peace, public order, the family, property, and the other interests the Lockean commonwealth focuses on securing. Another need covers the minimal moral conditions by which the society perpetuates Lockean liberalism going forward. While these conditions and Locke's formulations for them are broad in many respects, they still leave many private societies otherwise generally free. Such societies may thus organize around commonly agreed ends; may admit or exclude members depending on how they conform to common societal ends; and may govern internal affairs without outside interference.

Theoretically, the rights and responsibilities Locke recognizes in private societies issue from a more comprehensive meditation on the strengths and weaknesses of liberalism. At first glance, Locke seems to justify the right to private society in a fairly optimistic view of human nature. Society recognizes and builds on men's natural social and friendly affections, and it does so particularly by encouraging particular associations that reflect their members' individual characters, needs, and interests. Yet throughout his mature corpus, Locke acknowledges dangers with the wrong sorts of societies. Wrongly ordered societies may restrain free thought; may encourage partisanship and injustice, authoritarianism and fanaticism; and generally may destabilize the common opinions that glue together a liberal political order. Locke's liberalism recognizes in citizens the rights to think, believe, and associate as they please, but only to the extent that such rights threaten neither the basic material interests that government protects nor the moral and political consensus that makes liberalism possible.

Although this essay aims primarily to interpret and expand Locke's teaching, it also seeks to show why that teaching is worth recovering. Locke's critique of private societies may prove valuable to contemporary normative scholarship on association in two respects. First, Locke presents a tougher-minded theory of liberalism than one sees in contemporary practice and scholarship. Prevailing contemporary theories of liberalism may take for granted that the forms of government they advocate are more humane and attractive than governments that stress authority, tradition, and religion. Contemporary liberal governments may accommodate many different kinds of diversity—ethnic, religious, and especially ideological—without considering whether such diversity undermines their societies' commitment to liberalism. Locke did not have such luxuries. As a political practitioner, Locke needed to persuade his contemporaries that his version of liberalism was more acceptable than the throne and altar they already knew. As a political philosopher, Locke defended his theories of liberalism and associational freedom as comprehensive responses to permanent problems in human politics. Locke suggests that liberalism is always a precarious political order, which cannot survive without affirming several minimal moral and political conditions. He therefore challenges contemporary readers to consider whether contemporary theories of liberalism can adequately explain why they do not need to respect similar conditions.

Separately, Locke's accounts of liberalism and associational freedom deserve study because they appeal to an account of human experience that is psychologically and sociologically richer than one finds in many contemporary defenses. Prominent modern theories of liberalism justify liberalism on deontological grounds, on the grounds of broad claim-rights based in human free will without significant regard to human behavior. Such deontological foundations have been criticized for drawing on "bad sociology" or "naïve psychology." Those criticisms help discredit liberalism and open the door to theories of government that justify greater intervention with associational freedom.[6] Locke may provide a stronger and more satisfying account of associational freedom and of liberalism generally.

The essay proceeds primarily by interpreting Locke's specific discussions of associational freedom throughout his mature political, ethical, and philosophical writings. The essay also illustrates Locke's teachings by suggesting how they might help resolve two contemporary problems: identifying the circumstances in which governments may restrain residents from operating seditious associations; and determining whether the law should draw a principled public-private distinction in anti-discrimination law.

II. Tensions in Locke's Thought on Free Associations

Let us start with a first impression: that Locke seems not to have any consistent or systematic theory of private societies. While this impression is understandable, it is not accurate. In the *Letter Concerning Toleration*, Locke seems to use the private society as a standard for enlarging the freedom of churches. But as I have noted, Locke's argument suggests that private societies are entitled to broad practical discretion to organize and pursue their own affairs. Locke suggests that any private society "has power to remove any of its Members who transgress the Rules of its Institution" (*LT* 15). Moreover, in contrast with Boyd's reading, Locke's argument does not seem very prudential: Locke claims that this power to remove members is "the immutable Right of a spontaneous Society."[7] Throughout the *Letter*, Locke treats church denominations as the equivalent of secular societies, like "Meetings in Markets" or "Civil Assemblies" (*LT* 49). Whether or not this analogy demeans religious worship, the important point is that in the course of making

---

[6] Michael Walzer, "Liberalism and the Art of Separation," *Political Theory* 12, no. 3 (1984): 315, 324; Creppell, "Locke on Toleration," 201.

[7] *LT* 15. Popple's translation suggests that the right of private society is not only "immutable" but also "fundamental." Locke's Latin has no word corresponding to "fundamental."

an occasional argument about religious toleration, Locke presumes a broad right of private society.

Locke repeats the same maneuver in his *Two Treatises of Government*. He does not advance and defend his own theory of government, strictly speaking, until chapter 7 of the *Second Treatise*. Locke's treatment subordinates government by making the political community a species of the genus "society." This subordination is apparent in the title of chapter 7: "Of Political or Civil Society." It is also apparent in the chapter's seemingly syllogistic argument: Men have a natural right to consent before participating in *any* society; political society is another example of a society, on a par with marriages and employment relationships; men therefore may not be required to participate in political society without their consent (*TT* II.95; see also II.77–89). As a matter of first impression, Locke seems to justify government by asking whether it works for its citizens as well as private societies that they may enter and exit freely. This metaphor figures prominently in many other apologies for classical or libertarian liberalism.[8] The metaphor is also problematic. As for entry, Locke gradually qualifies the principle of "consent" in ways that undermine the force of his syllogism;[9] as for exit, Locke recognizes that the dissolution of a government is a measure of last resort (see *TT* II.223, 225). Again, however, the important point is that in the course of making occasional arguments about the purpose of government, Locke presumes a broad right of private society.

This right is not unqualified, however, for elsewhere in his corpus Locke is quite critical of private associations. In particular, in the *Essay Concerning Human Understanding*, Locke presents associations as impediments to free thinking. Most "Partisans of most of the Sects in the World . . . have [no] Opinions of their own," "are resolved to stick to a Party, that Education or Interest has engaged them in; and there, like the common Soldiers of an Army, show their Courage and Warmth as their Leaders direct, without ever examining or so much as knowing the Cause they contend for" (*ECHU* 4.20.18).

III. Locke's Liberalism in Its Christian Context

A. Locke's intentions

There are several ways to explain these various statements and the tensions between them. If one focuses on Locke's teachings specifically on association, one might conclude (as Horn does) that Locke means to protect religious and other spiritual associations and, at the same time (as

---

[8] See, for example, Robert Nozick, *Anarchy, State, and Utopia* (New York: Basic Books, 1974), 300–302.

[9] See Jeremy Waldron, "John Locke: Social Contract Versus Political Anthropology," *The Review of Politics* 51, no. 1 (Winter 1989): 3–28. For more general criticisms of the consent principle, consider John Rawls, "Justice as Fairness," *Philosophical Review* 67 (1958): 178.

Ruth Grant suggests), to banish from the commonwealth political parties and other associations that claim to participate actively in political life. More generally, perhaps the inconsistencies confirm that Locke was a strictly occasional writer, in which case it would be "pointless to look upon [Locke's] work as an integrated body of speculation and generalization." The inconsistencies might also confirm John Dunn's general impression of Locke, that his "ideas remain[ed] for his entire life profoundly and exotically incoherent." Or, even if we assume that Locke had intentions that were integrated and coherent in his time and day, it might be the case that our time and day differ too profoundly from his for us to appreciate his intentions in our present historical context.[10]

Yet one should not dismiss the possibility that Locke has a coherent and long-lasting intention. Whatever we may think of his intentions now, Locke's writings leave signs that he was quite ambitious. He begins the *Conduct of the Understanding* by suggesting that he hopes to improve upon principles of logic that had served the learned world for at least two thousand years before his time (*CU* 1). In a letter to a friend, Locke ranks the *Two Treatises* in the same company with Aristotle's *Politics* for its contributions to government.[11] As Peter Myers concludes, to read Locke solely in the context of the political, scientific, and theological problems of his generation in England may "impose[] an unwarranted degree of closure upon and diminish[] the stature" of Locke, and encourage interpreters to trivialize Locke's ambitious attempts "to effect profound theoretical innovations, to converse with writers long dead, and to enlighten distant audiences."[12]

To appreciate what gets lost if we trivialize Locke, consider his writings on private societies. Even if he seems to focus only on church and state in the *Letter Concerning Toleration*, in reality Locke anticipates political problems not strictly necessary to his argument about religion. He acknowledges that if "this Business of Religion were let alone," citizens would still discriminate against one another "upon account of their different Complexions, Shapes, and Features, so that those who have black Hair (for example) or gray Eyes, should not enjoy the same Privileges as other

[10] Ruth W. Grant, "Locke's Political Anthropology and Lockean Individualism," *Journal of Politics* 50, no. 1 (February 1988): 42, 59–60; John Dunn, *The Political Thought of John Locke: An Historical Account of the Argument of the "Two Treatises of Government"* (Cambridge: Cambridge University Press, 1969), 29, 266–67; Laslett, "Introduction," 3, 87. See also J. W. Gough, *John Locke's Political Philosophy*, 2d ed. (London: Oxford University Press, 1973), 14 (finding a "basic inconsistency between [Locke's] earlier belief in absolute moral principles and his tendency later to think in hedonistic terms"); and Raymond Polin, "John Locke's Conception of Freedom," in *John Locke: Problems and Perspectives*, ed. John W. Yolton (Cambridge: Cambridge University Press, 1969), 1 ("traditional interpreters of John Locke like to pretend that he professed simultaneously a theoretical philosophy of empirical style and a practical philosophy of innatist inspiration").

[11] Letter from John Locke to Richard King, August 25, 1703, cited in Andrzej Rapaczynski, *Nature and Politics: Liberalism in the Philosophies of Hobbes, Locke, and Rousseau* (Ithaca, NY: Cornell University Press, 1987), 15 and n. 11.

[12] Peter C. Myers, *Our Only Star and Compass: Locke and the Struggle for Political Rationality* (Lanham, MD: Rowman and Littlefield, 1998), 18.

Citizens; . . . [and] should either be excluded from the Benefit of the Laws, or meet with partial Judges" (*LT* 50–51). In addition, Locke's writings on private societies are also intertwined with deep questions of Enlightenment political philosophy: questions about how to reconcile the claims of Christianity with those of temporal politics. Those questions have philosophical import beyond Locke's day and age.

In what follows, I explain how I understand Locke's general intentions as a political philosopher and his general prescriptions for the problem of reconciling Christianity with temporal politics. This review will give readers early warning about how I read Locke generally and will offer background important for appreciating Locke's analysis of private associations. The background also helps clarify the relation between Locke's use of the "private society" metaphor in reference to churches and governments and his justifications of private societies generally. Here and throughout the remainder of the essay, I focus on Locke's mature, published, and relevant writings: *A Letter Concerning Toleration, The Reasonableness of Christianity,* the *Two Treatises of Government,* the *Essay Concerning Human Understanding,* and *Some Thoughts Concerning Education.* I pass over many of Locke's early writings because Locke's views on the church-state problem evolved as he matured. Early in his career (particularly in his *Two Tracts on Government*), Locke inclined to give the temporal sovereign absolute authority to prevent religious sectarian warfare. Locke preferred the liberal republic later in his career, and I focus here on the views Locke propounded in the works supporting liberal republicanism.[13]

These works are difficult to synthesize, however. Locke simultaneously makes occasional and philosophical arguments in all of these works, and each work treats one portion of the political universe from a different partial perspective.[14] Generalizing broadly, the *Letter Concerning Toleration* teaches potential legislators and princes how to resolve the competing claims of spiritual and temporal authority; the *Two Treatises* teach them how to structure political life once church-state questions have been resolved; *The Reasonableness of Christianity* teaches preachers and believers how to preach Christianity in the manner best suited for political, ethical, and spiritual life; *Some Thoughts Concerning Education* teaches parents how to raise their children; and the *Essay Concerning Human Understanding* teaches potential philosophers and scientists the epistemological foundations of decent ethics and politics.[15]

[13] See Robert P. Kraynak, "John Locke: From Absolutism to Toleration," *The American Political Science Review* 74, no. 1 (1980): 53–69.

[14] By describing Locke as a philosopher, this interpretation comes into some tension with more historically focused interpretations that prefer to read Locke primarily in the context of the problems of England in his day. See Laslett, "Introduction," 76; and Dunn, *The Political Thought of John Locke,* 16–18, 266–67.

[15] Although Locke's *Of the Conduct of the Understanding* targets the same audience, on the topics covered here that work is less relevant than and adds little to the *Essay.* I pass over Locke's subsequent letters on toleration for similar reasons.

To appreciate Locke's complete analysis of free association, the inter-
preter must consider different arguments in different works by adjusting for their differing intentions. This sort of interpretation is difficult,
for parallel arguments that seem complementary to one reader may
seem grossly inconsistent to another. Even so, I find, as Ruth Grant
suggests, that "[m]ost apparent inconsistencies evaporate[] on further
consideration of the context of conflicting statements, their place in the
argument, or Locke's word usage."[16]

B. Locke's ethical and political foundations

To begin with, Locke is a eudaimonistic consequentialist. That he is a
"consequentialist" means he justifies rights to the extent that they contribute to good consequences rather than the other way around, as
deontologists maintain. At one point in the *Two Treatises*, when speaking of man's dominion over animals, Locke assumes that man's right is
"to make use of those things that [are] necessary or useful to his Being"
(*TT* I.86). That he is a "eudaimonistic" consequentialist means that Locke
measures good consequences in reference to happiness. "Eudaimonistic" happiness refers primarily to a state of moral well-being of the sort
people associate with "mature" or "virtuous" individuals. Because it
focuses on the moral well-being of individuals, eudaimonistic happiness is not analyzed top down but bottom up: it refers not to the
general happiness of the society as an organic whole but rather to an
aggregation of the happinesses of individual citizens. Hence, while individual necessity and utility ordinarily set the standard for human action,
they are judged by reason, which directs them toward happiness—"the
utmost Pleasure we are capable of" (*ECHU* II.21.42) and man's "chief
end," which "Mankind . . . are and must be allowed to pursue" (*RC*
245).

This portrait goes against many other portraits of Locke. As I have
noted, some scholars maintain that Locke's ideas are incoherent. Many
reject the suggestion that Locke is a consequentialist and claim that he is
instead a deontologist; some of those claim that his deontology rests
solely on philosophical grounds, while others claim that it follows from a
combination of political philosophy and theology.[17] Yet if one reads Locke's

---

[16] Ruth W. Grant, *John Locke's Liberalism* (Chicago: University of Chicago Press, 1987), 8–9.
For similar approaches to interpreting Locke, consider Michael P. Zuckert, *Launching Liberalism: On Lockean Political Philosophy* (Lawrence: University Press of Kansas, 2002), 3–17;
Myers, *Our Only Star and Compass*, 13–26; Nathan Tarcov, *Locke's Education for Liberty* (Chicago: University of Chicago Press, 1984); Leo Strauss, *What Is Political Philosophy? and Other
Studies* (Chicago: University of Chicago Press, 1959), 93 n. 24; and Leo Strauss, "Persecution
and the Art of Writing," *Social Research* 8, no. 1 (1941): 488, 503 n. 21.

[17] Dunn, *The Political Thought of John Locke*, 29; see Gough, *John Locke's Political Philosophy*,
10–11, 19, 26; and Jeremy Waldron, *God, Locke, and Equality: Christian Foundations of John
Locke's Political Thought* (Cambridge: Cambridge University Press, 2002), 82.

mature political writings and his philosophical writings as complementary parts of an integrated whole, he instead propounds a "rule"-based consequentialist approach. This approach draws on human psychology and experience to prescribe broad rights designed to contribute to human happiness. Locke trenchantly criticizes the claim that men have any innate practical principles (see *ECHU* I.3). It is hard to explain why Locke would launch such a critique if he established the foundations of his political theory on deontology or revelation. He sets as a standard for human action "the highest perfection of intellectual nature," which "lies in a careful and constant pursuit of true and solid happiness" (*ECHU* II.21.51). Moreover, in his politics, he defines law "as the direction of a free and intelligent Agent to his proper Interest," prescribing "no farther than is for the general Good of those under that Law" (*TT* II.57).[18] But however Locke ultimately justifies the foundations of his politics and ethics, he makes many observations about human anthropology, psychology, and sociology. Even if I am wrong and Locke's political theory is foundationally incoherent, his observations may still be interesting and relevant to political theory in their own right.[19]

Locke also treats political opinion as a powerful force in practical political life. This characterization contradicts portraits suggesting that Locke is a "possessive individualist," whose theory of natural rights subordinates man's social tendencies by focusing too much on acquisitive and life-preserving passions.[20] Without a doubt, Locke does focus government on simple human interests like life and property, but not to the point that he focuses on human possessive and egoistic tendencies to the exclusion of social tendencies.[21] Among those social tendencies, Locke focuses

[18] On this point, I follow Thomas West, Ruth Grant, A. John Simmons, and Nathan Tarcov more than I do Michael Zuckert. Zuckert grounds Locke's normative claims in "self-ownership," which is not necessarily eudaimonistic. See Zuckert, *Launching Liberalism*, 4–5, 193–95; see also Thomas G. West, "Nature and Happiness in Locke," *The Claremont Review of Books* 4, no. 2 (2004) (reviewing Zuckert, *Launching Liberalism*), available online at http://www.claremont.org/publications/pubid.659/pub_detail.asp; Myers, *Our Only Star and Compass*, 137–72; Grant, *John Locke's Liberalism*, 23–25, 37–39; Simmons, *The Lockean Theory of Rights*, 52–53; and Tarcov, *Locke's Education for Liberty*, 210. See also Nomi M. Stolzenberg and Gideon Yaffe, "Waldron's Locke and Locke's Waldron: A Review of Jeremy Waldron's *God, Locke, and Equality*," *Inquiry* 49, no. 2 (2006): 186, 197–202 (criticizing Waldron for reading Locke as a deontologist and not a utilitarian).

[19] See Alasdair MacIntyre, "Hume on the 'Is' and the 'Ought'," in MacIntyre, *Against the Self-Images of the Age: Essays on Ideology and Philosophy* (South Bend, IN: University of Notre Dame Press, 1978): 109, 124; G. E. Anscombe, "Modern Moral Philosophy," *Philosophy* 33, no. 124 (1958): 1, 2 (general criticisms of Kantian deontology); and Creppell, "Locke on Toleration," 200–201 (on the relevance of Locke's observations on the human condition).

[20] See C. B. Macpherson, *The Theory of Possessive Individualism: Hobbes to Locke* (London: Oxford University Press, 1962), 220–21, 243, 247–51; Leo Strauss, *Natural Right and History* (Chicago: University of Chicago Press, 1953), 202–51; and Robert A. Goldwin, "John Locke," in Leo Strauss and Joseph Cropsey, eds., *History of Political Philosophy*, 3d ed. (Chicago: University of Chicago Press, 1987), 476.

[21] Walzer, "Liberalism and the Art of Separation," 315, 324; Creppell, "Locke on Toleration," 201. See also Grant, *John Locke's Liberalism*, 48–51.

heavily on most men's need for authoritative social opinion. He expects, "by the little that has hitherto been done in it, that it is too hard a task for unassisted reason to establish morality in all its parts upon its true foundation with a clear and convincing light" (*RC* 241). Instead, he acknowledges the force of the "Law of Opinion or Reputation," also called "the Law of Fashion" (*ECHU* II.28.5–10, 12), and he describes shame as "the common *measure of Virtue and Vice*" (*ECHU* II.28.11; see also I.3.22–26, IV.16.4, IV.20.2–3). The separation between reason and opinion shapes the character of political life. On the one hand, Locke expects that his *Essay Concerning Human Understanding*, a treatise on theoretical science and philosophy, will be thought among most readers "to deserve no consideration, for being somewhat out of the common road" (*ECHU*, Epistle to the Reader). On the other hand, he believes that *The Reasonableness of Christianity* will be extremely relevant to the vast run of mankind, for "[t]he greatest part cannot *know*, and therefore they must *believe*" (*RC* 243).

Locke is also pessimistic that politics can, within humane limits, direct citizens to pursue one or a few outstanding virtues. While Locke resembles many pre-Enlightenment political theorists in his eudaimonism and his respect for common opinion, on this topic he breaks with his predecessors and anticipates contemporary liberal thought. Many prominent ancient and medieval Christian philosophers were teleologists, which is to say that they presumed that men, like other things in the world, are naturally directed to one or a few purposes. In contrast, Locke criticizes "the philosophers of old" for "in vain enquir[ing], whether *Summum bonum* consisted in Riches, or bodily Delights, or Virtue, or Contemplation: and they might have as reasonably disputed, whether the best Relish were to be found in Apples, Plumbs, or Nuts, and have divided themselves into Sects upon it" (*ECHU* II.21.55). Locke agrees with the philosophers he criticizes inasmuch as they are all eudaimonists, but he parts with them to the extent that they claim that men are naturally inclined toward one or a few forms of human excellence. For Locke, men differ profoundly in their capacities. Some are endowed so that, realistically, they will appreciate riches and bodily delights but not contemplation; others are endowed so that they are "not content to live lazily on scraps of begged opinions" and instead set their "own thoughts on work, to find and follow truth" (*ECHU*, Epistle to the Reader). Because of these and many other differences, Locke concludes that teleological political philosophy has a tendency to be inhumane. It encourages political rulers to force many citizens to follow standards of excellence and happiness that they are simply not equipped to attain.[22]

Locke therefore sets lower standards for politics. Aristotle maintained, in principle, that the citizens who are superior in virtue deserve to rule

---

[22] Myers, *Our Only Star and Compass*, 20–21, 107–11, 149–55; Zuckert, *Launching Liberalism*, 148–49, 162; West, "Nature and Happiness in Locke."

the city; Locke's most political writings, the *Two Treatises*, do not mention virtue (a fact which contributes to the perception that Locke is a possessive individualist).[23] Locke's political theory focuses on the goods most useful to a broad cross-section of the citizenry, no matter what their particular talents and interests—life, liberty, security, property, and family (see *TT* I.86, I.88, II.17, II.124, II.135, II.199).[24]

C. Locke's diagnosis: Civil strife in the Christian world

Finally, Locke is a foul-weather friend and a fair-weather critic of Christianity. He finds Christianity's basic teachings to be just and humane. He regards Christianity as a more effective and humane way to inculcate basic practical morality in most men than other possible foundations for practical ethical and political morality (see *RC* 231, 239–45). At the same time, he takes pains that Christianity not be misunderstood in ways that make politics inhumane.[25] Christianity's universal and revelational claims create dangers in Christian nations. In contrast to pagan religions, which tended to emphasize external devotions to rituals and laws, Christianity emphasizes the internal aspects of faith—in Locke's description, "Faith only, and inward Sincerity" (*LT* 27; see *RC* 241, 243, 245). In addition, whereas pagan cults were tied to particular cities and made worship a matter of external practice, Christianity penetrates wider and deeper. Its revelation claims a universal reach; it purports to regulate not only external conduct but also inward belief and piety (*RC* 241; *LT* 28).

Christianity therefore creates the possibility that believers may disagree over points of dogma that are fairly abstract and difficult to resolve with unaided reason. Hence, Locke criticizes zealots who take less "care and industry to the rooting out of . . . Immoralities, than to the Extirpation of Sects" (*LT* 4). If Christian religion is as involved in real-world politics as pagan cults were tied to the ancient city, zealous believers will be tempted to use civil force to settle such dogmatic disputes. Because Christianity is a universal religion, believers will also be tempted to appeal to it as a justification to disobey their local civil laws and to treat their fellow citizens as enemies. They may ally more easily with members of their sect or denomination than they do with their countrymen. Hence, Locke concludes, "No Peace and Security, no not so much as Common Friendship, can ever be established or preferred amongst Men, so long as this Opinion

---

[23] Aristotle, *Politics*, 1255a3–a20; Goldwin, "John Locke," 484.

[24] Myers, *Our Only Star and Compass*, 168–69, 179–226; West, "Nature and Happiness in Locke."

[25] The following discussion relies substantially on insights from Zuckert, *Launching Liberalism*, 146–68; Harry V. Jaffa, *A New Birth of Freedom: Abraham Lincoln and the Coming of the Civil War* (Lanham, MD: Rowman and Littlefield, 2000), 121–52; Harvey C. Mansfield, Jr., *Taming the Prince: The Ambivalence of Executive Power* (New York: Free Press, 1989), 68–71, 91–118.

prevails, That Dominion is founded in Grace, and that Religion is to be propagated by force of Arms" (*LT* 18).

Jeremy Waldron reads Locke as making a narrower argument—as seeking to avoid the question of whether the commonwealth is competent to identify orthodox belief, and to stress instead that the commonwealth is not competent to *compel* such belief.[26] But Locke is making the broader criticism that Waldron reads him to avoid: "[I]t is unavoidable to the greatest part of Men, if not all, to have several *Opinions,* without certain and indubitable Proofs of their Truths; and it carries too great an imputation of ignorance, lightness, or folly, for Men to quit and renounce their former Tenets" (*ECHU* 4.16.4). Because opinions about the best and happiest way of life are so problematic, Locke "esteem[s] it above all things necessary" to separate politics from quests for the highest virtues—specifically by "distinguish[ing] exactly the Business of Civil Government from that of Religion, and . . . settl[ing] the just Bounds that lie between the one and the other. If this be not done, there can be no end put to the Controversies that will be always arising, between those that have, or at least pretend to have, on the one side, a Concernment for the Interest of Mens Souls, and on the other side, a Care for the Commonwealth" (*LT* 6).

D. Locke's prescription: Liberalism

Broadly speaking, in order to settle these problems Locke bifurcates what was one "city" in classical and medieval Christian political philosophy into two separate spheres—one for public affairs, and another for private. The deepest manifestation of this change is that Locke propounds his political program on foundations not of natural law or duties but of natural rights. The *Second Treatise* begins by insisting that men are "naturally in . . . a *State of perfect Freedom* to order their Actions, and dispose of their Possessions, and Persons as they think fit" (*TT* II.4). This liberty is an ordered liberty. The natural freedom sketched at the beginning of the *Second Treatise* is "within the bounds of the Law of Nature" (*TT* II.4). "[T]he great privilege of finite intellectual Beings," and "the great inlet, and exercise of all the *liberty* men have" lies in their capacity to "*suspend* their desires, and stop [those desires] from determining their *wills* to any action, till they have duly and fairly *examined* the good and evil of it" (*ECHU* II.21.52). This presumption of liberty also manifests itself in the principle of consent, under which all governments must operate by election or representation (see *TT* II.22, 95–99).

Because politics is ordered toward securing liberty, it bifurcates what counts as one realm of politics in many political theories into two separate

---

[26] Jeremy Waldron, "Locke: Toleration and the Rationality of Persecution," in Susan Mendus, ed., *Justifying Toleration: Conceptual and Historical Perspectives* (Cambridge: Cambridge University Press, 1988), 61, 64–67, 80–82.

realms. One sphere consists of the public realm, the "commonwealth," the realm of public affairs, which are limited to the securing of the low and solid material interests around which most or all citizens can agree. Locke refers to these interests by formulations like "Safety and Security," or "no other end but preservation" (*TT* II.94, 133, 135). These public interests, when secured, in turn secure and order for individual citizens private zones of practical discretion. Citizens may use such discretion first to secure their individual shares of material interests and then to pursue happiness as their reason and conscience help them to understand it.

That privatizing formula has public repercussions. For example, the public protects private property understood as individual zones of labor and creativity. Privately, property helps individual citizens to take care of their own needs. Publicly, the wealth created by private property in turn secures the citizenry from domination abroad and from dependency on "Quarrelsom and Contentious" elites at home (*TT* II.34, 42). Culturally, when the government secures "property" to its citizenry, it teaches the vulgar mass of citizens the virtues of responsibility and self-ownership. It teaches each citizen to value "honest industry" and how to become "Master of himself, and Proprietor of his own Person" (*TT* II.42, 44).[27] Privately, the Lockean nuclear family frees individual families to rear their children without interference by politics or rule by clan patriarchs. Publicly, in turn, because clans are disintegrated into clusters of autonomous nuclear families, the Lockean order undercuts quarrelsome noble dynastic families and makes the private home a source of self-reliant republican virtues (see *TT* II.77–78; *STCE* 70).[28]

Similarly, not only does the separation of church and state free a people from what Locke calls the "inhumane Cruelty" to which devout Christianity can encourage believers who disagree over articles of faith (*LT* 2), it also encourages church and government each to specialize in its own area of competence. Christianity is freed to focus on "the regulating of Mens Lives according to the Rule of Vertue and Piety" through the power of persuasion (*LT* 1–2; see also 3); the commonwealth is better focused on using the power of "command" and "Penalties" to protect material interests (*LT* 8). Religious toleration also perpetuates liberalism, for it gives every heterodox church a political interest in stopping the civil government and the dominant church from overstepping the liberal settlement of church and state. Toleration encourages dissident churches, "like so many guardians of the public peace, [to] watch one another, that nothing may be innovated or changed in the form of the government" (*LT* 52).

---

[27] See Zuckert, *Launching Liberalism*, 190–97, 323–26; Myers, *Our Only Star and Compass*, 190–96; and Tarcov, *Locke's Education for Liberty*, 8, 209–11.

[28] See Tarcov, *Locke's Education for Liberty*, 5, 209–11; West, "Nature and Happiness in Locke"; Mary B. Walsh, "Locke and Feminism on Private and Public Realms of Activities," *Review of Politics* 57, no. 2 (Spring 1995): 251, 261–62; and Thomas G. West, "Vindicating John Locke: How a Seventeenth-Century 'Liberal' Was Really a Social Conservative" (available online at http://www.frc.org/get.cfm?i=WT01F1&v=PRINT).

E. Liberalism and the private society

We may now appreciate why Locke uses the notion of a private society as a rhetorical measuring standard for churches in the *Letter Concerning Toleration* and for governments in the *Two Treatises*. As between a citizen and the government, Locke teaches his readers to judge their governments by whether those governments secure their happiness as well as their employers, their social clubs, and the many other private associations they may enter or exit freely. That standard makes consent and liberty as fundamental in politics as they are in these more social settings. Of course, Locke is quite aware that many individuals are bad judges of comprehensive questions (see *ECHU* 4.20). By the same token, he accepts that many citizens will use their consent and liberty irresponsibly in important ways. But the governors suffer from that problem as well as the governed, and Locke focuses the temporal order on securing forms of happiness that the governed are better-equipped to appreciate.

As between churches and the broader society, the private-society ideal works in two conflicting ways. It elevates the position of many heterodox churches. The ideal encourages the government to leave such churches alone to govern themselves as nonreligious societies do; the ideal also reinforces the basic principle that opinions about piety and salvation are presumptively off limits to politics. By the same token, however, the private-society ideal also limits the power of churches. It limits church proselytization only to "Exhortations, Admonitions, and Advices" (*LT* 13). If that ideal does not totally discredit the idea of an established state sect, at least it eliminates one of the main attractions for establishment: state compulsion to guarantee membership and revenues. More generally, the private-society ideal also undermines the legitimacy of some religions in a liberal society. If a religion, on the authority of revelation, maintains that believers may not leave the fold because they conscientiously disagree on articles of faith, or if it bars them from keeping their beliefs and their politics reasonably separate, Locke's teaching suggests that the religion is not compatible with republican liberalism.

IV. LOCKE'S ANALYSIS OF PRIVATE SOCIETIES

Now that we have established how Locke uses the private society to shape his general political theory, let us change course and consider how Locke's general politics shape the private society. The right of private society is another application of Locke's general presumption of liberty. The natural right of association has solid and wide eudaimonistic foundations, comparable to those of other Lockean natural rights like property and family. All men have social tendencies, and those tendencies are useful for men's accomplishing their many possible ends. Man was designed "for a sociable Creature . . . not only with an inclination, and under a necessity to have fellowship with those of his own kind; but furnished . . . also with Language, which was to be the great Instrument, and common Tye of Society" (*ECHU* III.1.1; see *TT* II.77; *STCE*, Dedication to Edward Clarke).

Locke confirms that the right of private society runs wide because he cites a wide range of examples: conjugal society (*TT* II.78); master-servant arrangements (and, by extension, more sophisticated business organizations) (*TT* II.83); political society (*TT* II.87–89); societies "of Philosophers for learning, or Merchants for Commerce, or of men of leisure for mutual Conversation and Discourse" (*LT* 10); churches, "Meetings in markets," "Concourse[s] of People in Cities," and many other "Civil assemblies" that he does not specifically mention (*LT* 49). Of course, some of these (e.g. the institution of marriage) have purposes considerably more focused and specific than the others (see *TT* I.88). But excepting those special cases, the rest of these associations aim toward different common ends. Their memberships have different needs, talents, life circumstances, or opinions about the most needful things. In all cases, however, the associations form for legitimate purposes, and in the process allow the participants to cultivate useful social faculties and to satisfy the reasonable desire for friendship.

This justification for associational freedom may be criticized in one of a few different ways. First, anyone who finds this portrait accurate may wonder why Locke's political philosophy is not more communitarian. If, as Locke suggests, man is driven by natural "inclination" into society, one may reasonably wonder why Locke proposes a liberal political order that is so skeptical that the government may pursue communal understandings of excellence. Others, however, might find Locke's portrait incomplete. Modern theories of liberalism are often criticized as question-begging. For example, libertarian Robert Nozick and modern liberal John Rawls both claim that citizens have a deontological right, as rational and autonomous beings, to choose their own conceptions of the good life. Both have been criticized for underestimating the extent to which culture and private associations shape individuals' conceptions of the good life and their attitudes toward fellow citizens. Michael Sandel illustrates a second critique, which suggests that Nozick's and Rawls's theories need more communitarian support. Andrew Koppelman illustrates a third, which contends that the government must transform civic culture to protect victims of social discrimination. Perhaps Locke's account is open to similar criticisms.[29]

---

[29] See Aristotle, *Politics*, 1252b27–1253a38; Aristotle, *Nicomachean Ethics*, 1155a22–28, 1167a26–30; John Rawls, *A Theory of Justice* (Cambridge, MA: Harvard University Press, 1971), 23–32; Nozick, *Anarchy, State, and Utopia*, 28–33, 300–304; Michael J. Sandel, *Liberalism and the Limits of Justice*, 2d ed. (Cambridge: Cambridge University Press, 1992), 9–14, 60–67; and Andrew Koppelman, *Antidiscrimination Law and Social Equality* (New Haven, CT: Yale University Press, 1996), 181–205.

Locke rejects the first criticism and sympathizes considerably with the latter two. Locke wants to build a just political order on the reasonable parts of human sociability; but he is quite aware of the problematic parts, and he fears that if society aims too high it will end up too low. Because he is a eudaimonist, when he philosophizes about rights he takes into account experiential observations from human anthropology, sociology, and psychology. Although his sociological assessment seems fairly rosy when he treats private societies most comprehensively, his sociology looks far more sober if one consults his mature works as a whole.[30]

The *Second Treatise* does not dwell at length on the destructive sides of human sociability, but it does acknowledge them subtly and indirectly. When Locke dedicates an entire chapter of the *Second Treatise* to conquest, he acknowledges that one group of people may be motivated by love of domination or hatred to subjugate another group (see *TT* II.175–96). Locke confirms the same point earlier, when he describes the foundations of political societies: such societies form out of families and extended clans because such smaller groups have "some Acquaintance and Friendship together" and "greater Apprehensions of others, than one another" (*TT* II.107). The social passions impel men to establish political communities. But the most natural political communities are tight-knit, closely tied to the extended family, and xenophobic. In an extended political community, these same social passions can encourage factiousness at home as easily as domination abroad. When Locke acknowledges offhand at one point that a person may owe "defence to his Child or Friend," he suggests that citizens are inclined to place loyalty to family and group over loyalty to country (*TT* II.70). Indeed, for Locke civil government is necessary precisely because "Self-love will make Men partial to themselves *and their Friends*" in the state of nature, at which point justice is impossible to enforce (*TT* II.13; emphasis added). These passages confirm the anti-teleological thrust of Locke's political theory. In his *Nicomachean Ethics*, Aristotle presumes that friendship promotes political concord and provides a precondition of decent political life.[31] In the *Two Treatises*, by contrast, Locke speaks of friendship only in contexts where it generates political discord.

If Locke hints at such themes in the *Two Treatises*, in the *Essay Concerning Human Understanding* he asserts them unabashedly, focusing especially on how political parties inhibit free thought. When explaining the various sources of human error, he identifies one as the greatest—as the one "which keeps in ignorance, or error, more people than all the others together." This is

the *giving up Our assent to the common received Opinions*, either of our Friends, or Party; Neighborhood, or Country. How many Men have

---

[30] From this paragraph until the end of this section, my argument has been informed substantially by Myers, *Our Only Star and Compass*, 123–29, 196–97.

[31] See Aristotle, *Nicomachean Ethics*, 1155a20–b1.

no other ground for their tenets, than the supposed Honesty, or Learning, or Number of those of the same Profession? As if honest, or bookish Men could not err; or Truth were to be established by the Vote of the Multitude: yet this with most Men serves the Turn. (*ECHU* 4.20.17)

Locke suspects that men who belong to parties "have no thought, no opinion at all" (*ECHU* 4.20.18).[32]

Man's factional and sectarian impulses are amplified to even worse extremes by other human faculties and passions. Man is needy in a harsh and chaotic natural world; he is terrified of his needs; his faculty for imagination amplifies that terror; and these faculties create an overwhelming need for man to find in societies comprehensive authority to structure and situate his life. These characteristics, if not checked, can drive entire societies toward religious and nationalist extremism, which encourages societies to brand outsiders as enemies and perhaps even as subhuman. In the most extreme cases, religious dogmas justify believers' cannibalizing their own children.[33]

Given this dour assessment, why does Locke still defend a broad natural right of association? Locke's answer is a specific application of his general justification for liberal republican self-government: In the right political conditions, man has enough reason and capacity for self-control to avoid becoming a slave to such extreme passions and group beliefs. In Lockean ethics, reason and temperance may, however precariously, control all the extreme passions. As Locke explains, "the great principle and foundation of all virtue and worth is placed in this, that a man is able to *deny himself* his own desires, cross his own inclinations, and purely follow what reason directs as best though the appetite lean the other way" (*STCE* 33; see also 122). Likewise, in Lockean politics, reason and temperance may establish liberal republican self-government as the precarious mean between despotism and the anarchical state of nature. Liberal republican government is an imperative for Locke, because such government contributes to human happiness more realistically and comprehensively than any other practical form of government. But the imperative binds only if the political community has been educated well enough to exercise the freedom liberalism provides with the moral responsibility and self-restraint liberalism requires. Otherwise, liberalism would be ineffective, if not suicidal.

Locke's natural right to private society should be understood in the same terms. When Locke teaches that this right follows from man's better social tendencies, he presumes that he is speaking to an audience

---

[32] See Grant, "Locke's Political Anthropology and Lockean Individualism," 59–60.
[33] See *TT* I.58–59; Myers, *Our Only Star and Compass*, 126; and Creppell, "Locke on Toleration," 213–16.

generally civilized enough to steer away from human tendencies toward faction, sectarianism, tribalism, and religious fanaticism. Locke presumes that the broad public is educated in morals by Christianity as understood in *The Reasonableness of Christianity*, and that elites are educated through religion and a sound program of liberal ethical and political philosophy as set forth in his writings on education and toleration, and in the *Two Treatises*. Locke's justification for free associations cannot be understood apart from this civil education.

This education starts with Locke's teaching on property. Recall that Locke teaches citizens to be "Master[s]" and "Proprietor[s]" over their own livelihoods (*TT* II.44), and that he does so before he justifies the family or political society. Men must learn to take responsibility for their own lives and plans, Locke suggests, before they can be happy in the close society of family or the complex society of politics. What is a suggestion in Locke's politics is a crucial theme of Locke's teaching on education, one goal of which is "a mind free, and master of it self, and all its actions" (*STCE* 66). Now, self-mastery cannot and will not free a citizen entirely from following and needing respect from dominant social opinions. Nonetheless, it will to a significant extent make man more selective in the opinions he chooses to follow, and more resilient in the face of criticism.

Locke also prescribes that a liberal society teach citizens to treat one another with more respect and tolerance. Locke's defense of Christianity stresses love of one's neighbor among Christ's core teachings, and Locke praises Christianity because Christ and the apostles did not present "anything tending to their own self-interest, or that of a party, in their morality" (*RC* 208–9, 212, 243). Locke's theory of politics starts from the principle of "*Equality*," whereby all "Creatures of the same species and rank . . . should . . . be equal one amongst another without Subordination or Subjection" (*TT* II.4).

With the political virtue of toleration Locke also introduces a new ethical virtue, "civility" (see *STCE* 93, 109). Civility is a middling virtue: Locke defines it as "a disposition of the mind not to offend others" or to avoid "making anyone uneasy in conversation," and also as "that general good will and regard for all people which makes anyone have a care not to show in his carriage any contempt, disrespect, or neglect of them, but to express, according to the fashion and way of that country, a respect and value for them, according to their rank and disposition" (*STCE* 143). Civility is a weak but solid substitute for friendship. Because the citizens of Locke's commonwealth acknowledge that they may not agree on the most needful things in human life, it is unrealistic for all citizens to become friends with all others. Citizens may find profound friendship with their associates in private life; they must learn to treat their fellow citizens with minimal respect.

Locke explains this moderate approach most comprehensively in the *Essay Concerning Human Understanding*. In the *Essay*, Locke is particularly harsh on parties, for there he is speaking from the vantage point of the scientists and philosophers who prize truth over good company. But even to this ascetic audience, Locke stresses that social groups are unavoidable and that moderation is the only practical and decent response:

> [I]t would, methinks, become all Men to maintain *Peace,* and the common Offices of Humanity, *and Friendship, in the diversity of Opinions,* since we cannot reasonably expect, that anyone should readily and obsequiously quit his own Opinion, and embrace ours with a blind resignation to an Authority, which the Understanding of Man acknowledges not. For however it may often mistake, it can own no other Guide but Reason, nor blindly submit to the Will and Dictates of another. (*ECHU* 4.16.4)

V. The General Right of Private Society

Now that we have traced Locke's justifications for private societies in broad outline, let us consider in more detail the extent of and limits on their rights. (I examine the extent of these rights in this section, and their limits in the next.) The rights are broad. Associations may form for any legitimate and noninjurious end.[34] By definition, an association is a "Society of Members voluntarily united toward" a common end—in Locke's words, "how free soever, or upon whatsoever slight occasion instituted" (*LT* 10).

The right of association entails two subsidiary rights. One consists of the power to admit or exclude potential members depending on whether and how much they agree with the society's purpose and rules. Here again, Locke applies to churches a more general right that he presumes exists among societies. The "Laws of the Society" are the "condition of Communion, and the Bond of the Society." "[I]f the Breach of them were permitted without any Animadversion, the Society would immediately be dissolved" (*LT* 13–14).

The other subsidiary right consists of a society's right to establish and enforce its own rules of governance—on membership and many other subjects. Here, Locke sweeps into freedom of association a right that is sometimes kept separate from it. For example, in a recent article on constitutional freedom of association, David McGowan distinguishes between the right of association and a zone of "managerial discretion" in which the association is free to govern itself without outside interference.[35] Locke holds that the latter is already swept into the former: "[S]ince the joyning together of several Members into this Church-Society, as has already been

---

[34] Here, "noninjurious" is a term of art meant to exclude acts that threaten harms the public may properly protect against, to be sketched in Section VI.

[35] See David McGowan, "Making Sense of *Dale,*" *Constitutional Commentary* 18 (2001): 121, 125, 157 (discussing *Boy Scouts of America v. Dale,* 530 U.S. 640, 648–53 [2000]).

demonstrated, is absolutely free and spontaneous, it necessarily follows, that the Right of making its Laws can belong to none but the Society it self, or at least (which is the same thing) to those whom the Society by common consent has authorized thereunto" (*LT* 10–11). The discretion must be lodged among the members and the association, and not in the hands of any government officer or anyone else: "No Church or Company, I say, can in the least subsist and hold together, but will presently dissolve and break to pieces, unless it be regulated by some Laws, and the Members all consent to observe some Order. Place, and time of meeting must be agreed on; Rules for admitting and excluding Members must be establisht; Distinction of Officers, and putting things in to a regular Course, and such like, cannot be omitted" (*LT* 10).

Perhaps this conception of association sweeps too broadly. Horn prefers to read Locke as ranking associations by the extent to which they pursue (low) material interests or (high) spiritual interests. Some elements of American federal constitutional law make a similar move, by ranking associations in terms of the purposes they serve. According to this ranking, businesses and other mere commercial associations get little protection, while religious and advocacy associations get extremely strong protection. More influential elements of American law rank associations in terms of their tendency to relate to "intimate" or "expressive" functions. Associations with these functions (say, nuclear families and political parties) get strong constitutional protection; associations that lack such functions get little protection.[36]

Locke rejects such rankings. When he speaks of "civil assemblies," he refers interchangeably to churches, political meetings, groups "of Philosophers for learning, or Merchants for Commerce, . . . of men of leisure for mutual Conversation and Discourse," or even "Compan[ies] for Trade and Profit" and "clubs for Clarret" (*LT* 10, 51). In Locke's judgment, human nature is too diverse for political authorities to enforce any one path (or a few paths) to complete human happiness, and Christianity makes the dangers of centralized virtue regulation especially extreme. Locke avoids both the general and the specific problems by distracting government from moral improvement and focusing it on rights protection. For men to improve themselves, they need to be allowed the freedom not to do so. Just as "[n]o man can be forced to be Rich or Healthful, whether he will or no," so "[t]he Care therefore of every man's Soul belongs unto himself, and is to be left unto himself" (*LT* 21). In addition, businesses and other commercial associations help individuals secure

---

[36] See *Dale*, 530 U.S. at 649–50; *Roberts v. United States Jaycees*, 468 U.S. 609, 617–23 (1984); and ibid. at 634–646 (O'Connor, J., concurring in the judgment). Here and henceforth, I use judicial opinions as expressions of conventional political wisdom, to show how contemporary political opinions contrast with Locke's. I do not cover the many legal issues that would need to be addressed before determining whether each of these cases was correctly decided as a matter of constitutional law.

reasonable and useful material interests that are necessary to the good life. Such interests may not be as noble or beautiful as cultivating the intellect or attaining salvation for the soul, but it would be snobbish to say that the former interests are unimportant. In addition, social clubs and businesses offer opportunities for friendship, cooperation, and responsibility no matter how high or low their organizing goals happen to be.

VI. Public Limitations on the Rights of Private Societies

A. Associational wrongs to individual rights

Locke qualifies the right of private society in several important respects. These qualifications identify the principles by which legitimate association may be distinguished from harmful association, and the private freedom of societies from their public responsibilities. Locke's understanding should be distinguished from the more utilitarian understanding that prevails in many contemporary discussions. For example, modern American constitutional law analyzes challenges to freedom of association in terms of a utilitarian calculus, in which a government interest may outweigh the private interest in association if the government's objective is important and compelling enough and its means narrowly tailored to advance that objective.[37] Locke's natural-rights theory presumes that individual and public interests do not conflict when both are understood correctly. Normally, the end of government consists of "the *preservation of all*, as much as may be." In extreme cases, the public interest may diverge from an individual's interest, as when the sheriff tears down the house of an innocent owner to stop a spreading fire (*TT* II.159). But excepting such extreme cases, if conduct is properly part of the right of private society, government interest may not take priority over that right. Government restraints on association are therefore justifiable in normal circumstances only if those restraints count as police "regulations"—that is, laws that require associates to keep their society "regular" in light of the moral laws, interests, and rights that justify and limit the bounds of private society.

Consider, by way of example, the principle that associations must answer for their torts and crimes on terms similar to those that apply to their individual members. When Locke concludes that the associational freedom of churches entitles them to expel members, he adds the proviso that "in all such Cases care is to be taken that the Sentence of Excommunication, and the Execution thereof, carry with it no rough usage, of Word or Action, whereby the ejected Person may any wise be damnified in Body or Estate" (*LT* 14). In contemporary American constitutional discourse, a church's actions have value as exercises of the freedom of association, but

---

[37] See *Dale*, 530 U.S. at 648; *Roberts*, 468 U.S. at 623.

the state has a stronger interest in preventing battery, property damage, or libel. In Locke's usage, by contrast, the moral foundations of the right to associate cease before the associates may tortiously or criminally injure neighbors through the vehicle of their association. Battery, trespass, and libel laws, however, do not seriously interfere with the activities or ends of associations; they simply stop associates from using their association to commit torts or crimes that they could not commit individually.

B. Associational wrongs to public opinion

Locke lays down other principles that limit private societies' activities or ends far more substantially. In the *Letter Concerning Toleration*, Locke identifies four separate grounds the civil magistrate may cite to refuse to tolerate churches. (I set out these grounds in subsection C below.) Taken together, these grounds are a metaphor for Lockean liberalism generally. Each of these grounds for denying toleration to churches is really a principled restraint on the natural right of any society to associate. Each of the grounds focuses on preserving a certain set of opinions. Locke hopes to free liberal citizens to pursue or believe "speculative" opinions, without fear of coercion by the state or retaliation by private groups who disagree passionately about those opinions. His liberal project is also willing to tolerate a wide range of "practical" opinions, meaning opinions bearing directly on individual ethics or the commonwealth's politics (see *LT* 39–40). But the Lockean commonwealth requires that the people assent to the practical opinions necessary to perpetuate liberalism.

In this respect, Locke is *not* a modern liberal pluralist. He rejects the pluralist view "that it is none of the government's business what citizens believe" or "that the shaping of citizens' beliefs is not a task of a liberal state."[38] In this respect, Locke has far more in common with pre-Enlightenment political philosophers than he does with, say, Nozick or Rawls. Locke assumes that political philosophy is primarily the study of a political community's comprehensive political opinions. He also assumes that, when political philosophy becomes prescriptive, it must teach political opinions that persuade a people first to embrace and then to perpetuate the best possible regime. Locke holds that three factors contribute to the ethical and political rules a society enforces on its members. These factors are religion, the positive law, and common opinions, and of these the last does most to establish "the common *measure of Virtue and Vice*" (*ECHU* II.28.11). Thus, because liberal toleration is more just and humane than its alternatives, a liberal people and magistrate must continually superintend public opinion, inculcate the citizenry in the moral and political conditions of liberal toleration, and remind the citizens how precarious and precious such toleration is.

---

[38] Koppelman, *Antidiscrimination Law and Social Equality*, 1.

Locke's qualifications on associational freedom may thus be understood as the product of a more general and relatively tough-minded
calculation regarding how to tolerate the widest freedom of thought consistent with the community's responsibility to perpetuate the conditions
in which such freedom is possible. The social compact runs both ways. If
the civil government breaches any of the terms of the social compact, it
dissolves itself from within, and the populace may properly replace it by
appealing to the natural right of revolution (see *TT* II.199, 221–26).[39] By
the same token, however, if citizens associate privately on terms inconsistent with the social compact, they threaten the compact, and the commonwealth may properly quell their associations.

This suggestion may seem contrary to much of the argument of the
Letter Concerning Toleration, for Locke insists more than once that "[t]he
business of Laws [is] not to provide for the Truth of Opinions, but for the
Safety and Security of the Commonwealth, and of every particular mans
Goods and Person" (*LT* 40; see also 6). Nevertheless, later in the *Letter*, he
qualifies this claim significantly:

> Rectitude of morals, in which consists not the least part of religion
> and sincere piety, looks to civil life also and in it lies the safety of
> souls at the same time as that of the commonwealth. Moral actions
> belong therefore to the jurisdiction of both courts, outward as well as
> inward; and are subject to the rule of both, the civil governor as well
> as the domestic—namely, the magistrate and the conscience.[40]

In this passage, Locke concedes that the magistrate of the Lockean
commonwealth is not *entirely* focused on "the Temporal Good and outward Prosperity of the Society" (*LT* 43). But the concession is subtle.
Locke holds that the civil magistrate is not responsible for all of social
morality, particularly social opinions about piety, intellectual excellence,
or other individual practical virtues. William Popple's translation of the
Letter confuses this point, when it translates "rectitudo morum" (translated above as "rectitude of morals") to mean "a good life." In the *Essay
Concerning Human Understanding*, Locke doubts that practical philosophy
can identify any "highest good" ("summum bonum"). Locke applies this
skepticism in the *Letter*. He instructs the civil magistrate to tolerate claret
clubs and other societies of moral idlers, and also to tolerate "speculative
opinions," which leave "to every Man the care of his own Eternal Happiness" (*LT* 39–40, 42).

With that qualification in mind, when Locke says that the civil magistrate has an interest in the "rectitude of morals," he refers to the public

---

[39] I thank Eric Miller and Andy Koppelman for encouraging me to make this point
explicit.

[40] Locke, *Epistola de Tolerantia*, 122. For Popple's translation, see *LT* 40–41.

morals relating not to speculative opinions but to "practical" ones, which specifically "contribute to the Comfort and Happiness of this Life" (*LT* 42).

C. Four types of harm to public opinion

Locke lays down four specific grounds on which the civil magistrate may properly rely for refusing to tolerate private societies. First, Locke recommends banning churches and other societies from organizing to propagate "Opinions contrary to human Society, or to those moral Rules which are necessary to the preservation of Civil Society" (*LT* 45). As part of his jurisdiction to protect lives, liberty, property, child-rearing families, and so forth, the civil magistrate has jurisdiction to stop citizens from associating toward the end of teaching that it is good to kill, enslave, or steal from citizens, or to be sexually promiscuous. Thus, to take one of many possible examples, the Lockean commonwealth has jurisdiction to restrain associations encouraging adultery, incest, sodomy, or polyamory. Such associations encourage the wider society to accept practical opinions that undermine the status of the traditional family and marriage, on which the liberal commonwealth depends to raise and educate children in sound republican habits.[41]

Second, the commonwealth need not tolerate atheists. Many contemporary authorities suggest that liberal law and policy should "mandate[] governmental neutrality between ... religion and nonreligion."[42] For Locke, however, it is crucial for the liberal civil society to inculcate liberal morality in the public. Even granting that some individual atheists may be far more moral than many religious believers, Locke doubts that the broad public will learn the moral habits liberalism requires without a humane and equality-respecting religion like Christianity (see *RC* 243). Locke thus worries that atheists "undermine and destroy all Religion" (*LT* 48).

Of course, one may wonder, as John Dunn does, whether Locke's attitude toward atheists is "odious." One may also wonder whether Locke can credibly banish atheists given how he recasts Christianity and propounds a rationalist theory of politics.[43] Nevertheless, in his political teachings, Locke prescribes against atheism to preserve public respect for

---

[41] See *TT* I.59; *Davis v. Beason*, 133 U.S. 33, 342–43 (1890); *Reynolds v. United States*, 98 U.S. 145, 164–64 (1879); and Horn, *Groups and the Constitution*, 24–25.

[42] *McCreary County v. American Civil Liberties Union*, 545 U.S. 844, 860 (2005) (quoting *Epperson v. Arkansas*, 393 U.S. 97, 104 [1968]).

[43] Dunn, "The Claim to Freedom of Conscience," 180–82; compare Zuckert, *Launching Liberalism* (suggesting that Locke's rationalism and skepticism undermine general public respect for Christianity and encourage deism and agnosticism) with Myers, *Our Only Star and Compass*, 46–50 (reading Locke as concluding that human faculties point toward the existence of God, even as Locke rests the grounds of human obligation on rationally knowable foundations). For examples of American cases upholding anti-blasphemy laws in the face of constitutional challenges on similar grounds, consider *Updegraph v. Commonwealth*, 11 Serg. & Rawle 394 (Pa. 1824); and *People v. Ruggles*, 8 Johns. R. 290 (N.Y. 1811).

morality and religious teachings consistent with liberalism. When Lockean liberalism replaces throne and altar with government by consent, it increases the risk that political society will be unstable (see *TT* II.223). Locke thinks that government by consent can be stable, but not without widespread support for humane religion. Even if common opinion supports government more strongly than religious or positive law, a civil society still gambles dangerously with its social capital if it moves all its bets from religion to popular opinion.[44]

A third limit on the extent of toleration is that the magistrate may ban churches and other societies whose membership rules specify that "all those who enter into it, do thereby, *ipso facto*, deliver themselves up to the Protection and Service of another Prince" (*LT* 47). Here, Locke cites as an example Muslims beholden to the Ottoman Empire, but in the process he invites his readers to think of Roman Catholics who hold that their articles of faith require them to support the temporal claims of the Church's hierarchy. Elsewhere in the *Letter*, Locke suggests that he is willing to tolerate the Latin Mass and transubstantiation doctrine; by extension, he is willing to tolerate Catholics (see *LT* 40, 52).[45] In return, however, Catholics must forsake any elements of Catholic teaching that make it legitimate to overthrow a sovereign government that is not in conformity with Church teaching. More generally, this proviso can fairly be understood to cover banning associational support for the interests of foreign governments and international totalitarian movements with ideological or political agendas inimical to the interests of the liberal commonwealth.

Finally, Locke proposes to ban churches and other societies whose members "arrogate to themselves, and to those of their own Sect, some peculiar Prerogative, covered over with a specious shew of deceitful words, but in effect opposite to the Civil Right of the Community" (*LT* 46). As he explains elsewhere, "No private Person has any Right, in any manner, to prejudice another Person in his Civil Enjoyments, because he is of another Church or Religion. All the Rights and Franchises that belong to him as a Man, or as a Denison, are inviolably to be preserved to him" (*LT* 14). Locke offers as examples a church that teaches its members to break promises with nonmembers, or to consider overthrowing the government over religious questions. "These therefore, and the like, who attribute . . . [to] themselves, any peculiar Priviledge or Power above other Mortals, in Civil Concernments . . . I say these have no right to be tolerated by the Magistrate; as neither those that will not own and teach the Duty of tolerating All men in matters of meer Religion" (*LT* 46–47).

---

[44] See *ECHU* I.3.6; *RC* 243; and Waldron, *God, Locke, and Equality*, 224–26, 235.

[45] Here Locke contradicts the position he took in his 1667 "Essay on Toleration," in John Locke, *Political Essays*, ed. Mark Goldie (Cambridge: Cambridge University Press, 1997), 134–59. In the text, I also contradict and correct an error I made in Eric R. Claeys, "Justice Scalia and the Religion Clauses: A Comment on Professor Epps," *Washington University Journal of Law and Policy* 21 (2006): 349–58, 355 and n. 28. See Waldron, *God, Locke, and Equality*, 218–23.

This last proviso complicates Locke's teachings considerably, because it threatens to retract much of the immutability of the natural right to society. If one reads Locke's proviso broadly, the more that private societies advocate particular political programs, the more they expose themselves to government supervision. This suggestion is somewhat overdrawn, for the proviso applies only when societies claim political rights and benefits inconsistent with the rights a Lockean common-wealth is pledged to secure. Yet in the hurly-burly of practical politics, it can be difficult for political parties to distinguish between disagree-ments over first principles and disagreements over their application. For instance, during the 1790s, American Federalists and Republicans accused one another of subverting the new U.S. Constitution, and some Federalists assumed that the federal government would not abridge associational freedom if it suppressed political protest by nascent Repub-lican Party groups.[46] The potential for disagreements of this sort helps explain why Grant reads Locke as being hostile to political parties, and why Boyd reads Locke as propounding a prudential view of private association. Even so, these readings go too far. Locke's teachings leave private societies with a wide right of association, not qualified by pru-dential concerns in any significant way, as long as they stay out of politics. If societies do engage in politics, Locke concedes, they do risk political supervision. But it is impossible to avoid this problem com-pletely, and Locke's prudential teaching encourages the civil magistrate to tolerate associational dissent as long as it is not too dangerous or violent. Locke suggests that there is no reason not to tolerate heterodox practical opinions, "tho not absolutely free from all Error, if they do not tend to establish Domination over others, or Civil Impunity" for the association in which they are propagated (*LT* 48).

VII. Contemporary Implications

Obviously, Locke's theory of private society is bound to be contro-versial. Although space prevents me from exploring all the controver-sies in an exhaustive way, I can at least consider two revealing points of contact between Locke's teaching and contemporary policy: associa-tional freedom's tension with anti-sedition policy (on the one hand) and with antidiscrimination policy (on the other). The observations that follow are only suggestive, not comprehensive. Even so, each of these examples highlights a different contrast between Locke's teaching and contemporary practice. Antidiscrimination policy highlights how and why Locke conceives of associational freedom more broadly than many

[46] See Jaffa, *New Birth of Freedom*, 30–72; Robert M. Chesney, "Democratic-Republican Societies, Subversion, and the Limits of Legitimate Political Dissent in the Early Republic," *North Carolina Law Review*, 82 (2004): 1525.

contemporary authorities do; anti-sedition policy highlights how and why Locke conceives of the commonwealth's power to police that freedom more broadly than contemporary authorities do.

A. Seditious associations

The Smith Act, passed in 1940, makes it a federal crime for anyone knowingly or willfully to organize an association advocating the forcible or violent overthrow of the United States or any state. Although many prosecutions under this act have been held unconstitutional, the act has been neither repealed nor declared unconstitutional in all of its possible applications. In the 1990s, the U.S. Congress added to the federal criminal code 18 U.S.C. section 2339B, which makes it a federal crime for anyone knowingly to provide material support to a foreign terrorist organization as designated by the Secretary of State. These laws are more or less consistent with three of Locke's provisos (discussed in Section VI.C above), relating to groups that threaten the public morals, claim special privileges or exemptions, or advance foreign interests.[47]

These laws (and executive policies that enforce them) raise an obvious practical problem: that the government may overzealously punish legitimate free speech and association in its efforts to stamp out anarchism and terrorism. The U.S. Supreme Court has struggled over how to reconcile this risk with the government's stated mission.[48] But the laws and policies also prompt an existential question: Can a government that claims to be tolerant claim it has a strong interest in refusing to tolerate groups because of their message?

Many prominent pluralist theories of liberalism are open to this objection. United States constitutional law raises the same problem when it holds that First Amendment doctrine aims in large part to foster a "marketplace of ideas." If the goal of constitutional democracy is to foster a competition of different ideas without regard to which idea prevails, it is hard to explain why Communism, Islamic jihadism, or other illiberal idea systems should be kept out of the market. This paradox has led Larry Alexander to wonder whether political liberalism is "nothing more than an unprincipled *modus vivendi* responsive to religious and cultural pluralism or,

---

[47] See 18 U.S.C. sec. 2385 (West 2007); *Yates v. United States*, 354 U.S. 298 (1957); 18 U.S.C. sec. 2339B(a)(1) and (g)(6) (West 2007); and Robert M. Chesney, "Civil Liberties and the Terrorism Prevention Paradigm: The Guilt by Association Critique," *Michigan Law Review* 101, no. 6 (2003): 1408, 1432–52.

[48] See *United States v. Robel*, 389 U.S. 258 (1967); *Keyishian v. Board of Regents*, 385 U.S. 589 (1967); *Elfbrandt v. Russell*, 384 U.S. 11 (1966); *Noto v. United States*, 367 U.S. 290 (1961); *Scales v. United States*, 367 U.S. 203 (1961); and David Cole and James X. Dempsey, *Terrorism and the Constitution: Sacrificing Civil Liberties in the Name of National Security* (New York: The New Press, 2002), 153–55.

alternatively, a description of a denatured way of life characteristic of Western modernity, one devoid of deep conviction."[49]

Locke's teachings provide a partial response to such doubts. Although Locke's philosophy is moderate in other respects, his tough-minded eudaimonism precludes existential doubt. The liberal polity need not tolerate illiberal groups. Again, Locke's theory is consequentialist; it builds generally on a comprehensive empirical and psychological analysis of human political life; and it justifies freedom not in any general theory of autonomy or the will, but rather in an account of the human interests most reasonably conducive to human happiness. Because of these qualities, Locke's liberalism is not indifferent to different conceptions of the good life. In Locke's terms, while individuals enjoy freedom to speculate about salvation and other topics, their freedom to do so is qualified by the common good, which is in turn defined as an aggregation of all the society's members' individual interests in being free to work, raise families, and pursue their own individual conceptions of excellence or salvation. Similarly, in contrast to the Supreme Court's marketplace-of-ideas metaphor, Locke doubts that a liberal people can cycle through different theories of government without corrupting the moral character they need to remain liberal.

Locke's liberalism thus has little difficulty explaining why Communists or Islamic jihadists need not be tolerated. Locke is reasonably sure that man knows too little about ultimate questions relating to the good life for politics to settle these questions in a decent way. He is also reasonably sure that citizens can coexist and even flourish if they agree to focus their government on liberty, property, and family, and then to pursue higher forms of excellence in smaller groups. Communists and Islamic jihadists are too sure they have comprehensive answers to ultimate questions. Both claim that their possession of these answers gives them the authority to impose tyranny. Both groups reject the public-private distinction and the freedom citizens enjoy thanks to that distinction. Both deny basic rights protecting reasonable human interests, including respect for life, liberty, property, and free thought not consistent with their dominant teachings. Both hold that their claims to truth justify claiming "peculiar Prerogatives" that justify their not extending respect and decent treatment to fellow citizens who do not support their causes (*LT* 46). While Locke limits the ends for which his liberal commonwealth may act, he does so to make it more competent and forceful within its rightful sphere — including taking those actions necessary to prevent illiberal elements from subverting the system. A Lockean civil magistrate may choose to tolerate illiberal fringe elements, when the society is fairly secure and

---

[49] *Keyishian v. Board of Regents*, 385 U.S. 589, 605–6 (1967); *Abrams v. United States*, 250 U.S. 616, 630 (1919) (Holmes, J., dissenting); Larry Alexander, "Illiberalism All the Way Down: Illiberal Groups and Two Conceptions of Liberalism," *Journal of Contemporary Legal Issues* 12 (2002): 625–30.

government suppression seems too likely to encourage censorship of legitimate freedom. But whether the magistrate should be so restrained is a question of prudence. If the society is genuinely threatened, the magistrate should take all actions appropriate to the threat.[50]

There is a catch here: To give the liberal commonwealth more certitude in the rightness of its cause against totalitarians, Locke's theory of association also gives the commonwealth stronger regulatory powers to use against associations of non-Lockean liberals. Contemporary welfare-state liberalism was developed in large part on the basis of a common political understanding holding (in John Dewey's formulation) that "[n]atural rights and natural liberties exist only in the kingdom of mythological social zoology," and that "organized society must use its powers to establish the conditions under which the mass of individuals can possess actual as distinct from merely legal liberty."[51] It would not be difficult to extend Locke's provisos to ban groups dedicated to implementing Dewey's principles in practice.

In many cases, Locke's teachings about prudence help establish a spectrum for judging different forms of political dissent. While modern welfare-state liberals may reject Locke's political foundations and many of the implications of his theory, they still respect democracy, elected representation, liberty, religious toleration, and many other implications of Locke's program. Welfare-state liberals and Lockean liberals have far more in common with each other than either does with Communists or jihadists. Those commonalities provide important reasons why welfare-state liberals might be tolerated in a Lockean commonwealth. At the same time, it is striking that, on Locke's view, toleration of welfare-state liberals is supported only by a prudential argument and not by an immutable right.

Nonetheless, it is not clear that any other theory of government can do better. Many contemporary theories of liberalism are committed to pluralism and neutrality between competing visions of the good life. These theories are broad enough to finesse deep divisions about politics within the political community, but they are correspondingly shallow in response to existential threats from outside that community. Lockean liberalism is

---

[50] See Harry V. Jaffa, *Original Intent and the Framers of the Constitution: A Disputed Question* (Washington, DC: Regnery Gateway, 1994), 329–42; Harry V. Jaffa, "On the Nature of Civil and Religious Liberty," in Jaffa, *Equality and Liberty: Theory and Practice in American Politics* (Oxford: Oxford University Press, 1965), 169–89; and John Marshall, "Report of the Minority on the Virginia Resolutions," reprinted in *The Founders' Constitution*, ed. Philip B. Kurland and Ralph Lerner (Chicago: University of Chicago Press, 1987), 5: 136–39. For examples of national anti-sedition policies that worked relatively effectively, consider Karl Loewenstein, "Legislative Control of Political Extremism in European Democracies, I and II," *Columbia Law Review* 38, no. 5 (1938): 591–622 and 725–74. Loewenstein suggests that many European democracies during the interwar period effectively suppressed fascist and socialist parties until they were conquered by Nazi Germany and the Axis. If Loewenstein is correct, these countries' internal policies toward seditionists were effective regardless of whether the countries could be overwhelmed by superior external force.

[51] John Dewey, *Liberalism and Social Action* (Amherst, NY: Prometheus Books, 1999), 27, 35.

deep enough to respond to such existential threats from without, but it is not broad. Rather than minimizing as "inner splits" profound theoretical differences among species of liberalism, Lockean liberalism highlights the political differences among liberals.[52] Maybe a liberal polity cannot have it both ways.

B. Antidiscrimination policies and the public-private distinction

Antidiscrimination laws bar employers, social clubs, and other groups from denying access on the basis of race, religion, sex, sexual preference, or other similar characteristics. These laws are usually justified as part of a broader project to eradicate animosity in all forms toward groups that are targets of discrimination. Such animosity often starts in small, private groups. To wipe out discrimination root and branch, then, antidiscrimination policies typically require that such groups open their membership to members of targeted groups.

As Andrew Koppelman has recognized, an antidiscrimination program thus "presses against the public/private distinction" symbolized in freedom of association. When an association claims that it should be free to regulate its membership, choose its ends, or enforce its policies without government interference, it claims that its internal governance belongs entirely in the private sphere. Antidiscrimination policies, by contrast, claim that, in some cases, such groups pursue ends and policies inconsistent with the public's interest in ending racial and other forms of discrimination. Many contemporary theories of liberalism have difficulty explaining why the private sphere is or ought to be autonomous from the claims of the public. Consider Robert Nozick's theory of liberalism, which entitles every citizen to wide discretion to believe what he wants and associate with whom he wants. As Koppelman and Stephen Macedo have suggested, the citizens of Nozick's ideal polity may not sufficiently appreciate the deontological respect for persons that provides the foundations of their freedom. But as soon as a Nozickian polity seeks to foster such appreciation, it blurs the line between public and private in free thought and association.[53]

Locke's defense of private societies may provide a stronger defense for associational privacy and a deeper justification for the public-private distinction. Because Locke's approach is consequentialist, it anticipates and provides a response to a claim central to antidiscrimination policy: that in order to make sure citizens do not use their freedom to discriminate against fellow citizens, a decent political community must intervene closely

---

[52] Ibid., 35.

[53] Koppelman, *Antidiscrimination Law and Social Equality*, 181; Nozick, *Anarchy, State, and Utopia*, 30–33, 299–306; see Koppelman, *Antidiscrimination Law and Social Equality*, 181–90, citing Stephen Macedo, *Liberal Virtues: Citizenship, Virtue, and Community in Liberal Constitutionalism* (Oxford: Clarendon Press, 1990), 55.

in its citizens' preferences and associations. Locke recognizes that a civil society has a huge interest in shaping its citizens' preferences—although not to the degree that contemporary antidiscrimination policies typically require. As I noted in Section VI, the Lockean commonwealth has an interest in preventing groups from committing crimes and torts that individuals are barred from committing. It also has an interest in stopping groups from undermining foundational liberal moral opinions, including, specifically, preventing groups from claiming "any peculiar Priviledge or Power above other Mortals, in Civil Concernments" or a right "to establish Domination over others" (*LT* 46-47, 49). The Lockean liberal order does not require citizens to like one another, but it does require them to be civil to one another and to respect one another's equal liberties to be let alone to pursue basic material interests. Thus, in principle, the Lockean commonwealth may prosecute and disband a group dedicated to the violent intimidation of members of a particular race or religion—before that group even commits any act of violence—simply to teach the broader community that such intimidation will not be tolerated.

At the same time, it is harder for the Lockean commonwealth to justify a policy forcing a private business or social club to admit members that it does not want, even if the association is denying membership on the basis of race or another similar characteristic. The refusal to admit an applicant does not count as domination over the applicant or as an assertion of any special privilege to the applicant's detriment. The applicant remains left alone. The applicant still has his liberty, his property, and his freedom to join many other associations to pursue his ends. Since the association is not inflicting any harm on the applicant or the public morals, it remains absolutely free—whether it is a local church, the Boy Scouts, or an employer employing individuals from the same religion and ethnic background—to control its membership without state interference. Here is where Locke's presumption of associational freedom applies with force. It matters little that the business or social club is not advocating a political program or promoting religious worship—if anything, the lack of advocacy favors associational freedom. The business's commerce and the social club's fraternity are ends as intelligible, legitimate, and deserving of legal noninterference as loftier ends, and neither commerce nor fraternity claims special privileges inconsistent with the equal civil rights of nonmember citizens.

Locke's analysis of human psychology and politics explains why a liberal society might want to refrain from enforcing policies against discrimination by associations. One strand of this analysis relates back to Locke's analysis of civility. Otherwise-decent citizens differ too much in their backgrounds, characters, interests, and religious backgrounds to make it realistic for the law to force them to associate. Citizens will have their own close friendships with their family members, workmates, churchmates, and so forth, but they will not like and will probably actively mistrust many of their fellow citizens. The law can teach such citizens not to threaten their neighbors, but it cannot force them to like one another. Thus, as Robert Putnam has suggested, compulsory association often fosters social isolation and depletes a country's store of social capital. A country may decide to enforce antidiscrimination laws anyway, to break up local patterns of ethnic and religious discrimination and to create patterns of social trust that transcend ethnic and religious backgrounds. But Putnam confirms with empirical data what Locke suggests by general observation: the society will pay a cost for making many useful and pleasant social groupings less so, and it ought to discount this cost from whatever benefits it hopes to promote by restraining the power of free associations to exclude outsiders.[54]

Along with civility comes a cluster of values associated with personal responsibility, spiritedness, and self-reliance. To justify wide-ranging power to monitor employment discrimination and private-group exclusion, antidiscrimination advocates often appeal to norms like equal dignity, concern, or respect: a freedom from insults, hate, and other social stigmas that make individuals think that the wider society values them little or not at all.[55] Locke's version of dignity sets lower goals. In a Lockean society, individuals can and should find enough affirmation from family, religion, and friends. Lockean citizens do not need to tolerate physical or reputational attacks by outsiders who dislike them, but they do need to disregard insults and other lesser expressions of animosity with spiritedness and a thick skin. At a high level of generality, when the Lockean citizen is excluded from a private association on the basis of race, religion, or another similar characteristic, the appropriate response is to brush off the implied insult and find more friendly associates.

In other words, Locke treats the public-private distinction more sensitively than antidiscrimination advocates often do. Koppelman and other antidiscrimination scholars portray liberalism as naïve. When liberalism claims that freedom of thought and association are entirely private affairs, these scholars argue, it ignores the fact that private associations shape the public culture. To this extent, Locke's theory accords with antidiscrimination scholars against Nozick and many other contemporary defenders of liberalism. But Locke differs with antidiscrimination scholars about what form of public culture is most likely to facilitate the private happiness of citizens and a humane and tolerant public life. When Locke draws a distinction between rights invasions and mere insults, he sets standards that teach individual citizens to be self-reliant and free. Antidiscrimination scholars may overlook such qualities or take them for granted: they

---

[54] See Robert D. Putnam, "*E Pluribus Unum:* Diversity and Community in the Twenty-First Century," *Scandinavian Political Studies* 30, no. 2 (2007): 137, 146–59.

[55] See, for example, Koppelman, *Antidiscrimination Law and Social Equality,* 57–76; and Ronald Dworkin, "Reverse Discrimination," in Dworkin, *Taking Rights Seriously* (Cambridge, MA: Harvard University Press, 1978), 227–28.

may be promoting a conception of dignity so open-ended as to encourage individuals to see themselves as victims, to habituate them to using the law as a bludgeon for social advancement, and to institutionalize ethnic and religious competition. Similarly, Locke's political theory limits the role of elites to a greater extent than antidiscrimination theory does. Locke's conceptions of dignity and self-reliance encourage a public culture in which individual citizens shrug off insults and focus on taking care of their own interests. By contrast, a capacious theory of dignity encourages elites to become "quarrelsome and contentious" over ethnic and religious grievances. While more needs to be said, these insights suggest why Locke may provide a more serious response than many contemporary liberal theorists to conventional antidiscrimination criticisms of liberalism.

At the same time, Locke's theory is exposed to a different set of problems. To get the advantages of psychological sophistication, Locke opens his approach to empirical criticisms. Locke presumes that individuals can coexist peaceably within a democratic republic even if they dislike one another for religious reasons and, depending on the political community, even if they mistrust one another because of racial and ethnic attachments. These predictions may be accurate in some cases, but not necessarily in all. Locke's arguments are thus exposed to criticisms similar to those leveled at Richard Epstein's book *Forbidden Grounds*, which defends the freedom of a business to deny employment to any applicant for any reason. This defense of at-will employment is similar to Locke's account of free association generally. Both are consequentialist; both draw broad lessons from relevant history; and both fill in the gaps by inducing likely general principles from general observations about human selfishness and sociality. Epstein's argument has been criticized thoroughly for going against the empirical evidence. According to the critics, before the U.S. Congress enacted the Civil Rights Act of 1964, white prejudices against blacks were too deep to dislodge privately and socially and too deep to allow blacks to create their own economic opportunities without government intervention. Because Locke's defense of free association relies similarly on soft empirical generalizations, it must confront similar empirical criticisms.[56]

VIII. Conclusion

John Locke uses the private society as a metaphor for political legitimacy. The local civic association illustrates in practice the theoretical standards he sets for judging how well a political community treats its churches

---

[56] See Richard A. Epstein, *Forbidden Grounds: The Case Against Employment Discrimination Laws* (Cambridge, MA: Harvard University Press, 1992), 13–143; Drew S. Days, III, "Reality," *San Diego Law Review* 31, no. 1 (1994): 169, 170–80; Richard McAdams, "Epstein on His Own Grounds," *San Diego Law Review* 31, no. 1 (1994): 241, 249–64; Samuel Issacharoff, "Contractual Liberties in Discriminatory Markets," *Texas Law Review* 70, no. 5 (1992): 1219, 1225–34; and J. Hoult Verkerke, "Free to Search," *Harvard Law Review* 105, no. 8 (1992): 2080, 2088–96.

and its citizens. These metaphorical usages illustrate Locke's teachings vividly, but they have the unfortunate side effect of obscuring his teachings specifically about associational freedom. This essay helps put Locke's specific teachings about private society back in proper perspective, where they may be appreciated justly on their own merits.

Locke justifies associational freedom as an outlet for the better social faculties in man's nature, but he also places necessary limits on this freedom in order to check the vicious social tendencies that encourage group fanaticism and totalitarianism. His concept of associational freedom is broader than the concept that informs much contemporary practice. This concept helps us appreciate better not only associational freedom in itself but also essential safeguards like the private-public distinction as it bears on associations. At the same time, Locke's concept of associational harms is broader than, and focused differently from, its counterpart in contemporary practice. This concept challenges us to think more probingly about the minimal conditions of citizenship in a liberal society.

Law, George Mason University

THE MADISONIAN PARADOX OF FREEDOM
OF ASSOCIATION*

By Richard Boyd

In this connection it is well to remember that in the early days of our Republic—when the element of commitment was strong—there was a considerable suspicion of private associations, lodges, and societies. Madison in *The Federalist* (No. X) wrote of the "dangerous vice" of "faction." Our Constitution contains no explicit guaranty of the right to form associations, but speaks instead in the First Amendment of "the right of the people peaceably to assemble, and to petition the Government for a redress of grievances." The Founding Fathers seem to have contemplated that as soon as "the people" had respectfully filed their petition, they would quietly and submissively retire to their homes. Some of the attitudes that we now confidently ascribe to totalitarianism and its intolerance of dissent were not absent in the early, anxious days of our own country.

—Lon Fuller, "Two Principles of Human Association"[1]

I. Introduction

Despite influential criticisms of liberalism as reducible to an "unencumbered" or "possessive individualism," many prominent liberal thinkers in the latter half of the twentieth century have regarded freedom of association as both a necessary and a sufficient condition for a good society.[2] The philosopher Michael Oakeshott not only thought that a free society was integrated by a wide variety of "enterprise associations" formed for the more satisfactory pursuit of individual ends, but indeed thought that the freedom of association was perhaps the single most important of liberal freedoms.[3] Freedom of association distinguished what F. A. Hayek

* This essay benefited greatly from my conversations with Eric Kasper, Jacob Levy, James Morrison, Howard Schweber, Greg Weiner, the other contributors to this volume, and the careful reading of Ellen Frankel Paul.

[1] Lon Fuller, "Two Principles of Human Association," in *The Principles of Social Order*, ed. Kenneth I. Winston (Durham, NC: Duke University Press, 1981), 77.

[2] Influential equations of liberalism with individualism include C. B. Macpherson, *The Political Theory of Possessive Individualism: Hobbes to Locke* (Oxford: Oxford University Press, 1962); Michael Sandel, "The Procedural Republic and the Unencumbered Self," *Political Theory* 12 (February 1984): 81–96; and Charles Taylor, "Atomism," in Taylor, *Philosophical Papers, Volume 2: Philosophy and the Human Sciences* (Cambridge: Cambridge University Press, 1985).

[3] Michael Oakeshott, *On Human Conduct* (Oxford: Clarendon Press, 1991); Oakeshott, "The Political Economy of Freedom," in Oakeshott, *Rationalism in Politics and Other Essays*

doi:10.1017/S0265052508080254

termed the "true individualism" of Edmund Burke, Alexis de Tocqueville, and Lord Acton from the "false individualism" of the French Revolutionaries, who sought to demolish every intermediary link between individual and state.[4] Likewise, the contemporary political theorist George Kateb has argued that being a free individual necessarily means one has the right to choose those with whom one wants to associate (or not to associate).[5] Either to deny or to compel association with others negates the ability to control one's own identity and life-choices. This kind of "compulsory-voluntary association" is anathema to a free society.[6]

Nonetheless, as Lon Fuller's provocative quotation above reminds us, classical liberal philosophers of the seventeenth and eighteenth centuries were often lukewarm to the idea of free association—and perhaps rightly so. Individuals need to be able to associate in order to fulfill their desires and, if necessary, oppose the actions of government or other vested interests in society. But with the augmented power of concerted action comes the potential to threaten other individuals, groups, or even the political authority upon which liberty itself rests. No surprise, then, that at least some of those Founders to whom Fuller refers were deeply ambivalent about the free association of citizens—whether into conspiratorial political factions, divisive religious sects, or monopolistic economic corporations.

Above and beyond the fact that the abuses of the freedom of association are arguably more destabilizing than other liberties like speech, religion, or the press—and, thus, the former might conceivably be more legitimately bounded or circumscribed—there are also questions about the moral status of the freedom of association.[7] Is there a right to associate

---

(Indianapolis, IN: Liberty Fund, 1991), 391–92. Although Oakeshott is often regarded as a "conservative" based on his early essays in defense of tradition, there is now widespread agreement about Oakeshott's place within the liberal tradition. While recognizing that liberty is an inherited tradition, Oakeshott also defends a purposively neutral rule of law intended to encourage pluralism and the maximum degree of individual flourishing. See, for example, Josiah Lee Auspitz, "Individuality, Civility, and Theory: The Philosophical Imagination of Michael Oakeshott," *Political Theory* 4 (August 1976): 261–94; Paul Franco, *The Political Philosophy of Michael Oakeshott* (New Haven, CT: Yale University Press, 1990); Terry Nardin, *The Philosophy of Michael Oakeshott* (University Park, PA: Penn State University Press, 2001); Richard Boyd, "Michael Oakeshott on Civility, Civil Society, and Civil Association," *Political Studies* 52 (October 2004): 603–22; Richard Flathman, *Reflections of a Would-Be Anarchist: Ideals and Institutions of Liberalism* (Minneapolis: University of Minnesota Press, 1998); and Flathman, *Pluralism and Liberal Democracy* (Baltimore, MD: Johns Hopkins University Press, 2005).

[4] F. A. Hayek, "Individualism: True and False," in Hayek, *Individualism and Economic Order* (Chicago: University of Chicago Press, 1948), 4–6. On apparent and real taxonomical differences between Hayek's "liberalism" and Oakeshott's "conservatism," see Richard Boyd and James Morrison, "F. A. Hayek, Michael Oakeshott, and the Concept of Spontaneous Order," in Louis Hunt and Peter McNamara, eds., *Liberalism, Conservatism, and Hayek's Idea of Spontaneous Order* (New York: Palgrave, 2007), chap. 4.

[5] George Kateb, "The Value of Association," in Amy Gutmann, ed., *Freedom of Association* (Princeton, NJ: Princeton University Press, 1998), esp. 48.

[6] Oakeshott, *On Human Conduct*, 115, 119, 157–58, 314–17.

[7] It is one thing to suggest that individuals ought not to be compelled to associate against their will, and another, very different matter to say that they have an inalienable and

that is conceptually analogous to other basic liberties like speech, religion, or press? Pope Leo XIII boldly adduced a natural human right to associate in his 1891 encyclical "Rerum Novarum," and the doctrine has been a mainstay of Catholic social thought.[8] But it is telling that classical liberals rarely cited freedom of association among their lists of canonical liberties like speech, conscience, press, property, etc.[9] The United States Constitution makes no explicit provision for the freedom of association, and the French government ceded the right of voluntary association only with the Law of July 1, 1901 (belatedly accorded full constitutional status in 1971). This was after having abolished a wide range of voluntary associations during the Revolutionary years of 1791 to 1793.[10] We have come a long way indeed from the complaints of Thomas Hobbes, David Hume, Adam Smith, and James Madison about seditious "sects" and divisive "factions" to Article 20.1 of the United Nations Universal Declaration of Human Rights stipulating a universal human right to "freedom of peaceable assembly and association."[11]

The historical and conceptual question, then, is whether and in what respects freedom of association *differs* from other core liberal freedoms. Why were classical liberal thinkers generally unwilling to extol it even as they lionized inalienable natural rights of speech, press, conscience, and private property? And why has the question of freedom of association in

---

absolute right to associate with others under all conditions and for all purposes. Like any other liberal freedom, the freedom of association cannot be construed as absolute and unbounded. The circumstantial boundaries of freedom of association have been considered in much more detail by Peter de Marneffe, "Rights, Reasons, and Freedom of Association," in Gutmann, ed., *Freedom of Association*, 145–73. De Marneffe's point about the necessary limits of freedom of association and its similarity to other freedoms in this respect is well-taken, but in what follows I want to emphasize the *differences* between freedom of association and other core liberal freedoms.

[8] Pope Leo XIII, Papal Encyclical of May 15, 1891, "Rerum Novarum," section 51.

[9] Modern liberals are another story altogether. Among those modern liberals who make freedom of association one of the basic liberties are John Stuart Mill, "On Liberty" (1859), in *On Liberty and Other Essays*, ed. John Gray (Oxford: Oxford Classics, 1991), 17; and John Rawls, *Political Liberalism* (New York: Columbia University Press, 1993), 291, 309, 313, 332, 335, 337, 341. By "classical liberalism," I refer to seventeenth- and eighteenth-century doctrines of limited government that regarded liberty primarily as the absence of restraint and saw this liberty as grounded in inalienable natural rights. "Modern liberalism," of course, envisions a broader role for the state in providing enabling conditions for individuals to make proper use of their liberty; generally disregards the idea that freedom is rooted in metaphysical natural rights; and, accordingly, condones trade-offs of individual liberty in the interest of securing other goods like justice, equality, diversity, development, or social utility. There are ongoing scholarly disagreements about whether Mill is better described as a "classical" or a "modern" liberal, but I incline toward the latter interpretation. See Richard Boyd, *Uncivil Society: The Perils of Pluralism and the Making of Modern Liberalism* (Lanham, MD: Rowman and Littlefield, 2004), chap. 5. For a somewhat different but very helpful taxonomy of this divide between "pluralist" and "rationalist" liberalisms, see Jacob T. Levy, "Liberalism's Divide, After Socialism and Before," *Social Philosophy and Policy* 20, no. 1 (2003): 278–97.

[10] See, for example, Kung Chuan Hsiao, *Political Pluralism* (New York: Harper, 1927), 263.

[11] Universal Declaration of Human Rights, adopted and proclaimed by the United Nations General Assembly Resolution 217 A (III) of December 10, 1948, article 20, section 1.

American constitutionalism so often been filtered through the murky lens of other cognate freedoms like expression or intimacy? In what follows, I want to suggest that some insights (if not definitive answers) are to be found in the intellectual history of liberalism. Indeed, I will push Fuller's observation further, drawing attention to the ways in which these assorted misgivings about the free association of citizens were not just an artifact of the "anxious days" of our own Founding, but were a common political and sociological refrain in the tradition of Anglo-American liberalism.

Fuller may be hyperbolic in characterizing the ideas of James Madison or others of the Founding generation as akin to "totalitarianism" or an "intolerance of dissent," but Madison's complaints about faction in *Federalist* No. 10 and elsewhere in his political writings seem to be an especially fruitful case for understanding classical liberal arguments both for and against the freedom of association. Given the suspicion of association and faction voiced in *The Federalist*, it seems reasonable to conjecture, as Fuller implies, that Madison would have supported provisions to curb freedom of association, as did many of his contemporaries and political opponents. However, despite Madison's well-known complaints about the incendiary effects of faction, he proved to be a staunch defender of the freedom of association over and against some of the very same attitudes Fuller alludes to in the above-cited quotation. I want to explore this paradox further, teasing out the considerations by which Madison could simultaneously lament the destructive effects of freedom of association while defending the principles upon which it is based.

II. THOMAS HOBBES AND THE DANGERS OF ASSOCIATIONAL LIBERTY

Madison's ambivalence makes perfect sense in light of his precursors in the Anglo-American tradition. Maybe the most adamant critic of the freedom of association was Thomas Hobbes, whose 1651 work *Leviathan* described associations as "lesser commonwealths in the bowels of a greater, like worms in the entrails of a natural man." [12] It is at the very least anachronistic and at worst wrongheaded to characterize the absolutist Hobbes as a "liberal," but his assumptions that government originates in the will of the people, that subjects are equal in the eyes of the law, and that the ends of civil association should be limited to the task of maintaining peace and security were noteworthy developments in the tradition of Anglo-American liberalism.[13] More pertinent to the subject of

---

[12] Thomas Hobbes, *Leviathan*, ed. Edwin Curley (Indianapolis, IN: Hackett, 1994), chap. 29, 218.

[13] Debates about whether Hobbes is a "liberal," properly speaking, are endless. I have surveyed these debates and answered largely in the negative. See Richard Boyd, "Thomas Hobbes and the Perils of Pluralism," *Journal of Politics* 63 (May 2001): 392–413. Nonetheless, as Stephen Holmes has argued, even if Hobbes's politics are illiberal, there are still concep-

associations, however, Hobbes's deep-seated pessimism about the irrational and disruptive proclivities of individuals in groups sets the tone for
the next century and a half of theorizing about the problems inherent to
the freedom of association.

For all of his vaunted individualism, Hobbes operates under the sociological assumption that groups amount to more than just the sum of
their parts, and that they should be regarded as such by the sovereign.
Religious fanaticism, panic terror, rage, or other violent and uncivil behavior "happens to none but in a throng, or multitude of people." [14] Normally reasonable, clear-thinking individuals are liable to be carried away
by the proximity of those around them. Overcome by "madness," and
spurred on by the "neighbourhood also of those that have been enriched
by it," otherwise decent individuals will descend to moral atrocities they
would never dare if left to their own devices:

> Though the effect of folly, in them that are possessed of an opinion of
> being inspired, be not visible always in one man, by any very extrav-
> agant action that proceedeth from such passion, yet when many of
> them conspire together, the rage of the whole multitude is visible
> enough. For what argument of madness can there be greater, than to
> clamour, strike, and throw stones at our best friends? Yet this is
> somewhat less than such a multitude will do. [15]

Moreover, sectarian and partisan conflicts have an emotional intensity
rarely encountered in other spheres of civil life: "there are no wars so
sharply waged as between sects of the same religion, and factions of the
same commonweal, where the contestation is either concerning doctrines
or political prudence." [16]

Under ideal conditions, Hobbes concedes a good deal of freedom to
individuals within what he calls the "silence of the law." [17] Unfortunately,
he leaves no analogous room for the freedom of private associations. [18]
Combinations for "kindred," "religion," or "of state" are all "unjust, as

---

tual reasons to look at Hobbes as one of the progenitors of key ideas in the liberal tradition.
Cf. Stephen Holmes, "Hobbes's Irrational Man," in Holmes, *Passions and Constraint: On the
Theory of Liberal Democracy* (Chicago: University of Chicago Press, 1995), 69–70. Ironically,
Hobbes's illiberal complaints about the dangerous and destabilizing effects of groups on
both individual liberty and political authority have become a mainstay of the liberal tradition. My subsequent discussion of Hobbes and his hostility to the freedom of association
draws upon, but does not reproduce, Boyd, *Uncivil Society*, esp. chaps. 1–3.

[14] Hobbes, *Leviathan*, chap. 6, 31.

[15] Ibid., chap. 8, 41–42; chap. 29, 214.

[16] Thomas Hobbes, "Philosophical Rudiments Concerning Government and Society," in
The English Works of Thomas Hobbes, ed. Sir William Molesworth (London: J. Bohn, 1839),
vol. II, 7–8.

[17] Hobbes, *Leviathan*, chap. 21, 138, 143.

[18] I owe this observation to Oakeshott, "Introduction to *Leviathan*," in Oakeshott, *Rationalism in Politics*, 282.

being contrary to the peace and safety of the people."[19] Private groups should be regarded as conspiratorial if only because they are invisible to the prying eyes of the sovereign: "For all uniting of strength by private men is, if for evil intent, unjust; if for intent unknown, dangerous to the public and unjustly concealed."[20] Whether the associations Hobbes had in mind were dissenting religious sects, fractious political parties, roving bands of soldiers, universities, municipalities, or other potentially divisive entities within the body politic, associational life would always be a limiting condition on the sovereign authority he believed absolutely necessary to secure liberty.

III. CLASSICAL LIBERALISM AND ASSOCIATIONAL FREEDOM

One of the central developments in the history of religious toleration—and *ipso facto* of classical liberalism—was John Locke's break from Hobbes's empirical assessment of the necessarily violent and illiberal nature of groups. While concurring with Hobbes that a liberal regime must draw the line at tolerating (religious) groups whose uncivil behaviors or beliefs are inimical to political society itself, Locke argues that precisely because religious congregations are no different from any other kind of "free and voluntary Society," they deserve to be tolerated under most ordinary circumstances.[21] He adamantly denies Hobbes's allegation that assemblies of individuals are necessarily "Conventicles, and Nurseries of Factions and Seditions."[22] "You'll say," Locke anticipates, *"That Assemblies and Meetings endanger the Publick Peace, and Threaten the Commonwealth."* But "if this be so," he replies, "Why are there daily such numerous Meetings in Markets, and Courts of Judicature? Why are Crowds upon the Exchange, and a Concourse of People in Cities suffered?"[23] Why, then, are political and religious groups singled out as factious and seditious?

Any tendency of groups to become violent and seditious has nothing to do with the activities toward which they are devoted: "Some enter into Company for Trade and Profit: Others, for want of Business, have their Clubs for Clarret. Neighbourhood joyns some, and Religion others. But there is one only thing which gathers People into Seditious Commotions, and that is Oppression."[24] Rather than anything "peculiar unto the Genius of such Assemblies," the tendency of religious groups to become factious is one of the "unhappy Circumstances of an

---

[19] Hobbes, *Leviathan*, chap. 22, 154.
[20] Ibid., chap. 22, 152–55.
[21] On some *civil* grounds for limiting toleration, see esp. John Locke, *A Letter Concerning Toleration*, ed. James Tully (Indianapolis, IN: Hackett, 1983), 39, 49–51.
[22] Ibid., 51.
[23] Ibid.
[24] Ibid., 52.

oppressed or ill-settled Liberty."[25] Almost any group affiliation could become a source of conflict if the state were to make it the basis of legal discrimination. "Suppose this Business of Religion were let alone," Locke hypothesizes, "and that there were some other Distinction made between men and men, upon account of their different Complexions, Shapes, and Features." Under conditions of differential treatment, such persons, "united together by one common persecution," would become just as dangerous and disruptive.[26] Conversely, if the state eliminated special privileges, on the one hand, or disproportionate burdens, on the other, then supposedly intractable religious or ethnic affiliations would become matters of complete indifference, no more or less contentious than other private decisions about how to spend one's money, manage one's estates, or marry off one's daughter.[27]

Notwithstanding Locke's sociological optimism about the peaceful qualities of groups, even his own defense of religious and political associations is framed in terms of a prudential policy of toleration rather than a natural and inalienable right of free association. Indeed, Hobbes's original pessimism about associational freedom never entirely disappears from the classical liberal tradition. Even after the immediate threat of civil war and revolution has passed, eighteenth-century philosophers like David Hume share Hobbes's worries about the divisive and irrational properties of individuals in groups. Hume in particular is adamant that "factions subvert government, render laws impotent, and beget the fiercest animosities among men of the same nation."[28] Hume's most extended and best known ruminations on the problems of associational life are his essays on political parties. There he distinguishes between parties of interest, affection, and principle. The former are both the most common and potentially manageable, whereas the latter "parties of principle, especially abstract speculative principle," represent the "most extraordinary phenomenon, that has yet appeared in human affairs."[29]

Hume is every bit as concerned as Hobbes about the violent and disruptive nature of groups, but his argument is finer-grained. Hume distinguishes, for instance, between different kinds of parties—of affection, interest, and principle—which pose different degrees of danger to civil society. Likewise, he can praise the more generalized benefits of a "civil society"—in the form of sociability, humanity, politeness, refinement, and the arts of conversation—even while acknowledging the divisive tendencies of certain kinds of ideological political and religious groups. Hume even hints at some rudimentary institutional and socio-

---

[25] Ibid., 51.
[26] Ibid., 52.
[27] Ibid., 34.
[28] David Hume, "Of Parties," in Hume, *Essays: Moral, Political, and Literary*, ed. Eugene Miller (Indianapolis, IN: Liberty Press, 1985), 55.
[29] Ibid., 59–61.

logical remedies to the problem of groups, attempting to render freedom of association of as little threat to political authority as possible.
First, like Locke, Hume believes that removing invidious legal distinctions is likely to blunt the edges of resentment that sometimes generate
factional groups.[30] Second, he believes that a commercial society will
polish away the "barbarous" rough edges of sectarianism and partisanship, recasting incommensurable conflicts of principle into more reasonable and "mensurable" conflicts of interest.[31] Third, he believes that
publicity—or public deliberation about ideas and principles—helps to
diffuse the negative energies of fanatical political groups.[32] Lastly, he
believes that the increased humanity of a more cosmopolitan society
discourages the jealousy and parochialism that make different groups—
religious, ethnic, or national—suspicious of one another and liable to
uncivil behavior.[33]

IV. James Madison, Faction, and American Constitutionalism

I would submit that the American Founders inherited two different and
contradictory sensibilities from the tradition of Anglo-European liberalism. The first, obviously, is solicitude for liberty and the desire to protect
traditional liberties from encroachments by the state. The second and less
observed attitude is a generalized suspicion of groups, especially those
founded on high degrees of emotional commitment. Not only did such
groups threaten the fragile new political order established by the U.S.
Constitution, as Fuller notes above, but they were objectionable from a
classical republican standpoint as well, taking something away from the
commitments that all good republican citizens were supposed to share
with one another and the new republic as a whole.[34]

---

[30] David Hume, *Dialogues Concerning Natural Religion,* ed. Richard Popkin (Indianapolis, IN: Hackett, 1980), 82–85.

[31] David Hume, "Of the Rise and Progress of the Arts and Sciences," in Hume, *Essays,* 118–20, 125–35; Hume, *Dialogues,* 80.

[32] David Hume, "Of Refinement in the Arts," in Hume, *Essays,* 271–75; David Hume, "Of Commerce," in Hume, *Essays,* 264.

[33] David Hume, "Of the Jealousy of Trade," in Hume, *Essays,* 327–31; David Hume, "Of National Characters," in Hume, *Essays,* 202–3, 206–7.

[34] On this "republican" antipathy toward groups, see especially Jean-Jacques Rousseau, *The Social Contract,* ed. Victor Gourevitch (Cambridge: Cambridge University Press, 1997), Book II, chap. 3, 59–60. On the differences between classical liberalism and the "classical republicanism" from which it is now commonly distinguished, see especially J. G. A. Pocock, *The Machiavellian Moment: Florentine Political Thought and the Atlantic Republican Connection* (Prince-
ton, NJ: Princeton University Press, 1975). Two influential works that treat the American Rev-
olution as largely a product of classical republican ideas of duty, civic virtue, and the public
good are Gordon Wood, *The Creation of the American Republic, 1776–1787* (New York: Norton,
1969); and Bernard Bailyn, *The Ideological Origins of the American Revolution* (Cambridge, MA:
Belknap, 1967). The American Revolution and Founding are now generally acknowledged to
have been products of multiple intellectual traditions, including Lockean liberalism, classical

Even before the Constitutional Convention of 1787, many complained of the factional and conspiratorial dangers of the Society of the Cincinnati, a hereditary association of Revolutionary War officers established in May of 1783 by Major-General Henry Knox, and later presided over by George Washington and Alexander Hamilton. While its nominal goals were the advancement of the cause of union and the charitable support of former army officers and their families, it was widely perceived as an elite conspiracy intended to pervert the new republic in the interest of its own members.[35] Some, like Benjamin Franklin and Thomas Jefferson, objected most keenly to the Society's aristocratic overtones, while others like South Carolina's Aedanus Burke specifically protested the voluntary or "self-created" character of the free association, sure evidence of its "fiery, hot ambition, and thrill for power" that could only end up as a "source of *civil dissension and misery.*"[36] According to Madison's notes from the Constitutional Convention, Elbridge Gerry of Massachusetts feared that "the power of some one set of men dispersed through the Union & acting in Concert" might delude the masses during popular elections. "Such a Society of men," Gerry complained, already "existed in the Order of the Cincinnati. They are respectable, United, and influential. They will in fact elect the chief Magistrate in every instance, if the election be referred to the people."[37]

This prejudice against groups as factional and conspiratorial, destined to unbalance the delicate Hobbesian equilibrium between liberty and authority, persists into debates surrounding the ratification of the American Constitution. The most famous attempt to balance this tension is James Madison's discussion of faction in *Federalist* No. 10, which sheds light on several aspects of the nature and limits of freedom of association. First, at least in this discussion, Madison is remarkably indifferent to the dimension of association with which we are most often concerned today: namely, the ends or purposes of association. He may be able to skirt this thorny matter of sorting out the various ends—whether of "good" or

---

republicanism, and Christianity. See especially James T. Kloppenberg, *The Virtues of Liberalism* (New York: Oxford University Press, 1998).

[35] These sentiments are expressed most succinctly by South Carolina's Supreme Court justice Aedanus Burke, *Considerations on the Society or Order of Cincinnati; Lately Instituted by the Major-Generals, Brigadier-Generals, and Other Officers of the American Army, Proving That It Creates a Race of Hereditary Patricians or Nobility* (Philadelphia, PA: Robert Bell, 1783). For an excellent treatment of these attitudes, see Markus Hünemörder, *The Society of the Cincinnati: Conspiracy and Distrust in Early America* (New York: Berghahn Books, 2006).

[36] Benjamin Franklin, "Letter to Sarah Bache," January 26, 1784, in *The Works of Benjamin Franklin*, ed. Albert Henry Smyth (New York: MacMillan, 1905–1907), vol. 9, 161–66; Thomas Jefferson, "Letter to George Washington," April 16, 1784, in Jefferson, *Writings*, ed. Merrill D. Peterson (New York: Library of America, 1984), 790–93; Jefferson, "Answers and Observations for Démeunier's Article on the United States in the *Encyclopédie Méthodique* (1786)," in Jefferson, *Writings*, 582–88; Burke, *Considerations on the Society or Order of Cincinnati*, 3–5.

[37] As recorded in James Madison, "Journal of the Constitutional Convention," July 25, 1787, in *The Writings of James Madison*, ed. Gaillard Hunt (New York: Putnam, 1903), vol. IV, 66–67.

"bad," "civil" or "uncivil" groups—because his working definition already presupposes that the ends of factions are contrary to the common good: "By a faction I understand a number of citizens, whether amounting to a majority or minority of the whole, who are united and actuated by some common impulse of passion, or of interest, adverse to the rights of other citizens, or to the permanent and aggregate interests of the community." [38]

A capable student of David Hume, Madison is well aware that factions may be subdivided into those whose animating causes are based in principle ("a zeal for different opinions concerning religion, concerning government, and many other points, as well of speculation as of practice"), in affection ("an attachment to different leaders ambitiously contending for pre-eminence and power"), or in interest ("the most common and durable source of factions, has been the various and unequal distributions of property").[39] Nonetheless, after briefly cataloging these various *causes*, which captivated Hume in and of themselves, Madison focuses almost exclusively on the *effects* of faction. Whether factions have their roots in the religious sects of a particular part of the country, the ambitions of local demagogues, or the more fundamental but less intractable conflicts between propertied and propertyless becomes secondary to the question of the remedies best calculated to alleviate their most pernicious effects.

Madison is less concerned than we might expect with the relative intensity of group commitments. While distinguishing between commitments founded in "passion" and those arising from "interest," and indicating a general preference for the latter over the former, the question of the degree of commitment of association gets transformed into a matter of numbers and of scale, that is, majority faction versus minority faction. It is simply given that "factious leaders may kindle a flame within their particular states" and that religious sects "may degenerate into a political faction in parts of the confederacy." Using a metaphor of the body politic and its susceptibility to disease (in the style of Thomas Hobbes), Madison reasons that just as "such a malady is more likely to taint a particular county or district, than an entire state" so too any "improper or wicked project, will be less apt to pervade the whole body of the union, than a particular member of it." [40]

---

[38] James Madison, *Federalist* No. 10, in James Madison, Alexander Hamilton, and John Jay, *The Federalist Papers*, ed. Isaac Kramnick (New York: Penguin, 1987), 123.

[39] Madison, *Federalist* No. 10, 124. There is a long tradition emphasizing the influence of David Hume, in particular, and the Scottish Enlightenment, in general, on the political thought of James Madison. Perhaps the single most influential treatment is Douglass Adair, "That Politics May Be Reduced to a Science: David Hume, James Madison, and the Tenth *Federalist*," in *Fame and the Founding Fathers: Essays by Douglass Adair*, ed. Trevor Colburn (Indianapolis, IN: Liberty Press, 1998). See also Edmund S. Morgan, "Safety in Numbers: Madison, Hume, and the Tenth *Federalist*," *Huntington Library Quarterly* 49 (1986): 95–112; and Mark G. Spencer, "Hume and Madison on Faction," *William and Mary Quarterly* 59 (2002): 869–96.

[40] Madison, *Federalist* No. 10, 128.

In one sense, then, these small, localized groups are likely to be more intensely committed (and thus dangerous) than large groups whose very scale and abstraction dispels the emotional attachments of their members. However, in another light, their intimacy and intensity limits their dangers to the nation as a whole, as a "greater variety of parties," "dispersed over the entire face" of the union, provides security against the dominance of any single overbearing majority faction. Not only does the "encreased variety of parties" that one finds on a national scale function to check the influence of any single one of them, but the vast scale of national politics frustrates the intimate "concert" and conspiracy of "secret wishes" that make parties dangerous.[41] The scale of an extended republic prevents local flare-ups from turning into a "general conflagration."[42] The institutional safeguards set in place by the new Constitution—the extended republic, representation, and federalism—all make this contagion less likely to spread throughout a vast extended republic like the United States. Local majorities are transformed into national minorities, who must then recombine or associate themselves with other minority groups in order to achieve their goals. Because these new compound, national majorities will inevitably be the product of compromise, deliberation, and aggregation, they will tend to lack the uncompromising intensity of local majorities.

Like Hobbes and Hume before him, Madison acknowledges the sociological effects of group affiliations on individual citizens. This social psychology of group conflict runs consistently throughout Madison's remarks on faction—before, during, and after the Constitutional Convention—coming to fruition in his celebrated *Federalist* No. 10. Not only is rectitude "as little regarded by bodies of men as by individuals," but "respect for character is always diminished in proportion to the number among whom the blame or praise is to be divided." If the moral conscience is often "inadequate in individuals," even less is to be expected from it among groups.[43] Moral and religious inhibitions on the "injustice and violence of individuals," already uncertain, "lose their efficacy in proportion to the number combined together."[44] Even individuals acting on the most pious oaths have been known to "join without remorse in acts, against which their consciences would revolt if proposed to them under the like sanction, separately in their closets."[45] Far from moderating the evil tendencies of collective action, religious enthusiasm only exacerbates those tendencies, as "its force like that of other passions, is increased by the sympathy of a

[41] Ibid.
[42] Ibid.
[43] James Madison, Speech of Wednesday, June 6, 1787, "Journal of the Constitutional Convention," in *The Writings of James Madison*, ed. Gaillard Hunt (New York: Putnam, 1902), vol. III, 104.
[44] Madison, *Federalist* No. 10, 126.
[45] James Madison, "Vices of the Political System of the United States," April 1787, in *The Writings of James Madison*, ed. Gaillard Hunt (New York: Putnam, 1901), vol. II, 367.

multitude."[46] Although it has proven difficult to establish any direct intellectual influence, Madison's sociological assumptions about the special dangers of group conflict are highly reminiscent of the writings of Thomas Hobbes surveyed above.[47]

Federalist No. 10 also tells us something provisional about the derivative or second-order status of freedom of association. Madison famously notes that "liberty is to faction what air is to fire, an aliment without which it instantly expires." Nonetheless, Madison cautions, "it could not be a less folly to abolish liberty, which is essential to political life, because it nourishes faction than it would be to wish the annihilation of air, which is essential to animal life, because it imparts to fire its destructive agency."[48] Faction may be one of the most dangerous diseases of government, but it must be tolerated because of the intrinsic value of "liberty," broadly understood. Freedom of association, as we will see, comes to be framed again and again less as a desideratum in and of itself than as a vexing offshoot whose existence is mainly justifiable as a subset or cognate of other more central and enumerable liberties.

Indeed, the roots of faction reach deep into human nature, according to Madison. Diversity of opinion stems from diversity of interests. This will always be the case because of the "diversity in the faculties of men, from which the rights of property originate" and whose "protection" ranks as the very "first object of government."[49] Something as innocuous as the "possession of different degrees and kinds of property" leads to "a division of the society into different interests and parties."[50] Unless one is willing to go so far as to redistribute property, Madison reasons, one must suffer the effects of faction and partisanship.

These "latent causes of faction" may be "sown in the nature of man," but their "degrees of activity" and the forms in which they express themselves depend on the "different circumstances of civil society."[51] Circumstances as different as the rivalries between charismatic leaders, a "zeal for different opinions concerning religion," or even the most "frivolous and fanciful distinctions" have all, at different moments,

---

[46] Ibid.

[47] Although commentators have gestured toward Hobbesian sensibilities at work in *The Federalist*, any direct connection to Madison or others of the Founding generation has proven difficult to establish, perhaps because of Hobbes's political and religious disreputability. On Hobbes's relative lack of influence (at least as measured by citations) on the Founding generation, see Donald Lutz, "The Relative Influence of European Writers on Late Eighteenth Century American Political Thought," *American Political Science Review* 78 (March 1984): 189–97. Attempts to explore these linkages include James R. Stoner, Jr., *Common Law and Liberal Theory: Coke, Hobbes, and the Origins of American Constitutionalism* (Lawrence: University Press of Kansas, 1994); and Frank M. Coleman, *Hobbes and America: Exploring the Constitutional Foundations* (Toronto: University of Toronto Press, 1978).

[48] Madison, *Federalist* No. 10, 123.

[49] Ibid., 124.

[50] Ibid.

[51] Ibid.

"divided mankind into parties, inflamed them with mutual animosity, and rendered them much more disposed to vex and oppress each other than to co-operate for their common good."[52] Nonetheless, of all these circumstances, "the most common and durable source of factions has been the various and unequal distribution of property."[53] More than almost anything else, then, a commitment to the sanctity of the right to private property both condones the freedom of association and dictates the need to find some way to control its most obnoxious effects.

Madison seems in *The Federalist* to take it for granted that the existence of faction is simply the price one has to pay for a society that sanctifies natural inequalities of property, but in his 1792 essay "Parties," he acknowledges the possibility of changing (or at least moderating) distributional conflicts. That is, while government needs to protect property rights, it need not accept vast extremes of wealth and poverty as a given. These conflicts could be minimized by guaranteeing political equality to all persons and groups, and, conversely, avoiding all invidious distinctions that arise when public measures "operate differently on different interests."[54] More radically, Madison alludes to the "silent operation of laws, which, without violating the rights of property, reduce extreme wealth towards a state of mediocrity, and raise extreme indigence towards a state of comfort."[55] Although he does not specify here what such laws might consist of, his later writings are more explicit about the salutary effects of laws of inheritance such as those enacted in the state of Virginia that abolished primogeniture and entail, encouraging the free exchange of small tracts of property and facilitating social mobility.[56] Thus, despite Madison's demurrer in *The Federalist*, the subtle legislator *can* act to mitigate the causes of faction, and not just its effects.

Madison's discussion of the problems of majority faction appeals to institutional solutions. Or, to put this differently, freedom of association can exist because its most egregious effects are controlled by political institutions (the Constitution's extended republic, representation, and federalism). However, as Madison notes in 1792, the rise of political parties in the United States creates a new dilemma. Whereas the logic of the extended republic was to convert local majorities into national minorities, the logic of the two-party system operates in precisely the opposite direction. The basic structure of society means that parties are "unavoidable" because of a "difference of interests, real or supposed." These opposing

---

[52] Ibid.

[53] Ibid.

[54] James Madison, "Parties," *National Gazette*, January 23, 1792, in *Madison: Writings*, ed. Jack Rakove (New York: Library of America, 1999), 504.

[55] Ibid.

[56] Elizabeth Fleet, "James Madison's 'Detached Memoranda,'" *William and Mary Quarterly* 3 (October 1946): 552.

interests and parties are rooted in the very "nature of things," by which Madison presumably means the permanent and naturally opposed interests of rich and poor. Above and beyond crafting political institutions that render these parties "checks and balances to each other," such as those constitutional mechanisms outlined and defended in *Federalist* No. 10, the dangers of political parties may require ongoing management that is as much social as political.[57]

This is a consistent lament throughout Madison's contributions to the Constitutional Convention and his subsequent struggles, as a member of Congress and later as president, against the dominance of the Federalist Party. "All civilized Societies," Madison worries during the Constitutional Convention, are "divided into different Sects, Factions, & interests, as they happened to consist of rich & poor, debtors & creditors, the landed, the manufacturing, the commercial interests, the inhabitants of this district or that district, the followers of this political leader or that political leader—the disciples of this religious Sect or that religious Sect."[58] However, the situation of parties in the early republic provides a basis for his concerns that the institutional design of the extended republic may have been inadequate to stem the influence of majority faction, in particular the designs of the wealthy to oppress the poor.

As described in a later 1792 essay of Madison's titled "A Candid State of Parties in the United States," the short history of the American regime may be subdivided into three distinct eras of partisanship. In the pre-Revolutionary era, there were divisions between those who sought the independence of the Colonies and Loyalists who resisted the break from the British Empire. In the immediate post-Revolutionary era, there were divisions between Federalist defenders of the Constitution and its Antifederalist critics. After the successful ratification of the Constitution, the American regime saw the rise of two much more natural and permanent sources of partisanship in the antagonism between the Federalist Party, rooted in the interests of the wealthy and privileged classes, and Jefferson's Democratic-Republicans, seeking to represent the republican interests of the many.[59]

Ironically, despite everything Madison argues about the dangers of majority faction in *The Federalist*, the main problem with the American party system is not that those republican citizens who constitute a natural majority throughout the entire society will impose their interests on the wealthy minority. The real threat is that the "antirepublican (or Federalist) party, as it may be called, being the weaker in point of numbers," will seek to strengthen itself with "men of influence" who are always "the

---

[57] Madison, "Parties," 504–5.

[58] Madison, Speech of Wednesday, June 6, 1787, "Journal of the Constitutional Convention," 103.

[59] James Madison, "A Candid State of Parties," *National Gazette*, September 26, 1792, in Rakove, ed., *Madison: Writings*, 530–31.

most active and insinuating."[60] Being a natural minority in society, this moneyed interest will seek to exploit differences among those who have a common love of republican opinions by "reviving exploded parties, and taking advantage of all the prejudices, local, political, and occupational, that may prevent or disturb a general coalition of sentiments."[61]

Although the ultimate sources of faction flow out of government's responsibility to secure the rights of private property, freedom of association is also mutually intertwined with the freedoms of speech, religious conscience, and press. If it is admitted that the government has the power to encroach upon any one liberty, Madison repeatedly enjoins, then the next logical step is tyranny. By its very nature, liberty—whether of speech, press, or conscience—must be absolute. In this respect, even if the freedom of association is more liable to abuses than other rights—as Madison himself sometimes seems to believe—it would nonetheless be a dangerous precedent to limit it. Madison emphatically rejects the Hobbesian line of reasoning by which any freedom that might conceivably threaten the peace and security of the regime can be taken away. In particular, as we will see below, to allow the federal government to censor the publications of some more extreme Revolutionary associations would set a dangerous precedent that any otherwise legal association could be singled out for repression: "To consider a principle, we must try its nature, and see how far it will go; in the present case ... the effects of the principle contended for, would be pernicious."[62]

V. Madison's Defense of Freedom of Association

We have seen that Madison's empirical assumptions about the dangerous and destabilizing nature of freedom of association are not so different from those of classical liberals like Hobbes, Hume, and others who were ambivalent about groups. In light of Madison's lifelong preoccupation with the perils of party and faction, one might be surprised by the zeal with which he defended the rights of allegedly seditious and divisive groups. Unlike John Locke, who downplayed the dangers posed by religious or political groups, Madison bites the bullet and defends associational freedom *despite* the fact that he regarded groups and factions as a perpetual danger to the constitutional order. Most famous, of course, is Madison's opposition to the Alien and Sedition Acts of 1798. Less well-known, however, and leading up to this stand-off with John Adams and the Federalist Party is Madison's support in 1794 for what he terms the "self-created societies" of the Democratic-Republican Party which had

---

[60] Ibid., 531.
[61] Ibid., 532.
[62] James Madison, "Speech in Congress on 'Self-Created Societies,'" February 27, 1794, in Rakove, ed., *Madison: Writings*, 552.

come out publicly in favor of the republican principles of the French Revolution and which President Washington had accused of fomenting the Whiskey Rebellion.[63]

This case of the "self-created societies" gets right to the heart of some crucial distinctions at stake in free association. The first is the preeminence of the criterion of the rule of law. So long as nothing that the Revolutionary societies had done was illegal, Madison vehemently opposes Federalist efforts to silence or censure them. "The law," Madison notes, "is the only rule of right: what is consistent with that is not punishable; what is not contrary to that, is innocent, or at least not censurable by the legislative body."[64] At least initially, the question is not framed in terms of whether there exists an inalienable freedom of association—analogous to the constitutional freedoms of speech and assembly enumerated in the Bill of Rights—that will be violated by the actions of the government. The matter is rather that the Constitution gives the legislature no more authority to censure the publications of otherwise legal private societies than it grants Congress to deal with undeniable crimes like murder or arson.[65] Any particular act of censure along these lines is the equivalent of a bill of attainder—specifically prohibited in the Constitution.

Reflecting on the issue privately in a letter to Thomas Jefferson, however, Madison frames the issue squarely within the idiom of inalienable rights: "The attack made on the essential & constitutional right of the Citizen in the blow levelled at the 'self-created Societies,' does not appear to have had the effect intended. It is and must be felt by every man who values liberty whatever opinions he may have of the use or abuse of it by those institutions."[66] Freedom of association is just like any other right in the sense that "[animadversions] on the abuse of reserved rights" such as the freedom of association may be taken to "extend to the liberty of speech and of the press."[67] As Jefferson wryly observes in his response to Madison, there is a supreme irony in the Federalist

---

[63] Branded by their Federalist critics as offshoots of French Jacobinism, these Revolutionary societies and their "Committees of Correspondence" arose in the early 1790s as an indigenous response—both elite and popular—to the pro-British economic and foreign policy of the Federalist administrations. After Washington denounced them publicly in his speech of November 19, 1794, Congress debated a motion to censure them, which was eventually defeated in the House of Representatives. Cf. *The Writings of George Washington*, ed. John C. Fitzpatrick (Washington, DC: Government Printing Office, 1940), vol. 33, 474–79, 505–9, 522–24; vol. 34, 17–19, 28–37. For a history of this controversy, see especially Stanley Elkins and Eric McKitrick, *The Age of Federalism* (New York: Oxford University Press, 1993); Philip S. Foner, ed., *The Democratic-Republican Societies, 1790–1800: A Documentary Sourcebook* (Westport, CT: Greenwood Press, 1976); Eugene Link, *Democratic-Republican Societies, 1790–1800* (New York: Columbia University Press, 1942); and Thomas P. Slaughter, *The Whiskey Rebellion: Frontier Epilogue to the American Revolution* (New York: Oxford University Press, 1986).

[64] Madison, "Self-Created Societies," 552.

[65] Ibid.

[66] James Madison, "Letter to Thomas Jefferson," December 21, 1794, in *The Writings of James Madison*, ed. Gaillard Hunt (New York: Putnam, 1906), vol. VI, 228.

[67] Madison, "Self-Created Societies," 551.

attempts to censure the publications of these "democratical societies, whose avowed object is the nourishment of the republican principles of our constitution," when the Federalists themselves are "the fathers, founders, & high officers" of "the society of the Cincinnati, a *self-created* one, carving out for itself hereditary distinctions, lowering over our Constitution eternally, meeting together in all parts of the Union, periodically, with closed doors, accumulating a capital in their separate treasury, corresponding secretly & regularly." [68]

Another principle that emerges from Madison's writings is the legal commensurability between the actions of individuals and groups. Whether an enterprise is undertaken by "self-created societies" or by solitary individuals makes no difference, according to Madison. Regardless of whether the censure of such an enterprise "falls on classes or individuals it will be a severe punishment." [69] Just as the fact of association affords no additional protections to the illegal actions of individuals, neither should the fact that otherwise legal actions are undertaken collectively subject them to any stricter scrutiny.

These same considerations inform Madison's better-known opposition to the Alien and Sedition Acts. Collectively, these four acts passed in 1798 by John Adams and his Federalist allies tightened standards for the naturalization of citizens, gave the president absolute power to deport aliens accused of seditious behavior or citizens of countries at war with the United States, and prohibited American citizens from criticizing acts of the president or Congress.[70] Like the earlier Federalist attack on the "self-created societies" in 1794, these laws were ostensibly passed to stave off the threat of domestic insurrection allegedly being fomented by the French, against whom Adams was expecting an imminent war. In practice, however, the laws targeted Adams's Democratic-Republican critics in the press, who were branded "seditious" Jacobins and French sympathizers. In particular, the so-called Sedition Act ("An Act for the Punishment of Certain Crimes against the United States"), enacted July 14, 1798, provides a punishment for any persons, whether United States citizens or not, who *"shall unlawfully combine or conspire together,* with intent to oppose any measure or measures of the government of the United States . . . or to intimidate or prevent any person holding a place or office in or under the government of the United States, from undertaking, performing or executing his trust or duty." Likewise, it deems a "high misdemeanor" any

[68] Thomas Jefferson, "Letter to James Madison," December 28, 1794, in Jefferson, *Writings,* 1015.

[69] Madison, "Self-Created Societies," 552.

[70] For a comprehensive survey of the Alien and Sedition Acts and the political circumstances that gave rise to them, see John Chester Miller, *Crisis in Freedom: The Alien and Sedition Acts* (Boston: Little, Brown, 1951); James Morton Smith, *Freedom's Fetters: The Alien and Sedition Laws and American Civil Liberties* (Ithaca, NY: Cornell University Press, 1956); and John Ferling, *Adams vs. Jefferson: The Tumultuous Election of 1800* (New York: Oxford University Press, 2004).

effort to "counsel, advise, or attempt to procure *any insurrection, riot, unlawful assembly, or combination,* whether such conspiracy, threatening, counsel, advice, or attempt shall have the proposed effect or not."[71]

Madison's draft of the Virginia Resolutions opposing these acts centers on two major claims. First, there is the familiar Madisonian idea that these laws usurp a "power no where delegated to the federal government" in the Constitution, one which would effectively blur the distinction between legislative, judicial, and executive powers.[72] In the case of the Alien Enemies Act, the notion that an individual or group might be judged by the president alone to be "dangerous to the public safety" or merely "suspected of secret machinations" and deported without legal proceedings represents a dangerous blurring of powers, for Madison. "They leave everything to the President. His will is the law."[73]

The second complaint in the case of the Sedition Act is that this law violates First Amendment freedoms (particularly those of speech and press) guaranteed in the Bill of Rights. It is this right of "freely examining public characters and measures, and of free communication among the people thereon, which has ever been justly deemed, the only effectual guardian of every other right."[74] While Madison acknowledges in the case of the Sedition Act that Congress undoubtedly has the power to suppress insurrections, "it would not be allowed to follow, that they might employ all the means tending to prevent them."[75] A legitimate constitutional "power to act on a case when it occurs" does not imply a correlative "power over all the means that may *tend to prevent* the occurrence of the case."[76]

Interestingly, although the problem of association is explicitly mentioned in the Alien and Sedition Acts themselves, Madison says little about the associational dimension of the question. The allegedly usurped rights are of those of speech, communication, and the press—albeit taking place *among citizens,* whether formally associated or not. Even so, Madison's comments defending the Virginia Resolutions reveal that the freedom of the press may have an easily overlooked associational dimension. Given the impracticality of citizens actually gathering together to debate public policy or to examine the characters of their representatives, freedom of the press provides an important surrogate to formal association. The duration, scale, power, and magnitude of the new federal government demands some effective "channel" for "circulating an adequate knowledge" of public characters and measures.[77] Free communication is

[71] Sedition Act, Fifth Congress, Session II, July 14, 1798.
[72] James Madison, "Virginia Resolutions Against the Alien and Sedition Acts," December 21, 1798, in Rakove, ed., *Madison: Writings,* 590.
[73] James Madison, "Report on the Alien and Sedition Acts," January 7, 1800, in Rakove, ed., *Madison: Writings,* 630.
[74] Madison, "Virginia Resolutions," 590.
[75] Madison, "Report on the Alien and Sedition Acts," 627.
[76] Ibid.
[77] Ibid., 651.

not in itself incendiary and seditious, Madison argues; it is the *repression* of free "information and communication among the people" that is most likely to "prepare a convulsion that might prove equally fatal" to the new republic.[78] Free speech and communication, then, not only operate as functional surrogates to association but also, perhaps, ameliorate some of the most destructive tendencies of faction. The implication seems to be that people must resort to association only in the absence of communication. As was the case for the Scottish philosophers who inspired Madison's political theory, publicity and the public sphere become functional equivalents of direct political action.[79]

Madison's criticism of the Alien and Sedition Acts focuses preponderantly on their abridgment of First Amendment freedom of the press, but he argues that to allow any freedom of the Bill of Rights to be abridged is to jeopardize all the other rights outlined therein. If the federal government is ceded a right to regulate or constrain—even without completely abridging—the freedom of the press, then what prevents Congress from claiming an analogous prerogative to "regulate and even abridge" the free exercise of religion, so long as Congress stops short of actually prohibiting it? Any "indifference . . . now shewn to a palpable violation of one of those rights, the freedom of the press; and to a precedent therein . . . may be fatal to the other, the freedom of religion."[80] By this logic, Madison justifies an absolutist reading of the First Amendment protections accorded to speech, press, conscience, and religion. Interestingly, however, he makes no analogous argument on behalf of the similarly enumerated right of free assembly. This may be because he did not regard any of the recent government actions as sufficiently threatening of freedoms of assembly and petition, although surely the Alien and Sedition Acts could reasonably be construed as abbreviating the right of individuals to assemble as well as to express

---

[78] Ibid., 653.

[79] In addition to the many scholarly contributions stressing the influence of David Hume's writings (cited in note 39 above), Madison was more broadly influenced by the Scottish Enlightenment through his tutor, Donald Robertson, and Princeton's John Witherspoon. See especially Roy Branson, "James Madison and the Scottish Enlightenment," *Journal of the History of Ideas* 40 (Spring 1979): 235–50; and Gary Wills, *Explaining America: The Federalist* (New York: Penguin, 1981). On the more general influence of the Scottish Enlightenment on the American Founding, see Gary Wills, *Inventing America: Jefferson's Declaration of Independence* (Garden City, NY: Doubleday, 1978). On the idea that politeness and sociability become surrogates for political activity in the Scottish Enlightenment, see Nicholas Phillipson, "Politics, Politeness, and the Anglicisation of Early Eighteenth-Century Scottish Culture," in Roger A. Mason, ed., *Scotland and England, 1286–1815* (Edinburgh: John Donald, 1987); Nicholas Phillipson, "Scottish Public Opinion and the Union in the Age of Association," in Nicholas Phillipson and Rosalind Mitchison, eds., *Scotland in the Age of Improvement* (Edinburgh: Edinburgh University Press, 1970); and John Robertson, "The Scottish Enlightenment at the Limits of the Civic Tradition," in Istvan Hont and Michael Ignatieff, eds., *Wealth and Virtue: The Shaping of Political Economy in the Scottish Enlightenment* (Cambridge: Cambridge University Press, 1986).

[80] Madison, "Report on the Alien and Sedition Acts," 657.

their frustrations with their representatives and their policies. Or perhaps Madison's curious silence on this associational dimension of the
question was in deference to the intrinsically self-limiting character of
the "right of the people *peaceably* to assemble."[81] Here the text of the
Bill of Rights is of no immediate help to Madison's argument, as it
seems (uniquely in the case of freedom of assembly?) to introduce qualifications and correlative duties of civility for instances of organized
political dissent.

VI. Freedom of Association and Freedom of Religion

Madison's ambivalence toward groups and the freedom of association that sustains them is not limited to the kinds of political groups
we ordinarily think of as factions. As Madison noted late in his life in
his "Detached Memoranda" (ca. 1819), the power of monopolies, local
corporations, ecclesiastical establishments, charitable foundations, and
other kinds of associations may pose a challenge to the well-being of
the nation and the rights of other groups. "The ordinary limitation on
incorporated Societies is a proviso that their laws shall not violate the
laws of the land," Madison observes, in keeping with his earlier criterion of the legal commensurability between individuals and groups.
However, certain kinds of corporations and voluntary associations may
take actions or accumulate large amounts of property in defiance of the
public good even if their actions are "not in strict construction violating any law of the land."[82] While he has in mind here the powers of
chartered banks or other corporations whose interests may be at odds
with those of the community as a whole, he is also concerned about
"Ecclesiastic Bodies," whose "silent accumulations & encroachments"
have gone unnoticed and unchecked.[83] These "encroachments" may
consist of attempts by religious groups to intertwine themselves with
the state, as we will see below, but the less obvious "evil which ought
to be guarded [against]" is their "indefinite accumulation of property
from the capacity of holding it in perpetuity." Indeed, Madison notes,
the "power of all corporations, ought to be limited in this respect."
Even some of the greatest "Charitable establishments" of Great Britain
pose a threat in this regard.[84]

Despite all of these worries, however, not only is Madison a strong
defender of the freedom of religious association but his defense of religious liberty is closely allied to his respect for the associational capacities
of ordinary citizens. Responding to Patrick Henry's proposed bill to lay a

---

[81] United States Constitution, First Amendment.
[82] Madison, "Detached Memoranda," 552–53.
[83] Ibid., 554.
[84] Ibid., 556–57.

religious assessment for the support of the Episcopal Church and its ministers on all the citizens of Virginia, Madison's 1785 "Memorial and Remonstrance Against Religious Assessments" lends credence to the view that Madison saw the segregation of religion from politics as the arrangement most conducive to both individual liberty and public order.[85] In Madison's (Lockean) view, it is the admixture of religion and politics that has resulted in the "Torrents of blood" spilt in Europe by "vain attempts of the secular arm, to extinguish Religious discord, by proscribing all differences in Religious opinion."[86] By contrast, allowing religious sects to form and dissolve freely within civil society according to the dictates of individual conscience has yielded "moderation and harmony" among the several sects.[87]

A number of key principles are at work here. The first is the notion of a freedom of association in religious matters based on a natural right more "fundamental" and "inalienable" than any other. Madison appeals to that "primitive State in which [Christianity's] Teachers depended on the voluntary rewards of their flocks," and individual believers were free to affiliate and disaffiliate at will.[88] However, religion is not simply one more mode of human association among many. Religion is a species of association more primeval even than our organization into "civil society" or government. Its obligations are "precedent, both in order of time and in degree of obligation, to the claims of Civil Society":

> Before any man can be considered as a member of Civil Society, he must be considered as a subject of the Governour of the Universe: And if a member of Civil Society, who enters into any subordinate Association, must always do it with a reservation of his duty to the General Authority; much more must every man who becomes a member of any particular Civil Society, do it with a saving of his allegiance to the Universal Sovereign.[89]

The argument here is frustratingly circular, one of Madison's rare admissions of the limits of free association. He takes it as a given that an individual entering into "any subordinate Association" must always concede that this engagement is subject to a more primary, reserved

---

[85] James Madison, "Memorial and Remonstrance Against Religious Assessments," June 20, 1785, in Rakove, ed., *Madison: Writings*. Madison's argument for separating church and state in this oft-cited text was sparked by Patrick Henry's proposed "Bill Establishing a Provision for Teachers of the Christian Religion" (1784–1785) in the General Assembly of Virginia, which would have levied a general assessment to support the promulgation of Christianity. Madison spearheaded efforts to defeat Henry's bill in 1785, paving the way for passage of Thomas Jefferson's "Act for Establishing Religious Freedom" in January 1786.

[86] Madison, "Memorial and Remonstrance Against Religious Assessments," 34.

[87] Ibid.

[88] Ibid., 33.

[89] Ibid., 30.

"duty to the General Authority." Analogously, our engagement in any particular civil society is always contingent on antecedent religious duties to our creator. Therefore, the laws of civil society can never trump or supersede our more primary religious engagements. The problem is that Madison's opening premise already concedes that our engagement in "*any* subordinate Association" (with the sole exception of a church?) is duly conditioned by a more primary duty to the "General Authority" of "Civil Society." Perhaps this is Madison's way of escaping the seemingly open-ended defense he offers of arguably destructive factions, parties, Revolutionary societies, etc. First, if and when these organizations *actually are* seditious—committing a criminal or treasonous act—their members fall under the civil jurisdiction. Presumably even religious sects would fall under this umbrella in their civil actions. Secondly, the assumption that any association is, in theory, subject to the "General Authority" of society does not imply that society should ever call in that reserved duty, especially in cases when the society may judge wrongly. "True it is," Madison concedes, "that no other rule exists, by which any question which may divide a Society, can be ultimately determined, but the will of the majority; but it is also true that the majority may trespass on the rights of the minority."[90] So while Madison inches away from the principle that something like an absolute and inalienable freedom of association exists, he nonetheless argues in practice that even the most minute abridgment of the freedom of association—or any other right—is a harbinger of tyrannies to come: "The Rulers who are guilty of such an encroachment, exceed the commission from which they derive their authority, and are Tyrants."[91]

The second key principle in Madison's discussion of religious assessments is the idea of equality in the eyes of the law. The proposal for a religious assessment "degrades from the equal rank of Citizens all those whose opinions in Religion do not bend to those of the Legislative authority."[92] Just as important as the task of protecting individual liberties, the "principle of equality . . . ought to be the basis of every law." According to Madison, then, the proposed bill is faulty in two respects: just as the bill "violates equality by subjecting some to peculiar burdens, so it violates the same principle, by granting to others peculiar exemptions. Are the Quakers and Menonists the only sects who think a compulsive support of their Religions unnecessary and unwarrantable?"[93]

At the margins, Madison's solicitude for absolute freedom of conscience runs up against the governing ideal of equal treatment in the eyes of the law. While Madison argued in his 1785 "Memorial and Remonstrance" that justice precluded laws imposing "peculiar bur-

[90] Ibid.
[91] Ibid., 30–31.
[92] Ibid., 33.
[93] Ibid., 31–32.

dens" on certain religious sects, he also rejected there the notion that any religious group ought to be granted "peculiar exemptions."[94] In the case of a 1790 bill in the U.S. Congress, however, Madison defends exemptions from military service for Quakers whose religion requires the duty of conscientious objection. Here, though, Madison stops short of offering a truly principled defense of the idea that one group deserves special treatment ("Compulsion being out of the question, we must, therefore, from necessity, exempt them"), arguing instead that Congress should "make a virtue of this necessity, and grant the exemption."[95]

Madison's discussion of religious association parallels his assumptions about parties and factions. First, there is the notion that conflict and oppression occur only when one group is in the position to impose its power on other minority groups. In the case of faction, we have seen, not only is no artificial support to be given to strengthening parties but the extension of the orbit of national politics is designed to remove the power that democratic institutions necessarily give to majorities over minorities. In the case of religion, however, the very nature of religious disagreement and plurality deprives even the largest religious sects of that power. Little more than denying secular support to religion is needed to guarantee that religions can peacefully coexist. This is easily accomplished "by neither invading the equal rights of any sect, nor suffering any sect to invade those of another."[96] Absent the political power to coerce religious affiliation, religions will freely and peacefully coexist.

VII. The Nature and Constitutional Limits
of the Freedom of Association

Although it is true that the United States Constitution makes no explicit *provision* of a constitutional right of free association, as noted above, neither did the American Founders ever go so far as to contemplate, as did the French Revolutionaries, the *prohibition* of the right of voluntary association.[97] However, the question remains why freedom of association lurks so uneasily in the background of other enumerated rights. As I have suggested, following Madison, there is the possibility that freedom of association was neglected because of its congruence with freedom of assembly, petition, speech, and conscience. Its existence was simply assumed to follow from or underlie the existence of those enumerated rights. A second and slightly different explanation might be that although the freedom of association is conceptually distinguishable from these other enumerated rights, it was considered either less central or less

[94] Ibid.
[95] James Madison, "Speech in Congress on Religious Exemptions from Militia Duty," December 20, 1790, in Rakove, ed., *Madison: Writings*, 479–80.
[96] Madison, "Memorial and Remonstrance Against Religious Assessments," 33.
[97] Hsiao, *Political Pluralism*, 263.

vulnerable and thus remained among those unenumerated rights whose existence was gestured to by the Ninth Amendment. Madison hints at this possibility in his correspondence with Thomas Jefferson on the case of self-created societies. Or, to frame the point in the reverse fashion, as Madison often did, the fact that the Constitution provided no power for Congress or the Executive to regulate or circumscribe the free association of individuals is much the same thing as saying that such a right is reserved to the people. Freedom of association exists, as Hobbes would say, not so much by nature as within the "silence of the law." Thirdly, and quite distinctly, the lack of any specific constitutional provision of a right of association could very well be indicative, as Lon Fuller hints, of a kind of elemental suspicion of this right. Members of the Founding generation— perhaps even James Madison—were uncomfortable suggesting that freedom of association enjoyed any kind of fundamental or basic constitutional sanction. To allow this would be inherently destabilizing. We have seen hints of this ambivalence even in the writings of the civil libertarian Madison.

Whatever their motivations, the fact that the Founders seem to have been content to treat freedom of association as a second-order or derivative right leads to another closely related question. Namely, if there is nothing in the Constitution that is conceptually distinguishable as a freedom of association, then out of what enumerated right does the freedom of association most naturally and appropriately spring? At some moments, Madison describes freedom of association as closely linked with freedom of opinion. Common opinions, whether religious or political, motivate individuals to join a party or sect. However, one might consider whether our acceptance of a natural freedom of opinion or conscience necessarily entails a right to associate, as Madison suggests. One can grant the freedom of individuals to *believe* anything they like (as did thinkers as different as Hobbes and John Stuart Mill) without at the same time acknowledging a correlative right for them to act upon these beliefs or communicate them to others—let alone to come together and cultivate these ideas in common.

To take an extreme example, one enjoys a constitutionally protected right to believe whatever one wants about the United States government (for example, that it is illegitimate and ought to be overthrown), but under certain circumstances either the communication of these ideas to others or the conspiracy of a group of individuals intent on actually achieving them may be prohibited. Thus, the notion that individuals are entitled to hold certain opinions may not provide a reliable or persuasive defense of the freedom of those same individuals to associate with others in the collective pursuit of those ends. Because (to use John Stuart Mill's categories) freedom of association is a "social act," it is in principle subject to limitations that are illegitimate in the case of purely self-regarding conduct such as holding beliefs or ideas that, absent their communication to others, can have no effects, positive or negative, on other persons.[98] This distinction seems to be borne out by the constitutional provision in Article III, Section 3 about the gravity of the crime of treason. The specification that charges of treason must be corroborated by two witnesses who have firsthand knowledge of the conspiracy not only works to help secure the rights of the accused against false allegations; it also implicitly acknowledges the fact that treason must be an "overt act" which ordinarily entails collusion or conspiracy with others, including "enemies" of the United States.

Nonetheless, if one understands First Amendment rights of speech and expression to be more positive or substantive than merely the absence of restraint, then one can argue that freedom of association is a necessary condition for the actualization of those guaranteed rights. Can we really be said to enjoy freedom of speech or expression if we are forced to speak alone? The voices of lone individuals are easily drowned out in the din of public life, whereas the voices of organized associations are more often heard. As Stephen Holmes has argued in his discussion of "positive constitutionalism," freedom of speech or expression may require certain enabling conditions in order to be anything more than an empty formality, and the freedom of association may be an important element of these enabling conditions.[99]

In addition to First Amendment freedoms of speech and conscience, the correlative rights of petition and assembly seem to be even more transparently linked to the right of association. That is to say that in addition to religious freedom and the freedom of speech and expression, with which freedom of association has been most commonly linked in American constitutional law, it arguably makes more sense to think about the freedom of association as existing in the penumbra of the enumerated political rights of petition and assembly. The freedom to petition one's government, after all, is an inherently social or collective enterprise, even if the individuals involved are never physically gathered together in one place. The very act of petition constitutes a symbolic linkage of individuals with one another. Even so, the fact that the right of petition presupposes an act of association—and is itself a species of association—does not necessarily imply a more general right of association. Put more generally, the fact that individuals must be free to come together in order to avail themselves of a certain kind of constitutionally protected right that entails an act of association need not imply that a more generalized right of association holds for a wider variety of contexts or ends.

The same may be true for the right of assembly. While the First Amendment offers a general and abstract right to "peaceably assemble," this

---

[98] On this distinction between purely self-regarding and other-regarding actions, see Mill, "On Liberty," esp. 14, 16–17, 62, 88, 104–5.
[99] Holmes, *Passions and Constraint*, esp. chap. 6.

right is by its very nature circumstantially qualified. While few today would countenance the idea that a supposedly constitutional right to free speech could be subject to the side constraint that the speech in question must be peaceful or civil, the freedom of assembly seems to be a different matter altogether, containing within itself an inherent limitation or qualification. What constitutes a "peaceable" instance of assembly—something that can often be determined only in retrospect—leaves considerable latitude for discretion on the part of authorities or local police powers.

Most broadly, Madison's emphasis on the legality principle of freedom of association rests on two key assumptions about the primacy of the rule of law and the equivalency between the actions of individuals and those of groups. The negative or proscriptive version of Madison's thesis is that if the actions of an individual are illegal, then the collective pursuit of this same means or end ought to be illegal as well. The fact that prohibited activities are central to the mission of a group should provide no additional guarantees or protections. This doctrine seems, on the face of it, to run counter to contemporary legal doctrines of centrality and differential burdens, by which certain activities deemed absolutely central to a group's mission or identity ought to be accommodated on grounds that the very existence of a group would be compromised if they were compelled to submit themselves to the same conditions governing the actions of individuals or other groups. By way of contrast, Madison's strict emphasis on legality rests on the assumption that there are no relevant differences between the actions of individuals and those of groups—or, for that matter, among the central missions of different groups. While Madison did contemplate situations where certain religious groups might necessarily be absolved of responsibilities because of their core beliefs, these are the exceptions that validate the more general rule. By and large, the assumption is that the liberties of individuals and groups ought to be roughly coextensive with one another.

All this goes to suggest that groups should be allowed *at least as many*, if not more, rights than their composite individuals. However, allowing a small and distinct minority (say, the Amish) to do something that individuals or other groups are prohibited from doing (or, conversely, absolving them of the responsibility to do something that everyone else is compelled to do) may not be symmetrical with the notion that groups should always be permitted the same liberties as individuals. It is worth considering whether the positive version of the legality principle is really consistent with the negative version of the thesis considered above. That is, does the claim that groups ought to be bound by the same legal *constraints* that limit the actions of individuals necessarily imply that groups are entitled to all the same *liberties*? Just because individuals enjoy certain liberties may not mean that groups should expect the same latitude. It is here, on the flip-side of this principle of the legal commensurability between individuals and groups, that Madison's argument encounters problems.

Groups are nothing more than collectivities formed by like-minded individuals, Madison reasons, and if individuals are allowed certain rights, then it follows that those same rights ought to be afforded to groups. If individuals are allowed freedom of conscience, opinion, or property, for example, then groups must be guaranteed those same rights. The problem with this view is that, contrary to Madison's assumptions, the collective actions of groups may be qualitatively *different* from those of individuals, both in degree and in kind. This was substantially Hobbes's point. With respect to degree, for example, the freedom of assembly must be limited in light of the sociological and political reality that individuals assembled in large groups may be transformed into angry and violent mobs. Traditionally reserved police powers of localities may, under certain circumstances, (rightly) trump the constitutionally protected right of assembly—a right that is qualified already as "peaceable." Freedom of speech must be circumscribed at the margins by considerations of the context in which that speech takes place— especially the likely effects of the speech on other individuals and any harms that may result. Likewise, the right to private property and the economic liberties of individuals may differ from those accorded to corporations or other large-scale economic entities because of the disproportionate power commanded by the latter. These may be more than differences of scale or degree. The opinions, speech, and property of individuals have commonly been regarded as "private," whereas analogous actions by collectivities can be construed as "public" by virtue of their direct, causal effects on other individuals. Not just sociologically or morally, as Madison himself acknowledges, but also legally, something seems to change qualitatively when the wills of individuals are melded together into collectivities.

This is not to say that Madison was necessarily wrong in his conclusions about the rights of "self-created Societies" or other political and religious associations. There is little evidence that the newspaper articles or public declarations in support of the French Revolution and its republican ideals were incongruent with the U.S. Constitution or the American regime, or even that the threat of alien sedition was of the order of magnitude claimed by Adams and others among the pro-British Federalist Party. Even so, it is quite possible that Madison may have been right in practice, but wrong in principle. Madison's assumptions that groups are nothing more than the sum of their individual members—and that groups are therefore entitled to precisely the same (unqualified) rights as individuals—may be faulty if pushed to the extreme. It is this dimension of the peculiar, potentially destabilizing, and qualitatively unique nature of freedom of association that the classical liberal tradition brings so powerfully to our attention.

VIII. Conclusion

James Madison's writings are noteworthy in bringing together two different and mutually antagonistic strands of the classical liberal tradition. On the one hand, Madison draws upon a long tradition of political thought that was wary of the potentially disruptive, seditious, and oppressive dangers of groups. Numerous remarks about the problem of faction and the collective psychology of groups clearly reflect this anti-associational bias. On the other hand, however, Madison stands out against many others of the Founding generation in his unwillingness to abridge the freedom of association in response to those same fears. In this respect, he fully accepts the empirical and sociological premises of the anti-associational tradition without jumping to the same easy normative conclusion, as did George Washington, John Adams, and other Federalists, that freedom of association ought to be curtailed. Constitutional design, Madison confidently predicted, would resolve the worst excesses of faction, sectarianism, and social conflict.

For Madison, as we have seen, although freedom of association remains a derivative or second-order liberty, existing in the penumbra of other more central and enumerable liberal freedoms, it is nonetheless vital that it be protected precisely because of its intimate relationship to first-order liberties of speech, press, religion, and property. Even if Madison stops well short of subsequent thinkers such as Edmund Burke, Alexis de Tocqueville, and Michael Oakeshott, who made strong and affirmative cases for the benefits of the freedom of association and an abundant plurality of political, civil, and religious groups, Madison's writings nonetheless represent an important step in overcoming classical liberalism's anti-associational prejudices.[100]

Government, Georgetown University

---

[100] For a more detailed treatment of the birth of an "associational" liberalism, see Boyd, *Uncivil Society*, esp. chaps. 4, 6–8.

FROM THE SOCIAL CONTRACT TO THE ART OF ASSOCIATION: A TOCQUEVILLIAN PERSPECTIVE*

By Aurelian Craiutu

Civilization is, before all, the will to live in common. . . . Barbarism is the tendency to disassociation.[1]

—José Ortega y Gasset

I. The Return of Civil Society

Most contemporary democratic theorists agree that an orderly and viable democracy ultimately depends on the existence of a vibrant associational life consisting of a multiplicity of social networks, associations, and groups. Indeed, it would be difficult to imagine the daily functioning of modern democratic societies without the existence of civil associations such as charitable foundations, trade unions, churches, business groups, and other voluntary associations. All of these are credited with enhancing the quality of democracy by cultivating citizenship and promoting open fora for public deliberation and self-government.

A case in point is offered by the former communist countries in Central and Eastern Europe, where the demise of communism has demonstrated the key role that civil society and its associations play in restoring political freedom and individual rights. Many Central and Eastern European intellectuals have courageously fought for the reconstruction of civil society and have maintained that only the restoration of an independent space between the state and individuals can guarantee the successful transition to an open society.[2] In Poland, for example, the Solidarity movement challenged the legitimacy of the official regime by forcing the Communist Party to recognize the existence and the right of an independent political entity with no ties to the official hierarchy. In an essay written in 1982, the prominent writer and dissident Adam Michnik described the strategy followed by the nascent Polish civil society as follows: "These groups promoted social self-help and self-defense, organized independent intellectual activities, and worked outside censorship to fashion programs for the fight for freedom. The essence of the programs put forward by the

* I would like to thank Ellen Frankel Paul and Harry Dolan for their comments on a previous draft of this essay.

[1] José Ortega y Gasset, *The Revolt of the Masses* (New York: Norton, 1964), 76.

[2] Krishan Kumar, *1989: Revolutionary Ideas and Ideals* (Minneapolis: University of Minnesota Press, 2001), 142.

doi:10.1017/S0265052508080266

opposition groups . . . lay in the attempt to reconstruct society, to restore social bonds outside official institutions."[3] Along with the courageous political program of the Charter 77 movement in Czechoslovakia,[4] the "politics of anti-politics" and the theory of the "parallel polis"[5] proposed by Vaclav Havel and Vaclav Benda in the late 1970s articulated an original view of civil society as the realm of the "power of the powerless." This conception of civil society embraced an original strategy of individual liberation based on the imperative of "living in truth."[6] The significance of the Polish Solidarity movement and the theory of anti-politics as strategies for the self-defense of society soon became powerful symbols for the fight against oppressive regimes throughout Eastern Europe. The example of Havel, Michnik, Andrei Sakharov, Lech Walesa, and their colleagues not only encouraged various dissident groups in Eastern Europe to express openly their own social and political agendas; it also reminded the friends of freedom in the West of the importance of civil society as a locus of resistance and freedom.[7]

If everyone agrees today that the existence of a vibrant civil society is an essential prerequisite of democracy, this broad consensus on the virtues of civil society should not make us forget that only a century and a half ago, in *On the Jewish Question* (1843), Karl Marx gave voice to an alternative view of civil society as a realm of egoism, greed, and narrow self-interest that arguably thwarts democracy and increases the mutual antagonism between classes. The recent revival of interest in voluntary associations and civil society is a testament to this significant paradigm shift that has coincided with the demise of Marxism in the Western world. What is truly remarkable is the fact that the return of civil society has found advocates on both sides of the political spectrum. They have praised civil society and its intermediary institutions for being an indispensable buffer against undue state interference and have emphasized the seminal role of civil society as an effective means of building the "social capital"[8] essential for strengthening democratic values and citizenship.

---

[3] Adam Michnik, *Letters from Prison and Other Essays* (Berkeley: University of California Press, 1985), 28.

[4] The Charter 77 movement was a prominent informal civic initiative in Czechoslovakia, named after Charter 77, a human rights declaration published in January 1977. Among the movement's founding members and architects were Václav Havel, Jan Patočka, and Pavel Kohout.

[5] "The Parallel Polis" was the title of a famous essay published by Vaclav Benda, a prominent member of the Charter 77 movement and a colleague of Havel.

[6] See Vaclav Havel, *The Power of the Powerless: Citizens Against the State in Central-Eastern Europe* (New York: M. E. Sharpe, 1990).

[7] For more information, see Vladimir Tismaneanu, *Reinventing Politics: Eastern Europe from Stalin to Havel* (New York: The Free Press, 1992), 113–74; Kumar, *1989: Revolutionary Ideas and Ideals*, 142–70.

[8] The high relevance of the concept of "social capital" is illustrated by its numerous practical applications, especially for the economics of development. For more information, see the Social Capital Gateway, http://www.socialcapitalgateway.org/index.htm (accessed November 3, 2007).

The strong interest in the notion of social capital is worth pointing out in the context of recent debates on pluralism and civility. Writing from a Marxist perspective in the early 1980s, French sociologist Pierre Bourdieu contrasted this concept with other forms of capital—cultural, economic, and symbolic. Social capital, Bourdieu wrote, is "the aggregate of the actual or potential resources which are linked to possession of a durable network of more or less institutionalized relationships of mutual acquaintance and recognition."[9] More recently, in *Bowling Alone: The Collapse and Revival of American Community* (2000), Harvard political scientist Robert Putnam distinguished between bridging and bonding social capital. "Of all the dimensions along which forms of social capital vary," Putnam wrote, "perhaps the most important is the distinction between bridging (or inclusive) and bonding (or exclusive). Some forms of social capital are, by choice or necessity, inward looking and tend to reinforce exclusive identities."[10] As such, bridging social capital is more likely to have liberal effects than bonding capital, because the former encompasses not only a set of viable social networks but also a set of attitudes and mental dispositions that promote social cooperation and toleration.[11]

Beginning with Alexis de Tocqueville's *Democracy in America* (1835, 1840), it has been customary to regard the United States as unusually "civic" in comparison to other countries. Its high degree of civicness has traditionally been attributed to the high density of networks of civic and social engagement.[12] Nonetheless, a growing number of scholars, from Francis Fukuyama and Michael Sandel to Robert N. Bellah and Robert Putnam, have lately challenged the traditional optimism regarding the vibrancy of civil society in America and raised serious doubts about the long-term prospects for American democracy. The signs of civil decline and political apathy in the United States range from increasingly lower voter turnout to declining participation in town meetings, Parent-Teacher Associations (PTAs), trade unions, and bowling leagues. Although religious groups, charitable institutions, and churches continue to retain significant influence in contemporary American society, the traditional communities which made up American civil society in the mid-twentieth century, from families and neighborhoods to workplaces, have been under constant assault.[13] In a 1995 essay, Putnam interpreted diminished civic

---

[9] Pierre Bourdieu, "Forms of Capital," in *Handbook of Theory and Research for the Sociology of Education*, ed. J. C. Richards (New York: Greenwood Press, 1983), 249.

[10] Robert Putnam, *Bowling Alone: The Collapse and Revival of American Community* (New York: Simon and Schuster, 2000), 22.

[11] See ibid., 22–24, 178–79, 357–63.

[12] The relationship between social trust and effective civil and political institutions is a complex one that goes beyond the narrow scope of this essay. It can be argued that a large degree of trust is needed first in order to form civil networks and associations; at the same time, it is equally possible to claim that a vibrant associational life promotes and enhances civic trust.

[13] On this issue, see Francis Fukuyama, *Trust: The Social Virtues and the Creation of Prosperity* (New York: Free Press, 1995), 269–323; Robert N. Bellah et al., *Habits of the Heart:*

engagement and lower social connectedness in the U.S. as the outcome of a host of social, cultural, and technological factors that radically altered American community life during the late twentieth century. "By almost every measure," Putnam argued, "Americans' direct engagement in politics and government has fallen steadily and sharply over the last generation, despite the fact that average levels of education—the best individual-level predictor of political participation—have risen sharply throughout this period. Every year over the last decade or two, millions more have withdrawn from the affairs of their communities."[14] Putnam maintained that the fast pace of economic growth and the major technological changes in the past few decades have had a complex impact on civil society broadly construed—leading, among other things, to a decline in civic engagement in America, depleted social capital, moral relativism, asocial individualism, increasing privatism, and civic apathy. Since civil society is "a realm that is neither individualist nor collectivist . . . [and] partakes of both the I and the we,"[15] these developments invite us to rethink the ethic of individualistic achievement and self-fulfillment and the unrivaled predominance of the language of individualism and individual rights in contemporary American society.

It is not a coincidence that, in the United States, the debate on civil associations has coincided with the revival of interest in the writings of Alexis de Tocqueville, particularly *Democracy in America*, in which he famously praised the Americans' propensity to form civil and political associations. Tocqueville regarded these associations as laboratories of democracy that teach citizens the art of being free and give them the opportunity to pursue their own interests in concert with others. Indeed, the strong relationship between democracy and civil and political associations was one of the most important insights of Tocqueville's *Democracy in America*, which has become the locus classicus for any discussion of civil society. As Don Eberly, the editor of *The Essential Civil Society Reader* (2000), pointed out a few years ago, "in Tocqueville, we find an uncanny foretelling of the American cultural and social debate at the turn of the twenty-first century. Without a vibrant and functioning civil realm, he held that the state would emerge to fill the vacuum, producing . . . a gentle despotism."[16] More so than any other political thinker, Tocqueville grasped the seminal role that civil and political associations play in the

---

Individualism and Commitment in American Life (New York: Harper and Row, 1985), 250–96; and William A. Schambra, "The Progressive Assault of Civic Community," in *The Essential Civil Society Reader: The Classic Essays*, ed. Don. E. Eberly (Lanham, MD: Rowman and Littlefield, 2000), 317–51.

[14] Robert Putnam, "Bowling Alone: America's Declining Social Capital," *Journal of Democracy*, 6, no. 1 (1995): 68.

[15] Jean Bethke Elshtain, "Democracy on Trial: The Role of Civil Society in Sustaining Democratic Values," in Eberly, ed., *The Essential Civil Society Reader*, 105.

[16] Don E. Eberly, "The Meaning, Origins, and Applications of Civil Society," in Eberly, ed., *The Essential Civil Society Reader*, 27.

framework of modern society, and understood that in order to remain civilized, modern democratic regimes must constantly cultivate and promote the art and freedom of association.

II. The French Background

Tocqueville's views on political and civil associations cannot be properly understood unless we take into account the wider political background of his native France. After all, since Tocqueville went to America (from May 1831 to February 1832) in order to find lessons that might be applied to the French context, the portrait of American democracy that he offered to his countrymen had a strong normative component. In particular, Tocqueville's discussion of the right of association and the spirit of association in America was meant to convince his countrymen back home about the long-term benefits of civil and political associations, an idea that had traditionally been received with skepticism by the French, who were fascinated by the ideology of unity and general will proposed by Jean-Jacques Rousseau's disciples during the French Revolution.

Drawing a famous distinction between the general will and the will of all in *The Social Contract* (1762),[17] Rousseau had argued that intermediary associations are not conducive to the pursuit of the common good because they tend to distort individual judgment. Doubting that individual differences could ever produce good decisions reflecting the general will, Rousseau feared that sectional associations would be formed at the expense of the larger association, and that prevailing opinions would be nothing more than private interests and private views. "If the general will is to be clearly expressed," he wrote, "it is important that there should be no sectional societies in the state, and that each citizen should make up his own mind for himself."[18] A few decades later, Rousseau's disciples, such as Abbé Sieyès,[19] took this argument a step further in emphasizing the indivisibility of the nation at the very moment when the representatives of the French nation attempted to replace the sovereignty of the monarch with their own sovereignty. "France," Sieyès proclaimed in September 1789, "is and must be a single whole."[20] His position expressed the French

---

[17] Rousseau wrote: "There is often a great difference between the will of all [what all individuals want] and the general will; the general will studies only the common interest while the will of all studies private interest, and is indeed no more than the sum of individual desires." Jean-Jacques Rousseau, *The Social Contract*, trans. Maurice Cranston (London: Penguin, 1968), 72.

[18] Ibid., 73.

[19] Emmanuel Joseph Sieyès (1748–1836) was one of the leading theorists of the French Revolution, and the author of a famous pamphlet, *What Is the Third Estate?* Published on the eve of the events of 1789, this pamphlet became the manifesto of the Revolution.

[20] As quoted in Pierre Rosanvallon, *Le modèle politique français: La société civile contre le jacobinisme de 1789 à nos jours* (Paris: Editions du Seuil, 2004), 28.

fascination with the mystique of unity and the general will that elevated the general interest above particular interests. In adopting this antiplural-ist stance, the French Revolutionaries proved to be remarkably persistent in their attempts to eradicate the causes of factions rather than control their effects. In so doing, they implicitly rejected the Madisonian idea that "the private interest of every individual may be a sentinel over the public rights."[21]

Yet the French political tradition was far from being monolithic in its skepticism toward intermediary associations, the kinds of associations suspected of corrupting or altering the general will and undermining the sovereignty of the nation. Tocqueville's description of the role played by civil and political pluralism in a democratic regime mirrored, to some extent, Montesquieu's arguments on intermediary bodies in a moderate monarchy.[22] To be sure, the connection between liberty, mod-eration, and pluralism loomed large in Montesquieu's *The Spirit of the Laws* (1748), as well as in his lesser-known (but equally important) book *Considerations on the Causes of the Greatness of the Romans and Their Decline* (1734).[23] Montesquieu distinguished between limited (constitu-tional) monarchy, tempered by pluralism and the rule of law, and rule by one man in the absence of the rule of law. He argued that if, in the state, there is only the momentary and capricious will of one person, nothing can be fixed and consequently there can be no fundamental law. Not surprisingly, Montesquieu preferred those political regimes that had an intricate structure consisting of overlapping centers of pow-ers and interests. In his view, such pluralist regimes were more likely to preserve political freedom than any other regimes, because they had a complex system of checks and balances that placed effective limits on the exercise of power (by one person or a group of persons). At the same time, Montesquieu pointed out that only such systems create the conditions for genuine competition for social supremacy among vari-ous interests, principles, ideas, and groups that reflect the diversity of

[21] The quote is from James Madison (*Federalist* No. 51) in Alexander Hamilton, James Madison, and John Jay, *The Federalist Papers*, ed. Clinton Rossiter (New York: The New American Library, 1961), 322. In *Federalist* No. 10, Madison made a persuasive plea for diversity and pluralism that ran against the vision proposed by Rousseau's *Social Con-tract*: "The smaller the society, the fewer probably will be the distinct parties and inter-ests composing it ... [and] the more easily will they concert and execute their plans of oppression. Extend the sphere and you take in a greater variety of parties and interests; you make it less probable that a majority of the whole will have a common motive to invade the rights of other citizens; or if such a common motive exists, it will be more difficult for all who feel it to discover their own strength and to act in unison with each other" (*The Federalist Papers*, 83).

[22] See, among others, Pierre Gouirand, *Tocqueville: Une certaine vision de la démocratie* (Paris: L'Harmattan, 2005), 215–40.

[23] Montesquieu, *The Spirit of the Laws*, trans. Anne Cohler, Basia Miller, and Harold Stone (Cambridge: Cambridge University Press, 1989); Montesquieu, *Considerations on the Causes of the Greatness of the Romans and Their Decline*, trans. David Lowenthal (Indianapolis, IN: Hackett, 1999).

mores, manners, and customs of a nation and serve as effective breaks on arbitary power, intolerance, and fanaticism. "Intermediate, subordinate, and dependent powers," Montesquieu wrote, "constitute the nature of monarchical government, that is, of the government in which one alone governs by fundamental laws." [24]

Montesquieu singled out pluralism as one of the most important sources of political moderation and claimed that those regimes that do not encourage and promote social diversity and political pluralism cannot be called moderate. He went to great lengths to point out that intermediary bodies—nobles, clergy, "depositories" of laws, *parlements*, courts of justice, corporations—performed a seminal role in limiting the authority of the monarch, acting as countervailing powers capable of effectively restraining the potentially capricious will of the king. This explains why, in well-ordered monarchies, things were rarely carried to excess: the tendency of those regimes to excess was effectively moderated by the existence of powerful intermediary bodies. In such regimes, Montesquieu explained, "temperings are proposed, agreements are reached, corrections are made; the laws become vigorous again and make themselves heard." [25]

In *The Spirit of the Laws*, Montesquieu also emphasized the role of good laws and ordinances in moderating the power of the monarch, and added that they were supposed to act in concert with customs, traditions, and the multitude of offices and magistracies. As such, in Montesquieu's eyes, a moderate government appeared as a well-ordered and balanced system whose equilibrium resulted from a sound balance of powers and institutionalized interactions between various intermediary bodies and interests in society. If properly channeled into adequate institutions and laws, Montesquieu argued, the dissonances and divisions of this system would increase its internal capacity for self-correction rather than undermine its vitality (as Rousseau would claim a decade and a half later in *The Social Contract*).[26]

---

[24] Montesquieu, *The Spirit of the Laws*, 18.

[25] Ibid., 57.

[26] The emphasis on commonality and harmony of interests was a constant theme in Rousseau's *Social Contract*. See, for example, the following passage from book II, chapter 1: "The first and most important consequence of the principles so far established is that the general will alone can direct the forces of the state in accordance with that end which the state has been established to achieve—the common good; for if conflict between private interests has made the setting up of civil societies necessary, harmony between those same interests has made it possible. . . . The private will inclines by its very nature towards partiality, and the general will towards equality" (69). I should also point out that the authors of *The Federalist Papers* were steeped in the writings of Montesquieu, and that the intense debates between the Federalists and the Antifederalists over whether the proposed U.S. Constitution should be ratified or not touched upon many of the points that had previously been raised by Montesquieu in *The Spirit of the Laws*. One such issue was whether or not a republic could be established over a large geographical area. Montesquieu and the Antifederalists answered in the negative, while Madison and Hamilton believed in the possibility of a large republic.

Alas, the French did not follow Montesquieu when they had a chance to implement a new political regime in the summer of 1789. Instead, they preferred Rousseau's theory of indivisible sovereignty and endorsed his celebration of unity and the general will. During the intense parliamentary debates of July and September 1789, Montesquieu's disciples and proponents of a constitutional monarchy (that mirrored the English model)[27] failed to persuade their compatriots about the need for bicameralism and an absolute royal veto, and were defeated by the populist rhetoric of their opponents, such as Sieyès and Mirabeau.[28] Rousseau's distrust of intermediary associations (factions) exercised a powerful influence on the revolutionary discourse on political associations and corporations, as demonstrated by the famous Chapelier Law of June 14, 1791. This law explicitly banned all kinds of corporations of citizens and emphatically declared that "citizens of the same occupation or profession, entrepreneurs, those who maintain open shop, workers, and journeymen of any craft whatsoever may not, when they are together, name either president, secretaries, or trustees, pass decrees or resolutions, or draft regulations concerning their alleged common interests."[29] The right of association was thus seen as inimical to the principles of liberty and the constitution; consequently, any corporations or groups that ignored the law were to be declared seditious assemblies and were to be punished accordingly. As Pierre Rosanvallon and Lucien Jaume have demonstrated, the mystique of unity and homogeneity that characterized the Jacobin discourse of democracy helps explain the peculiarities of the French political model and accounts for the presence of strong illiberal elements in modern French political culture, well beyond the horizon of the Revolution.[30]

The themes of intermediary powers and local associations never fully disappeared from the French post-revolutionary political vocabulary. During the Bourbon Restoration (1814–1830), both liberal and conservative writers praised the role of intermediary bodies as necessary countervailing powers in a constitutional monarchy. On the right, the brilliant polemicist Joseph Fievée argued: "We need powers between the general administration and the administered individuals; otherwise, neither

[27] The group of so-called French *monarchiens* included Jean-Joseph Mounier (1758–1806), Gérard de Lally Tollendal (1751–1830), Stanislas Marie Adelaide Clermont-Tonnerre (1757–1792), and Pierre Victor Malouet (1740–1814).

[28] Honoré Gabriel Riqueti, Comte de Mirabeau (1749–1791) was a prominent French orator and statesman who played a key role during the first two years of the French Revolution, when he was elected president of the National Assembly.

[29] *Readings in Western Civilization, vol. 7: The Old Regime and the French Revolution*, ed. Keith M. Baker (Chicago: University of Chicago Press, 1987), 248.

[30] See Lucien Jaume, *Le Discours jacobin et la démocratie* (Paris: Fayard, 1989); Jaume, *Échec au libéralisme: Les Jacobins et l'État* (Paris: Kimé, 1991); and Pierre Rosanvallon, "Fondements et problèmes de l'illibéralisme français," in *La France du nouveau siècle*, ed. Thierry de Montbrial (Paris: PUF, 2002). Rosanvallon gives a comprehensive account of French exceptionalism in his book *Le modèle politique français*.

liberty nor stability will ever exist in France." [31] Prominent liberal thinkers such as Benjamin Constant also praised the virtues of intermediary powers as indispensable protective screens in modern society. In his *Principles of Politics* (1815), Constant commented at length on the seminal importance of municipal powers and local institutions. In order to attach individuals to their own places in society, Constant argued, "it is essential to grant them, in their homes, in their communes, as much political importance as possible without injuring the general good." [32]

The twin issues of local associations and decentralization were present even on the agenda of the French Doctrinaires, who are often viewed as staunch partisans of centralization. [33] In one of his parliamentary speeches from 1821, Pierre-Paul Royer-Collard explicitly linked the art of being free to the preservation of local independent institutions—"true republics in the bosom of monarchy" [34] that had provided effective opposition to the power of the kings. Another Doctrinaire, Charles de Rémusat, stated: "The spirit of association marches forward with the spirit of liberty. England and America are its witnesses. Hence it is both advantageous and expedient to extend the empire of the spirit of association." [35] A similar point can be found in Prosper de Barante's important book *Des communes et de l'aristocratie* (1821). Under the Old Regime, local institutions developed into genuine "fragments of a constitution." [36] Although they were never fully established or recognized in legal terms, such institutions played an important role in bringing citizens together and allowing them to form common bonds. In the footsteps of Montesquieu, both Royer-Collard and Barante insisted that the Old Regime consisted of a surprisingly diverse society characterized by diverse customs, unwritten laws, and local associations—Barante refers to them as "communal societies"—all of which were destroyed under the centralized administration of Cardinal Richelieu (1585–1642) and the rule of Louis XIV (1638–1715). The disappearance of these institutions was a momentous event that paved the way for the irresistible growth of absolute power and administrative centralization in

[31] Joseph Fievée, quoted in Rosanvallon, *Le modèle politique français*, 180.

[32] Benjamin Constant, *Principles of Politics*, reprinted in Benjamin Constant, *Political Writings*, ed. Biancamaria Fontana (Cambridge: Cambridge University Press, 1988), 254.

[33] Although the French Doctrinaires did not form a political party in the proper sense of the word, they held important positions in Parliament, administration, and government during the Bourbon Restoration (1814–1830) and the July Monarchy (1830–1848). The group included François Guizot, Pierre-Paul Royer-Collard, Prosper de Barante, Hercule de Serre, Camille Jordan, and Charles de Rémusat. The word "Doctrinaires" was a misnomer, not only because it generated serious misinterpretations which (unfairly) portrayed Guizot and his colleagues as greedy opportunists or shameless hypocrites, but also because there were many differences among them that are not adequately conveyed by the word "Doctrinaires." For more information, see Aurelian Craiutu, *Liberalism Under Siege: The Political Thought of the French Doctrinaires* (Lanham, MD: Lexington Books, 2003), chap. 2.

[34] *La Vie politique de M. Royer-Collard: Ses discours et ses écrits*, vol. 2, ed. Prosper de Barante (Paris: Didier, 1861), 130–31.

[35] Charles de Rémusat, quoted in Rosanvallon, *Le modèle politique français*, 182–83.

[36] Prosper de Barante, *Des communes et de l'aristocratie* (Paris: Ladvocat, 1821), 7.

France. The French Revolution completed the process of social leveling, destroyed intermediary bodies, and ended the tradition of local freedoms and local institutions that had previously served as effective countervailing forces to the power of the monarchs. The outcome of this process was the emergence of an atomized society, *"la société en poussière,"* [37] and the destruction of local "communal societies" that were swallowed up in the centralized nation. As Barante remarked, the rule of the administrators began when the communes disappeared and were replaced by a new system in which the absolute will of the king prevailed. [38]

In spite of all this, it is revealing that only a few years before Tocqueville, another Frenchman who visited America, Victor Jacquemont (1801–1832), one of the most brilliant representatives of the new generation that came of age in the 1820s, made some interesting remarks (in correspondence with family members and friends) about the spirit of association in the New World—remarks that reveal some of the old French preconceptions concerning "uncivilized" American mores. [39] Jacquemont was impressed by the multifarious ways in which American citizens made continuous and systematic use of the right of association to found schools and build churches and roads. He attributed the Americans' propensity to form civil and political associations to the principle of equality which reigns supreme in a democratic society. Jacquemont pointed out that Americans of all ages and professions displayed an unusual ability to choose common goals and were able to pursue these goals effectively by the aid of various civil associations. Americans, he noticed, shied away from carrying out these activities in isolation and viewed civil associations as powerful means of action that created sound social bonds.

At the same time, however, Jacquemont feared that the spirit of association might turn into a caricature when everyone acquired the habit of association and carried it to the extreme. He wryly noted that "ten Americans do not know how to dine, play or meet for any reason without electing a president and a secretary." [40] He added that all these American organizations resembled small armies in which there were no soldiers and in which everyone was a general. This, he opined, was the effect of equality and republican education on mores. While applauding the habit of forming associations for pursuing common projects, Jacquemont doubted

[37] The term *"la société en poussière"* was used by Royer-Collard in one of his parliamentary speeches in 1820. See Barante, ed., *La Vie politique de M. Royer-Collard,* 131.

[38] Barante, *Des communes et de l'aristocratie,* 16–17.

[39] On Jacquemont, see Aurelian Craiutu, "A Precursor of Tocqueville: Victor Jacquemont's Reflections on America," in *America Through European Eyes,* ed. Aurelian Craiutu and Jeffrey C. Isaac (University Park: Penn State University Press, 2008). For a comprehensive analysis of Jacquemont's generation, see Alan B. Spitzer, *The French Generation of 1820* (Princeton, NJ: Princeton University Press, 1987).

[40] *Correspondance inédite de Victor Jacquemont avec sa famille et ses amis, 1824–1832,* ed. Prosper Mérimée, vol. 1 (Paris: Calmann-Lévy, 1885), 166.

that civil associations could ever serve as a substitute for what "civilized" Europeans called society in the proper sense of the word.[41] It was left to Tocqueville, who visited America four years after Jacquemont, to break with the French tradition of skepticism toward civil associations.

III. TOCQUEVILLE'S DEFINITION OF ASSOCIATIONS

In volume one of *Democracy in America*, Tocqueville defined an association as consisting "in the decision of a certain number of individuals to adhere publicly to certain doctrines, and to commit themselves to seek the triumph of those doctrines in a certain way" (*DA*, 216).[42] Associations bring together the efforts, ideas, and initiatives of many individuals and allow them to freely pursue common goals for the sake of the common good. "Men," wrote Tocqueville, "can see one another, pool their resources, and exchange views with a forcefulness and warmth that the written word can never achieve" (*DA*, 216).

Tocqueville espoused a fairly broad view of associations and devoted a lot of attention to studying the relationship between civil associations, the right to associate, and the spirit of association in a democratic regime. It is worth pointing out that, in Tocqueville's view, the word "association" applied to local institutions and municipal councils as well as to newspapers, political parties, or party conventions that "would have never existed or flourished but for the initiative of individuals" (*DA*, 215). He distinguished three stages in the exercise of the right of association. The first stage channels individual actions toward some common goal. The second stage has to do with "the ability to assemble," predicated upon the existence of centers of action and meeting places that allow people to interact with one another. The third stage refers to the tendency of people to form electoral bodies and choose delegates to represent them in a central assembly.

In his account of the American system of townships in *Democracy in America*, Tocqueville highlighted the seminal connection between municipal (local) institutions and political liberty. Local institutions, he remarked, constitute the strength of free nations and the key to their long-term survival: "It is at the local level that the strength of a free people lies. Local institutions are to liberty what elementary schools are to knowledge; they bring it within the reach of the people, allow them to savor its peaceful use, and accustom them to rely on it. Without local institutions, a nation may give itself a free government, but it will not have a free spirit" (*DA*, 68). On Tocqueville's view, local institutions also allowed people to exercise power

---

[41] Ibid., 167.

[42] All references are to Alexis de Tocqueville, *Democracy in America*, trans. Arthur Goldhammer (New York: The Library of America, 2004). References to this work will be given parenthetically in the text, with the title abbreviated as *DA*.

immediately, gave them a stake in the administration of local affairs, and taught them the art of self-government:

> The New Englander is attached to his town because it is strong and independent; he takes an interest in it because he helps direct its affairs; he loves it because it gives him no reason to complain about his lot in life. He invests his ambition and his future in the town and participates in all aspects of community life. In the limited sphere that is within his reach, he tries his hand at governing society. He becomes accustomed to the forms without which liberty advances only by way of revolution, becomes imbued with their spirit, develops a taste for order, comprehends the harmony of powers, and finally acquires clear and practical ideas about the nature of his duties and the extent of his rights. (*DA*, 77)

It was to Tocqueville's credit that he grasped that in modern democratic societies local institutions are more necessary in proportion as the social conditions become more egalitarian and democratic, and as the sphere and scope of state intervention increase steadily.

IV. CIVIL ASSOCIATIONS

Tocqueville's views on civil (and political) associations are articulated in several key chapters of *Democracy in America*.[43] During his nine-month visit to America in 1831–32, Tocqueville had a unique opportunity to observe the beneficial effects of the science of association for which his compatriot, Victor Jacquemont, had only lukewarm words (mixed with a good dose of skepticism). Tocqueville was unambiguous in his praise of American associations. He understood the seminal connection between the process of equalization of conditions and the art of association, and this led him to point out that the more stable a democratic regime is, the more developed the art of association is in that regime. In his travel notes, Tocqueville wrote: "The spirit of association, as I have already remarked elsewhere, is one of the distinctive characteristics of America; it is by this means that a country where capital is scarce and where absolutely democratic laws and habits hinder the accumulation of wealth in the hands of a few individuals, has already succeeded in carrying out undertakings and accomplishing things which the most opulent aristocracies would

---

[43] Specifically, volume 1, part II, chap. 4, and vol. 2, part II, chaps. 4–6. Richard Boyd devotes an entire chapter to examining Tocqueville's views of associations and pluralism in Boyd, *Uncivil Society: The Perils of Pluralism and the Making of Modern Liberalism* (Lanham, MD: Lexington Books, 2006), 209–38. On this topic, see also Dana Villa, "Tocqueville and Civil Society," in *The Cambridge Companion to Tocqueville*, ed. Cheryl B. Welch (New York: Cambridge University Press, 2006), 216–44; and Robert T. Gannett, "Bowling Ninepins in Tocqueville's Township," *American Political Science Review* 97, no. 1 (February 2003): 1–16.

certainly have not been able to undertake and finish in the same way."[44]
Tocqueville noted that in nineteenth-century America, civil and political
associations served as laboratories of democracy while also providing
indispensable social services to all citizens. "Americans of all ages, all
conditions, and all minds," he remarked,

> are constantly joining together in groups. In addition to commercial
> and industrial associations in which everyone takes part, there are
> associations of a thousand other kinds: some religious, some moral,
> some grave, some trivial, some quite general and others quite par-
> ticular, some huge and others tiny. Americans associate to give fêtes,
> to found seminaries, to build inns, to erect churches, to distribute
> books, and to send missionaries to the antipodes. This is how they
> create hospitals, prisons, and schools. If, finally, they wish to publi-
> cize a truth or foster a sentiment with the help of a great example,
> they associate. Wherever there is a new undertaking, at the head of
> which you would expect to see in France the government and in
> England some great lord, in the United States you are sure to find an
> association. (DA, 595)[45]

One of the main theses of *Democracy in America* is that a vibrant
associational life cannot exist in the absence of a genuine and vigorous
spirit of association. In America, Tocqueville argued, the existence of
effective associations was made possible by the art of self-government
and administrative decentralization. One of the most important consequences of self-government is "the ripening of individual strength which
never fails to follow therefrom. Each man learns to think and to act for
himself without counting on the support of any outside power which,
however watchful it be, can never answer all the needs of man in
society."[46] With one major exception (England), administrative decentralization and self-government hardly existed in the majority of European countries, where central power stifled local energies and restricted
local autonomy. Tocqueville noted that, in this regard, America was
fundamentally different from Europe; for, unlike the Europeans, American citizens learned early on in life to rely upon their own efforts in
order to cope with practical challenges. Because they were taught to
mistrust social authorities of all kinds, they developed a habit of cooperation and deliberation that permitted them to attend effectively to
important common concerns such as public safety, commerce, industry,
morality, and religion: "One encounters the same spirit in all aspects of

---

[44] Alexis de Tocqueville, *Journey to America*, ed. J. P. Meyer, trans. George Lawrence (New
Haven, CT: Yale University Press, 1962), 252.
[45] See also Tocqueville, *Journey to America*, 212–13.
[46] Ibid., 51.

social life. . . . There is nothing the human will despairs of achieving through the free action of the collective power of individuals" (*DA*, 215-16). More than any other country in the world, Tocqueville remarked, America had learned how to make the best use of the freedom to associate. In the New World, this freedom had not been used as a political weapon in the fight for power or against the government, but as an effective guarantee against the potentially despotic power of the majority.

The situation was radically different in the Old World, where most Europeans looked upon associations as weapons to be hastily used in political battles. When people did associate, Tocqueville pointed out, they did so as soldiers in an army in order to march against a common enemy: "The members of an association may regard legal resources as a useful means of action but never as the only path to success" (*DA*, 220). The main goal of these associations was not to debate and persuade others but to impose one's views upon them; as such, these associations required obedience or servility rather than reasoned argument and consent. Hence, the means that were chosen were not always peaceful and civil, but resembled most often the habits and rules of military life.

In America, far from triggering major political crises that might have thrown the country into anarchy, unlimited freedom of association had been instrumental in preventing social and political turmoil. This, Tocqueville noted, was a testament to the political experience of America, where the freedom to associate for political purposes was practically unlimited and universal suffrage successfully mitigated the potential violence of political associations. Because the members of civil and political associations knew that they never fully represented the majority, they developed respect for the rules of the political game and learned to compromise with their opponents. Tocqueville was quick to note the contrast with Europe, where most associations pretended to be the true representatives of the majority, and acted as if they were the "legislative and executive council of a nation" (*DA*, 222). This led them to believe that they were entitled to trample the laws under their feet when they thought it convenient to do so: "The members of such associations respond to orders as soldiers in the field. . . . Within such organizations a tyranny often prevails that is more unbearable still than the tyranny exerted over society by the government they attack" (*DA*, 222).

The salutary role played by civil associations in America, Tocqueville went on, went far beyond improving the daily lives of ordinary citizens. He claimed that in democratic times, the science of association had become "the fundamental science" (*DA*, 599), making possible progress in all the other sciences. The very survival of modern civilization ultimately depended on people developing the habit of forming associations in order to pursue common projects. For if men living in democratic countries failed to learn and practice the art of association, "civilization itself would be in peril" and society would risk relapsing into a new form of barbarism or despotism:[47] "If men are to remain civilized, or to become so, they must develop and perfect the art of associating to the same degree that equality of conditions increases among them" (*DA*, 599). This, Tocqueville added, is far from being an easy task, since of all forms of liberty, freedom of association is the last one that people learn to master properly. It requires a long and difficult apprenticeship that is not without its own perils and challenges.

Much like Montesquieu's intermediary bodies in aristocratic times, in democratic regimes civil and political associations serve as effective and indispensable countervailing forces to concentrations of political power (state power, corporations, or the tyranny of the majority). Civil associations, Tocqueville believed, are particularly needed in democratic times when people are equal, independent, and individually weak, and when they tend to prefer equality over liberty and wholeheartedly embrace individualism as a way of life. If left unchecked, this passion for equality could develop into a real threat to liberty, while individualism, a peculiarly democratic phenomenon fueled by the passion for equality, tends to degenerate into pure egoism or selfishness.

V. Individualism and the Art of Association

Tocqueville's analysis of individualism as one of the central values of democratic societies is too well-known to require further elaboration. What is perhaps less well-known is the fact that this issue was far from being of mere theoretical interest to the French. It was the image of the atomized society—*la société en poussière*—that came to dominate the political debates in Restoration France (especially in the late 1810s and early 1820s), debates with which Tocqueville was entirely familiar by the time he visited America in 1831–32.[48] The voices denouncing the perils of individualism spanned across the political spectrum in post-revolutionary France. "We cannot hide it from our eyes," Jean-Baptiste Villèle remarked. "Our long civil troubles had given birth amongst us not to a new nation, but to a collection of individuals."[49] It was this process of atomization of society that became the focus of criticism, not only from conservative thinkers such as Villèle but also from figures on the left of the political spectrum, such as the philosopher Pierre Leroux and the disciples of the social theorist Henri de Saint-Simon.

---

[47] Tocqueville's point that democracies may risk lapsing into a new form of despotism might remind the reader of Montesquieu's claim: "Rivers run together into the sea; monarchies are lost in despotism" (Montesquieu, *The Spirit of the Laws*, 125).

[48] On this topic, see Rosanvallon, *Le modèle politique français*, 158–64; and Aurelian Craiutu, "Tocqueville and the Political Thought of the French Doctrinaires," *History of Political Thought* 20, no. 3 (Fall 1999): 456–93.

[49] Villèle, quoted in Rosanvallon, *Le modèle politique français*, 160.

The most significant expression of this atomized society was individualism, a word that was not invented by Tocqueville himself but had previously been used by Joseph de Maistre to criticize the allegedly pernicious effects of Protestantism in political life.[50] In *The Old Regime and the Revolution* (1856), Tocqueville referred to a new type of individualism, which he dubbed "collective individualism," that accounted, in his view, for the emergence of an atomized society on French soil: "Our ancestors lacked the word 'individualism,' which we have created for our own use, because in their era there were, in fact, no individuals who did not belong to a group and who could consider themselves absolutely alone; but each one of the thousand little groups of which French society was composed thought only of itself. This was, if one can use the word thus, a kind of collective individualism, which prepared people for the real individualism with which we are familiar."[51]

Tocqueville proposed a new understanding of individualism and insisted that the science of association could serve as an effective means of combating and neutralizing individualism's pernicious consequences, which had broken society into its bare elements.[52] It is important to note that Tocqueville distinguished individualism from mere egoism and selfishness. Unlike egoism, individualism is a novel democratic phenomenon that manifests itself as "a reflective and tranquil sentiment that disposes each citizen to cut himself off from the mass of his fellow men and withdraw into the circle of family and friends, so that, having created a little society for his own use, he gladly leaves the larger society" (*DA*, 585). The advance of individualism occurred against the background of an atomized society which, in turn, arose as old aristocratic institutions (institutions that had previously linked every man to his fellow citizens) gradually disappeared: "Aristocracy linked all citizens together in a long chain from peasant to king. Democracy breaks the chain and severs the links" (*DA*, 586). As the contemporary French political philosopher Pierre Manent has perceptively noted, democracy threatens to dissolve the social contract between individuals, throwing them back into a state of nature.[53] "Not only does democracy cause each man to forget his forebears," Tocqueville wrote, "but it makes it difficult for him to see his offspring and cuts him off from his contemporaries. Again and again it leads him back to himself" (*DA*, 587). As a result, individuals living in democratic times are separated from each other, owe nothing to anyone, and expect nothing from anyone: "They

[50] See Koenraad Swart, "Individualism in the Mid-Nineteenth Century (1826–1860)," *Journal of the History of Ideas* 23, no. 1 (January–March 1962): 78.

[51] Alexis de Tocqueville, *The Old Regime and the Revolution*, vol. 1, trans. Alan S. Kahan (Chicago: University of Chicago Press, 1998), 163. According to Swart ("Individualism in the Mid-Nineteenth Century," 79), the term "individualism" made its first appearance in a French dictionary in 1836.

[52] On this topic, see also Boyd, *Uncivil Society*, 214–18.

[53] Pierre Manent, *Tocqueville and the Nature of Democracy* (Lanham, MD: Rowman and Littlefield, 1996), chaps. 2–3.

become accustomed to thinking of themselves in isolation and are pleased to think that their fate lies entirely in their own hands" (*DA*, 586–87).

How can this democratic phenomenon be properly combated? Does democracy naturally tend toward social anomie? And what remedies can be used to stave off a phenomenon that imprisons individuals in the solitude of their own hearts and souls, and ultimately fosters individual powerlessness and civic apathy? For all its concerned tone, Tocqueville's diagnosis of democratic individualism was not a pessimistic one. The science of association, he noted, is itself a powerful remedy against social anomie and isolation. The need for associations arises from the individual weakness of each person, a feature that is inherent in the nature of democratic society, in which people are no longer united by firm and lasting ties or by subordination to prominent aristocratic individuals. Only voluntary associations can work against the weakness of individuals and bring them together to act in concert. If individuals in democratic societies are disposed to live apart, they also have numerous opportunities to draw near to their fellow citizens and participate in common projects. Moreover, the art of association has an ennobling effect upon the minds and souls of individuals living in democratic societies. Feelings and ideas are renewed and the heart itself expands as the result of social interaction and exchanges; through them, people lend one another mutual assistance and combine their efforts and energies in the pursuit of common goals. Associations teach their members new ways of improving both the common property and their own lot. What's more, associations increase individuals' self-confidence and respect for others, impart new knowledge, and enlighten individuals while also cultivating their taste for even greater enterprises.

Tocqueville highlighted this advantage of democracy in a seminal passage from *Democracy in America* that deserves to be quoted in full:

> Under democratic liberty, projects are not executed with the perfection that intelligent despotism can achieve. Democracy will often abandon its projects before harvesting their fruits, or it will embark on dangerous adventures. In the long run, however, it achieves more than despotism. It does each thing less well, but it does more things. Under its rule, it is not so much what the public administration does that is great, but above all, what people do without it, and independent of it. Democracy does not give the people the most skillful government, but what it does even the most skillful government is powerless to achieve: it spreads throughout society a restless activity, a superabundant strength, an energy that never exists without it, and which, if circumstances are even slightly favorable, can accomplish miracles. These are its true advantages. (*DA*, 280–81)

Some of these miracles, Tocqueville argued, are performed by civil and political associations supported by local liberties. What makes these associations effective in America is the unique combination of local liberties, self-government, political rights, and decentralization. As I have already noted, associations reconstitute a new social contract between individuals whom equality had formerly placed side by side and had left without any common ties. By reminding them that they are not—and can never be—independent of their fellow men, civil and political associations tame their selfishness, purify their interest, and moderate their indifference toward anything that goes beyond their narrow sphere. By linking private and common interests, associations encourage democratic individuals to take an interest in their fellow citizens, and predispose them to seek their fellow citizens' cooperation.

From temperance societies and lobbying groups to professional organizations and church support groups, these associations, whether broad or narrow in scope, make people constantly feel the need for each other, bring them together, and force them to acquaint, help, and adapt themselves to one another. In doing so, associations allow individuals to see the connection between their private interests and the public affairs which they undertake in common. As Tocqueville observed:

> The free institutions that Americans possess, and the political rights of which they make such extensive use, are, in a thousand ways, constant reminders to each and every citizen that he lives in society. They keep his mind steadily focused on the idea that it is man's duty as well as his interest to make himself useful to his fellow man. Since he sees no particular reason to hate others, because he is neither their slave nor their master, his heart readily inclines to the side of benevolence. Men concern themselves with the general interest at first out of necessity and later by choice. What was calculation becomes instinct, and by dint of working for the good of one's fellow citizens, one ultimately acquires the habit of serving them, along with a taste for doing so. (*DA*, 593–94)

VI. Political Associations

Although Tocqueville carefully distinguished between civil and political associations, he believed that, in the end, they all act as "vast free schools" (*DA*, 606) in which people learn the art of being free. As such, the relation between the two types of associations is both natural and necessary: "Civil associations facilitate political associations, but then again, political association singularly develops and perfects civil association" (*DA*, 604). Politics provides an arena in which large associations such as political parties make the practice of association more general and more widespread. Yet, at the same time, political associations, by drawing together a large number of individuals, may disturb social order if their energies are applied to subverting the constitutional foundations of society.

Tocqueville was concerned by the abuse of freedom of association, and, as we have already seen, he acknowledged that the proper exercise of this liberty requires a long experience and an advanced degree of civilization that teach people how to tolerate differences of opinion and how to practice self-restraint. Under certain circumstances, Tocqueville pointed out, a democratic nation may seek to confine the freedom of association within certain limits in order to protect itself against abuses of that freedom. When the differences between political associations are fundamental and irreconcilable, absolute freedom of association can jeopardize social order and disturb the regular functioning of representative government. In such cases, there is no peaceful contestation of power by opposition parties, but only an all-out war between them that makes any compromise impossible or extremely difficult. This, Tocqueville added, was not the case in the United States, where the differences of opinion were mere differences of hue rather than fundamental differences of political principles.

Tocqueville's endorsement of political parties in America should not make us forget that his views on political parties were anything but orthodox; in fact, the type of politics that he was longing for turned out to have little place for ordinary party politics and political bargaining. Tocqueville was and remained to the very end a highly independent mind, unable to give his full allegiance to any political party of his times. His reputation derived mostly from the formidable success of volume one of *Democracy in America*, but even that had to be taken with a grain of salt. As he acknowledged to his friend Eugène Stoffels in 1836, "I please many persons of conflicting opinions, not because they understand me, but because they find in my work, by considering it only from a single side, arguments favorable to their passion of the moment." [54]

In other letters, Tocqueville called himself a "liberal of a new kind" who followed no group and had no party behind him. In a letter to his mentor, Pierre-Paul Royer-Collard, composed in 1841, Tocqueville wrote, not without a peculiar mixture of pride and sadness: "The liberal but not revolutionary party, which alone suits me, does not exist." [55] Nine years later, he made the same point in a letter to Louis de Kergorlay, in which he described himself again as a man without party or cause "other than that of liberty and human dignity." [56] Not surprisingly, the conception of freedom that Tocqueville endorsed was a highly idiosyncratic one. When challenged to describe it, he proudly wrote: "Do not ask me to analyze this sublime desire, it must be felt. It enters of itself into the great hearts that God has prepared to receive it; it fills them, it fires them. One must

[54] Alexis de Tocqueville, *Selected Letters on Politics and Society*, ed. Roger Boesche, trans. Roger Boesche and James Toupin (Berkeley: University of California Press, 1985), 99–100.
[55] Ibid., 156.
[56] Ibid., 257.

give up on making this comprehensible to the mediocre souls who have never felt it." [57]

As a deputy representing his constituency from Normandy,[58] Tocqueville could ally himself neither with radical democrats, whose extreme zeal for equality he viewed with skepticism, nor with the nostalgic conservatives and prophets of the past, who failed to understand that a new science of politics and new concepts were needed for a new epoch. Not surprisingly, Tocqueville refused to associate himself in a permanent manner with any of the political men of his times, especially Adolphe Thiers and François Guizot,[59] who were, to use his own words, "fundamentally antipathetical"[60] to his independent way of feeling and thinking. Moreover, Tocqueville displayed the same uneasiness vis-à-vis the dominant parties and groups that divided France: "I do not see a single one to which I would want to be tied. I do not find in any of them, I do not say *everything* that I would want to see in political associates, but even the principal things for which I would willingly give up the lesser."[61]

Tocqueville's skepticism toward political parties during the July Monarchy (1830–1848) should not come as a surprise to any attentive reader of *Democracy in America*, who will remember that Tocqueville distinguished between two types of parties which he dubbed "minor" and "great" parties. The political parties that he called "great" were those that dedicated themselves "to principles [rather] than to their consequences; to generalities and not particulars; to ideas and not to men" (*DA*, 199). Such parties, Tocqueville argued, were distinguished by their noble features and pursuits, and their adherents were moved by genuine convictions and generous passions rather than purely by private interests and petty intrigues. Minor parties lacked true ideals and their members were often carried away by a factitious spirit and partisan zeal that corrupted their language and made their actions erratic and uncertain. "Great parties," Tocqueville wrote, "stand society on its head; minor parties agitate it. Great parties tear society apart; minor parties corrupt it. The former may at times save society at the cost of disrupting it, while the latter provoke agitation without profit" (*DA*, 199). America, he went on, once had great parties at the moment of its founding, but they had disappeared over time, being replaced by smaller parties that lacked the loftiness of purpose of their predecessors.

---

[57] Tocqueville, *The Old Regime and the Revolution*, 1: 217.

[58] Tocqueville was elected a member of the Chamber of Deputies in 1839; he was reelected during the Second Republic (1841–1851). Tocqueville's political career came to an end after the coup d'état of December 2, 1851, by Louis Napoleon.

[59] Louis-Adolphe Thiers (1797–1877) was a prominent French politician and historian who served as prime minister during the July Monarchy (from 1832 to 1836). François Guizot (1787–1874) was the most famous of the French Doctrinaires (see note 33 above). During the July Monarchy, he served as minister of education, minister of foreign affairs, and prime minister.

[60] Tocqueville, *Selected Letters on Politics and Society*, 154.

[61] Ibid., 155–56.

France, too, seems to have followed the same declining pattern. It once had noble and generous passions, but their hour was long gone. In *The Old Regime and the Revolution*, Tocqueville described the actors involved in the initial phase of the revolution in the following glowing terms: "People had real convictions, everybody followed his own convictions boldly, passionately."[62] The heroes of 1789, Tocqueville argued, were concerned with lofty and ambitious goals and were animated by sincere and generous emotions. Their youthful enthusiasm was combined with true independence of mind and passionate faith in themselves; they believed in a noble cause that convinced them to act boldly in order to correct the mistakes of the past. They were sincerely interested in public affairs, forgetful of their individual interests, and absorbed in the contemplation of a great plan aiming at the common good. "I have never met," Tocqueville wrote in *The Old Regime*, "with a revolution where one could see at the start, in so many men, a more sincere patriotism, more disinterest, more true greatness. . . . This is 1789, a time of inexperience doubtless, but of generosity, of enthusiasm, of virility, and of greatness, a time of immortal memory."[63]

Not surprisingly, the daily politics of the July Monarchy, a period of bourgeois individualism and acquisitiveness, failed to quench Tocqueville's thirst for noble actions. True politics, Tocqueville believed, could not exist in a world dominated by the bourgeoisie. "You know what a taste I have for great events," he confessed to his mentor Royer-Collard, "and how tired I am of our little democratic and bourgeois pot of soup."[64] On numerous occasions, Tocqueville voiced his concern about the emergence of a prosaic society entirely dominated by the values and principles of the bourgeoisie. The reign of the middle class, Tocqueville wrote in his *Recollections*, was exclusive and corrupt; public morality was degraded, and a general flatness and mediocrity threatened to create a flaccid humanity, incapable of any great heroic actions.[65] If a society could be compared to a garden, then France was entirely laid out to produce carrots and cabbages rather than peaches and oranges. Tocqueville, who had once compared himself to Don Quixote, dreamt of something far nobler than that.

VII. Conclusion: The Contemporary Relevance of Tocqueville

To what extent do Tocqueville's views on civil society, formulated almost two centuries ago, remain relevant for our times? For all his criticism of

---

[62] Alexis de Tocqueville, *The Old Regime and the Revolution*, vol. 2, trans. Alan S. Kahan (Chicago: University of Chicago Press, 2001), 237.

[63] Tocqueville, *The Old Regime and the Revolution*, 1: 208, 244.

[64] Tocqueville, *Selected Letters on Politics and Society*, 143.

[65] Alexis de Tocqueville, *Recollections*, ed. J. P. Mayer and A. P. Kerr (New Brunswick, NJ: Transaction, 1997), 5–6.

American restlessness, Tocqueville saw American society as fundamentally sound because it was capable of generating and educating virtuous citizens who knew how to combine self-interest with concern for the public good. If this was not a brilliant society, at least it was a decent one, or to put it differently, it was a society that developed a set of peaceful virtues suited to individuals living in democratic times.

Needless to say, some of us might be reluctant to endorse such an optimistic view today. A growing body of evidence shows a significant decline of family life, increasing civic apathy, and pervasive selfishness, made possible by a radical interpretation of individual rights.[66] Moreover, associational life in early twenty-first-century America is quite different from that of the 1830s, when Tocqueville visited America. Long gone are the famous temperance societies that impressed the French visitor, who was struck by the fact that responsible adults pledged to use the force of association to resist one of the most intimate urges of each human being.[67] While many contemporary civil associations foster character traits needed for the proper functioning of democratic regimes, such as independence of spirit, general tolerance for pluralism, and respect for diversity, membership in many associations today is mostly nominal, the payment of membership dues often being the only sign of participation in these associations.

Furthermore, there is a certain irony in Tocqueville's strong endorsement of civil and political associations and his critique of individualism, for Tocqueville himself often remained aloof from the political parties of his time and took great pride in stressing his independence from them. A proud and extremely ambitious person who was, however, haunted by a permanent lack of confidence in himself, Tocqueville devoted a great deal of time to cultivating deep friendships with a few friends, such as Gustave de Beaumont and Louis de Kergorlay, and enjoyed discharging the duties imposed by his aristocratic position on his Normandy estate. But when he stepped out of this intimate circle, Tocqueville often found it difficult to cooperate with other colleagues. As his biographer André Jardin remarked, "in his periods of euphoria, he allowed himself to be carried away by an enthusiasm that made him lose his sense of reality."[68]

Two revealing examples of Tocqueville's curious combination of strong ambitions and political ineffectiveness are his involvement in the publishing of the newspaper *Le Commerce,* and his attempt to build a new political movement on the left in the mid-1840s.[69] Tocqueville became

---

[66] On this topic, see Mary Ann Glendon, *Rights Talk* (New York: The Free Press, 1991).

[67] In his travel notes, Tocqueville wrote: "The effect of temperance societies is one of the most notable things in this country" (Tocqueville, *Journey to America,* 212).

[68] André Jardin, *Tocqueville: A Biography* (New York: Farrar, Straus, Giroux, 1988), 373.

[69] For more detail, see *The Tocqueville Reader,* ed. Oliver Zunz and Alan S. Kahan (Oxford: Blackwell, 2002), 221–26.

involved in the publication of *Le Commerce: Journal politique et littéraire* in the summer of 1844 and hoped that the newspaper would soon become "the only authentic representation of liberal ideas" in France.[70] In spite of Tocqueville's initial hopes, however, *Le Commerce* did not bear the expected fruit. Not only was he forced to withdraw from the editorial board a year later because of financial difficulties, but his short involvement in the publication of the newspaper led to a temporary rift with his best friend, Gustave de Beaumont.

The new political direction that Tocqueville dreamt of giving to the French left in the mid-1840s also failed, because it did not manage to articulate a viable political alternative to the political parties of that time. As I have already mentioned, Tocqueville's search for an alternative to the politics of the July Monarchy was motivated by his deep-seated distrust of a politics based exclusively on self-interest. He felt estranged from the values of the bourgeoisie, which he chastised for lacking both true virtue and greatness. In his *Recollections,* Tocqueville described the spirit of the bourgeoisie as "active and industrious, often dishonest, generally orderly, but sometimes rash, because of vanity and selfishness, timid by temperament, moderate in all things, except a taste for well-being, and mediocre."[71] He felt alienated by the pervasive obsession with money, the increasing commercialization of life, and the general abasement of mind and taste brought about by the rise of the middle class.[72]

Yet, unlike Marx who rejected civil society (which in his view was nothing but the realm of greed and selfishness), Tocqueville correctly grasped that the long apprenticeship of liberty depends to a significant degree on the science of association that draws precisely on those bourgeois virtues—self-restraint, temperance, self-interest rightly understood—that Marx despised and rejected. Tocqueville acknowledged that civil associations perform many functions in democratic societies, from serving as centers of opposition to tyranny (of the state or of the majority) and neutralizing the effects of social anomie and civic apathy, to fostering necessary civil (bourgeois) virtues. As such, associations help transform unenlightened self-interest into self-interest rightly understood, help moderate and purify the excesses of individualism, and help promote civic solidarity by bringing people together and giving them the opportunity to act in concert. In doing so, civil and political associations help heal the fragmentation created by conditions in

---

[70] Quoted in Roger Boesche, "*Le Commerce:* A Newspaper Expressing Tocqueville's Unusual Liberalism," in Roger Boesche, *Tocqueville's Road Map: Methodology, Liberalism, Revolution, and Despotism* (Lanham, MD: Lexington Books, 2006), 190.

[71] Tocqueville, *Recollections,* 5.

[72] On Tocqueville's "strange liberalism," see Boesche, *Tocqueville's Road Map,* 17–58; and Aurelian Craiutu, "Tocqueville's Paradoxical Moderation," *The Review of Politics* 67, no. 4 (2005): 599–629.

modern society and help generalize norms of reciprocity and informal norms of cooperation.

At the same time, it would be incorrect to assume that, in Tocqueville's view, civil and political associations served as a panacea for all the problems of democracy. To his credit, he was fully aware that they did not; in fact, both in *Democracy in America* and in his private correspondence, he insisted that mores are more important than laws, associations, and institutions in promoting and sustaining democracy over time. As he wrote to his friend Francisque de Corcelle in 1853, political societies are not what their laws and institutions make them, "but what sentiments, beliefs, ideas, habits of the heart, and the spirit of the men who form them, prepare them in advance to be, as well as what nature and education have made them."[73]

Last but not least, civil and political associations are themselves subject to professionalization and the iron law of oligarchy. As the effects of pork-barrel politics also extend to political associations, many of them tend to become rigid and excessively bureaucratic, and fall prey to factional politics. In other words, paraphrasing Tocqueville, one might say that the mere fact of associating is often less important in practice than what is associated with it—which is another way of saying that not all forms of associations are likely to promote democracy and democratic values.[74] As the contemporary political philosopher Richard Boyd has perceptively argued, "more is not always better,"[75] and we should seek to go beyond counting associations when attempting to assess the vitality of civil society today. Civil society, Boyd writes, consists "rightly speaking, only of those associations that contribute to the virtues of civility," associations that successfully promote social trust and civic solidarity. At the same time, there are many associations and groups which are not oriented to issues outside of themselves and, as such, tend to prove divisive and uncivil, fostering intolerance, exclusion, and generalized mistrust of outsiders and of government.[76] These uncivil associations—some of which exclude and harass nonmembers and seek to promote racist ideologies or illegitimate hierarchies—may foster a strong sense of identity and community within their frameworks, but their legacy is a predominantly negative one because their activities deepen social, political, economic, cultural, and intergenerational divisions.

---

[73] Tocqueville, *Selected Letters on Politics and Society*, 294.

[74] Jeffrey C. Alexander, "Tocqueville's Two Forms of Association," *The Tocqueville Review/La Revue Tocqueville* 27, no. 2 (2006): 181.

[75] Boyd, *Uncivil Society*, 41. On this issue, see also Nancy Rosenblum, *Membership and Morals* (Princeton, NJ: Princeton University Press, 2000), 3–69, 239–84; and Mark Warren, *Democracy and Association* (Princeton, NJ: Princeton University Press, 2000), 134–204.

[76] Jean Cohen, "Does Voluntary Association Make Democracy Work?" in Neil Smelser and Jeffrey C. Alexander, eds., *Diversity and Its Discontents: Cultural Conflict and Common Ground in Contemporary American Society* (Princeton, NJ: Princeton University Press, 1999), 269–70.

As Tocqueville reminds us, this is a small price to pay if we want to remain civilized and avoid relapsing into barbarism. Although we shall never be able to reach a consensus about the ends of politics, we might be able to agree on the means of civil politics. Without the virtue of civility[77] and the mediating structures that stand between the private sphere of individuals and the impersonal structures of today's world, there can be no genuine freedom in modern societies.

Political Science, Indiana University, Bloomington

---

[77] For an extensive treatment of civility, see Boyd, *Uncivil Society*, 25–30, 248–52.

THE RAWLSIAN VIEW OF PRIVATE ORDERING*

By Kevin A. Kordana and David H. Blankfein Tabachnick

I. Introduction

While the right to freedom of association has been the subject of interesting and important work in constitutional law scholarship,[1] the topic is also illustrative of important fault lines between and within various liberal schools of thought. Within any scheme of political and legal institutions, questions arise, for example, as to the justification of various forms of private ordering—for example, the firm. Unsurprisingly, different conceptions of liberalism offer different answers to such questions. Lockean liberals and libertarians might be expected to view such questions as requiring the working out of the relationship between one's natural (economic) rights and other social values. Contemporary egalitarian liberals with a more skeptical view of a natural right to private property typically hold a more distributive view of institutional design and regulation (e.g., Rawlsians).

Interestingly, the answer to the question of the status of the right to freedom of association is not only sharply controversial between liberal camps (e.g., Rawlsians and Lockeans), but, surprisingly, appears to be quite controversial even *within* the contemporary egalitarian camp: Rawlsianism. Indeed, the Rawlsian texts appear not to be consistent with regard to the status of the right to freedom of association. John Rawls's early work omits mention of freedom of association as among the basic liberties, but in his later work he explicitly includes freedom of association as among these liberties.

In addition, contemporary literature on Rawlsianism is highly divided over the status of "private ordering" in Rawlsianism. If we narrow our focus to questions of economic association, that is, private ordering (e.g., contract, partnership, and corporate law), we find a similar ambiguity in the Rawlsian texts. This ambiguity has engendered widespread confusion

* We are grateful to John G. Bennett, Harry Dolan, John Marshall, Ellen Frankel Paul, Thomas Pogge, and A. John Simmons for written comments on a previous draft, and to John D. Arras, Guido Calabresi, Anthony Kronman, Daniel Markovits, Jeffrey Paul, Robert Post, Seana Shiffrin, Michael Smith, the other contributors to this volume, and participants in University of Virginia School of Law and Yale Law School workshops, for valuable discussions.

[1] See, e.g., Seana V. Shiffrin, "What Is Really Wrong with Compelled Association?" *Northwestern Law Review* 99, no. 2 (2005): 839; Amy Gutmann, ed., *Freedom of Association* (Princeton, NJ: Princeton University Press, 1998); Geoffrey R. Stone, "The Equal Access Controversy," *Northwestern Law Review* 81, no. 1 (1986): 168; and Kenneth L. Karst, "The Freedom of Intimate Association," *Yale Law Journal* 89, no. 4 (1980): 624.

doi:10.1017/S0265052508080278

over the scope of the two principles of justice—leading to the contemporary dispute over the breadth of what Rawls calls the "basic structure" and the question of whether the principles of justice are properly understood to govern private ordering. This ambiguity has, as we will argue, engendered further discussion in private law theory over the question of whether Rawlsianism (properly understood) is neutral between conceptions of the private law and economic associations: for example, the dispute over the *ex ante* and *ex post* conceptions of contract theory.[2]

In what follows, we discuss the right to freedom of association in Rawlsianism and explain what we take to be the source of the ambiguity in question. We argue that the ambiguity owes to the fact that (for Rawls) the right to freedom of association is best understood as a complex right: a conjunction (or bundle) of two distinct sorts of liberties: *basic* (noneconomic) liberties conjoined with *nonbasic* (economic) liberties. We then maintain, however, that disambiguating the right to freedom of association in this fashion exposes two further puzzles in Rawlsianism and the literature on Rawls and private ordering: first, the dispute over the breadth of the basic structure and the question of whether private ordering is properly understood as governed by the two principles of justice; and second, if private ordering is indeed within the bounds of the basic structure and subject to the two principles of justice, whether the first principle of justice is properly understood to play a significant role in Rawlsian private ordering.

We maintain that the solutions to these significant puzzles turn upon what appears to be a conflation in Rawlsianism over two distinct conceptions of "freedom"—on one hand, what we call "pre-institutional" (or natural) freedom, and on the other, "post-institutional" (or constructed) freedom. While Rawls accepts the distinction between pre- and post-institutional conceptions of freedom and acknowledges that (going forward from the original position) he is entitled only to the "post-institutional" conception, in discussing these matters he illicitly slips into propounding a pre-institutional (seemingly, Lockean) conception. We maintain that recognition of this conflation explains the confusion surrounding the basic structure and the role the two principles of justice play in private ordering and thus sheds light on the Rawlsian view of freedom of association.

---

[2] In the *ex post* conception of contract law, the standard of justice invoked is endogenous to the terms of the contract (i.e., the will of the consenting parties). A particular contract is fair, *because* it was consented to (of course, consent requires some measure of information, capacity, and lack of duress). A promise, itself, is taken to be the procedure which generates the fair terms of contractual liability. In the *ex ante* conception, normative values or standards that are exogenous to the contract (i.e., external to the promise, or to the will of the parties) may be invoked as the basis of contractual liability; these standards are duty-imposing despite the fact that they do not arise from an explicit promise or from the will of the parties. Typically, such liability involves an appeal to general welfare, economic efficiency, or distributive justice.

II. Rawls and the Right to Freedom of Association

The status of a right to freedom of association in a Rawlsian scheme of legal and political institutions is, from Rawls's texts, neither obvious nor uncontroversial. In *A Theory of Justice*, Rawls, patterning the United States Constitution, indicates that the basic liberties to be constructed and protected by the first principle of justice include "freedom of . . . assembly," [3] but he does not mention freedom of association explicitly. However, in *Political Liberalism*, when discussing the basic liberties Rawls includes "the political liberties and freedom of association." [4] In *Justice as Fairness: A Restatement*, Rawls notes that "liberty of conscience and freedom of association are to ensure the opportunity for the free and informed exercise of [the] capacity [to form and pursue a conception of the good]." [5]

Given this ambiguity, it is an open question for Rawlsianism whether or not freedom of association is properly understood as a basic right, constructed by the first principle of justice in its provision of a package of liberties adequate to the full exercise of the two moral powers: "the capacity for a sense of justice" and "the capacity for a conception of the good." [6] This ambiguity leads to a dilemma for Rawlsianism: either the right to freedom of association is best understood as a basic, though noneconomic right, constructed by the first principle of justice and thus constitutionally protected, *or* it is best viewed as one of many conceivable *nonbasic* and therefore *non*guaranteed *economic* rights constructed by the second principle of justice in conjunction with the entire economic scheme. In Rawls's earlier work, he appears to have grasped the second horn of the dilemma, but then in his later work he seems to have been drawn to the first.

In our view, the source of the ambiguity and the resultant dilemma is the fact that freedom of association for Rawls is best understood as a complex right; it conjoins a set of personal liberties (e.g., the freedom of assembly and the freedom to form intimate relationships) with a set of economically oriented liberties (i.e., the rights of private ordering). Given the complex nature of the right to freedom of association and the ambiguity surrounding this right, the ambiguity in the Rawlsian

[3] John Rawls, *A Theory of Justice* (Cambridge, MA: Harvard University Press, 1971), 61.

[4] John Rawls, "The Basic Liberties and Their Priority," in Rawls, *Political Liberalism* (New York: Columbia University Press, 1989), 291.

[5] John Rawls, *Justice as Fairness: A Restatement*, ed. Erin Kelly (Cambridge, MA: Harvard University Press, 2001), 113.

[6] Rawls, in *Political Liberalism* and in *Justice as Fairness*, treats the first principle of justice not as a maximizing principle, as it was in *A Theory of Justice*, but rather as a principle for the provision of *adequate* liberty to the exercise of what he calls the two moral powers. Rawls's revised first principle of justice states: "Each person has an equal right to a fully adequate scheme of equal basic liberties which is compatible with a similar scheme of liberties for all" (Rawls, "The Basic Liberties and Their Priority," 291). With regard to the revised formulation of the first principle of justice, see also Rawls, *Justice as Fairness*, 42: "Each person has the same indefeasible claim to a fully adequate scheme of equal basic liberties, which scheme is compatible with the same scheme of liberties for all." On the two moral powers, see Rawls, "The Basic Liberties and Their Priority," 332.

text is understandable. The constitutive personal and economic components of the right to freedom of association interestingly straddle the (arguably) most central distinction in Rawlsianism—the bifurcation between basic (personal) and nonbasic (economic) liberties.[7]

The Rawlsian texts are sometimes vague about the extent to which property constructions (i.e., the details of ownership and liability) are made at the level of the first or of the second principle of justice. For example, in writing about the "distribution of native endowments," Rawls writes: "It is not said that this distribution is a common asset: to say that would presuppose a (normative) principle of ownership that is not available in the fundamental ideas from which we begin the exposition."[8] He goes on to say that by "agreeing to [the difference] principle, it is as if [we] agree to regard the distribution of endowments as a common asset. What this regarding consists in is expressed by the difference principle itself."[9] This might be interpreted to mean that property constructions are largely second-principle matters. Theories of property and ownership are not available at the first-principle level, and instead emerge as constructions of the difference principle.

However, in the very next paragraph, he writes:

> Note that what is regarded as a common asset is the distribution of native endowments and not our native endowments per se. It is not as if society owned individuals' endowments taken separately, looking at individuals one by one. To the contrary, the question of ownership does not arise; and should it arise, it is persons themselves who own their endowments: the psychological and physical integrity of persons is already guaranteed by the basic rights and liberties that fall under the first principle of justice.[10]

While we offer below a reading that provides a unified Rawlsian interpretation of these passages, it might seem that this latter paragraph suggests that (some) property constructions are a first-principle matter: native endowments are "owned" by their holders as a first-principle matter. The key to understanding what Rawls means here is to understand that the first-principle right to "psychological and physical integrity" need not entail a full-blown property right—that is, persons might be understood

---

[7] In defending this bifurcation in previous work, we ourselves uncritically followed the later Rawls in placing the freedom of association squarely on the basic liberties side of the divide. We maintained, following the later Rawlsian texts, that the "more fundamental non-economic basic liberties that *are* central or necessary to the full exercise of the two moral powers [include] (for example, freedom of thought and conscience, freedom of religion, and freedom of association)." Kevin A. Kordana and David H. Tabachnick, "On Belling the Cat: Rawls and Tort as Corrective Justice," *Virginia Law Review* 92, no. 7 (2006): 1302.

[8] Rawls, *Justice as Fairness*, 75.

[9] Ibid.

[10] Ibid.

as having, as a first-principle matter, the right to bodily organs vital to survival, but not necessarily the right to "own" their particular organs. When Rawls, in the second paragraph, uses the term "own," he must be understood as using that term in the pre-institutional sense in which his critics, such as Robert Nozick, use it. Crucially, however, this usage is not available in Rawls's own theory, where property rights are post-institutional creations. Property constructions in native endowments might, then, emerge from the difference principle, as stated in the first passages. But they are not *entirely* a second-principle construction, in the sense that their construction at the second-principle level must satisfy the first principle's demand for a scheme adequate to the exercise of the two moral powers.

Return now to the right to freedom of association. On the one hand, it appears that the personal rights concerning, for example, the right of assembly or the right to form intimate relationships, are what Rawls calls basic liberties—properly understood as subject to the first principle of justice and to be constitutionally protected. On the other hand, the right to freedom of association also appears to be comprised of an economic component which, if it is to exist for Rawls, is properly understood to be under the governance of the second principle of justice, constructed so as to maximize the position of the least well-off in conjunction with the complete scheme of economic institutions, subject to the lexically prior demands of equal opportunity and the first principle of justice.[11]

The Rawlsian texts, interestingly, invite the view—and Rawls himself at times appears to hold the view—that the right to freedom of association must be included among the *basic* liberties. We have, however, argued elsewhere[12] for what we call the "high" Rawlsian position: namely, the view that all robust economic constructions and baselines—the full details of tax and transfer policies, property rules, the rules of contract law and tort law, etc.—are properly understood, for Rawls, as second-principle matters. In the high Rawlsian view, the *economic* component of the right to freedom of association turns on a distributive baseline set by the second principle of justice. Our idea is that even conceptions and details of "economic freedom" are underdetermined at the stage of the first principle of justice. For Rawls (unlike Locke or Nozick), of course, the outcomes of "free"

---

[11] The second principle of justice states: "Social and economic inequalities are to satisfy two conditions: first, they are to be attached to offices and positions open to all under conditions of fair equality of opportunity; and second, they are to be to the greatest benefit of the least-advantaged members of society (the difference principle)." Rawls, *Justice as Fairness*, 42–43.

[12] The "high Rawlsian" position is (roughly) the view that the specific details of any economic liberties (including private law doctrine: contract, tort, etc.) are, for Rawls, a second-principle construction, to be constructed by the difference principle (constrained by equality of opportunity). See Kordana and Tabachnick, "On Belling the Cat: Rawls and Tort as Corrective Justice," 1300–1306; Kevin A. Kordana and David H. Tabachnick, "Rawls and Contract Law," *George Washington Law Review* 73, no. 3 (2005): 609–10; and Kevin A. Kordana and David H. Tabachnick, "Taxation, the Private Law, and Distributive Justice," *Social Philosophy and Policy* 23, no. 2 (2006): 146.

consensual market transactions have no particular normative privilege. Indeed, the very notion of "freedom" as it pertains to economic arrangements in any purported right to freedom of association requires a distributive or economic baseline.

For Rawls, economic freedom is post-institutional freedom or what we have described as a set of "options open," constructed by the difference principle.[13] In our view, for Rawls, the very question of the economic associations in which one is "free" to engage *is itself* a question requiring an economic baseline. For Rawls, of course, it is the difference principle, not the first principle of justice, which sets such baselines. To invoke a right to freedom of association (in the economic realm) at the first-principle stage is to invoke an alternative or exogenous economic baseline which is unavailable to Rawlsianism. Since the right to freedom of association is, as we have argued, in some measure a function of *economic* liberties constructed as a second-principle matter, the first principle of justice cannot serve as the basis for the full-blown right.

Despite what we have described as the high Rawlsian position, there remains a question over the precise role (if any) that the first principle of justice might play in the construction of property baselines and economic liberties, given the demand for what Rawls calls "personal property." Rawls admittedly *appears* reluctant to commit to relegating *all* property matters to the second principle of justice. He notoriously maintains that the right to hold what he describes as personal property is basic and under the control of the first principle of justice, but he is also clear that the robust details of this rudimentary right are to be constructed by the second principle of justice.[14]

He writes, "Two wider conceptions of the right of property as a basic liberty are to be avoided. One conception extends this right to include certain rights of acquisition and bequest."[15] The point of our high Rawlsian position is that the details of any economic scheme are second-principle constructions. Rawls's notion of "personal property" is a rudimentary right best understood as the very minimal demand for the "material basis" of "independence" and "self-respect,"[16] consistent with Rawls's general property skepticism and the full range of possible economic schemes. Any robust details of the economic component of the right to freedom of

---

[13] Kordana and Tabachnick, "Rawls and Contract Law," 620–23.

[14] Rawls writes that "[a]mong the basic rights is the right to hold and to have the exclusive use of personal property. . . . Having this right and being able effectively to exercise it is one of the social bases of self-respect. Thus this right is a general right: a right all citizens have in virtue of their fundamental interests. . . . [W]ider conceptions of property are not used because they are not necessary for the adequate development and full exercise of the moral powers, and so are not an essential social basis of self-respect. They may, however, still be justified. . . . The further specification of the right to property is to be made at [the stage of the second principle's implementation]." Rawls, *Justice as Fairness*, 114.

[15] Rawls, "The Basic Liberties and Their Priority," 298.

[16] Rawls, *Justice as Fairness*, 114.

association—for example, the right to form a firm—would go well beyond the mere minimal right to "personal property." Rawls writes that a second conception of property as a basic liberty which is to be avoided is "the equal right to participate in the means of production and natural resources."[17] For Rawls, there is, at the stage of the first principle of justice, the open possibility of even perfect equality in economic matters (as a second-principle construction); any economic right to freedom of association must not be so robust as to dictate details of a specific economic scheme.[18]

Return to the ambiguity surrounding the right to freedom of association in Rawlsianism. Assuming that the two principles of justice govern private ordering and that (following the high Rawlsian position) robust conceptions of property or economic relations must be governed by the second principle of justice, one may justifiably conclude that private ordering is best understood as a second-principle construction. The ambiguity in Rawls's texts likely arises from the fact that the right to freedom of association is comprised of both personal and economic liberties and is properly understood as straddling the first-principle/second-principle bifurcation; this, in turn, helps resolve the ambiguity. There is for Rawls no commitment to freedom of association in private ordering at the first-principle stage. Any basic right to freedom of association must protect *merely* personal (noneconomic) liberties. Thus, the full-blown right to freedom of association for Rawls, were it to exist, would be in a significant measure a second-principle construction.

III. Disagreements about the "Basic Structure"

For Rawlsian political theory, the two principles of justice are taken to apply to the basic structure of society.[19] There is, however, significant disagreement over the breadth of the basic structure and its relationship to private ordering. Arguably, Rawls has, in different passages, espoused differing conceptions of the breadth of the basic structure, some narrow and some broad.[20] Attention to the question of the breadth of the basic

---

[17] Rawls, "The Basic Liberties and Their Priority," 298.

[18] Rawls, *A Theory of Justice*, 61; Rawls, "The Basic Liberties and Their Priority," 298.

[19] Rawls, *A Theory of Justice*, 7.

[20] "[T]he whole concept of basic institutions in Rawls's theory is vaguer than one might expect, given the role he insists they are supposed to play in any adequate theory of social justice." Hugo Adam Bedau, "Social Justice and Social Institutions," in Peter A. French et al., eds., *Midwest Studies in Philosophy: Studies in Ethical Theory* (Notre Dame, IN: Notre Dame Press, 1978), 169. Thomas Pogge writes that what he takes to be a broad conception of the basic structure found in *A Theory of Justice* "conflicts with a narrower understanding of the term which dominates Rawls's discussion in 'The Basic Structure as Subject.'" Thomas Pogge, *Realizing Rawls* (Ithaca, NY: Cornell University Press, 1989), 23. G. A. Cohen describes Rawls's account of the basic structure as embodying a "fatal ambiguity." G. A. Cohen, "Where the Action Is: On the Site of Distributive Justice," *Philosophy and Public Affairs* 26, no. 1 (1997): 11. A. John Simmons writes: "[O]n what constitutes 'the basic structure of society' . . . Rawls may not have been entirely consistent." A. John Simmons, "The Duty to

structure may be motivated by a variety of concerns: we focus, in what follows, upon one—namely, the question of whether or not the principles of justice apply to private ordering.

There are several accounts of the breadth of the basic structure. In the narrow view, the basic structure is comprised only of constitutional essentials and society's system of taxation and transfer. In this view, private ordering lies outside the bounds of the basic structure, beyond the reach of the distributive aims of the two principles of justice. The two principles of justice, in this view, are thought to swing clear of private ordering.[21] If the narrow view of the basic structure is correct, Rawlsian political philosophy is, as it is often thought to be, silent or neutral with regard to the structure of private ordering (e.g., the institutions of contract, tort, and bankruptcy). Rawlsianism, then, would be neutral with regard to the contemporary debates in legal theory between, for example, the autonomy and wealth-maximization conceptions of contract law or the deterrence and corrective-justice conceptions of tort law.[22]

The narrow view is contrasted with other, broader, conceptions. In the *wide* view, chiefly associated with *A Theory of Justice*, the two principles of

---

Obey and Our Natural Moral Duties," in Christopher Heath Wellman and A. John Simmons, *Is There a Duty to Obey the Law?* (New York: Cambridge University Press, 2005), 157.

[21] "Is it possible to justify [Rawls's] preference for taxation and the non-distributive conception of contract law that it entails?" Anthony T. Kronman, "Contract Law and Distributive Justice," *Yale Law Journal* 89, no. 3 (1980): 500. "Rawls . . . restrict[s] his principles of justice to something called the 'basic structure,' specifically exempting all issues involving the fairness of particular transactions." Bruce A. Ackerman, *Social Justice in the Liberal State* (New Haven, CT: Yale University Press, 1980), 195. "The principles of justice are meant to regulate the effects of basic institutions and do not apply to private arrangements and transactions." David Lyons, *Ethics and the Rule of Law* (New York: Cambridge University Press, 1984), 131–32. Arthur Ripstein, arguably defending the narrow view, writes that "particular transactions can be judged on their own terms, rather than being subordinated to distributive justice." Arthur Ripstein, "The Division of Responsibility and the Law of Tort," *Fordham Law Review* 72, no. 5 (2004): 1815. Thomas Nagel, articulating Rawls's view though not commenting on its merits, writes: "[Rawls's] two principles of justice are designed to regulate neither the personal conduct of individuals living in a just society, nor the governance of private associations, nor the international relations of societies to one another, but only the basic structure of separate nation-states." Thomas Nagel, "The Problem of Global Justice," *Philosophy and Public Affairs* 33, no. 2 (2005): 123.

For the alternative view, in which private ordering is subject to the two principles of justice, see Kordana and Tabachnick, "Rawls and Contract Law," 619. Samuel Scheffler maintains that there is no reason to believe that the rules of contract law cannot be properly understood as constitutive of the basic structure and subject to the principles of justice. He argues: "There is no reason why the specific institutional mechanisms that are used to ensure background justice must be fixed or invariant. . . . The distinction between tax and contract is illustrative, not definitional or essential." Samuel Scheffler, "Is the Basic Structure Basic?" in Christine Sypnowich, ed., *The Egalitarian Conscience: Essays in Honour of G. A. Cohen* (New York: Oxford University Press, 2006), 42 n. 6.

[22] For a summary and overview of competing conceptions of contract theory, see Peter Benson, "Contract," in Dennis Patterson, ed., *A Companion to Philosophy of Law and Legal Theory* (Cambridge, MA: Blackwell Publishers, 1996); and Jody S. Kraus, "Philosophy of Contract Law," in *The Oxford Handbook of Jurisprudence and Philosophy of Law*, ed. Jules Coleman and Scott Shapiro (New York: Oxford University Press, 2002), 687.

justice are taken to apply to all institutions which significantly affect the distribution of primary goods and one's life prospects. Rawls himself mentions, for example, the monogamous family and the social practice of promising.[23] In the *coercive conception*, the principles of justice are taken to apply to all of society's coercive political and legal institutions.[24] If such a broader conception of the basic structure is correct, private ordering—given its (at least partially) coercive nature, the significant role it plays in the distribution of primary goods, and the effect it has on one's life prospects—is properly understood as within the bounds of the basic structure and is, therefore, constructed in service to the distributive aims of the two principles of justice.[25] Rawlsianism then would not properly be understood as silent with regard to private ordering; a distributive-justice conception would be required.

Rawls recognizes the significance of this issue. Seemingly in response to Robert Nozick's criticisms[26] that Rawlsian distributive justice can be made to seem objectionable because it is inconsistent with the purport-edly appealing features of Nozick's Lockean-libertarian conception of transfer,[27] Rawls addresses the relationship between the basic structure and private ordering in a complex and controversial passage on pages 268–69 of *Political Liberalism*, in "The Basic Structure as Subject." Rawls writes:

> Thus . . . we arrive at the idea of a division of labor between two kinds of social rules, and the different institutional forms in which these rules are realized. The basic structure comprises first the institutions that define the social background and includes as well those operations that continually adjust and compensate for the inevitable tendencies away from background fairness, for example, such operations as income and inheritance taxation designed to even out the ownership of property. *This structure* also enforces through the legal system another set of rules that govern the transactions

---

[23] Rawls, *A Theory of Justice*, 7, 345.

[24] Cohen, "Where the Action Is: On the Site of Distributive Justice," 11.

[25] For Rawls, *each* of the two principles of justice is distributive. If private law rules are to be constructed instrumentally in service to their distributive demands, Rawlsianism would, then, produce a distributive-justice conception of the private law. To what degree *each* of the two principles of justice would share in the private law construction is an open question, given that the rules of the private law may define some aspects of personal liberty and that they also construct economic liberties and define economic baselines. Our point is that, whatever the result, the conception of private law is distributive. Any coincidental pattern-ing of, say, Charles Fried's "will theory" of contract, or of Lockean conceptions of property, would be a matter of mere overlap; such rules would have been constructed in service to the distributive aims of the two principles of justice and not *directly* drawn from comprehensive deontic principles. See Charles Fried, *Contract as Promise: A Theory of Contractual Obligation* (Cambridge, MA: Harvard University Press, 1981).

[26] Robert Nozick, *Anarchy, State, and Utopia* (New York: Basic Books, 1974), 167.

[27] John Rawls, "The Basic Structure as Subject," in Rawls, *Political Liberalism*, 263 n. 6.

and agreements between individuals and associations (the law of contract, and so on). The rules relating to fraud and duress, and the like, belong to these rules, and satisfy the requirements of simplicity and practicality. They are framed to leave individuals and associations free to act effectively in pursuit of their ends and without excessive constraints.

To conclude: we start with the basic structure and try to see how this structure itself should make the adjustments necessary to preserve background justice. What we look for, in effect, is an institutional division of labor between the basic structure and the rules applying directly to individuals and associations and to be followed by them in particular transactions. If this division of labor can be established, individuals and associations are then left free to advance their ends more effectively within the framework of the basic structure, secure in the knowledge that elsewhere in the social system the necessary corrections to preserve background justice are being made.[28]

This passage has, unfortunately, neither helped to clarify Rawls's own thinking on the issue, nor helped to clarify the most philosophically defensible Rawlsian position. Indeed, the passage has contributed to disagreement and prompted further commentary. G. A. Cohen has suggested, for example, that "[p]uzzlement with respect to the bounds of the basic structure is not relieved by examination of the relevant pages of *Political Liberalism*."[29] Thomas Pogge has maintained that Rawls's views on the issue "are not merely vague but also ambiguous."[30]

Other commentators, however, have found in this passage from *Political Liberalism* strong support for the narrow conception of the basic structure. If the passage provides the needed textual and philosophical support for the narrow view, then the two principles of justice are, as is often conventionally thought to be the case, not properly understood to apply to the private law. The seemingly invited conclusion is that Rawlsianism is consistent with any number of (even nondistributive) private law conceptions (e.g., the autonomy conception of contract or the corrective-justice conception of tort law).

If, however, the passage can be shown to be consistent with a broader view of the basic structure, then Rawlsianism is not properly understood as neutral in this regard; private law institutions are subject to the two principles of justice. Liam Murphy, for example, while seeming to acknowledge that Rawls narrows the conception of the basic structure in the second paragraph of the passage, argues that contract law is most plausibly understood as within the bounds of the basic structure,

---

[28] Ibid., 268–69 (emphasis added).
[29] Cohen, "Where the Action Is: On the Site of Distributive Justice," 19 n. 36.
[30] Pogge, *Realizing Rawls*, 21.

and concludes that the second (narrowing) paragraph of the passage must be an unintended mistake. Murphy thus stipulates that "Rawls did not after all intend the account of the basic structure offered in 'The Basic Structure as Subject' to differ significantly from that offered in *A Theory of Justice*."[31]

In what follows, we explain why this passage has led commentators to reach such divergent conclusions about the basic structure and its relationship to the various conceptions of the private law. We argue that the disagreement is explained by an instructive confusion in the passage over the distinction between what we characterize as "pre-institutional" and "post-institutional" freedom. Once this distinction is drawn, the disagreement can be explained.[32] The passage, we argue, illicitly shifts from invoking the post-institutional sense of "freedom" to invoking the pre-institutional sense, thereby causing significant though understandable disagreement. Rawls's problematic lapse into the pre-institutional conception of "freedom" provides reasonable interpretive grounds for the narrow understanding of the basic structure. If Rawls, however, had instead remained consistent, invoking the sense of "free-dom" to which he is entitled at this stage of his theory—the post-institutional conception—such sharp disagreement need not have arisen.

Once these two senses of freedom are distinguished and Rawlsianism, despite the confusion of the passage, is shown to require freedom in the post-institutional sense, we argue that the sharp disagreement over the relationship between the basic structure and the private law is explained. The passage can be coherently read to provide a plausible account of a broader conception of the basic structure that encompasses the private law, which entails that the private law, for Rawlsianism, is properly understood to answer to the distributive aims of the two principles of justice.

---

[31] Liam B. Murphy, "Institutions and the Demands of Justice," *Philosophy and Public Affairs* 27, no. 4 (1998): 258, 261 and n. 30.

[32] Rawls accepts, although at times seems to underappreciate, the distinction between (roughly) the pre-institutional and post-institutional conceptions of freedom, and he acknowledges that it is the distribution of *post*-institutional "liberties" (or what we call "post-institutional freedom") that is the concern of the first principle of justice, as opposed to "liberty as such" (or what we call "pre-institutional freedom"). For example, H. L. A. Hart argues that there are "important differences between Rawls's doctrine of liberty and Kant's conception of mutual freedom under universal law," insightfully pointing out that the first principle of justice "refers not to 'liberty' but to basic or fundamental *liberties*, which are understood to be legally recognized and protected from interference." H. L. A. Hart, "Rawls on Liberty and Its Priority," in Norman Daniels, ed., *Reading Rawls* (Stanford, CA: Stanford University Press, 1975), 234–35 and n. 6.

Rawls acknowledges the distinction: "Hart noted, however, that in *Theory* I sometimes used arguments and phrases which suggest that the priority of liberty *as such is meant;* although, as he saw, this is not the correct interpretation. . . . With Hart's discussion I agree, on the whole." Rawls, "The Basic Liberties and Their Priority," 292 and n. 7 (emphasis in the original). Rawls reiterates this point of agreement with Hart in *Justice as Fairness*, writing that "no priority is assigned to liberty as such, as if the exercise of something called 'liberty' had a preeminent value and were the main, if not the sole, end of political and social justice." Rawls, *Justice as Fairness*, 44.

IV. "Freedom" in Rawlsianism

There are two important senses of "freedom" at work in Rawlsianism. The first is a commitment to freedom as a component of the plurality of values that constitute the original position.[33] This conception of freedom informs the original position (hereafter, OP). It is, however, understood to be—in the first instance—silent with regard to any particular economic construction or the specific details of economic rights and liberties, quite unlike the Lockean pre-institutional account of natural freedom and right. There is, however, also in Rawls a second, post-institutional conception of freedom or, as Rawls calls it, a set of "liberties," constructed by the two principles of justice. It is important to recognize the role that each of these two conceptions of freedom plays in Rawlsianism. The first conception is, of course, a component of Rawls's initial justificatory project—if persons are taken to be morally bound by the OP-derived principles of justice, there must be an antecedent commitment, in some measure, to the idea of persons conceived of as free and equal. It is only against the backdrop of this set of values that sense can be made of the justificatory force that Rawls attributes to the OP-derived principles. Thus, the value of the person conceived of as free and equal is a crucial component of Rawlsianism that resides in the initial justificatory framework that (purportedly) legitimates the principles derived in the OP.

Once the two principles of justice are derived, however, *direct* appeal to the value of freedom, equality, any comprehensive moral doctrine, or any natural freedom or right is illicit. Going forward from the OP, the two principles of justice, for Rawls, *define* the conception of justice. The liberal commitment to freedom, however, has purportedly not simply fallen out of the picture; instead, Rawls takes it to be "built into" the two principles of justice themselves, in conjunction with the other values embedded in the OP construction. The two principles of justice, once derived, in turn construct society's complete set of legal and political institutions.

Thus, moving forward from the OP with the two principles of justice in place, there emerges a second, institutional, conception of freedom in Rawlsianism—namely, what we have called "post-institutional freedom." This post-institutional freedom is the institutional set of legal and political "liberties" (or options open) constructed instrumentally in service to the demands of the two principles of justice, taken in lexical priority.[34] It is this post-institutional freedom or set of liberties that, for

---

[33] The original position is Rawls's hypothetical social choice scenario, in which idealized actors, maximizing their self-interest under conditions of imperfect knowledge, select principles of justice to govern social, political, and legal institutions.

[34] Jonathan Wolff has also identified in Rawlsianism what we are describing as post-institutional freedom, calling it "formal liberty." He writes: "After all, a Rawlsian pattern will allow a great deal of room for transfers, although some will probably be prohibited, while others made compulsory by taxation. . . . The right to liberty is, on this view, purely formal. It is, in essence, merely the right to do what you have a right to do." Jonathan Wolff,

Rawls, constructs and frames the crucial liberal distinction between the public and private realms. These liberties are constructed instrumentally in service to the demands of Rawls's distributive principles. The post-institutional private realm so constructed is neither derived directly from nor taken to map in a one-to-one fashion Kantian or Lockean conceptions of autonomy or natural freedom.[35]

V. The Ambiguity between Pre-Institutional and Post-Institutional Freedom

While Rawls accepts the distinction between what we call pre-institutional and post-institutional conceptions of freedom, he is not always clear as to which sense of the term he is invoking. The ambiguity is first introduced in *Political Liberalism* on pages 265–66 in a paragraph in which Rawls raises the issue of freedom of contract. In his response to Nozick, Rawls briefly adopts, for the sake of argument, the libertarian (pre-institutional) account of freedom and its associated entitlement conception of justice (or fairness). Rawls writes: "[S]uppose we begin with the initially attractive idea that social circumstances and people's relationships to one another should develop over time in accordance with *free* agreements *fairly* arrived at and fully honored" (emphasis added). He continues: "Straightaway we need an account of when agreements are *free* and the social circumstances under which they are reached are *fair*" (emphasis added), without which "the accumulated results of many separate and ostensibly fair agreements . . . are likely in the course of time to alter citizens' relationships . . . so that the conditions for free and fair agreements no longer hold." Here, Rawls must have in mind that what is needed at the start is a post-institutional account of when agreements and social circumstances are *free* and *fair*.[36] That is, we need an account of institutional design in which the rules that govern contractual freedom (i.e., the institutional rules of contract law), in conjunction with all other background rules, are constructed in service to the demands of the two principles of justice.

However, Rawls goes on to say that "the role of the institutions that belong to the basic structure is to secure background conditions against which the actions of individuals and associations take place." Here the sense of "freedom" he has in mind is ambiguous. That individual actions

---

Robert Nozick: Property, Justice, and the Minimal State (Stanford, CA: Stanford University Press, 1991), 96.

[35] Analogously, in discussing the distinction between natural (here, Lockean) and Rawlsian accounts of justice, A. John Simmons writes that, for Locke, "justice consists of satisfying pre-existing rights," while, for Rawls, "some independently-defended standard of justice generates rights to just institutional arrangements." A. John Simmons, "Liberties and Markets," *Virginia Law Review* 92, no. 7 (2006): 1629.

[36] Rawls, *Political Liberalism*, 265–66. For Rawls, contra Nozick's entitlement theory of justice, the two principles of justice define the conception of fairness.

are taking place "against" "background conditions" could indicate a commitment to pre-institutional freedom for individual actions. In a post-institutional sense, individual actions might better be described as taking place within the set of institutional rules that has been created, rules which offer various options for individuals to pursue (while foreclosing other options).

The paragraph concludes, in an even more explicitly pre-institutional vein, that "[u]nless this structure is appropriately regulated and adjusted, an initially just social process will eventually cease to be just, however *free* and *fair* particular transactions may look when viewed by themselves" (emphasis added). Rawls has seemingly returned to the pre-institutional conception of "free" and "fair" with which he began the paragraph and does not appear to complete the thought with which he immediately followed: that "straightaway" we need an account of what it means for contractual relationships to be "free" and "fair" (in the Rawlsian post-institutional sense). In other words, individual transactions which do not accord with post-institutional demands would not even properly be understood as "fair," from that post-institutional perspective. It would only be in the pre-institutional (Lockean) conception of freedom that they would be properly understood as "fair." In subsequent passages of "The Basic Structure as Subject," as we discuss in detail, Rawls continues to equivocate between these two important senses of "freedom," an equivocation which has caused quite understandable disagreement over the bounds of the basic structure and its relationship to private law rules.

Now, return to the lengthy passage from pages 268–69 of *Political Liberalism* (quoted in Section III above). In the first paragraph, Rawls draws a distinction between rules that assist in maintaining "background fairness" and rules that address "transactions . . . between individuals." The latter, he states, are to answer to the demands of "simplicity and practicality" and are "framed to leave individuals . . . free . . . in pursuit of their ends." On the one hand, if one were to interpret "free" here in the pre-institutional sense, as is suggested by the word "leave" applied to "free," the paragraph could reasonably be taken to support the narrow view of the basic structure. In this view, the rules of taxation and transfer lie within the basic structure and answer to the demands of the two principles of justice. Rules of contract law, however, lie outside the (narrow) basic structure, and may be derived either from pre-institutional Kantian notions of autonomy or natural freedom, or from the demands of "simplicity and practicality"—from the passage, it is unclear.

On the other hand, this first paragraph need not be read to invoke the narrow conception of the basic structure[37] and the pre-institutional

---

[37] Liam Murphy, for example, argues that this paragraph can be viewed as invoking a single (basic) structure which includes both tax and transfer and the rules of property and contract. Murphy, "Institutions and the Demands of Justice," 261 and n. 30.

conception of freedom. If one were to interpret "free" here in the post-institutional sense, as is suggested by the word "framed" (i.e., constructed) as applied to "free," then a measure of contractual freedom has been constructed in service to the demands of the two principles of justice. In this view, the rules of contract law lie within the basic structure, and the extent to which such rules respond to the demands of "simplicity and practicality" must be viewed as simply a conjecture. In essence, Rawls can be read here as speculating that the preponderance of equity-oriented moves (i.e., those directed at achieving and maintaining "background fairness") are best achieved in areas such as taxation, as opposed to the rules of the private law.[38] The extent to which this is true is, of course, an empirical question. Rawls's distinction between "two kinds of . . . rules" should be read as mere conjecture about optimal institutional design, rather than as a philosophical or principled distinction between rules guided by differing principles.[39] We return to this issue in greater detail in Section VI below. At the level of principle, for Rawls, *all* rules of legal and political institutions are to be constructed—in conjunction with one another—to best meet the demands of the two principles of justice.[40]

That Rawls (incorrectly) has in mind the pre-institutional conception of freedom seems even more likely when we turn to the second paragraph of the passage from pages 268–69 of *Political Liberalism*. Here, he speaks of "an institutional division of labor between the basic structure and the rules applying directly to individuals . . . and to be followed by them in particular transactions." This seems to provide grounds for narrowing the conception of the basic structure—contract law, for example, would seem to apply to individuals and particular transactions and therefore be contrasted with the rules of (and lie outside the bounds of) the basic structure. Furthermore, Rawls goes on to state that given this division of labor, "individuals . . . are then left free to advance their ends." Here, Rawls seems to invoke the pre-institutional conception of freedom, since post-institutional freedom would be *constructed* in service to the demands of the difference principle, not simply "left free." Pre-institutional freedom, in contrast, is "natural" freedom—which makes perfect sense in the context of being "left free" or left unfettered.

---

[38] Cf. Louis Kaplow and Steven Shavell, "Why the Legal System Is Less Efficient Than the Income Tax in Redistributing Income," *Journal of Legal Studies* 23 no. 2 (1994), 667.

[39] Rawls, *Political Liberalism*, 268. Rawls frequently makes such conjectures concerning institutional design. See, for example, Rawls, *A Theory of Justice*, 277, where he surmises that the government's "distribution branch . . . imposes a number of inheritance and gift taxes, and sets restrictions on the rights of bequest." *No* particular tax policies, however, are obviously required at the level of the two principles of justice, which construct the (distributive) scheme of political and legal institutions. For a discussion of the instrumental nature of tax policy, see Liam Murphy and Thomas Nagel, *The Myth of Ownership: Taxes and Justice* (New York: Oxford University Press, 2002), 15.

[40] On this matter, we are in agreement with Murphy, "Institutions and the Demands of Justice," 259.

Rawls's central concern in the passage seems to be to respond to Nozick's charge that the two principles of justice will demand unacceptable interference with individual transactions,[41] which for Nozick, of course, are to be left free in the pre-institutional sense. Rawls could have met this objection, however, *without* narrowing the basic structure had he (correctly) stuck with the post-institutional conception of freedom throughout the passage.[42] This would have led Rawls to adopt the distributive-justice conception of contract (and the rest of the private law), in which individual transactions occur within the range of freedom constructed, in conjunction with the rules of all legal and political institutions, in service to the distributive demands of the two principles of justice. Such transactions are "freely" undertaken by parties exercising their post-institutional freedom, consistent with the constitutive rules of the basic structure.

In responding to Nozick's objection, Rawls seems inadvertently to lapse into Nozick's own pre-institutional conception of natural freedom that serves as the basis of the libertarian right to contract. Rawls mistakenly, given his avowed commitment to a post-institutional conception of freedom, places the private law outside the bounds of the basic structure, such that it may, then, be drawn directly from pre-institutional notions of freedom rather than constructed by the demands of the two principles of justice.

In meeting Nozick's objection, however, Rawls need not have adopted Nozick's libertarian conception of freedom. Rawls should have argued instead that the rules of economic arrangements, including the private law, although constructed in service to the demands of the two principles of justice, need not license unjustifiable, unannounced, or unpredictable governmental interference with individual transactions.[43] For Rawlsianism, because the two principles of justice define the conception of justice

[41] Assuming a Lockean baseline in natural (or pre-institutional) freedom, Nozick writes that "[t]o maintain a pattern one must either continually interfere to stop people from transferring resources as they wish to, or continually (or periodically) interfere to take from some persons resources that others . . . chose to transfer to them." Nozick concludes by posing a question which takes as an assumption Lockean rights in ownership: "Why not have immediate confiscation?" Nozick, *Anarchy, State, and Utopia*, 163.

[42] In an attempt to avoid Nozick's charge, Rawls narrows the scope of the basic structure, so as to leave private transactions "free" in the Nozickian (pre-institutional) sense. Rawls writes, "The difference principle holds, for example, for income and property taxation, for fiscal and economic policy. It applies to the announced system of public law and statutes and *not to particular transactions* or distributions. . . . The objection that the difference principle enjoins continuous corrections of particular distributions and capricious interference with private transactions is based on a misunderstanding." Rawls, *Political Liberalism*, 283 (emphasis added).

[43] Such institutions may well embody equity-oriented demands (e.g., minimum wage laws, substantive unconscionability doctrine, etc.) which, to be sure, are unacceptable given Nozick's libertarian commitments. See Kordana and Tabachnick, "Taxation, the Private Law, and Distributive Justice," 153. The point is not that Rawls's two principles of justice will produce private law rules patterning the libertarian conception of private law, but rather that there is a plausible distributive-justice account of the private law open to Rawls, one that is not unjustifiably unstable or unpredictable. Of course, the ultimate character of private law rules is, for Rawls, an instrumental question.

and the complete set of legal and political rules constructed instrumentally in service to them, any "interferences" with pre-institutional conceptions of contract rights are *justified*.

Return now to the disagreement engendered by the passage on pages 268–69 of *Political Liberalism*. On the one hand, proponents of the narrow view, in which the principles of justice do not apply to the private law, understandably ground their interpretation in a pre-institutional reading of the passage. In their view of Rawlsianism, the private law is not subject to the two principles of justice and may be drawn from values distinct from them (e.g., natural freedom, Kantian autonomy, or conceptions of natural justice). The resulting conclusion is that any number of private law conceptions may be consistent with Rawlsianism. In this view, the character of the private law is determined by the most plausible conception of the "natural" values one takes to be at stake.

On the other hand, while commentators holding broader conceptions of the basic structure have been correct in their conclusion that Rawlsianism *must* adopt a distributive-justice conception of the private law,[44] such views have not provided an account or explanation of the narrowing which has engendered the alternative view of the passage. Our account isolates and explains the source of this important and indeed reasonable disagreement in the literature and shows that there is, after all, a Rawlsian conception of the private law. Going forward from the original position, the conception of "freedom" in Rawlsianism, properly understood, is most consistent with both a broader conception of the basic structure and the distributive-justice conception of the private law. Rawlsianism, then, is not properly understood as neutral with regard to private law conceptions.

The Rawlsian idea appears to be that the moral values of freedom and equality that inform the OP demand "institutional background conditions" that ensure that agreements satisfy our pre-OP notions of freedom and equality. Private agreements and arrangements, however, cannot be guaranteed to be free and fair without background institutions that set the conception of freedom or fairness. The idea is that there is an initial normative demand to *begin* with an institutional account of fair background conditions which define the *post*-institutional conception of freedom. This account is *motivated*, of course, by Rawls's pre-OP commitment to persons conceived of as free and equal. However, in the discussion of freedom and fairness, Rawls inadvertently slips into the Lockean notion of pre-institutional freedom, as opposed to his own set of (noneconomic) values that inform the OP.

The Rawlsian view appears to be this: For agreements to count as free or fair, they must satisfy "institutional" (fair background) requirements, which themselves are motivated (though underdetermined) by

[44] Murphy, "Institutions and the Demands of Justice," 260.

the values that inform the OP. The post-institutional conception of justice—including the details of the economic scheme and the economic or property-oriented baselines—is then defined by the two principles of justice. Thus, the pre-OP values require that persons be treated fairly and as equals, but treating people fairly and as equals *requires* a basic structure (i.e., a set of political and legal institutions) that satisfies the two principles of justice.

The key to understanding the conflation is that while the values Rawls takes to inform the OP are, in a Rawlsian sense, "pre-institutional," they are normatively prior to all economic constructions, which require the full set of political and legal institutions. These pre-OP values are not *pre-institutional* in the Lockean sense—they are void of all economic notions of freedom and property-oriented conceptions (in the absence of the full set of political and legal institutions). The difficulty with the passage, for Rawls, arises in that, in addressing Nozick, he appears to inadvertently slip into Nozick's own (full-blown) pre-institutional account of freedom and fairness—which derives, of course, from the Lockean entitlement conception of justice, which takes the existence of natural rights in property as a normative given.

VI. INSTITUTIONAL DESIGN AND TYPES OF LEGAL AND POLITICAL RULES

It is important to emphasize that even though private ordering is *not* outside the basic structure, there may, as a matter of institutional design, be identifiable differences between types of legal rules in the Rawlsian scheme of institutions designed in service to the two principles of justice. That is to say, a legal anthropologist might be able to make useful distinctions between "enabling rules" (e.g., rules of partnership law or of bequest, should they be constructed), rules that seem to be aimed directly at maintaining justice in distributive shares (e.g., income taxation), and rules that seem to be aimed at justice, but in a less than systematic way— that is to say, rules that need not affect broad groups of persons (as would income taxation). Examples of such rules might be strict liability for harms resulting from the use of lead paint or limitations on employment contracts with minors. However, the crucial mistake to be avoided would be to think that different groups of rules, so delineated, respond to different imperatives. All categories of rules have been constructed in service to the demands of the two principles of justice. The fact that some rules might more directly "pattern" the difference principle, and others not so obviously (since they find their home in an entire scheme of rules and institutions which, as a *whole*, best answers the demands of the two principles of justice), while perhaps of interest to note, does not mean that some rules are created with some other end in mind or in compliance with some principle other than to comply with the demands of Rawlsian justice.

Thus, the "division of labor" between kinds of rules spoken of by Rawls on page 268 of *Political Liberalism* must be viewed as a commentary on institutional design at a *practical* level. It does not mean that only some rules respond to the demands of justice, while other rules can be selected with some other end in mind. Similarly, in *Justice as Fairness*, Rawls writes that "[t]he difference principle might, then, roughly be satisfied by raising and lowering [the decent social] minimum and adjusting the constant marginal rate of taxation. The principle cannot be satisfied exactly. . . . No fine-tuning is possible anyway."[45] Again, this cannot mean that rules other than those of taxation are not selected in service to the demands of the two principles of justice. Instead, it must be read as a practical commentary on institutional design in terms of what rules (here, income taxation) might most obviously pattern the difference principle. In terms of inter-schemic comparisons, if a scheme with a given tax system and no enabling rules renders the position of the least well-off lower than a scheme with the same tax system and enabling rules, then the latter scheme *must* be selected over the former. This is the sense in which all the rules in the system are selected in service to the demands of the two principles of justice, even though some rules (e.g., enabling rules) might not obviously pattern the difference principle.

Rawls writes elsewhere of the distinction between principles for individuals and principles for social institutions.[46] Importantly, however, what we have termed "private ordering" falls on the social institution side of this divide. In other words, because the enabling and regulation of private ordering—essentially, the construction of complex rules governing property—has pervasive effects on the position of the least well-off, such rules must answer to the demands of the two principles of justice. There is no commitment, in Rawlsianism, to any notion of "privacy" with respect to property matters.[47]

VII. CONCLUSION

Despite the ambiguity in the Rawlsian texts, the right to freedom of association for Rawls is not, in its entirety, a basic right. The right's economic component—that is, the component of the right governing private ordering—is quite distinct from Lockean (or libertarian) conceptions. While certain liberties concerning economic associations might be constructed as a component of the complete scheme of economic institutions, this is

---

[45] Rawls, *Justice as Fairness*, 161.

[46] Rawls, *A Theory of Justice*, 108–9.

[47] Contrast Arthur Ripstein, who reads the phrase "division of labor between two kinds of social rules" (Rawls, *Political Liberalism*, 268) as indicating that rules governing individual transactions fall on the "individual" side of the division, and hence are not regulated by the two principles of justice which govern the basic structure. Ripstein, "The Division of Responsibility and the Law of Tort," 1812–13.

true only as a matter of the demands of the second principle of justice. We have argued that the distinct components of this right illuminate a further important ambiguity in Rawlsianism, and we have argued that the puzzle surrounding this ambiguity may be resolved, once one recognizes the proper role of property in the Rawlsian scheme.

Law, University of Virginia
Law, Yale University

INDEX